P9-CQG-993

Fodor's 2023
ROME

Welcome to Rome

Italy's vibrant capital lives in the present, but no other city on Earth evokes its past so powerfully. For over 2,500 years, emperors, popes, artists, and common citizens have left their mark here. Ancient ruins, art-stuffed churches, and the Vatican's treasures vie for your attention, but Rome is also a wonderful place to practice the Italian-perfected *il dolce far niente*, the sweet art of idleness. Your most memorable experiences may include sitting at a caffè or strolling in a beguiling piazza. As you plan your upcoming travels to Rome, please confirm that places are still open and let us know when we need to make updates by writing to us at editors@fodors.com.

TOP REASONS TO GO

★ **History:** The Colosseum and the Forum are just two amazing archaeological musts.

★ **Food:** From pasta and pizza to innovative fare, great meals at trattorias or enotecas.

★ **Art:** Works by Michelangelo, Raphael, Bernini, and Caravaggio dazzle around the city.

★ **Churches:** Places of worship from the Byzantine to baroque eras hold artistic bounty.

★ **Landmarks:** The Pantheon, St. Peter's Basilica, the Spanish Steps—to name only a few.

★ **Shopping:** Chic boutiques around Piazza di Spagna, flea market finds in Trastevere.

Contents

MAPS

Fodor's Features

Chapter 1

EXPERIENCE ROME

24 ULTIMATE EXPERIENCES

Rome offers terrific experiences that should be on every traveler's list. Here are Fodor's top picks for a memorable trip.

1 Piazza Navona

One of the most popular public spaces in Rome, the magnificent, oval-shaped Piazza Navona is lined with restaurants, gelaterias, souvenir shops, and baroque art by both Bernini and Borromini. *(Ch. 5)*

2 MAXXI Museum

It's easy to forget that Rome has some wonderful modern art museums; the best is the Zaha Hadid–designed MAXXI (Museum of 21st Century Art). *(Ch. 8)*

3 Gelato

Gelato is generally denser and less fatty than normal ice cream. Rome has no shortage of excellent gelaterias, but it's smart to stick to the old-school shops. *(Ch. 3–11)*

4 Palazzo Barberini/ Galleria Nazionale

This impressive palace was once home to the powerful Barberini family, and today, you'll find within a splendid collection of art, including works from famed Italian artists like Raphael and Caravaggio. *(Ch. 7)*

5 Via Appia Antica

Known as the Queen of Roads, this ancient road is lined with ruins and the underground graves of Rome's earliest Christians; the spooky yet mesmerizing catacombs can still be visited today. *(Ch. 11)*

6 The Jewish Ghetto

Rome's Jewish population lived in this closed community from the 16th century until 1870. It still is the cultural home of Jewish Rome, with historic synagogues and excellent Jewish bakeries. *(Ch. 5)*

7 Churches

Roman churches, from Santa Maria della Vittoria to San Luigi dei Francesi, are full of impressive art and architecture from Renaissance and baroque masters. *(Ch. 3–11)*

8 Shopping in Piazza di Spagna

Piazza di Spagna and nearby Via dei Condotti and Via del Corso are where you can find major intentional chains and the flagship stores of Italian designer brands. *(Ch. 6)*

9 The Roman Forum

The Forum was once a political playground, a center of commerce, and a place where justice was dispensed during the days of the Roman Republic and Empire. *(Ch. 3)*

10 The Vatican Museums

As the home base for the Catholic Church and the papacy, the Vatican sees millions of visitors each year, who come to explore its museums and Michelangelo's Sistine Chapel. *(Ch. 4)*

11 Espresso and Caffè

When in Rome, you must drink espresso (drip coffee and Starbucks don't even exist here). Stop by a classic caffè and sit down to enjoy one of the city's most beloved traditions. *(Ch. 3–11)*

12 Campo de'Fiori

Shopping for fresh fruit and vegetables at the mercato (market) is a way of life for many Romans; one of the city's most popular is the daily (except Sunday) Campo de'Fiori. *(Ch. 5)*

13 Priory of the Knights of Malta

By the nondescript door to the Priory of the Knights of Malta up on the Aventine Hill, peep through the keyhole and you'll spy a perfect view of Saint Peter's Basilica across the city. *(Ch. 10)*

14 Ostia Antica

Located about 40 minutes outside Rome, this ancient port city is one of the best-preserved archaeological sites in Italy. *(Ch. 12)*

15 The Pantheon

This best-preserved pagan temple of ancient Rome was rebuilt in the 2nd century AD, and has survived intact because it was consecrated as a Christian church. *(Ch. 5)*

16 Trastevere

This charming, village-like neighborhood is a maze of cobblestone streets, traditional Roman trattorias, and medieval houses. *(Ch. 9)*

17 The Colosseum

The most internationally recognized symbol of Rome, this mammoth amphitheater was the site of gladiatorial combats and animal fights. *(Ch. 3)*

18 St. Peter's Basilica

Within the world's most important Catholic church, visit the site of the martyrdom and burial of St. Peter and marvel at Michelangelo's cupola. *(Ch. 4)*

19 Aperitivo

After work, Romans love to meet for aperitivo, the Italian happy hour. Any bar worth its salt offers snacks and a collection of cocktails, including the classic Aperol Spritz. *(Ch. 3–11)*

20 The Spanish Steps

Connecting the ritzy shops at the bottom with the ritzy hotels at the top, this is one of Rome's liveliest spots, with tourists and locals congregating on the steps and around the fountain at their base. *(Ch. 6)*

21 Capitoline Museum

On the smallest and most sacred of Rome's seven hills, you'll find the world's first public museum, a greatest-hits collection of Roman art through the ages. *(Ch. 3)*

22 La Cucina Roman

Roman specialties tend to be simple, with a few ingredients prepared using tried-and-true methods. Classics include fried artichokes, carbonara, and cacio e pepe. *(Ch. 3–11)*

23 Trevi Fountain

One of the few fountains in Rome actually more absorbing than the people crowding around it, the Fontana di Trevi is nothing short of magical. *(Ch. 6)*

24 Galleria Borghese

Only the best could satisfy the aesthetic taste of Cardinal Scipione Borghese, whose artistic holdings within this museum evoke the essence of baroque Rome. *(Ch. 8)*

WHAT'S WHERE

1 Ancient Rome. No other archaeological park in the world has so compact a nucleus of fabled sights; nearby Monti has artisan shops, restaurants, bars, and high-end boutiques.

2 The Vatican. An independent sovereign state, the pope's residence draws millions to St. Peter's Basilica and the Vatican Museums. Borgo and Prati are the neighborhoods right outside the Vatican.

3 Piazza Navona, Campo de' Fiori, and the Jewish Ghetto. The Piazza Navona and Campo de' Fiori are busy meeting points, surrounded by restaurants and caffè, with the Pantheon nearby. The Jewish Ghetto is the historic center of Jewish life in Rome, and still home to Rome's main synagogue.

4 Piazza di Spagna. The Spanish Steps are iconic, and the surrounding area is the place to window-shop, thanks to upscale fashion boutiques. The Trevi Fountain is a short walk away.

5 **Repubblica and Quirinale.** These areas bustle with government offices during the day, but are also home to several churches and sights, including Bernini's baroque Sant'Andrea al Quirinale.

6 **Villa Borghese and Around.** The Villa Borghese, Rome's vast city park, is home to dazzling museums while nearby Piazza del Popolo is prime people-watching territory.

7 **Trastevere.** This picturesque neighborhood attracts locals and visitors to its restaurants and wine bars. The Janiculum Hill has incomparable views.

8 **Aventino and Testaccio.** These neighborhoods are off the usual tourist track but have the vibrancy of true Rome. Aventino is an elegant residential area, while Testaccio is traditionally working-class, although rapidly gentrifying, and has a hip nightlife scene.

9 **Esquilino and Around.** These are some of Rome's least touristy and most beloved neighborhoods, with plenty of ancient sights and spectacular churches. The verdant Via Appia Antica leads past the landmark church of Domine Quo Vadis to the catacombs and beyond.

What to Eat and Drink in Rome

SALUMI AND PROSCIUTTO AT ROSCIOLI
This family-run deli/restaurant originally opened as a grocery store and today the counter is still piled high with 300 types of cheeses, 150 varieties of salami and cold cuts, and confections of olive oil, mustards, and sauces.

PIZZA
In Rome, there are two pizza styles to know: *pizza tonda* (round pizza) and *pizza al taglio* (by the slice). The latter has a thicker, focaccia-like crust and is cut into squares; these are sold by weight and generally available all day. The typical Roman pizza tonda has a very thin crust and is cooked in a wood-burning oven that reaches extremely hot temperatures; these pizzerie, like Pizzeria ai Marmi, tend to open for dinner only.

CACIO E PEPE
Meaning "cheese and pepper," this is a simple pasta dish from the *cucina povera*, or rustic cooking, tradition. It's a favorite Roman primo, usually made with *tonnarelli* (fresh egg pasta a bit thicker than spaghetti), coated with pecorino-cheese sauce and lots of freshly ground black pepper. You can find it at most classic Roman trattorias.

GELATO
For many visitors, their first taste of Italian gelato is revelatory. Its consistency is a cross between regular American ice cream and soft-serve, and the best versions are extremely flavorful, and always made fresh daily. When choosing a gelateria, avoid the places hawking industrially made gelato in unnatural colors and flavors and opt for the places serving the artisan stuff.

FRITTI
The classic Roman starter (especially at a pizzeria) is *fritti*, an assortment of fried treats, usually crumbed or in batter. Popular options include *filetti di baccala* (salt cod in batter), *fiori di zucca* (zucchini flowers, usually stuffed with anchovy and mozzarella), and *supplì* (rice balls stuffed with mozzarella and other ingredients).

AMARO COCKTAILS
You can find cocktails that include *amaro*, the popular bittersweet Italian liqueur, in most cocktail bars in Rome (it's a main ingredient in drinks like the Aperol Spritz and Negroni). But the best place to sample this Italian staple is Il Marchese, Europe's first amaro bar, where you can choose from around 550 different bottles.

ESPRESSO
Few Romans can live without *il caffè*, and there is no shortage of coffee bars to satisfy cravings. Real Italian espresso is a thimbleful of aromatic black liquid, prepared by a barista in a variety of ways, but either enjoyed standing at the bar or leisurely while sitting down (to-go cups are not a thing here).

ARTICHOKES
Winter through spring is artichoke season in Rome, and restaurants all over the city put them on menus as appetizers or side dishes. There are two styles to know: *carciofi alla romana*, i.e., Roman-style artichokes, which are stuffed with garlic and wild Roman mint and cooked in olive

Italian espresso

oil and water, and *carciofi alla giudia*, Jewish-style artichokes, which are smashed so the leaves open up and then fried to crispy perfection. The former can be found in trattorias all over the city, but the place to get the latter is in the Jewish Ghetto.

PASTA ALL'AMATRICIANA

A classic Roman pasta, the origins of *amatriciana* are in the Lazio town of Amatrice, hence the name. Sometimes served with *bucatini* (spaghetti-like but hollow), *mezze maniche* (short grooved pasta tubes), or rigatoni, it always consists of a tomato-based sauce with *guanciale* (cured pork cheek) and pecorino cheese. You'll find it just about everywhere Roman classics are served.

CODA ALLA VACCINARA

Rome's largest slaughter-house in the 1800s was in the Testaccio neighbor-hood, and that's where you'll still find dishes like "oxtail in the style of the cattle butcher." This dish is made from ox or veal tails stewed with tomatoes, carrots, celery, and wine, and usually seasoned with cinnamon. It's simmered for hours, and then finished with raisins and pine nuts or bittersweet chocolate.

LA GRICIA

This dish is often referred to as a "white amatriciana," because it's precisely that: pasta (usually spaghetti or rigatoni) served with pecorino cheese and guanciale—thus amatriciana without the tomato sauce. It's a lighter alternative to carbonara (it doesn't contain eggs), and its origins date back farther than the amatriciana.

TRAPIZZINO

A cross between a *tramezzino* (a triangle-shaped sandwich made with two slices of white, crust-less bread) and pizza, the *trapizzino* is an original street-food creation that was born in Rome and has since expanded to Florence, Milan, New York, and beyond. The concept is simple: triangle-shaped pizza dough stuffed à la minute with fillings drawn from the tradition of Rome's cucina povera. Fillings differ, but you might find eggplant parmigiana, burrata and anchovies, tripe, or meatballs in tomato sauce. A chain fittingly called Trapizzino invented them; locations include a shop in Trastevere and a stall inside the Mercato Centrale in Termini station.

What to Buy in Rome

JEWELRY

Over the years, several delightful boutiques featuring unique handmade jewelry have made their debut in the Eternal City. Don't leave Rome without stepping foot in a specialized *oreficeria*.

LAZIO WINE

Lazio might not have the reputation of Piedmont or Tuscany when it comes to wine, but some local wineries are finally putting the region on the map. Roman wines can be purchased at *enotecas* (wine shops) across the city, and even in wine bars and supermarkets. Options include the versatile Cesanese, an earthy red wine.

GOURMET FOOD PRODUCTS

Thanks to the impressive selection of Italian produce, Rome luckily has no shortage of specialty food stores, gourmet outlets, and artisan shops. From Roman wine biscuits to locally produced olive oil, vinegar, condiments, and coffee, the city is a great place to stock up on some basics for your kitchen.

PECORINO ROMANO

Rome's famed sheep's milk cheese, known as pecorino romano, is the star of many classic Roman dishes, from cacio e pepe to supplì. You can purchase some to take back home with you from multiple delicatessens and cheese shops around town, including La Tradizione by the Vatican.

HANDMADE CHOCOLATE

Roman desserts aren't quite as famous as their Parisian counterparts, but they still have their charm thanks to tasty concoctions like amaretti or *brutti ma buoni* cookies (which literally translates to "ugly but good"). But for the best tasty treat to bring home, try some handmade chocolate from an old-school chocolate shop. Walking into Pasticceria Valzani in Trastevere is like stepping back in time: it first opened in the 1920s and hasn't been touched since. Or check out Moriondo and Gariglio, which first opened in 1850 in Turin before setting up shop in Rome with this opulent red store. Today, their chocolates are still prepared according to 19th-century recipes.

SHOES

When it comes to sexy stilettos, strappy sandals, or stylish *stivali* (boots), Rome has a *scarpa* (shoe) for every Cinderella. The best place to get your feet wet is in the swanky Piazza di Spagna area, but other high-end boutiques can be found around the Piazza Navona and Campo de' Fiori.

DESIGNER CLOTHING

Italians know fashion; that much is indisputable. There are plenty of upmarket flagship stores of world-famous brands in Rome, including the likes of Prada, Fendi, and Valentino. But be sure to browse the city's smaller boutiques, too; you'll be sure to find a piece or two from a lesser-known designer to liven up your wardrobe.

CERAMICS AND DECORATIVE ARTS

Unique pottery, beautiful ceramics, and other decorative arts are at the top of most souvenir shoppers' lists, and Rome is a great place to search for Italian-made items. The best finds are at Rome's many artisan shops tucked away on winding cobblestone streets. Whether you fancy a quasi-authentic Roman mask or a marble plaque carved by hand with a funny saying , you won't go home empty-handed.

LEATHER ITEMS

Italian leather is renowned the world over for its high quality, supple feel, and sturdy craftsmanship. Roman stores that carry leather products abound, from high fashion designers to boutique shops. Everything from handbags and wallets to belts and jackets can make a unique (but be warned, very pricey) souvenir.

RELIGIOUS ITEMS

With the Vatican positioned in the heart of the city, religious tourism is a bit of a big deal in Rome. That means items like religious art or rosary beads can readily be found around town, particularly near St. Peter's Square and the Vatican Museums. In these areas, market stands and street sellers beckon with everything from kitschy priest calendars to more-devout Catholic items. Higher-quality rosary beads, Bibles, and artwork can be purchased at the Vatican Museums gift shop.

ANTIQUES AND PRINTS

Rome is one of Italy's happiest hunting grounds for antiques and bric-a-brac. You'll find streets lined with shops groaning under the weight of gilded Rococo tables, charming Grand Tour memorabilia, fetching 17th-century engravings of realistic scenes, and many intriguing curios.

VINTAGE CLOTHING

For many, looking good means not looking like anyone else. Luckily Rome has a wide range of vintage shops (mainly in the Monti and Piazza Navona areas), where you can find some great couture from the *Dolce Vita* days and other classic time periods. Spend some time going through the racks, and you'll never know what treasures you might find.

Roman chocolate

FLEA MARKETS

Treasure seekers and bargain hunters alike will appreciate Rome's *mercati all'aperto* (open-air markets). Roman flea markets are great spots to unearth some really good finds, whether you're hunting for something borrowed or something new. Every Sunday, all of Rome tends to gravitate to Trastevere for the Porta Portese flea market, where tents overflow with cheap luggage, new and used clothes, vintage World War II memorabilia, and nearly everything else you can think of.

GLOVES

You just wouldn't be an Italian *signora* without a pair of fashionable handmade gloves, and you'll find plenty to choose from in Rome. Whether you're looking for cashmere, silk, lambskin, or other types of leather, there is a sea of colors and styles to choose from. Gloves make wonderful presents to bring back home, too.

Best Museums in Rome

CAPITOLINE MUSEUMS
Second in size only to the Vatican Museums, the Capitoline Museums were the world's first public art museums. The two buildings on Michelangelo's famous piazza house a collection spanning from Ancient Rome to the baroque era, with masterpieces including Caravaggio's *The Fortune Teller* and *St. John the Baptist*.

GALLERIA NAZIONALE D'ARTE MODERNA E CONTEMPORANEA
Located within Villa Borghese, this art museum in a huge white Beaux Arts building hosts one of Italy's most important collections of 19th- and 20th-century art. You'll find works by Degas, Monet, Courbet, Cézanne, and Van Gogh, but the emphasis is on understanding Italian Modernism through a historical lens.

MACRO
Housed in the former Peroni brewery, this modern and contemporary art museum focuses on Italian art from the 1960s through the present. The building, with its striking red structure and glass walkways, was designed by French architect Odile Decq and is worth a visit in and of itself.

GALLERIA BORGHESE
It would be hard to find a more beautiful villa filled with a must-see collection of masterpieces by Bernini, Caravaggio, Raphael, Rubens, and Titian. Cardinal Scipione Borghese had the gorgeous Renaissance villa built in 1612 to display his collection, though it has undergone many changes since.

MUSEO NAZIONALE ETRUSCO DI VILLA GIULIA
The pre-Roman civilization known as the Etruscans appeared in Italy around 2,000 BC, though no one knows exactly where they originated. To learn more about them, plan a visit to this museum in Villa Giulia, which was built for Pope Julius III in the mid-1500s.

PALAZZO DORIA PAMPHILJ
For a glimpse into aristocratic Rome, it's hard to beat this museum in the 15th century palazzo of the Doria Pamphilj family. Wander through the Hall of Mirrors—fashioned after the one at Versailles, naturally—but don't miss the Old Master paintings.

Vatican Museums

VATICAN MUSEUMS
One of the largest museum complexes in the world, the Vatican palaces and museums comprise some 1,400 rooms, galleries, and chapels. By far the most famous is the Sistine Chapel painted by Michelangelo and a team of other painters, but the Raphael Rooms come in a close second when it comes to must-see works.

MAXXI
Tucked away in the quiet Flaminio neighborhood, the Museo Nazionale delle Arti del XXI Secolo (National Museum of 21st Century Arts)—or MAXXI, for short—proves that there's more to Rome than ancient and baroque art.

CENTRALE MONTEMARTINI
Nowhere else is the theme of gods and machines more apparent than at this museum. Rome's first power plant now houses the runoff from the Capitoline Museums' collection; the sculptures of men in togas and women in dresses form a poignant contrast to the machinery.

Best Ancient Sites in Rome

COLOSSEUM

Perhaps the monument most symbolic of ancient Rome, the Colosseum is one of the city's most fascinating—and popular—tourist attractions. It officially opened in AD 80 with 100 days of games, including wild-animal fights and gladiatorial combat.

FORO DI TRAIANO

Trajan's Forum was the last of imperial Rome's forums—and the grandest. Comprising a basilica, two libraries, and a colonnade surrounding a piazza, it's connected to a market that once bustled with commercial activity.

PANTHEON

Built as a pagan temple to the gods, the Pantheon is Rome's best-preserved ancient site, perhaps because it was later consecrated as a church. Step inside and you'll be amazed at its perfect proportions and the sunlight streaming in from the 30-foot-wide oculus. It's truly a wonder of ancient engineering.

ROMAN FORUM

One of the Eternal City's most emblematic sites, the Roman Forum stretches out between the Capitoline and Palatine Hills. This vast area filled with crumbling columns and the ruins of temples, palaces, and shops was once the hub of the ancient world and the center of political, commercial, and religious life in the city.

CIRCUS MAXIMUS

It might be hard to imagine now, but the grassy area between the Palatine and Aventine Hills was once the site of the largest hippodrome in the Roman Empire. The huge oval course was rebuilt under Julius Caesar and later enlarged by subsequent emperors. During its heyday, it hosted epic chariot races and competitions that sometimes lasted as long as 15 days.

BOCCA DELLA VERITÀ

Legend has it the mouth in this ancient stone face will bite off the hand of a liar, and tourists line up to stick their hand inside the mouth and put it to the test. (Gregory Peck's character tricks Audrey Hepburn's Princess Ann into thinking he lost a hand inside it in a scene from *Roman Holiday*.) You'll find the enigmatic face in the portico of the Church of Santa Maria in Cosmedin, near the Circus Maximus.

The Roman Forum

TEATRO MARCELLO
It may look a bit like a smaller version of the Colosseum, but the Teatro Marcello was once ancient Rome's largest and most important theater. Julius Caesar ordered the land for the theater to be cleared, but he was murdered before it was built. It was inaugurated in AD 12 by Augustus and hosted performances of drama and song. It's kept that purpose even today, at least during the summer, when it hosts concerts.

APPIA ANTICA
Head to the southeastern edge of the city to Appia Antica Park and you can walk on the same stones that ancient Roman soldiers and citizens once trod—which are incredibly well-preserved. This ancient thoroughfare once stretched all the way to Brindisi, some 300 miles away on the Adriatic Coast. Today, the first 10 miles are part of a regional park, and it's a perfect spot for bike rides and picnics in the grass under the shadow of Rome's emblematic umbrella pines.

ARA PACIS AUGUSTAE
Now housed in a modern glass-and-travertine building designed by renowned American architect Richard Meier, the Ara Pacis Augustae has some of the most incredible reliefs you'll see on any ancient monument. It was commissioned to celebrate the Emperor Augustus's victories in battle and the Pax Romana, a peaceful period that followed. It's centrally located on the Tiber River and definitely worth a visit.

BATHS OF CARACALLA
A testament to ancient Rome's bathing culture, this site was essentially a massive spa, with saunas, baths, what would be an Olympic-size pool, and two gymnasiums for boxing, weightlifting, and wrestling.

Best Churches in Rome

SANTA MARIA DEL POPOLO

It would be easy to pass by this church on the corner of Piazza del Popolo, but go inside and you'll find artistic treasures worth seeing. Raphael designed an entire chapel within the church, but perhaps the most amazing works are the two altar paintings by Caravaggio depicting the *Crucifixion of Saint Peter* and the *Conversion of Saint Paul*. The church also contains 16th-century stained glass, which is rare in this part of Italy.

BASILICA DI SAN PIETRO

The world's largest church and one of the world's holiest places for Catholics, St. Peter's Basilica was built on the site of Saint Peter's tomb. The greatest architectural achievement of the Renaissance, it's a testament to the Catholic Church's wealth and power.

SAN LUIGI DEI FRANCESI

Among art lovers, the secret's out about this small church dedicated to Saint Louis, the patron saint of France. Inside, the Contarelli Chapel is adorned by three Caravaggios, each one more splendid than the last. Gaze up at his three depictions of Saint Matthew (the *Calling of Saint Matthew*, *Saint Matthew and the Angel*, and the *Martyrdom of Saint Matthew*) and you'll understand why Caravaggio was the master of chiaroscuro.

SAN GIOVANNI IN LATERANO

Built by the Emperor Constantine 10 years before the Basilica di San Pietro was constructed, this monumental church is actually the ecclesiastical seat of the Pope. Before you enter, look up to admire the 15 monumental statues depicting the 12 apostles, plus Jesus Christ, the Virgin Mary, and John the Baptist. The intricate mosaic floors are the work of the Cosmati family. To learn more about them, join Personalized Italy's Cosmatesque Tour of Rome led by a charming art historian who illuminates the incredible craftsmanship that went into this and other churches.

PANTHEON

Originally a pagan temple and later consecrated as a church, the Pantheon counts itself among Rome's most famous monuments for good reason. It's considered the world's only architecturally perfect building by some, because of its proportions (the diameter is equal to its height). Of Rome's many ancient sites, it's the best preserved. It's also the final resting place of Raphael and other important figures from Italy's history.

SCALA SANTA

Devout Catholic pilgrims travel from far and wide to climb the Scala Santa—the marble staircase from Pontius Pilate's palace in Jerusalem—on their knees. At the top lies the Sancta Sanctorum (Holy of Holies), a small chapel ornately decorated with marble, elaborate frescoes, and Cosmatesque mosaic floors, which was the Pope's chapel before the Sistine Chapel. You can reach the top via the non-sanctified side stairs to admire the incredible chapel.

Basilica di San Pietro

BASILICA DI SAN CLEMENTE

The Basilica di San Clemente is known as the "lasagna church" because the deeper you descend, the farther back in time you go. The 12th-century church was built on top of a 4th-century church, which was built on top of a 2nd-century pagan temple dedicated to the cult of Mithras as well as a collection of 1st-century Roman houses. Pay the nominal entry fee to access the lower levels, where the mysterious cult once worshipped and you'll feel like you're peeling back the layers of ancient history.

SANTA MARIA DELLA VITTORIA

Bernini's genius is on full display in this church near Piazza della Repubblica. Though the church's architect was Carlo Maderno, Bernini was responsible for the Cornaro Chapel, where you can admire his somewhat controversial sculpture, the *Ecstasy of Saint Teresa*. Meant to depict the saint abandoning herself to the divine love of god, her facial expression seems to resemble a rather earthlier pleasure. Pay this church a visit and decide for yourself.

SAN PIETRO IN VINCOLI

The reason to visit this otherwise unremarkable church in Monti is to lay eyes on Michelangelo's *Moses*. Pope Julius II had commissioned the statue for his tomb, but after he died, his successor—a rival from the Medici family— abandoned the tomb and left the statue here instead. Scholars debate whether the two things on Moses's head are meant to be horns or rays of light. Either way, the statue is one of Michelangelo's best.

SANT'AGOSTINO

This church tucked behind Piazza Navona contains a triple-whammy of incredible art. Not only is it home to Caravaggio's *Madonna of the Pilgrims*, but also Raphael's *Isaiah*, which may have been inspired by Michelangelo's prophets on the ceiling of the Sistine Chapel (the artist snuck a peek despite orders of secrecy) and Sansovino's sculpture *St. Anne and the Madonna with Child*. It's definitely worth a detour.

Under-the-Radar Things to Do in Rome

Gardens on Aventine Hill

STREET ART IN OSTIENSE, TESTACCIO, AND PIGNETO

Beyond the *centro storico* (historic center), the gritty neighborhoods of Ostiense, Testaccio, and Pigneto may not be at the top of your Rome bucket list, but they're a must-see for fans of street art. Entire buildings are covered top-to-bottom in murals and well-known street artists have left their mark.

THE KEATS-SHELLEY MEMORIAL HOUSE

You don't have to be a fan of the English Romantic poets to visit this house museum at the foot of the Spanish Steps, but it certainly helps. The home at 26 Piazza di Spagna was the final resting place of the poet John Keats, who died of tuberculosis at the tender age of 25.

CULTURAL PROGRAMMING AT THE VILLA MEDICI

You wouldn't know it from the outside, but this gorgeous Renaissance palace on the Pincio Hill houses the Academy of France in Rome, which hosts visiting artists and scholars and puts on cultural events.

Ostiense street art

THE CAPUCHIN CRYPT

As if preserving saintly relics wasn't creepy enough, the Capuchin order of monks used the bones of some 4,000 friars to decorate the crypt under the Church of Santa Maria della Concezione. This site isn't for the faint of heart. A sign that reads "What you are, we once were. What we are, you will someday be" serves as a poignant reminder of our mortality.

CONCERTS AT THE ORATORIO DEL GONFALONE

Hidden behind a nondescript door in the centro storico lies a room decorated wall-to-wall with incredibly well-preserved frescoes depicting scenes of the passion of the Christ. Painted in the 16th century by a team of mannerist painters, the site has been called "the Sistine Chapel of mannerism."

SHOPPING ON VIA DI MONSERRATO

Via del Corso and Via dei Condotti may be Rome's most famous shopping streets, but for truly unique finds, you need to get off the beaten path and head to Via di Monserrato. This charming cobblestoned street is home to a collection of high-end boutiques.

PARCO DEGLI ACQUEDOTTI

On the city's southeastern outskirts, this massive green park is a peaceful oasis where locals come to jog, walk their dogs, and just hang out. The aqueducts are relics of the Ancient Roman Empire and you can walk along the remains of an ancient cobblestone road that once formed part of the Appia Antica.

GARDENS ON AVENTINE HILL

If you happen to be in Rome in the spring, when the Roseto Comunale on the Aventine Hill is in bloom, it's worth a stop. Once a Jewish cemetery, the garden's paths are fittingly shaped like a menorah. With more than 1,000 different varieties of roses, it's one of the most romantic spots in Rome.

QUARTIERE COPPEDÈ

This charming micro-neighborhood near Villa Torlonia may be a bit off the beaten path, but it's a fascinating spot for architecture fans. A collection of 27 buildings were designed in a whimsical art nouveau style by architect Gino Coppedè in the 1910s. Don't miss the Fontana delle Rane (a.k.a. Fountain of the Frogs).

Best Free Things to do in Rome

VITTORIANO MONUMENT
This building has polarized locals since its construction, but it still has some of the best views in the city. A monument to Italy's first king, Victor Emmanuel II, it also holds the Tomb of the Unknown Soldier and its eternal flame.

PANTHEON
There has been much talk about imposing an entry fee for the Pantheon, but for now, there's no cost to visiting one of Rome's most impressive monuments.

SPANISH STEPS
The largest staircase in Europe definitely deserves a visit, and luckily it doesn't cost a thing. Located within the elegant Piazza di Spagna, you can walk up the stairs for great views from the famed church, Trinità dei Monti. Bernini's fountain, La Barcaccia, stands at the bottom of the stairs and is a great example of baroque art and design.

PIAZZA NAVONA
For the finest example of baroque Roman architecture, head to Piazza Navona. Here you'll find one of Bernini's most important masterpieces, the Fountain of the Four Rivers, topped by the obelisk of Domitian. The square is filled daily with street performers and artists. You can also enter the church Sant'Agnese in Agone by Borromini from the piazza.

CAMPO DE' FIORI
It may not be the most authentic, but Campo de' Fiori is the oldest and most famous market in Rome. Watch the stand owners boisterously interact as they show off their wares, and admire the monument to the philosopher Giordano Bruno; it's the big statue in the middle of the square. Around the corner, you'll find some of Rome's best *pizza bianca* (focaccia-style bread) at Forno Roscioli or Forno Campo de' Fiori.

KEYHOLE OF THE KNIGHTS OF MALTA
High up on Aventine Hill, within the Villa del Priorato dei Cavalieri di Malta (belonging to the Knights of Malta), lies a special and unusual attraction. Through the tiny keyhole of a nondescript door, you can view the gorgeous dome of St. Peter's Basilica. This enchanting view gives you a unique taste of three separate nations: Malta, Italy, and the Vatican.

ORANGE GARDEN
Located on elegant Aventine Hill, the Orange Garden (as it's known by locals) is officially named Savelli's Park, named for the family who lived there throughout the 13th century. Orange plants were planted during this time, hence the reason for its colloquial name. Today, it's an enchanting garden space perfect for a stroll or picnic. But most of all, visitors love coming here for the spectacular panoramic views of the city.

TIBER ISLAND
The only island in Rome, Tiber Island sits in the middle of the Tiber River between the Jewish Ghetto and Trastevere. The small boat-shaped island is home to a hospital (here since the 16th century), a church, a pharmacy, and two

Via Margutta

restaurants. It's connected to the mainland by bridges on either side, one of which is pedestrian-only. From here, city views stretch out across the river, and in the summer months, there is an outdoor cinema and seasonal restaurants and bars.

GIANICOLO

While not officially one of the famed Seven Hills of Rome, the Janiculum (Giani-colo in Italian) is certainly the one Romans are fondest of. From it, sprawling panoramic views of the city stretch out like a postcard; it's often the location for a wedding photo shoot, first kiss, or proposal. Walk the paths that feature signifi-cant historical statues and busts, and take in the beauty of the Fontana di Acqua Paola; referred to by

locals as the *fontanone* (the big fountain), it's said to be where you go to weep and mourn a broken heart.

ROME'S BASILICAS

It's completely free to walk right into Rome's four major papal basilicas. These churches are the four highest-ranking Roman Catholic church buildings in the world, and include Archbasilica of Saint John Lateran (which is the official seat and parish of the Pope), Saint Peter's Basilica, the Basilica of Saint Paul Outside the Walls, and the Basilica of Santa Maria Maggiore. Each is unique in their archi-tecture and style, and you could easily spend an entire day exploring them all.

VIA MARGUTTA

Walk in Audrey Hepburn and Gregory Peck's footsteps à la *Roman Holiday* on a stroll down one of the city's prettiest streets. Via Margutta (at number 51, to be precise) was the location of Peck's character's apartment in the film, and where many scenes were shot. This short street with a long history is now filled with antiques stores and galleries.

VILLA BORGHESE

As the most famous park in Rome, Villa Borghese is a lush oasis in the northern part of the city center. It has a man-made lake where you can rent canoes, and there are plenty of spaces for a picnic. You could easily spend the entire day here, and there's a caffè for light meals and snacks, too.

Rome Today

Rome, the Eternal City, is 28 centuries old and yet is still constantly reinventing itself. The glories of ancient Rome, the pomp of the Renaissance Papacy, and the futuristic architecture of the 20th and 21st centuries all blend miraculously into a harmonious whole here. The fact that you can get Wi-Fi in the shadow of 2,000-year-old ruins sort of sums things up, and it's this fusion of old and new and the casual way that Romans live with their weighty history that make this city so unique.

NEW ARCHITECTURE

Rome may be firmly anchored in the distant past, but that's never been an obstacle to its journey into the new millennium. Just look at some of the architectural marvels that have emerged in the last 20 years: the Auditorium Parco della Musica (Renzo Piano, 2002), the new Jubilee Church (formerly Chiesa di Dio Padre Misericordioso; Richard Meier, 2003), the Museo dell'Ara Pacis (Richard Meier, 2006), MACRO (Odile Decq, 2010), and the MAXXI—Museo Nazionale delle Arti del XXI Secolo (Zaha Hadid, 2010). In 2011, Rome also built a new bridge: the grandiose Ponte della Musica over the Tiber River. Looking like two giant white harps rising from the ground, it can be used only by pedestrians and cyclists. And the Massimiliano Fuksas–designed Roma Convention Center, nicknamed "La Nuvola" for its futuristic suspended cloud shape, opened in 2016.

NEW MODES OF TRANSPORTATION

Romans are anxiously awaiting the completion of the new Metro Linea C, which will cut through the city center at Piazza Venezia and link with both the A and B lines at Ottaviano for St. Peter's and the Colosseum, respectively. Although it is expected to considerably ease surface-traffic congestion, progress on the new line has gone slowly, because every time a shaft is sunk in Roman ground, it reveals some new important archaeological site and all work halts for the ensuing excavation. Currently only the peripheral section of Line C is running, connecting with Line A at San Giovanni and continuing eastward to Pigneto and beyond.

More eco-friendly modes of transportation are popping up, too. Electric scooters are now ubiquitous in Rome, and e-bikes by Uber Jump can be found around the city. The main electric scooter companies are Helbiz, Lime by Uber, and Bird, all of which can be rented by downloading the respective company's app. Just be careful—riding on the sidewalks is prohibited and drivers can be rather aggressive.

THE PANDEMIC

Italy was famously the first European country to declare a nationwide lockdown in March 2020. You could get whiplash trying to keep track of the various restrictions imposed since then. At the time of writing, however, Italy has entered a period of seeming stability. The country has one of the highest vaccination rates in the world, no doubt because Prime Minister Mario Draghi has mandated it for all workers and people over 50.

Vaccinated Italians have a "super green pass" in the form of a QR code, which is required to ride public transit, eat and drink at restaurants and bars, visit museums and other attractions, go to the cinema, theater, sporting events, concerts, spas, nightclubs, and check into hotels. For Americans, a CDC-issued proof of vaccination is accepted in its place. And at the time of writing, a mask must be worn anytime you enter an enclosed public space, including public transit. But these rules could change, and often do, so before you travel, check the website for the Ministero della Salute (⊕ *salute.gov.it*).

Another big change to come out of COVID-19 restrictions is the need to book timed tickets at many museums and attractions in advance. For a while, advanced booking was required across the board in order to enforce reduced capacity and ensure social distancing. Many museums have since dropped this requirement, but others have kept it, so it's best to check in advance before showing up.

NEW FOOD TRENDS

While it's still true that Romans love Roman food, the city's food scene is becoming (slightly) more international. It might never have the diversity of New York or London, but some of Rome's trendiest restaurants and bars serve Mexican tacos and margaritas, California-inspired cuisine, Danish bread and pastries, and even ramen. You'll also find a sometimes puzzling tendency at restaurants to offer traditional Roman or Italian cuisine and a few surprising items, like sushi or burgers. Once you've had your fill of traditional trattoria fare, it's nice to try something different.

MORE HOTEL OPTIONS

While the pandemic caused a lot of hotel closures, over the past year there's been a flurry of new openings, with lots more to come—and they're seriously upping the ante for travelers looking for a fabulous place to stay.

International hospitality companies are investing big in the Eternal City, opening trendy new hotels, some bringing unprecedented levels of luxury and others offering great style at relatively low price points. Yes, there have always been hotels by Marriott and Hilton, but recent openings include properties by British brands Hoxton and Soho House, French brand Mama Shelter, and American brands like W. Thai brand Anantara has taken over Palazzo Naiadi on Piazza della Repubblica, and Six Senses is revamping a historic palazzo just off Via del Corso. Also watch out for trendy hotels by EDITION and Nobu as well as ultra-luxurious openings by Bulgari and Rosewood.

The influx of new places to stay coupled with pandemic-induced woes means that some older hotels will go out of business, but others like the illustrious Hotel de Russie are gussying up their spaces and refreshing their offerings. Overall, it's good news for travelers.

What to Read and Watch Before You Go

LA DOLCE VITA

Just as the names Raphael, Botticelli, Michelangelo, and Da Vinci reign over the Italian art world, filmmakers like Fellini, Rossellini, De Sica, and Antonioni are essential for appreciating Italian (and Roman) cinema. Federico Fellini's classic *La Dolce Vita* follows the busy days and nights of journalist Marcello, taking viewers throughout Rome and its most notable landmarks. Among the film's more artistic and nuanced aspects are gorgeous scenes of nightlife, dining, and general folly in the ancient city's ruin and splendor.

HISTORY OF THE DECLINE AND FALL OF THE ROMAN EMPIRE BY EDWARD GIBBON

Okay, so maybe you do get through all six volumes of this classic text, or maybe they just sit on your bookshelf looking pretty (we're not here to judge). But while there have since been many historical and archaeological discoveries that add to and challenge the conclusions Gibbon made in the late 1700s, this text remains famous and respected for its comprehensive attempt to understand ancient Rome and the causes of its decline. For a more contemporary and abridged source of Roman history, try *SPQR: A History of Ancient Rome* by Mary Beard.

BICYCLE THIEVES

Many Roman films capture a spirit of unsettling resistance, confusion, and pain during the aftermath of Mussolini's fascist regime—a time that came to define much of contemporary Italy and its art. Vittorio de Sica's neorealist masterpiece captures this atmosphere through the story of a father, son, and one stolen bicycle, taking us through the desperate, dusty streets of life in Rome after World War II.

THE YOUNG POPE

While it's unclear how realistic the Vatican politics depicted in this HBO series actually are, this tale about the rise of an unlikely, power-hungry young pope and his ensuing deviance, manipulations, and power-grabs make for great television. The clever writing and skilled performances (especially by a creepy Jude Law as Pius XIII, the world's first American pope) elevate the show, as does the gorgeous cinematography.

AENEID BY VIRGIL

Because so much of Roman literature (and history) has been built upon the early greats, it's helpful to get some classical poetry under your belt before a trip to Rome. Virgil, Ovid, Horace, or Catullus (and even Dante or Keats) will do just fine, but the *Aeneid* is arguably the most Roman poem in existence. The long harrowing journey of Aeneas and his soldiers, as they head out of Troy and toward the Italian peninsula, is outlined in this long epic poem, which ends with the early finding (and founding) of Rome, making it a unique literary origin story.

ROMAN HOLIDAY

When all the fascism and papal politics start to get too heavy, turn instead to a light Roman film, the classic *Roman Holiday*. In it, the charms of Gregory Peck and Audrey Hepburn and their whirlwind romance make great vacation fodder, as they ride Vespas through Roman streets, and gallivant through the Piazza del Popolo, around the Coliseum, and other landmarks.

A CLASH OF CIVILIZATIONS OVER AN ELEVATOR IN PIAZZA VITTORIO BY AMARA LAKHOUS

While the plot centers around a murder that takes place in a small apartment building on the Piazza Vittorio, this novel is really about the tenants of said building, a culturally diverse group from all walks of life, whose differences shape the complexity of what it means to be Roman. An author of Algerian descent, Lakhous has a knack for voice and delving into shifting points of view, particularly shining a much needed light on the Muslim immigrant experience in Italy.

THE BORGIAS

This historical television drama series gives a fictionalized tale of the very real, very corrupt Borgia family that came from Spain and rose to power and the papacy in Renaissance Italy. While the show takes historical liberties to build drama, most of the juiciest scandals—torture, bribery, and even incest—are based on real events or longtime rumors about the infamous family.

LA GRANDE BELLEZZA (THE GRAND BEAUTY)

Paolo Sorrentino's Academy Award-winning film follows an aging writer in contemporary Rome as he examines both his past and present life choices. Moving through the protagonist's partying lifestyle, the film is a modern-day version of La Dolce Vita, providing many a lavish and indulgent landscape of Roman life.

THE AGONY AND THE ECSTASY BY IRVING STONE

Reading this 1961 novel provides great context for those who plan to visit the Vatican's most popular artistic sight, the Sistine Chapel. This fictionalized biography of Michelangelo's arduous process details the genius and struggle (along with the politics) that went into his masterful creation. As material for the novel, Stone sourced Michelangelo's original correspondence during the time (almost 500 letters), spent long periods in Rome and Florence, and even worked in a marble quarry and as a sculptor's apprentice.

EAT, PRAY, LOVE

Elizabeth Gilbert's memoir on what she ate, learned, and loved after leaving a failed marriage to travel the world is divided into three sections and her time spent in Italy, India, and Bali, respectively. The "Eat" portion of Gilbert's journey (the four months she spent in Rome) is perhaps the most enjoyable to read, and provides important travel advice: when in Rome, indulge with abandon. In the movie version, Rome and its feasts are less detailed but more cinematic (and on the plus side, you have Julia Roberts playing Gilbert).

LOVE AND ANARCHY

Much like her mentor Federico Fellini, Lina Wertmüller—one of Italy's most impressive female directors and the first woman to be nominated for the Best Director Oscar—has a knack for combining humor and folly with political critique and human heartbreak. The film's lovable, blundering star is a countryman determined to murder Mussolini, finding love and friendship in a Roman brothel along the way. This beautiful work is full of Roman sentiment, style, and history, making it a must-see in Italian cinema, as is Wertmüller's slightly darker work, Seven Beauties.

GLADIATOR

Russell Crowe takes on ancient Rome as a powerful general who, after a fall from political grace, is taken as a slave and forced to fight as a gladiator in the (digitally re-imagined) Colosseum. It's an epic film, full of high stakes and high emotions, and was a huge box-office hit when it opened in 2000. While it contains some historical inaccuracies, it's an enjoyable watch for those fascinated by the ins and outs of the political and social structures, power plays, and daily violence of ancient Rome.

Rome with Kids

There are plenty of ways to keep the younger set occupied in Rome—with the added bonus that getting them to eat isn't usually a problem, with pizza, pasta, and gelato on the menus.

ARCHAEOLOGY

If your kids are into archaeology or gladiators, traipsing the ruins of ancient Rome can provide hours of entertainment. Who can resist climbing the giant steps of the **Colosseum?** For the true enthusiast, the Roman Gladiator School offers group and private lessons in which your little one (or big one) can dress up like Spartacus and learn sword-fighting techniques and a bit about the lives of these warriors.

Roman Gladiator School. Two-hour lessons in how to be a gladiator include clothing to dress up in as well as "weapons" and shields—it's great fun and a great way to get some history lessons. The instructors are top-quality, and experienced at dealing with participants of varying levels. There's a viewing platform for those who prefer to observe their friends and family. ⊕ www.romegladiatorschool.com ✉ From €120.

EXPLORE THE PARKS

Take little ones to see the Teatrino Pulcinella's open-air puppet show weekends on the Janiculum Hill, where you can also enjoy a great view of the city, or to the San Carlino puppet theater weekends on Viale dei Bambini in **Villa Borghese Park.** (Tips for the puppeteers are greatly appreciated.) Villa Borghese is also home to other kid-oriented attractions such as the **Bioparco** (zoo), with more than 1,000 animals in peaceful landscaped surroundings. Rent a bike (at Bici Pincio at Via di Campo Marzo or on Viale Goethe) and explore the vast Borghese estate. You can also take a rowboat out on the Laghetto di Villa Borghese. At only €3.50 per person for 20 minutes, it's one of the best ways to explore the park's incredible sculptures, temples, and natural beauty.

CREEPY STUFF

Rome's catacombs (underground cemeteries) are intriguing enough to wipe the boredom off most teenagers' faces, and the best is the **Catacombe di San Callisto** on the Via Appia Antica. It's hard not to be impressed by the labyrinth of dark corridors and grisly tales of Christian martyrs. The **Capuchin Crypt** under Santa Maria della Concezione is gruesomely mesmerizing, with the skulls and bones of 3,700 friars arranged on the walls and ceiling in fanciful patterns. Take the kids to the Bocca della Verità (Mouth of Truth) at **Santa Maria in Cosmedin,** and warn them that it bites off liars' hands.

WATER FOUNTAINS

The public water fountains in Rome are free (and perfectly safe) to drink from; the only problem is figuring out how to do it without getting wet. A good trick is to block a hole under the spout with your finger to create a fountain, or bring bottles to fill up.

TRAVEL SMART

Updated by
Laura Itzkowitz

★ CAPITAL:	📠 COUNTRY CODE:	⊙ TIME:
Rome	39	Six hours ahead of New York
👥 POPULATION:	⚠ EMERGENCIES:	🌐 WEB RESOURCES:
4,227,588	113	www.turismoroma.it
💬 LANGUAGE:	🚘 DRIVING:	www.romeguide.it
Italian	On the right	www.theamericanmag.com
$ CURRENCY:	⚡ ELECTRICITY:	www.060608.it
Euro	220V/50Hz; Continental-style plugs, with two or three round prongs	

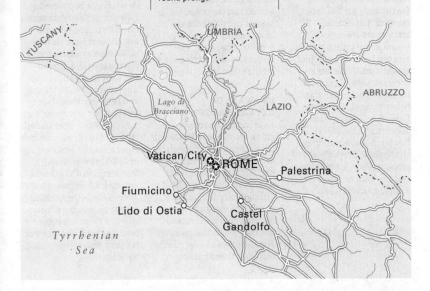

Know Before You Go

TAKE ADVANTAGE OF THE ROMA PASS.

In addition to single- and multi-day transit passes, a three-day Roma Pass (€52) covers unlimited use of buses, trams, and the Metro, plus free admission to two museums or archaeological sites of your choice and discounted entrance to others. A two-day pass is €32 and includes one museum.

NAVIGATING THE CITY IS ACTUALLY PRETTY EASY.

The *centro storico* (historic center) of Rome comprises what stood inside the 3rd-century walls of the city, and today contains most of the city's major tourist sights. The borders are roughly the Vatican to the west, Villa Borghese to the north, Termini station to east, and the Colosseum to the south. This large area is easier to navigate when divided into smaller modern neighborhoods. Fortunately for tourists, many of Rome's main attractions are concentrated in the centro storico and can be covered on foot. In addition, Rome has a good network of public transport, both above and below ground. The Metro Linea A will take you to Termini station, the Trevi Fountain (Barberini stop), the Spanish Steps (Spagna stop), St. Peter's (Ottaviano), and the Vatican Museums (Cipro), to name a few.

IT'S HELPFUL TO KNOW HOW TO READ ADDRESSES.

In the centro storico, most street names are posted on ceramic-like plaques on the side of buildings, which can make them hard to see. Addresses are fairly straightforward: the street name is followed by the street number, but it's worth noting that Roman street numbering, even in the newer outskirts of town, can be erratic. Usually numbers are even on one side of the street and odd on the other, but sometimes numbers are in ascending consecutive order on one side of the street and descending order on the other side.

BE AWARE OF EXTRA CHARGES.

As is common in many big cities, tourists can be taken advantage of in establishments near major sights, and Rome is no different, so always check your final bill carefully. It's common to see table service charges or cover charges on menus, but they should be specified and the cover charge should include a bread basket.

These charges mean tipping is not mandatory, although locals generally round up to the nearest euro of the total amount; at a casual trattoria or pizzeria, some coins on the table is good enough. If any surprise fees are on your final bill, don't be afraid to bring this up to the waitstaff. If you're at a bar having coffee, it's customary to leave a coin for your barista. Other charges to be aware of include paying to use the bathroom in some public places and the Tourist City Tax, imposed by the City of Rome—this is a compulsory per night, per person charge for all hotels, B&Bs, and even Airbnb bookings.

DRESS (AND ACT) APPROPRIATELY WHEN VISITING CHURCHES.

If you're planning to visit the Vatican, in particular St. Peter's Basilica, appropriate clothing and attire must be worn and, at a minimum, shoulders have to be covered. Low-cut or sleeveless tops, miniskirts, and hats are not allowed. Scarves and shawls are available for purchase in and around the Vatican if you turn up unprepared. Modest dress and behavior should also be observed when visiting other religious sites and all churches in the city. Do not enter a church while eating or drinking—keep all food items in a bag. Avoid entering altogether when a service is being held. All mobile phones must be on silent. If there are signs reading *No photography* or *No flash photography*, abide by these rules.

PRACTICE SOME BASIC ITALIAN ETIQUETTE.

Although you may find Rome much more informal than many other European cities, Romans will nevertheless appreciate attempts to abide by local etiquette. When entering an establishment, the key words to know are: *buongiorno* (good morning), *buona sera* (good evening), and *buon pomeriggio* (good afternoon). These words can also double as a goodbye upon exit. Italians greet friends with a kiss, usually first on the right cheek, and then on the left. When you meet a new person, shake hands and say *piacere* (*pee-ah-chair-ay*).

IT HELPS TO LEARN SOME ITALIAN, TOO.

You can always find someone who speaks at least a little English in Rome, albeit with an accent. Remember that the Italian language is pronounced exactly as it's written, so many Italians try to speak English as it's written—sometimes with bewildering results. You may run into a language barrier outside big cities, but a phrase book and close attention to the Italian use of expressive gestures will go a long way. Try to master a few phrases for daily use, and familiarize yourself with the terms you'll need to decipher signs and museum labels. Many museum exhibitions only have descriptions in Italian.

BE PREPARED FOR ROMAN TIME.

In Italy, almost nothing starts on time except for (sometimes) a theater, opera, or movie showing. Italians even joke about a "15-minute window" before actually being late somewhere. In addition, the day starts a little later than normal here with many shops not opening until 10 am, lunch never happening before 1 pm, and dinner rarely before 8 pm. On Sunday, Rome virtually shuts down, and on Monday, most state museums and exhibition halls, plus many restaurants are closed. Daily food shop hours generally run 10 am–1 pm and 4 pm–7:30 pm or 8 pm, but other stores in the center usually observe continuous opening hours. Pharmacies tend to close for a lunch break and keep night hours (*ora rio notturno*) in rotation. As for churches, most open at 8 or 9 in the morning, close noon to 3 or 4, then reopen until 6:30 or 7. St. Peter's, however, has continuous hours 7 am–7 pm (until 6 pm in the fall and winter); and the Vatican Museums are open Monday but closed Sunday (except for the last Sunday of the month).

IT'S USUALLY BEST TO AVOID AUGUST.

If you can avoid it, don't travel at all in Italy in mid-August, when much of the population is on the move, especially around Ferragosto, the August 15 national holiday, when cities such as Rome are deserted and many restaurants and shops are closed. If you've done the tourist circuit several times, though, you may enjoy a quieter, emptier version of the city during this time. Other national holidays are New Year's Day (January 1); Epiphany (January 6); Easter Sunday and Monday; Liberation Day (April 25); Labor Day (May 1); Republic Day (June 2); Ferragosto (August 15); All Saint's Day (November 1); Immaculate Conception (December 8); Christmas Day and the feast of Saint Stephen (December 25 and 26). Rome-specific holidays are Rome's birthday (April 21) and St. Peter and Paul Day (June 29).

THERE ARE WAYS TO AVOID THE CROWDS.

Millions of tourists visit Rome each year and you should plan your sightseeing ahead of time, especially for the most popular sights like the Colosseum and the Vatican. While travelers seem to be catching on to what used to be low season in Rome, January, February, and November are still when the city is a little quieter than usual. Advance tickets and private tours that let you skip the ticket lines are highly recommended to ensure hours aren't lost queuing for the major attractions. While the city center is the most aesthetically spectacular part of the city, spend some time in the less busy neighborhoods like Testaccio, Monti, or San Giovanni if tourist crowds aren't your thing.

Getting Here and Around

Air

Flying time to Rome is 7½–8½ hours from New York, 9–10 hours from Chicago, 11–12 hours from Los Angeles, and 2½ hours from London.

AIRPORTS

The principal airport for flights to Rome is Leonardo da Vinci Airport, more commonly known as Fiumicino (FCO). It's 30 km (19 miles) southwest of the city. There is a direct train link with Rome's Termini station on the Leonardo Express train, and a local train to Trastevere and Ostiense stations. Rome's other airport is Ciampino (CIA), on Via Appia Nuova, 15 km (9 miles) south of downtown. Ciampino is a national and international hub for many low-cost airlines. There are no trains linking the Ciampino airport to downtown Rome, but there are a number of shuttle buses running daily.

TRANSFERS BETWEEN FIUMICINO AND DOWNTOWN

If you're driving into the city, follow the signs for Rome and the GRA (the ring road that circles Rome). The direction you take on the GRA depends on where your lodging is located. If you're staying in the centro storico, follow indications for Roma Centro. Get a map and directions from the car-rental service, and if you aren't using one on your phone, considering renting a GPS as well.

A law implemented by the Comune di Roma requires all Rome taxi drivers to charge a fixed fare of €48 (including four passengers and luggage handling) if your destination is within the Aurelian walls (this covers the centro storico, most of Trastevere, most of the Vatican area, and parts of San Giovanni). If you aren't sure if your hotel falls within the Aurelian walls, ask when you book your room. If your hotel is outside the walls, the cab ride can run you about €60 plus *supplementi*

(extra charges) for luggage. (Of course, this also depends on traffic.) The ride from the airport to the city center takes about 30–45 minutes. Private limousines can be booked at booths in the Arrivals hall; they charge more than taxis but can carry more passengers. The Comune di Roma now has a representative in place outside the International Arrivals hall (Terminal 2), where the taxi stand is located, to help tourists get into a taxi cab. Use only licensed white taxis. When in doubt, always ask for a receipt and write the cab company and taxi's license number down (it's written on a metal plate on the inside of the passenger door). Avoid unauthorized drivers who may approach you in the Arrivals hall; they charge exorbitant, unmetered rates.

Airport Connection charges €22 for one passenger, €28 for two, and minimal fees for each additional passenger. Booking ahead is required. **Airport Shuttle Express** offers a daily service from/to FCO. The shuttles stop at all major hotels in the center of Rome. It costs €20 one-way for one passenger, €30 for two, and €10 for each additional passenger. (The rate includes two bags per person.) **Airport Shuttle** provides door-to-door shuttle service, at a cost of €25 for one person and €6 for each additional passenger (up to eight). Advance booking is recommended.

Two trains link downtown Rome with Fiumicino—a nonstop express and a local. Inquire at the APT tourist information counter in the International Arrivals hall (Terminal 2) or train information counter near the tracks to determine which takes you closest to your destination in Rome. The 32-minute nonstop Airport–Termini express (called the **Leonardo Express**) goes directly to Tracks 23 or 24 at Termini station, which is well served by taxis and is a hub of Metro and bus lines.

Departures to Termini station run every 15 minutes beginning at 6:08 am from the airport, with a final departure at 11:23 pm. Trains depart Termini station from Tracks 23 and 24 to the airport starting at 5:20 am and the last train leaves at 10:35 pm. Tickets cost €14.

Trenitalia's **FL1,** the commuter rail, leaves from the same tracks and runs to Rome and beyond. The main stops in Rome are at Trastevere (26 minutes), Ostiense (31 minutes), and Tiburtina (48 minutes); at each you can find taxis and public transport connections to other areas of Rome. FL1 regional trains run from Fiumicino between 5:57 am and 10:42 pm, with departures every 15 minutes; the schedule is similar going to the airport. Tickets cost €8. For either train, you can buy your ticket at a vending machine or at ticket counters at the airport and at some stations (Termini, Trastevere, Tiburtina). At the airport, stamp the ticket at the gate. Remember when using the train at other stations to stamp the ticket in the little yellow or red machine near the track *before* you board. If you fail to stamp your ticket before you board, you could receive a hefty fine, as much as €100 on top of the ticket price. If you book your ticket online, you don't need to stamp or even print it. You can show the PDF to the ticket controller using your smartphone.

At night, take **COTRAL buses** from the airport to Tiburtina station or Termini station in Rome (50 minutes) and vice versa. Timetables are subject to last-minute changes, so be sure to check before traveling. Tickets either way cost €5 (€7 if purchased on board).

TRANSFERS BETWEEN CIAMPINO AND DOWNTOWN
By car, go north on the Via Appia Nuova into downtown Rome. The taxi fare law implemented by the Comune di Roma that affects Fiumicino applies to this airport, too. All taxi drivers are supposed to charge a fixed fare of €30 (including luggage handling) if your destination is within the Aurelian walls. If your hotel is outside the walls, the cab ride can run you about €60, plus supplementi for luggage. The ride takes about 30 minutes. Take only official white cabs with the "taxi" sign on top; unofficial cabs often overcharge disoriented travelers.

Airport Connection Services has shuttles that cost €22 for the first passenger and €28 for two. **Airport Shuttle** charges €25 for the first person, and €6 for each additional passenger. The **ATRAL bus** connects Ciampino airport with Termini station via a bus to Ciampino station and then a train. Buses depart from in front of the airport terminal frequently 6:15 am–11:30 pm. The fare is €2.70, and tickets can be bought on the bus. Travel time is approximately 40 minutes.

TRANSFERS BETWEEN AIRPORTS
It's not easy to move from one airport to another in Rome—the airports aren't connected by a railway system or by the Metro. The only way to make the transfer is by car, taxi, or a combination of bus, Metro, and train. The latter option is not advisable because it would take you at least two to three hours to get from one airport to the other. A taxi ride from Fiumicino Leonardo Da Vinci Airport to Ciampino Airport will take approximately 45 minutes and could cost roughly €50.

 ## Bus
An extensive network of bus lines that covers all of Lazio (the surrounding geographical region of which Rome is the capital) is operated by **COTRAL** (Consorzio Trasporti Lazio). There are several main bus stations. Long-distance and suburban COTRAL bus routes terminate either

Getting Here and Around

near Tiburtina station or at outlying Metro stops, such as Rebibbia and Ponte Mammolo (Linea B) and Anagnina (Linea A).

ATAC, Rome's city transport service, offers reasonable fares for travel in and around Rome, especially with the BIRG (Biglietto Integrale Regionale Giornaliero), which allows you to travel on all the lines (and some railroad lines) up to midnight on the day of the ticket's first validation. The cost of a BIRG depends upon the distance to your destination and how many "zones" you travel through. Because of the extent and complexity of the system, it's a good idea to consult with your hotel concierge, review ATAC's website, or to telephone COTRAL's central office when planning a trip. COTRAL has several buses that leave daily from Rome's Ponte Mammolo (Linea B) Metro station for the town of Tivoli, where Hadrian's Villa and Villa D'Este are located. Flixbuses leave from Rome's Tiburtina Metro and train station (Linea B) and will take you to Siena and other towns in Tuscany.

While the bus may be an affordable way of moving around, keep in mind that buses can be crowded due to commuter traffic. Just because you've managed to purchase a ticket doesn't mean you're guaranteed a seat. Make sure to arrive early and stand your ground in line. If you are not able to procure a seat, you may be standing for the entire ride.

If you're taking a city bus, make sure the bus you're waiting for actually runs during that part of the day or on that particular day of the week. For example, *notturno* buses (late-night buses)—distinguished by the "N" sign just above the bus number—don't run until after midnight and then only a few times per hour. Tourists often get confused while waiting at the bus stop, since the notturno bus schedules are listed side by side with

the regular day bus schedules. Also, be aware that *deviata* buses are those that have been rerouted due to road construction or public demonstrations. And *festivi* buses are ones that only run on Sunday and holidays. Neither notturno buses nor festivi buses run as often as other buses do on weekdays and Saturday. Regular buses will either say *feriali*, which means "daily," or won't have any special distinction.

Car

Driving in Rome is generally not recommended. The main access routes from the north are the A1–E35 (Autostrada del Sole) from Milan and Florence and the A12–E80 highway from Genoa. The principal route to or from points south, including Naples, is the A1–E45. All highways connect with the Grande Raccordo Anulare Ring Road (GRA), which channels traffic into the city center. Markings on the GRA are confusing: take time to study the route you need. Be extremely careful of pedestrians and mopeds when driving: Romans are casual jaywalkers and pop out frequently from between parked cars. People on scooters tend to be the most careless drivers, as they weave in and out of traffic. For driving directions, check out ⊕ *www.tuttocitta.it.*

PARKING

Be warned: parking in Rome can be a nightmare. The situation is greatly compounded by the fact that private cars without permits are not allowed access to the centro storico on weekdays 6:30 am–6 pm, Saturday 2 pm–6 pm, or Friday and Saturday nights (11 pm–3 am). Other areas, including Trastevere, Testaccio, and San Lorenzo, are closed to cars at various times. Check the **Roma Mobilità** website for the most up-to-date information. These areas, known as

Zona Traffico Limitato (ZTL), are marked by electric signs, and bordering streets have video cameras for photographing license plates. Fines are sent directly to car-rental companies and added to your bill. There is limited free parking in Rome; most parking is metered, on a pay-by-the-hour basis. Spaces with white lines are free parking; spaces with blue lines are paid parking; and spaces with yellow lines are for the handicapped only. All other color-coded spaces are usually reserved for residents or carpooling and require special permits. If you park in one of these spaces without a permit, your car could be ticketed or towed. Make sure to check with your hotel regarding appropriate places to park nearby. Meter parking costs €1–€1.50 per hour (depending on what area you're in) with a limit on total parking time allowed in many areas. Parking facilities near historic sights exist at the Villa Borghese and the Vatican.

RULES OF THE ROAD

Driving is on the right. Regulations are largely similar to those in Britain and the United States, except that the police have the power to levy on-the-spot fines. Speed limits are 50 kph (31 mph) in Rome, 110 kph (70 mph) on state and provincial roads, and 130 kph (80 mph) on autostrade, unless otherwise marked. Talking on a mobile phone while driving is strictly prohibited, and if caught, the driver will be issued a fine. Not wearing a seat belt is also against the law. The blood-alcohol content limit for driving is 0.5 gr/l with fines up to €6,000 and the possibility of 12 months imprisonment for surpassing the limit. Fines for speeding are uniformly stiff: 10 kph (6 mph) over the speed limit can warrant a fine in the hundreds and even thousands of euros; over 10 kph, and your license could be taken away.

Whenever the city decides to implement an "Ecological Day" in order to reduce smog levels, commuters are prohibited from driving their cars during certain hours of the day and in certain areas of the city. These are usually organized and announced ahead of time; however, if you're planning to rent a car during your trip, make sure to ask the rental company and your hotel if there are any planned, because the traffic police won't cut you any breaks, even if you say you're a tourist.

CAR RENTALS

When you reserve a car, ask about cancellation penalties, taxes, drop-off charges (if you're planning to pick up the car in one city and leave it in another), and surcharges (for being under or over a certain age, for additional drivers, or for driving across regional or country borders or beyond a specific distance from your point of rental). All these things can add substantially to your costs. Request car seats and extras such as GPS when you book. Make sure to ask the rental car company if they require you to obtain an International Driver's Permit beforehand (most do). These can generally be obtained for a fee through AAA in the United States. Rates are sometimes—but not always—better if you book in advance or reserve through a rental agency's website. There are other reasons to book ahead, though: for popular destinations, during busy times of the year, or to ensure that you get certain types of cars (automatic transmission, vans, SUVs, exotic sports cars).

Rates in Rome begin at around €40 per day for an economy car with air-conditioning, a manual transmission, and unlimited mileage. This includes the 20% Value-Added Tax (VAT, or "IVA" in Italian) on car rentals. All international car-rental agencies in Rome have a number of

Getting Here and Around

locations. It's usually cheaper to rent a car in advance through your local agency than to rent on location in Italy. Or book ahead online—you can save as much as €10 per day on your car rental. Within Italy, local and international rental agencies offer similar rates. Whether you're going with a local or international agency, note that most cars are manual; automatics are rarer, so inquire about those well in advance.

In Italy, your own driver's license is acceptable if accompanied by an official translation in Italian. But to be extra safe, an International Driving Permit is a good idea; it's available from the American or Canadian Automobile Association and, in the United Kingdom, from the Automobile Association or Royal Automobile Club. These international permits are universally recognized, and having one in your wallet may save you a problem with the local authorities.

In Italy you must be 21 years of age to rent an economy or subcompact car, and most companies require customers under the age of 23 to pay by credit card. Upon rental, all companies require credit cards as a warranty; to rent bigger cars (2,000 cc or more), you must often show two credit cards. Debit or check cards are not accepted. Call local agents for details. There are no special restrictions on senior-citizen drivers.

Ⓜ Public Transport

Although most of Rome's sights are in a relatively circumscribed area, the city is too large to be seen solely on foot. Try to avoid rush hour when taking the Metro (subway) or a bus, as public transport can be extremely crowded. Midmorning or midday through early afternoon tends to be less busy. Otherwise, it's best to take

a taxi to the area you plan to visit if it is across town. You should always expect to do a lot of walking in Rome, especially considering how little ground the subway actually covers, so plan on wearing a pair of comfortable, sturdy shoes to cushion the impact of the *sampietrini* (cobblestones). You can get free city and transit maps at municipal information booths.

Rome's integrated transportation system includes buses and trams (ATAC), the Metropolitana (the subway, or Metro), suburban trains and buses (COTRAL), and the commuter rail run by the state railway (Trenitalia). A ticket (BIT), valid for 100 minutes on any combination of buses and trams and one entrance to the Metro, costs €1.50. Tickets are sold at tobacco shops, newsstands, some coffee bars, automatic ticket machines in Metro stations, some bus stops, in machines on some buses, and at ATAC ticket booths. You can purchase individual or multiple tickets. It's always a good idea to have a few tickets handy so you don't have to hunt for a vendor when you need one. All tickets must be validated by time-stamping in the yellow meter boxes aboard buses and in Metro stations, immediately prior to boarding. Failure to validate your ticket will result in a fine of €54.90. You can now pay for fines on the ATAC website. Pay immediately, or the fine will increase to €104.90 if you pay after five days. You can also pay fines in post offices, authorized shops, or by wire transfer. Do not pay the ticket inspectors in cash; some may be equipped for payment by mobile POS.

A Roma24H ticket, or *biglietto integrato giornaliero* (integrated daily ticket), is valid for 24 hours (from the moment you stamp it) on all public transit and costs €7. You can also purchase a Roma48H (€12.50), a Roma72H (€18), and a CIS (Carta Integrata Settimanale), which is valid for one week (€24). Each option gives unlimited travel on ATAC buses, COTRAL urban bus services, trains for the Lido and Viterbo, and Metro. There's an ATAC kiosk at the bus terminal in front of Termini station. If you're going farther afield, or planning to spend more than a week in Rome, think about getting a BIRG (daily regional ticket) or a CIRS (weekly regional ticket) from the railway station. These give you unlimited travel on all state transport throughout the region of Lazio. This can take you as far as the Etruscan city of Tarquinia or medieval Viterbo.

The Metro is the easiest and fastest way to get around Rome. There are stops near most of the main tourist attractions; street entrances are marked with red "M" signs. The Metro has three lines: A and B, which intersect at Termini station, and also C. Linea A (red) runs from the eastern part of the city, with stops at San Giovanni in Laterano, Piazza Barberini, Piazza di Spagna, Piazzale Flaminio (Piazza del Popolo), and Ottaviano/San Pietro, near the Basilica di San Pietro and the Musei Vaticani. Linea B (blue) has stops near the Colosseum, the Circus Maximus, the Pyramid (Ostiense station and trains for Ostia Antica), and the Basilica di San Paolo Fuori le Mura. Linea C runs from the eastern outskirts of the city through Pigneto and meets Linea A at San Giovanni. The Metro opens at 5:30 am, and the last trains leave the last station at either end at 11:30 pm (on Friday and Saturday nights the last trains leave at 1:30 am).

Although not as fast as the Metro, bus and tram travel is more scenic. With reserved bus lanes and numerous tram lines, surface transportation is surprisingly efficient, given the volume of Roman traffic. At peak times, however, buses can be very crowded. If the distance you have to travel is not too great, walking can be a more comfortable alternative. ATAC city buses are red or gray; trams are green. Remember to board at the rear and to exit at the middle: some bus drivers may refuse to let you out the front door, leaving you to scramble through the crowd to exit the middle or rear doors. Don't forget that you must buy your ticket before boarding, and be sure to stamp it in a machine as soon as you enter. The ticket is good for a transfer and one Metro trip within the next 100 minutes. Buses and trams run 5:30 am–midnight, after which time there's an extensive network of night buses with service throughout the city.

The bus system is a bit complicated to navigate due to the number of lines, but ATAC has a website (⊕ *www.atac. roma.it*) that will help you calculate the number of stops and bus route needed, and even give you a map directing you to the appropriate stops. To navigate the site, look for the British flag in the upper right-hand corner to change the website into English. Or do as the locals do and use the Moovit app.

🛵 Scooter

After a few days in the city, you'll quickly notice that mopeds/scooters are everywhere. Riders are required to wear helmets, and traffic police are tough in enforcing this law. Producing your country's driver's license should be enough to convince most rental firms that they're not dealing with a complete beginner; but if you're unsure of exactly how to ride a moped, think twice, as driving one in Rome is not like you see it in the movies. It can be very dangerous, and Roman drivers tend to be ruthless; at least ask the attendant for a detailed demonstration. If you don't feel up to braving the

Getting Here and Around

Roman traffic on a moped, you can hire a Segway or electric bicycle to explore the seven hills of Rome.

Taxi

The best way to find a taxi in Rome is generally to hire one at a taxi stand. Taxis do not cruise, but they may stop if you flag them down. You can also call for one by phone, in which case you'll be charged a supplement (the meter will already be running when you're picked up). The various taxi services are considered interchangeable and are referred to by their phone numbers rather than names. Taxicabs can be reserved the night before only if you're traveling to or from the airport or the train station. Only some taxis are equipped to take credit cards; inquire when you phone to make the booking.

The base meter fare is €3 during the day, €6.50 10 pm–6 am, and €4.50 on Sunday and holidays. Supplemental charges, such as for luggage or even for pick up at Termini station, are added to the meter fare. When in doubt, ask for a receipt (*ricevuta*). This will encourage the driver to be honest and charge you the correct amount. Women traveling alone via taxi 10 pm–6 am are entitled to a 10% discount; the same discount applies if your destination is a public hospital (make sure to ask for it). Use only licensed, metered white cabs, identified by a numbered shield on the side, an illuminated taxi sign on the roof, and a plaque next to the license plate reading "*servizio pubblico*." Avoid unmarked, unauthorized, unmetered cabs (numerous at Rome airports and train stations), whose drivers actively solicit your trade and may demand astronomical fares.

While ride-sharing apps like Uber and Lyft are not yet big in Rome, a new app, Mytaxi, is a quick and easy way to book an official taxi with a smartphone. You can choose to pay by app or with cash, and can rate your driver after the ride.

🚆 Train

State-owned Trenitalia trains are part of the Metrebus system and also serve some destinations on side trips outside Rome. The main Trenitalia stations in Rome are Termini, Tiburtina, Ostiense, and Trastevere. Suburban trains use all of these stations. The Ferrovie COTRAL line departs from a terminal in Piazzale Flaminio, connecting Rome with Viterbo.

Only Trenitalia trains such as Frecciarossa, Frecciargento, and Intercity Plus have first- and second-class compartments. Local trains can be crowded early in the morning and in the evening as many people commute to and from the city, so try to avoid traveling at these times. Plan on arriving early to secure a seat or be ready to stand. On long-distance routes (to Florence and Venice, for instance), you can either travel by the cheap (but slow) *regionale* trains, or the fast, but more expensive, Intercity, Frecciarossa, or Frecciargento, which require seat reservations, available at the station when you buy your ticket, online, or through a travel agent. The state railways' excellent and user-friendly site will help you plan any rail trips in the country.

Since 2012, Italy's rails have had a private competitor, Italo, whose gorgeous and very fast trains travel between large cities including Naples, Rome, Florence, Bologna, Milan, Venice, and Torino. In Rome, Italo trains stop at Termini and Tiburtina stations.

Essentials

Dining

In Rome, simple yet traditional cuisine reigns supreme. Most chefs prefer to follow the mantra of freshness over fuss, and simplicity of flavor and preparation over complex cooking techniques. Rome has been known since antiquity for its grand feasts and banquets, and dining out has always been a favorite Roman pastime. Until recently, the city's *buongustaii* (gourmands) would have been the first to tell you that Rome is distinguished more by its enthusiasm for eating out than for a multitude of world-class restaurants—but this is changing. There is an ever-growing promotion of slow-food practices, a focus on sustainably and locally sourced produce. The economic crisis forced the food industry in Rome to adopt innovative ways to maintain a clientele who were increasingly looking to dine out but wanting to spend less; the result has been the rise of "street food" restaurants, selling everything from inexpensive and novel takes on the classic *suppli* (Roman fried-rice balls) to sandwich shops that use a variety of organic ingredients.

Generally speaking, Romans like Roman food, and that's what you'll find in many of the city's trattorias and wine bars. For the most part, today's chefs cling to the traditional and excel at what has taken hundreds, sometimes thousands, of years to perfect. This is why the basic trattoria menu is more or less the same wherever you go. And it's why even the top Roman chefs feature their versions of simple trattoria classics like carbonara, sometimes in a "deconstructed" or slightly varied way. To a great extent, Rome is still a town where the Italian equivalent of "What are you in the mood for?" still gets the answer, "Pizza or pasta."

Nevertheless, Rome is the capital of Italy, and because people move here from every corner of the Italian peninsula, there are more variations on the Italian theme in Rome than you'd find elsewhere in Italy: Sicilian, Tuscan, Pugliese, Bolognese, Marchegiano, Sardinian, and northern Italian regional cuisines are all represented. And reflecting the increasingly cosmopolitan nature of the city, you'll find a growing number of good-quality international foods here as well—particularly Japanese, Indian, and Ethiopian.

Oddly enough, though, for a nation that prides itself on *la bella figura* ("looking good"), most Romans don't fuss about music, personal space, lighting, or decor. After all, who needs flashy interior design when so much of Roman life takes place outdoors, when dining alfresco in Rome can take place in the middle of a glorious ancient site or a centuries-old piazza?

RESTAURANT TYPES

Until relatively recently, there was a distinct hierarchy delineated by the names of Rome's eating places. A **ristorante** was typically elegant and expensive, and a **trattoria** served more traditional, home-style fare in a relaxed atmosphere. An **osteria** was even more casual, essentially a wine bar and gathering spot that also served food, although the latest species of wine bars generally goes under the moniker of **enoteca.** All these terms still exist but their distinction has blurred considerably. Now, an osteria in the center of town may be pricier than a ristorante across the street.

Although Rome may not boast the grand **caffè** of Paris or Vienna, it does have hundreds of small places on pleasant side streets and piazze. The coffee is routinely of high quality. Locals usually stop in for a quickie at the bar, where prices are much lower than for the same drink taken at

Essentials

the table. If you place your order at the counter, ask if you can sit down: some places charge more for table service. Often you'll pay a cashier first, then give your *scontrino* (receipt) to the person at the counter who fills your order.

HOW TO ORDER: FROM PRIMO TO DOLCE

In a Roman sit-down restaurant, whether a ristorante, trattoria, or osteria, you're expected to order at least two courses. It could be a *primo* (first course, usually pasta or an appetizer) followed by a *secondo* (second course, really a "main course" in English parlance, usually meat or fish); an *antipasto* (starter) followed by a primo or secondo; or a primo or secondo and a *dolce* (dessert). Many people consider a full meal to consist of a primo, a secondo, and a dolce.

If you're not too hungry, try a pizzeria, where it's common to order just one dish. The handiest places for an afternoon snack are bars, caffè, and pizzerie. For a quick lunch or dinner, head to a *tavola calda*, kind of like a cafeteria where you can order from what's available at the counter and sit and eat at a table.

MEAL TIMES AND CLOSURES

Breakfast (*la colazione*) is usually served 7 am–10:30 am, lunch (*il pranzo*) 12:30 pm–2:30 pm, dinner (*la cena*) 7:30 pm–11 pm. Peak times are around 1:30 pm for lunch and 9 pm for dinner. Enoteche are sometimes open in the morning and late afternoon for snacks. Most pizzerie open at 8 pm and close around midnight or 1 am. Most bars and caffè are open 7 am–8 or 9 pm. Almost all restaurants close one day a week (in most cases Sunday or Monday) and for at least two weeks in August. The city is zoned, however, so that there are always some restaurants in each zone that remain open.

Local regulations are in the process of changing in Rome to give proprietors greater leeway in setting their hours. This is meant to allow establishments to stay open later and make more money in a down economy, and to offer patrons longer hours and more time to eat, drink, and be merry. It has yet to be seen whether Italians will find the law "flexible" and use it as an excuse to close early when they feel like it. *Tutto è possibile*: anything's possible in Rome.

Restaurant prices are the average cost of a main course at dinner or, if dinner is not served, at lunch.

WHAT IT COSTS in Euros			
$	**$$**	**$$$**	**$$$$**
AT DINNER			
under €15	€15–€24	€25–€35	over €35

Health

Smoking is banned in Italy in all public places. This includes trains, buses, offices, hospitals, and waiting rooms, as well as restaurants, pubs, and dance clubs (unless the latter have separate smoking rooms). Fines for breaking the law are exorbitant. You'll find that most people skirt the law by sitting outside on the many outdoor restaurant terraces. Sit inside if the smoke in outdoor seating areas bothers you. Many restaurants are now equipped with air-conditioning.

It's always best to travel with your own trusted medications. Should you need medication while in Italy, you should speak with a physician to make sure it is the proper kind and in case a prescription is necessary. Aspirin (*l'aspirina*) can be purchased at any pharmacy, as can over-the-counter medicines such as ibuprofen or acetaminophen. Other over-the-counter remedies, including cough syrup, antiseptic creams, and headache pills, are sold only in pharmacies. Pharmacists are happy to dispense advice and, in the city center especially, almost always speak some English.

At this writing, COVID-19 is still an ongoing concern in Italy, but restrictions are slowly being lifted.

 Immunizations

Proof of COVID-19 vaccination, recovery, or a negative test result is no longer required for visits to Italy.

🛏 Lodging

When it comes to accommodations, Rome offers a wide selection of high-end hotels, bed-and-breakfasts, and designer boutique hotels—options that run the gamut from whimsical to luxurious. Whether you want a simple place to rest your head or a complete cache of exclusive amenities, you have plenty to choose from.

Luxury hotels are justly renowned for sybaritic comfort: postcard views over Roman rooftops, silver flatware on white linen atop a groaning breakfast-buffet table, and the fluffiest towels. But in more modest categories, very often Rome's hotels are not up to the standards of space, comfort, quiet, and service taken for granted in the United States: you'll still find places with tiny rooms, lumpy beds, and anemic air-conditioning. The good news: if you're flexible, there are happy mediums aplenty.

One thing to figure out before you arrive is which neighborhood you want to stay

in. There are obvious advantages to staying in a hotel within easy walking distance of the main sights. If a picturesque location is your main concern, stay in one of the small hotels around Piazza Navona or Campo de' Fiori. If luxury is a high priority, head for Piazza di Spagna or beyond the city center, where quality/price ratios are higher and some hotels have swimming pools.

Prices are for a standard double room in high season.

WHAT IT COSTS in Euros			
$	$$	$$$	$$$$
LODGING FOR TWO			
under €125	€125– €200	€201– €300	over €300

🍸 Nightlife

For a great night out in Rome, all you need to do is to wander, because ready entertainment is sure to find you on every corner. It's important to follow Rome's rule of thumb: if you see an enoteca, stop in. Though most enoteche are tiny and offer a limited antipasti menu, they cover more ground in their wine lists and often have a charming gang of regulars. For the linguistically timid, there are also several stereotypical English and Irish pubs peppered around the city, complete with a steady stream of Guinness, darts, and rugby on their satellite televisions. Those oversize flat-screen TVs also show American football, baseball, and basketball—ideal for those who don't want to miss a playoff game.

Although Rome offers a cornucopia of evening bacchanalia, from ultra-chic to super-cheap, all that glitters is not gold.

Where Should I Stay?

	NEIGHBORHOOD VIBE	PROS	CONS
Around the Vatican: Borgo and Prati	Touristy near the Vatican but also with some upmarket restaurants and caffè; not especially atmospheric.	Close to the Vatican; pretty quiet at night.	Far from other tourist attractions and nightlife.
Piazza Navona, Campo de' Fiori, and Jewish Ghetto	Surrounding areas are filled with good restaurants and most of Rome's major attractions; the Jewish Ghetto is quieter.	Everything is within walking distance: good eats, shopping, and many of Rome's museums and monuments.	The height of hustle and bustle in Rome—convenient, but often pricey; street noise may be an issue.
Piazza di Spagna	Home to Rome's crème de la crème for lodging and shopping.	Where all the high rollers and A-listers like to reside.	Everything is expensive; not very close to central hot spots.
Repubblica	Repubblica, with its beautiful piazza, is near Termini station without the grungy feel.	Hotels are much cheaper than elsewhere in Rome; convenient to Termini station.	Cheap, basic accommodations; the area surrounding Termini station can be iffy.
Villa Borghese and Piazza del Popolo, Monte Mario, and Parioli	Somewhat removed from the hubbub, this area is a bit more refined, with fancy boutiques and hotels.	Close to the Piazza di Spagna and shopping; lots of dining options nearby.	Pricey and a bit remote from Piazza Navona and Campo de' Fiori.
Trastevere	Villagelike Trastevere has winding cobblestone alleys, beautiful churches, and authentic mom-and-pop trattorias.	Fun area with great restaurants, bars and caffè.	General area gets busy at night; can be rowdy and rambunctious on the weekends; full of students.
Aventino and Testaccio	Aventino is a relaxing hilltop retreat. Working-class Testaccio is the heart of Rome's nightlife.	Tranquility, amazing views, and spacious rooms await in Aventino. Party like a rock star in Rome's famous nightlife district, Testaccio.	Transportation difficult on the Aventine Hill; Testaccio is crowded on weekends.
Esquilino	These are some of the more hip and funky neighborhoods in Rome.	Hotels are cheaper here than elsewhere in Rome; close to Termini station.	Far from main tourist attractions.

Insiders and visitors alike understand that finding "the scene" in Rome is the proverbial needle in the haystack: it requires patience and pursuit. Your best asset will be your ability to talk, since word-of-mouth is the most accurate source. Entertainment guides like Roma 2night provide great logistical information including up-to-date listings of bars and clubs. Most visitors head out in the centro storico to find some fun; Piazza Navona, Pantheon, Campo de' Fiori, and even Trastevere may be filled with tourists, but more recently, several niche and boutique bars have opened. (In contrast, the Spanish Steps area is a ghost town by 9 pm.) If you want to get out of the comfort zone, head to the Testaccio, San Lorenzo and Pigneto areas. And wherever you go, remember: Romans love an after-party, so plenty of nightlife doesn't start until midnight.

When it comes to clubs, discos, and DJs in Rome, Testaccio is considered a mecca. Testaccio's Via Galvani is Rome's Sunset Strip, where hybrid restaurant-clubs, largely identical in music and crowd, jockey for top ranking. On average, drinks range between €10 and €15, and one is often included with the entrance (€10–€20). In summer, many clubs relocate to the beach or the Tiber, so call ahead to confirm location and hours.

🌐 Passports and Visas

All U.S., Canadian, Australian, and New Zealand citizens, even infants, need a valid passport to enter Italy for stays of up to 90 days. However, visas are not required for stays in Italy under 90 days.

🎭 Performing Arts

One of the pleasures of Rome is seeing a performance in one of the city's stunning venues, ancient or modern. This is the city where you might experience classical opera performed in the 3rd-century-AD Terme di Caracalla, or enjoy an experimental dance show in the postindustrial detergent factory Teatro India, or see a contemporary performance at the Renzo Piano–designed Auditorium Parco della Musica.

HOW TO FIND EVENTS

With its foot firmly in the 21st century, Rome has a pantheon of publications heralding its cultural events. For city-sponsored events, Rome's official website tries to remain as up to date as any governmental entity can. A broader range of event listings can be found in the Cronaca and Cultura section of Italian newspapers, including *Metro,* the free newspaper found at Metro stops and on trams.

On the Internet, check out this website written exclusively for the English-speaking community: ⊕ *romeing. it.* Its Italian-language counterpart **Roma 2night** (⊕ *www.2night.it*) has an even more robust selection of nightlife, along with food spots. The monthly English-language periodical **Wanted in Rome** (⊕ *www. wantedinrome.com*) is available at many newsstands and has good coverage of arts events. For directory information, like addresses, **060608** (⊕ *www.060608. it/en*) has listings of every cultural site (monument, church, museum, art space, etc.) in the city.

Essentials

Safety

Rome is like any other major Western city: generally quite safe, but the occasional pickpocketing or bag snatching does happen, especially in the busy summer months. Wear a bag or camera slung across your body bandolier-style, and don't rest your bag or camera on a table or underneath your chair at a sidewalk café or restaurant. If you have to bring a purse, make sure to keep it within sight by wearing it toward the front.

In Rome, beware of pickpockets on buses, especially No. 64 (Termini–Stazione di San Pietro); the No. 40 Express, which takes a faster route; and No. 46, which takes you closer to St. Peter's Basilica; on subways and in subway stations; and on trains, when making your way through the corridors of crowded cars. Pickpockets often work in teams and zero in on tourists who look distracted or are in large groups. Pickpockets may be active wherever tourists gather, including the Roman Forum, the Spanish Steps, Piazza Navona, and Piazza di San Pietro.

Women traveling alone will feel safe, but they should take the same precautions as in any other major Western city. While Italy is still a rather conservative country (and gay marriage is not legal here), LGBTQ+ travelers should feel safe and welcomed in Rome, although it doesn't have as big of a gay-friendly scene as other European cities.

Shopping

In Rome, shopping is an art form. Perhaps it's the fashionably bespectacled commuter wearing Giorgio Armani as he deftly zips through traffic on his Vespa, or all those Anita Ekberg, Audrey Hepburn, and Julia Roberts films that make us long to be Roman for a day. But with limited time and no Hollywood studio backing you, the trick is to find what you're looking for and still not miss out on the city's museums and monuments—and, of course, leave yourself plenty of euros to enjoy the rest of your trip.

Since you may be pressed for time, knowing how and where to put your best fashion foot forward is crucial. Luckily for shop-till-you-droppers, you can still fit your shopping sprees in between sights. A visit to the Trevi Fountain means not only reliving the movie classic *Three Coins in a Fountain,* but puts you within striking distance of some of the city's best shopping. Pose for a picture-perfect snapshot at Piazza di Spagna, as you keep your eye on that delicious handbag in the window at Dolce & Gabbana.

There may be no city that takes shopping quite as seriously as Rome, and no district more worthy of your time than Piazza di Spagna, with its abundance of shops and designer powerhouses like Fendi and Armani. The best of them are clumped tightly together along the city's three primary fashion arteries: Via dei Condotti, Via Borgognona, and Via Frattina. From Piazza di Spagna to Piazza Navona and on to Campo de' Fiori, shoppers will find an explosive array of shops within walking distance of one another: a shop for fine handmade Amalfi paper looks out upon the Pantheon, while slick boutiques anchor the corners of 18th-century Piazza di Spagna. Across town in the colorful hive that is Monti, a second-generation mosaic artist creates Italian masterpieces on a street named for a pope who died before America was even discovered. Even in Trastevere, one can find one of Rome's rising shoe designers creating next-century *nuovo chic* shoes nestled on a side street beside one of the city's oldest churches.

DUTY-FREE SHOPPING

Value-Added Tax (VAT, or IVA in Italian) is 22% on clothing and luxury goods, but is already included in the amount on the price tag for consumer goods. All non–EU citizens visiting Italy are entitled to a reimbursement of this tax when purchasing nonperishable goods that total more than €154.95 in a single transaction. If you buy goods in a store that does not participate in the "Tax-Free Italy" program, ask the cashier to issue you a special invoice known as a *fattura,* which must be made out to you and includes the phrase *Esente IVA ai sensi della legge 38 quarter.* The bill should indicate the amount of IVA included in the purchase price. Present this invoice and the goods purchased to the Customs Office on your departure from Italy to obtain your tax reimbursement.

ITALIAN SIZES

Unfortunately, Italian sizes are not standard—it is therefore always best to try things on. If you wear a "small," you may be surprised to learn that in Italy, you are a medium. Children's sizes are just as complicated; they are typically based on Italian children's ages. Check labels on all garments, as many are dry clean–only or non–tumble dry. When in doubt about the proper size, ask the shop attendant—most will have an international size chart

handy. At open-air markets, where there often isn't any place to try on garments, you'll have to take your best guess: if you're wrong, you may or may not be able to find the vendor the next day to exchange.

⑨ Tipping

In Italy, service is always included in the menu prices. It's customary to leave an additional 5%–10% tip, or a couple of euros, for the waiter, depending on the quality of service. Tip checkroom attendants €1 per person, restroom attendants €0.50. In both cases tip more in expensive hotels and restaurants. Tip €0.05–€0.10 for whatever you drink standing up at a coffee bar, €0.20–€0.50 or more for table service in a café. At a hotel bar, tip €1 and up for a round or two of cocktails, more in the grander hotels.

For tipping taxi drivers, it is acceptable if you round up to the nearest euro, minimum €0.50. Give a barber €1–€1.50 and a hairdresser's assistant €1.50–€4 for a shampoo or cut, depending on the type of establishment and the final bill; 5%–10% is a fair guideline.

On private sightseeing tours, tipping your guides 10% is customary. In museums and other places of interest where admission is free, a contribution is expected; give anything from €0.50 to €1 for one or two people, more if the guardian has been especially helpful. Service station attendants are tipped only for special services. On off-hours there may be station attendants not in uniform working just for tips. Give €0.50 to €1 if they fill up your tank.

In hotels, give the *portiere* (concierge) about 15% of his bill for services, or €2.50–€5 if he has been generally helpful. For two people in a double room,

Essentials

leave the chambermaid about €1 per day, or about €4–€6 a week, in a moderately priced hotel; tip a minimum of €1 for valet or room service. Increase these amounts by one half in an expensive hotel, and double them in a very expensive hotel. In very expensive hotels, tip doormen €0.50 for calling a cab and €1 for carrying bags to the check-in desk, bellhops €1.50–€2.50 for carrying your bags to the room, and €2–€2.50 for room service.

⊙ Tours and Guides

Some might consider them kitsch, but guided bus tours can prove a blissfully easy way to enjoy a quick introduction to the city's top sights—if you don't feel like being on your feet all day. Sitting in a bus, with friendly tour guide commentary (and even friendlier fellow sightseers, many of whom will be from every country under the sun), can make for a fun experience—so give one a whirl even if you're an old Rome hand. Of course, you'll want to savor these incredible sights at your own leisure later on.

The least expensive organized sightseeing tour of Rome is the one run by **CitySightseeing Roma**. Double-decker buses leave from Via Marsala, beside Termini station, but you can pick them up at any of their nine stopping points. A day ticket costs €30 and allows you to get off and on as often as you like. The price includes an audio guide system in six languages. The total tour takes about two hours and covers the Colosseum, Piazza Navona, St. Peter's, the Trevi Fountain, and Via Veneto. Tickets can be bought on board. Two- and three-day tickets are also available. Tours leave from Termini station every 20 minutes 9–7:30.

All operators can provide a luxury car for up to three people, a limousine for up to seven, or a minibus for up to nine, all with an English-speaking driver, but guide service is extra. Almost all operators offer "Rome by Night" tours, with or without dinner and entertainment. You can book tours through travel agents.

Big Bus Rome Tour

BUS TOURS | Double-decker buses make 8 stops around Rome, and ticket-holders can jump on and off. Discount prices can often be found on their website. ⊠ *Rome* ⊕ *www.bigbustours.com* ✉ *From €24.*

🗓 When to Go

Spring and fall are the best times to visit, with mild temperatures and many sunny days. Summers are often sweltering so come in July and August if you like, but we advise doing as the Romans do—get up and out early, seek refuge from the afternoon heat, resume activities in early evening, and stay up late to enjoy the nighttime breeze.

Most attractions are closed on major holidays. Come August, many shops and restaurants close as locals head out for vacation. Remember that air-conditioning is still a relatively rare phenomenon in this city, so carrying a small paper fan in your bag can work wonders. Roman winters are relatively mild, with persistent rainy spells.

Contacts

Air

AIRPORTS Ciampino.
☎ 06/65951 ⊕ www.adr.
it/ciampino. **Leonardo da
Vinci Airport/Fiumicino.**
☎ 06/65951 ⊕ www.adr.it/
fiumicino.

AIRPORT TRANSFERS
Airport Connection Services.
☎ 333/2411797 ⊕ www.
airportconnection.it. **Airport
Shuttle.** ☎ 06/42013469,
06/4740451 ⊕ www.
airportshuttle.it. **Airport
Shuttle Express.** ✉ Rome
☎ 06/65017448 ⊕ www.
airportshuttleexpress.it.

Ⓜ Public Transport

ATAC. ✉ Rome ☎ 06/46951
⊕ www.atac.roma.it.
COTRAL. ☎ 800/174471 in
Italy (from landline only),
06/72057205 ⊕ www.
cotralspa.it. **Flixbus.**
⊕ www.flixbus.it.

Scooter

**RENTAL AGENCIES
& TOURS Bici & Baci.**
✉ Rome ☎ 06/4828443
⊕ www.bicibaci.com.
Scooteroma. ✉ Rome
☎ 340/0751432,
338/8227671 ⊕ www.
scooteroma.com. **Treno
e Scooter.** ✉ Piazza dei
Cinquecento, in the
parking lot in front of
the train station, Termini
☎ 349/4169730 ⊕ rent.
trenoescooter.com.

Taxi

CONTACTS Mytaxi.
⊕ www.free-now.it. **Rome
Taxis.** ✉ Rome ☎ 06/6645,
06/3570, 06/4994, 06/4157
⊕ www.3570.it.

🚆 Train

Italo Treno. ☎ 892020 customer service line within
Italy, 06/0708 from abroad
⊕ www.italotreno.it. **Trenitalia.** ☎ 892021 customer
service line within Italy,
06/68475475 from abroad
⊕ www.trenitalia.it.

🏛 U.S. Embassy

U.S. Embassy Rome
✉ 121 Via Vittorio
Veneto, Piazza di Spagna
☎ 06/46741 ⊕ www.
usembassy.gov/italy
Ⓜ Barberini.

📍 Visitor Information

**060608 (Tourist Ser-
vices).** ☎ 06/0608
⊕ www.060608.it. **Roma
Sito Turistico Ufficiale.**
☎ 06/0608 ⊕ www.turis-
moroma.it/?lang=en.

Helpful Italian Phrases

BASICS

Yes/no	Sí/No	see/no
Please	Per favore	pear fa-**vo**-ray
Thank you	Grazie	**grah**-tsee-ay
You're welcome	Prego	**pray**-go
I'm sorry (apology)	Mi dispiace	mee dis-pee-**atch**-ay
Excuse me, sorry	Scusi	**skoo**-zee
Good morning/ afternoon	Buongiorno	bwohn-**jor**-no
Good evening	Buona sera	**bwoh**-na **say**-ra
Good-bye	Arrivederci	a-ree-vah-**dare**-chee
Mr. (Sir)	Signore	see-**nyo**-ray
Mrs. (Ma'am)	Signora	see-**nyo**-ra
Miss	Signorina	see-nyo-**ree**-na
Pleased to meet you	Piacere	pee-ah-**chair**-ray
How are you?	Come sta?	**ko**-may-**stah**
Hello (phone)	Pronto?	**proan**-to

NUMBERS

one-half	mezzo	**mets**-zoh
one	uno	**oo**-no
two	due	**doo**-ay
three	tre	Tray
four	quattro	**kwah**-tro
five	cinque	**cheen**-kway
six	sei	Say
seven	sette	**set**-ay
eight	otto	**oh**-to
nine	nove	**no**-vay
ten	dieci	dee-**eh**-chee
eleven	undici	**oon**-dee-chee
twelve	dodici	**doh**-dee-chee
thirteen	tredici	**trey**-dee-chee
fourteen	quattordici	kwah-**tor**-dee-chee
fifteen	quindici	**kwin**-dee-chee
sixteen	sedici	**say**-dee-chee
seventeen	dicissette	dee-chah-**set**-ay
eighteen	diciotto	dee-chee-**oh**-to
nineteen	diciannove	dee-chee-ahn-**no**-vay
twenty	venti	**vain**-tee
twenty-one	ventuno	**vent**-oo-no
thirty	trenta	**train**-ta
forty	quaranta	kwa-**rahn**-ta
fifty	cinquanta	cheen-**kwahn**-ta
sixty	sessanta	seh-**sahn**-ta
seventy	settanta	seh-**tahn**-ta
eighty	ottanta	o-**tahn**-ta
ninety	novanta	no-**vahn**-ta
one hundred	cento	**chen**-to
one thousand	mille	**mee**-lay
one million	un milione	oon **mill**-oo-nay

COLORS

black	Nero	**nair**-ro
blue	Blu	bloo
brown	Marrone	ma-**rohn**-nay
green	Verde	**ver**-day
orange	Arancione	ah-rahn-**cho**-nay
red	Rosso	**rose**-so
white	Bianco	bee-**ahn**-koh
yellow	Giallo	**jaw**-low

DAYS OF THE WEEK

Sunday	Domenica	do-**meh**-nee-ka
Monday	Lunedi	loo-ne-**dee**
Tuesday	Martedi	mar-te-**dee**
Wednesday	Mercoledi	**mer**-ko-le-**dee**
Thursday	Giovedi	jo-ve-**dee**
Friday	Venerdì	ve-ner-**dee**
Saturday	Sabato	**sa**-ba-toh

MONTHS

January	Gennaio	jen-**ay**-o
February	Febbraio	feb-**rah**-yo
March	Marzo	**mart**-so
April	Aprile	a-**pril**-ay
May	Maggio	**mahd**-joe
June	Giugno	**joon**-yo
July	Luglio	**lool**-yo
August	Agosto	a-**gus**-to
September	Settembre	se-**tem**-bre
October	Ottobre	o-**toh**-bre
November	Novembre	no-**vem**-bre
December	Dicembre	di-**chem**-bre

USEFUL WORDS AND PHRASES

Do you speak English?	Parla Inglese?	**par**-la een-**glay**-zay
I don't speak Italian	Non parlo italiano	non **par**-lo ee-tal-**yah**-no
I don't understand	Non capisco	non ka-**peess**-ko
I don't know	Non lo so	non lo **so**
I understand	Capisco	ka-**peess**-ko
I'm American	Sono Americano(a)	**so**-no a-may-ree-**kah**-no(a)
I'm British	Sono inglese	so-no een-**glay**-zay
What's your name?	Come si chiama?	**ko**-may see kee-**ah**-ma
My name is ...	Mi chiamo...	mee kee-**ah**-mo
What time is it?	Che ore sono?	kay **o**-ray **so**-no
How?	Come?	**ko**-may
When?	Quando?	**kwan**-doe
Yesterday/today/ tomorrow	Ieri/oggi/domani	**yer**-ee/ **o**-jee/ do-**mah**-nee

This morning	Stamattina/Oggi	sta-ma-**tee**-na/ o-jee
Afternoon	Pomeriggio	po-mer-**ee**-jo
Tonight	Stasera	sta-**ser**-a
What?	Che cosa?	kay **ko**-za
What is it?	Che cos'è?	kay ko-**zey**
Why?	Perchè?	pear-**kay**
Who?	Chi?	**Kee**
Where is ...	Dov'è...	doe-**veh**
the train station?	la stazione?	la sta-tsee-**oh**-nay
the subway?	la metropolitana?	la may-tro-po-lee-**tah**-na
the bus stop?	la fermata dell'autobus?	la fer-**mah**-ta del-ow-tor-**booss**
the airport	l'aeroporto	la-er-roh-**por**-toh
the post office?	l'ufficio postale	loo-**fee**-cho po-**stah**-lay
the bank?	la banca?	la **bahn**-ka
the hotel?	l'hotel...?	lo-**tel**
the museum?	Il museo	eel moo-**zay**-o
the hospital?	l'ospedale?	lo-spay-**dah**-lay
the elevator?	l'ascensore	la-shen-**so**-ray
the restrooms?	...il bagno	eel **bahn**-yo
Here/there	Qui/là	kwee/la
Left/right	A sinistra/a destra	a see-**neess**-tra/a **des**-tra
Is it near/far?	È vicino/lontano?	ay vee-**chee**-no/ lon-**tah**-no
I'd like ...	Vorrei...	vo-**ray**
a room	una camera	**oo**-na **kah**-may-ra
the key	la chiave	la kee-**ah**-vay
a newspaper	un giornale	oon jore-**nah**-vay
a stamp	un francobollo	oon frahn-ko-**bo**-lo
I'd like to buy ...	Vorrei comprare...	vo-**ray** kom-**prah**-ray
a city map	una mappa della città	**oo**-na **mah**-pa **day**-la chee-**tah**
a road map	una carta stradale	**oo**-na **car**-tah stra-**dahl**-lay
a magazine	una revista	**oo**-na ray-**vees**-tah
envelopes	buste	**boos**-tay
writing paper	carta de lettera	**car**-tah dah **leyt**-ter-rah
a postcard	una cartolina	**oo**-na car-tog-**leen**-ah
a ticket	un biglietto	oon bee-**yet**-toh
How much is it?	Quanto costa?	**kwahn**-toe coast-a
It's expensive/ cheap	È caro/ economico	ay **car**-o/ ay-ko-**no**-mee-ko
A little/a lot	Poco/tanto	**po**-ko/**tahn**-to
More/less	Più/meno	pee-**oo**/**may**-no

Enough/too (much)	Abbastanza/ troppo	a-bas-**tahn**-sa/tro-po
I am sick	Sto male	sto **mah**-lay
Call a doctor	Chiama un dottore	kee-**ah**-mah-oondoe-**toe**-ray
Help!	Aiuto!	a-**yoo**-to
Stop!	Alt!	ahlt

DINING OUT

A bottle of ...	Una bottiglia di...	**oo**-na bo-**tee**-lee-ah dee
A cup of ...	Una tazza di...	**oo**-na **tah**-tsa dee
A glass of ...	Un bicchiere di...	oon bee-key-**air**-ay dee
Beer	La birra	la **beer**-rah
Bill/check	Il conto	eel **cone**-toe
Bread	Il pane	eel **pah**-nay
Breakfast	La prima colazione	la **pree**-ma ko-la-**tsee**-oh-nay
Butter	Il Burro	eel **boor**-roh
Cocktail/aperitif	L'aperitivo	la-pay-ree-**tee**-vo
Dinner	La cena	la **chen**-a
Fixed-price menu	Menù a prezzo fisso	may-**noo** a **pret**-so **fee**-so
Fork	La forchetta	la for-**ket**-a
I am vegetarian	Sono vegetariano(a)	**so**-no vay-jay-ta-ree-**ah**-no/a
I cannot eat ...	Non posso mangiare	non **pose**-so mahn-gee-**are**-ay
I'd like to order	Vorrei ordinare	vo-**ray** or-dee-**nah**-ray
Is service included?	Il servizio è incluso?	eel ser-**vee**-tzee-o ay een-**kloo**-zo
I'm hungry/ thirsty	Ho fame/sede	oh **fah**-meh/**sehd**-ed
It's good/bad	È buono/cattivo	ay **bwo**-bo/ka-**tee**-vo
It's hot/cold	È caldo/freddo	ay **kahl**-doe/**fred**-o
Knife	Il coltello	eel kol-**tel**-o
Lunch	Il pranzo	eel **prahnt**-so
Menu	Il menu	eel may-**noo**
Napkin	Il tovagliolo	eel toe-va-lee-**oh**-lo
Pepper	Il pepe	eel **pep**-peh
Plate	Il piatto	eel pee-**aht**-toe
Please give me ...	Mi dia...	mee **dee**-a
Salt	Il sale	eel **sah**-lay
Spoon	Il cucchiaio	eel koo-kee-ah-yo
Tea	tè	tay
Water	acqua	**awk**-wah
Wine	vino	**vee**-noh

Great Itineraries

Rome is jam-packed with things to do and see. These are some of our suggested itineraries. Make sure to leave yourself time to just wander and get the feel of the city as well.

Rome in 1 Day

Rome wasn't built in a day, but if that's all you have to see it, take a deep breath, strap on some stylish-but-comfy sneakers, and grab a cappuccino to help you get an early start. Get ready for a spectacular sunrise-to-sunset tour of the Ancient City.

Begin by getting a coffee at the bar of the Caffè Sant'Eustachio right when it opens at 7:30 am. Close by are two opulently over-the-top monuments that show off Rome at its baroque best: the church of Sant'Ignazio, with its stunning painted ceiling, and the princely Palazzo Doria Pamphilj, packed with great Old Master paintings. Midmorning, head west a few blocks to find the fabled Pantheon, still looking like Emperor Hadrian might arrive shortly. A few blocks north is San Luigi dei Francesi, home to Caravaggio's earliest major commissions.

Just before lunch, saunter a block or so westward into the gorgeous Piazza Navona, studded with Bernini fountains. Then take Via della Cuccagna (at the piazza's south end) and continue several blocks toward Campo de' Fiori's open-air food market. This is a great place to stop for lunch.

Two more blocks toward the Tiber brings you to one of the most romantic streets of Rome—Via Giulia—laid out by Pope Julius II in the early 16th century. Walk past 10 blocks of Renaissance palazzi and ivy-draped antiques shops to take a bus (from the stop near the Tiber) over to the Vatican.

Gape at St. Peter's Basilica, then hit the treasure-filled Musei Vaticani (for the Sistine Chapel) in the early afternoon. During lunch, the crowds thin out some, but you can avoid lines entirely if you book online at ⊕ tickets.museivaticani.va (the €4 service fee is well worth the time saved). Wander for about two hours and then head for the Ottaviano stop near the museum and Metro your way to the Colosseo stop.

Climb up into the Colosseum and picture it full of screaming toga-clad citizens enjoying the spectacle of gladiators in mortal combat. Follow Via dei Fori Imperiali to the entrance of the Roman Forum. Photograph yourself giving a "Friends, Romans, Countrymen" oration (complete with upraised hand) by a crumbling column. At sunset, the Forum closes and the floodlights come on.

March down the Forum's ancient Via Sacra and back out into Via dei Fori Imperiali where you will head around "the wedding cake," the looming Vittorio Emanuele II Monument (Il Vittoriano), to the Campidoglio. Here, on the Capitoline Hill, tour the great ancient Roman art treasures of the Musei Capitolini, and admire the view over the Forum from the Tabularium and toward St. Peter's from the terrace by the museum's caffè. If you're not entering the museum, there is a spectacular view over the Forum from the Capitoline Hill (at the top of via Monte Tarpeo).

After dinner, hail a cab—or take a long stroll (passeggiata) down La Dolce Vita memory lane—to the Trevi Fountain, a gorgeous sight at night. Don't forget to toss a coin in over your shoulder to ensure a trip back to Rome.

Rome in 3 Days

More time in Rome will allow you to explore more of the Roman Forum and the Vatican Museums, check out some less touristy sights, and drink your way through hip neighborhoods like Trastevere.

DAY 1: ANCIENT ROME

Spend your first day in Rome exploring the likes of the Roman Forum, Musei Capitolini, and the Colosseum. This area is pretty compact, but you can easily spend a full morning and afternoon exploring its treasures. It's best to try to beat the crowds at the Colosseum by getting there right when it opens at 9 am (advance tickets help, too). A guided tour of the Forum is also a good way to make the most out of your afternoon. After your day of sightseeing, stop for a classic Roman dinner in nearby Monti.

DAY 2: THE VATICAN AND PIAZZA NAVONA

Another full day of sightseeing awaits when you make your way to the city-state known as the Vatican. You'll once again want to try to avoid the biggest crowds here, especially for a glimpse of the Sistine Chapel (the best way to do this is to make online reservations for an extra €4 ahead of time). Booking a tour of the Vatican Museums is a good way to take full advantage of the site; most tours last two hours. Be sure to stop in and marvel at St. Peter's Basilica, too. Stop for lunch in nearby Prati, but after you're done with the Vatican, cross the river to Piazza Navona. Spend some time exploring this glorious piazza and its sculptures, but make sure to stop by the Pantheon before heading to the area around Campo de' Fiori for dinner at an outdoor restaurant. Afterwards, there are plenty of nearby bars to keep you occupied.

DAY 3: PIAZZA DI SPAGNA, VILLA BORGHESE, AND TRASTEVERE

Start your morning with breakfast near the Trevi Fountain, before doing some window-shopping up Via Condotti and the many surrounding backstreets as you make your way to the Spanish Steps. Pose for some postcard-worthy photos there before heading to nearby Villa Borghese. If you're sick of museums, feel free to explore Rome's main park and enjoy the great views; if you're up for some more art, the Galleria Borghese is one of the city's best art museums. Afterwards, head to trendy Trastevere for dinner, and soak in the cobblestone streets and charming medieval houses as you bar-hop your last night in town.

If You Have More Time

If your trip to Rome is on the longer side, be sure to put aside one day for a trip out to Ostica Antica, an ancient port city that is now one of the best preserved archaeological ruins in all of Italy. A train to the site leaves every 15 minutes from the Porta San Paolo station; the trip takes a mere 35 minutes. Take your time exploring these impressive ruins, and be sure to stop for lunch in town, too. Other great day trips include the gorgeous villas in the town of Tivoli, the charming small villages of the Castelli Romani, and the whimsical gardens of Bomarzo.

If you want to make the most of your time in the city itself, take your time exploring the many churches and cathedrals like Sant'Ignazio or San Clemente. You can also stop by to explore gorgeous palaces like the Palazzo Doria Pamphilj and check out lesser known but just as impressive museums like the MAXXI or the MACRO. Visiting the ancient Roman road known as the Via Appia Antica and its spooky yet mesmerizing catacombs is another great way to spend an afternoon immersed in Roman history.

Rome of the Emperors: A Roman Forum Walk

Taking in the famous vista of the Roman Forum from the terraces of the *Campidoglio* (Capitoline Hill), you have probably already cast your eyes down and across two millennia of history in a single glance. Here, in one fabled panorama, are the world's most striking and significant concentrations of historic remains.

THE COLOSSEUM

To kick things off, start just south of the Forum at ancient Rome's hallmark monument, the **Colosseum** (with its handy Colosseo Metro stop). Convincingly austere, the Colosseum is the Eternal City's yardstick of eternity. Nowadays, you can take one of the elevators upstairs to level one to glimpse the extensive subterranean passageways that used to funnel all the unlucky animals and gladiators into the arena.

THE ROMAN FORUM

Leaving the Colosseum behind, admire the **Arch of Constantine,** standing just to the north of the arena. The largest and best preserved of Rome's triumphal arches, it was erected in AD 315 to celebrate the victory of the emperor Constantine (280–337) over Maxentius—it was shortly after this battle that Constantine converted Rome to Christianity. You have to walk down Via dei Fori Imperiali to the only Forum entrance, located about halfway down the street from the Colosseum and across from Via Cavour, to enter the Forum. From there, you can take a left up the ancient Via Sacra to start at the Forum's southwestern point with the **Temple of Venus and Roma.** Off to your left, on the spur of hillside jutting from the Palatine Hill, stands the famed **Arch of Titus.** Through the arch, photograph the great vista of the entire Forum as it stretches toward the distant Capitoline Hill.

Rome of the Emperors: A Roman Forum Walk

HIGHLIGHTS:
Arches of Septimius Severus, Titus, and Constantine; the Colosseum; the Via Sacra; the Roman Forum

WHERE TO START:
Piazza del Colosseo, with its handy Colosseo Metro stop

WHERE TO STOP:
Inside the archaeological ruins, there are drinking fountains and a couple of vending machines (on the Palatine and the via Nova in the Forum) for hot days. Just a five-minute walk from the Colosseum on Via di San Giovanni, fresh and creamy gelato and homemade Sicilian specialties await you at several genuine shops and restaurants.

LENGTH:
Two to five hours, depending on your pace and how detailed you wish the visit to be

BEST TIME TO GO:
To avoid the harsh midday sun start your tour of the Forum early or in the late afternoon.

WORST TIME TO GO:
Midday in high summer, when the sun is high and merciless in the Forum, particularly in the summertime—remember, there are no roofs and few trees to shelter under at these archaeological sites. The Palatine has more shade (and a small air-conditioned museum). Crowds are at their thickest after 10 am.

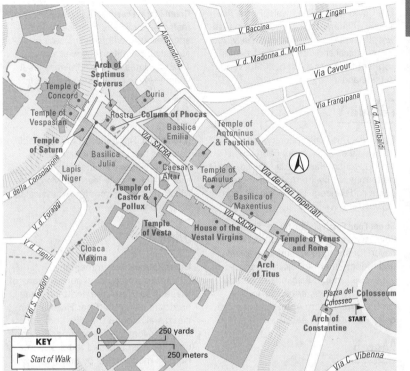

HAUNT OF THE VESTAL VIRGINS

Continue your walk toward the Capitoline Hill by strolling over to the **Temple of Castor and Pollux**, then head past the temple to the circular **Temple of Vesta**. In a tradition going back to an age when fire was a precious commodity, the famous vestal virgins kept the fire of Rome burning here. Of the original 20 columns only three remain, behind which stretch the vast remains of the **House of the Vestal Virgins**. Crossing the central square and walking back toward the towering Capitoline Hill, you are now entering the midsection of the open area of the Forum proper; you can see to your left the **Column of Phocas**.

SEVERUS AND SATURN

Continue back down the Via Sacra, where towers one of the Forum's extant spectaculars, the **Arch of Septimius Severus**. Continuing left and up the Via Sacra, you reach the base of the celebrated **Temple of Saturn**. For a better sense of the whole area—a sort of archaeological gestalt—climb onto the Palatine (the stairs are very steep; easier access is up the path by the Arch of Titus) to the terrace at the Horti Farnesiani Gardens for a breathtaking view to put your walking into panoramic context.

On the Calendar

The City of Eternal Festivals, Rome has a bevy of internationally recognized festivals. In the fall and spring especially, you can see local and international talent in some of the city's most beautiful venues, outside and in.

February

Equilibrio. This contemporary dance festival takes place every February at the Auditorium Parco della Musica, with performances by international choreographers and dancers. ⊕ *www.auditorium. com.*

Street Food Festival. For three days in February, Eataly's third floor becomes a haven for street food fans. Buy tokens and redeem them for Sicilian *panelle* (chickpea fritters), Tuscan *lampredotto* (tripe sandwiches), *arrosticini* (grilled lamb skewers) from Abruzzo, and more delicacies. ⊕ *www.eataly.net.*

March

Spring FAI Days. The Fondo Ambiente Italiano (FAI) produces two series of open days yearly throughout Italy: one in the spring and one in the fall. During FAI Days, incredible off-limits treasures of architecture and art are opened to the public. Locations in Rome include the Casino dell'Aurora Ludovisi, a 16th-century villa with the only ceiling painting attributed to Caravaggio, the prestigious Accademia Nazionale dei Lincei inside Palazzo Corsini (Galileo Galilei was a member), and the 16th-century Palazzo del Collegio Romano, which now houses the Ministry of Culture. ⊕ *www.fondoambiente.it.*

Green Market Festival. This relatively new festival is dedicated to artisan goods and wellness, with artisans selling sustainable creations as well as yoga, Tai Chi, Pilates, and mindfulness lessons. ⊕ *www.greenmarketfestival.it.*

April

Il Tempietto. This series of unforgettable concerts takes place throughout the year in otherwise inaccessible sites, like the 1st-century Teatro di Marcello. Music runs the gamut from classical to contemporary.

June

Estate Romana. A summer-long, city-sponsored cultural series, many of these events are free and take place outdoors along the Tiber River and in piazzas all around the city. Look for cinema events, art programs, theater, book fairs, and guided tours of some of Rome's monuments by night. ⊕ *www. culture.roma.it.*

I Concerti nel Parco. This beautiful evening-concert series is held under the stars in a small park near the Via Appia Antica. From June through August, the concerts are held at sunset and last late into the evening, showcasing a variety of musical genres from classical to contemporary. There are some winter events, including Christmas concerts, as well. ⊕ *www.iconcertinelparco.it.*

Rock in Roma. From June through August, various locations throughout Rome, including the massive Ippodromo, host rock's top acts from all over the world. ⊕ *www.rockinroma.com.*

Roma Incontra il Mondo. World-class headliners as well as its beautiful location in Villa Ada, a former monarch's residence, make Roma Incontra il Mondo one of Europe's most impressive world-music festivals. The summer concert series is held in the middle of the park and begins at 10 pm, followed by dancing until 2 am. ⊕ *www.villaada.org.*

Roma Summer Fest. Past editions of this music festival, which takes place at the Auditorium Parco della Musica from June through August, have included concerts by Elton John, Sting, Leonard Cohen, Bob Dylan, Patti Smith, and Arctic Monkeys. ⊕ *www.auditorium.com.*

Pride Week. Much like Pride celebrations across Europe and the U.S., Pride Week in Rome comprises concerts, book and film presentations, and culminates in a parade. Revelers decked out in drag or swaddled in rainbow flags march from Piazza della Repubblica down Via Merulana toward the Colosseum in an epic celebration of the city's LGBTQ+ community. The parade usually takes place the second Saturday of June.

September

RomaEuropa. For six weeks in early fall, the RomaEuropa festival ignites stages and theaters as a collective, multivenue avant-garde performing and visual arts program, showcasing international artists, installations, film, and performance. ⊕ *www.romaeuropa.net.*

October

Festa del Cinema di Roma. In the fall, cinephiles head to Rome for its annual film festival, two packed weeks of cinema celebration and celebrity spotting. The festival showcases Hollywood hits, Italian indie and experimental films, retrospectives and shorts, and conversations with global cinema icons. ⊕ *www.romacinemafest.it.*

November

Roma Jazz Festival. Throughout the month of November, the Auditorium Parco della Musica hosts this jazz festival that draws local and international musical acts. ⊕ *www.romajazzfestival.it.*

December

Vitala Festival. From December through June, this philanthropic festival presents concerts of soul, rock, and blues at Teatro San Genesio in Prati. ⊕ *www.facebook.com/vitalafestival.*

Natale Festival. For about a month, from early December through early January, the Auditorium Parco della Musica hosts a Christmas festival replete with pop, rock, jazz, and gospel concerts as well as ice-skating. ⊕ *www.auditorium.com.*

Chapter 3

ANCIENT ROME

Updated by
Laura Itzkowitz

⦿ Sights	🍴 Restaurants	🛏 Hotels	🛍 Shopping	🍸 Nightlife
★★★★★	★★☆☆☆	★★★☆☆	★★☆☆☆	★★☆☆☆

NEIGHBORHOOD SNAPSHOT

MAKING THE MOST OF YOUR TIME

This area is relatively compact, but extremely rich in history with plenty to see. Serious history buffs should allow a full day to do the area justice, including an hour in the Colosseum, a few hours in the Forum and on the Palatine Hill, and a couple more hours in the Musei Capitolini. Even for ancient Rome experts, taking a tour can be helpful, but be sure to book a guide in advance instead of picking up one of those trying to shill their expertise on-site.

The longest line in Rome, aside from the one at the Vatican Museums, is at the Colosseum, so book a timed slot online ahead of time (⊕ *www.coopculture. it*). Even with timed entrances, the security line can be long and the interior crowded. From April through October and on weekends year-round, it's usually best to try and book your visit for before 10 am or for an hour or so before closing, when many tour buses have started to depart. There is little to no shade in the Forum, so it gets very hot and dusty in summertime—another reason to either go early or start late.

Outside the main tourism area, make sure to give yourself some time to explore the neighborhood of Monti itself, which surrounds the Colosseum, with its artisans' shops, fine trattorias, and high-end boutiques—the best of old and new Rome, all in one tiny, proud *rione* (district).

TOP REASONS TO GO

The Colosseum: Clamber up the stands above the imperial box and imagine the gory games as Trajan saw them.

The Roman Forum: Walk through crumbling, romantic ruins—a trip back 2,000 plus years—to the heart of one of the greatest empires the world has ever seen.

The Campidoglio: Watch the sun go down over the Forum from the Campidoglio, the best view in town.

Capitoline Museums: See eye-to-eye with the ancients—the busts of emperors and philosophers are more real than ideal.

GETTING HERE

■ The Colosseo Metro station is right across from the Colosseum and a short walk from both the Roman and Imperial forums, as well as the Palatine Hill. Walking from the very heart of the historic center will take about 20 minutes, much of it along the wide Via dei Fori Imperiali. The little electric Bus No. 117 from the center or No. 175 from Termini will also deliver you to the Colosseum's doorstep. Any of the following buses will take you to or near the Roman Forum: Nos. 60, 75, 85, 95, and 175.

VIEWFINDER

■ As you walk down Via dei Serpenti in Monti, you'll see a slice of the Colosseum framed cinematically between the buildings on either side of the street, which becomes Via del Fagutale as you cross Via Cavour. At the end of the street, you'll find this little hill with fantastic views. When you're done taking photos, head down the steps on the left and you'll be right across the street from the Colosseum.

If you ever wanted to feel like a caesar—with all of ancient Rome (literally) at your feet—simply head to Michelangelo's famed Piazza del Campidoglio. There, make a beeline for the terrace flanking the side of the center building, the Palazzo Senatorio, Rome's ceremonial city hall. From this balcony atop the Capitoline Hill you can take in a breathtaking panorama.

Looming before you is the entire Roman Forum, the *caput mundi*—the capital of the known world—for centuries, and where many of the world's most important events in the past 2,500 years happened. Here, all Rome shouted as one, "Caesar has been murdered," and crowded to hear Mark Antony's eulogy for the fallen leader. Here, legend has it that St. Paul traversed the Forum en route to his audience with Nero. Here, Roman law and powerful armies were created, keeping the rest of the world at bay for a millennium. And here the Roman emperors staged the biggest blow-out extravaganzas ever mounted for the entire population of a city, outdoing even Elizabeth Taylor's entrance in *Cleopatra*.

But after a more than 27-century-long parade of pageantry, you'll find that much has changed in this area. The marble fragments scattered over the Forum area makes all but students of archaeology ask: is this the grandeur that was Rome? It's not surprising that Shelley and Gibbon once reflected, on the sense that *sic transit gloria mundi*—"thus passes the glory of the world." Yet spectacular monuments—the Arch of Septimius Severus, the Palatine Hill, and the Colosseum (looming in the background), among them—remind us that this was indeed the birthplace of much of Western civilization.

Before the Christian era, before the emperors, before the powerful republic that ruled the Mediterranean, Rome was founded on seven hills. Two of them, the Capitoline and the Palatine, surround the Roman Forum, where the Romans of the later Republican and imperial ages worshipped deities, debated politics, and wheeled and dealed. It's all history now, but this remains one of the world's most striking and significant concentrations of ancient remains: an emphatic reminder of the genius and power that made Rome the fountainhead of the Western world.

Outside the actual ancient sites, you'll find neighborhoods like Monti and Celio, riones which are just as much part of Rome's history as its ruins. These are the city's oldest neighborhoods, and today are a charming mix of the city's past and present. Once you're done exploring ancient

Rome, these are the easiest places to head for a bite to eat or some shopping.

The Campidoglio

Your first taste of ancient Rome should start from a point that embodies some of Rome's earliest and greatest moments: the Campidoglio. Here, on the Capitoline Hill (which towers over the traffic hub of Piazza Venezia), a meditative Edward Gibbon was inspired to write his 1764 tome, *The History of the Decline and Fall of the Roman Empire*. Of Rome's famous seven hills, the Capitoline is the smallest and the most sacred. It has always been the seat of Rome's government, and its Latin name echoes in the designation of the national and state capitol buildings of every country in the world. While there are great views of the Roman Forum from the terrace balconies to either side of the Palazzo Senatorio, the best view is from the 1st century BC Tabularium, now part of the Musei Capitolini. The museum caffè is on the Terrazza Caffarelli, with a magical view toward Trastevere and St. Peter's, and is accessible without a museum ticket.

Sights

Basilica di Santa Maria di Aracoeli
CHURCH | Sitting atop 124 steps, Santa Maria di Aracoeli perches on the north slope of the Capitoline Hill. The church rests on the site of the temple of Juno Moneta (Admonishing Juno), which also housed the Roman mint (hence the origin of the word "money"). According to legend, it was here that the Sibyl, a prophetess, predicted to Augustus the coming of a Redeemer. He in turn responded by erecting an altar, the Ara Coeli (Altar of Heaven). This was eventually replaced by a Benedictine monastery, and then a church, which was passed in 1250 to the Franciscans, who restored and enlarged it in Romanesque-Gothic style. Today,

the Aracoeli is best known for the Santo Bambino, a much-revered olivewood figure of the Christ Child (today a copy of the 15th-century original that was stolen in 1994). At Christmas, everyone pays homage to the "Bambinello" as children recite poems from a miniature pulpit. In true Roman style, the church interior is a historical hodgepodge, with classical columns and large marble fragments from pagan buildings, as well as a 13th-century cosmatesque pavement. The richly gilded Renaissance ceiling commemorates the naval victory at Lepanto in 1571 over the Turks. The first chapel on the right is noteworthy for Pinturicchio's frescoes of St. Bernardino of Siena (1486). ⊠ *Via del Teatro di Marcello, at top of long, steep stairway, Piazza Venezia* ☎ *06/69763839* Ⓜ *Colosseo.*

Carcere Mamertino (*Mamertine Prison*)
RUINS | The state prison of the ancient city has two subterranean cells where Rome's enemies, most famously the Goth, Jugurtha, and the indomitable Gaul, Vercingetorix, were imprisoned and died of either starvation or strangulation. Legend has it that in the lower cell saints Peter and Paul were imprisoned under Nero, and a miraculous spring of water appeared with which they baptized their jailers. A church, San Giuseppe dei Falegnami, now stands over the prison. The multimedia tour has received mixed reviews: it focuses on the Christian history of the site, and the audio is more fluffy than historical. ⊠ *Clivo Argentario 1, Piazza Venezia* ☎ *06/698961* ⊕ *www.omnia-vaticanrome.org* 🎫 *€10* Ⓜ *Colosseo.*

Le Domus Romane di Palazzo Valentini
RUINS | If you find your imagination stretching to picture Rome as it was two millennia ago, make sure to check out this "new" ancient site just a stone's throw from Piazza Venezia. As was common practice in Renaissance-era Rome, 16th-century builders simply filled in ancient structures with landfill, using them as part of the foundation for Palazzo

Valentini. In doing so, the builders also unwittingly preserved the ruins beneath, which archaeologists rediscovered during excavations in 2007. It took another three years for the two opulent, imperial-era *domus* (upscale urban houses) to open to the public on a regular basis.

Descending below Palazzo Valentini is like walking into another world. Not only are the houses luxurious and well preserved, still retaining their beautiful mosaics, inlaid marble floors, and staircases, but the ruins have been made to "come alive" through multimedia. Sophisticated light shows re-create what it all would have looked like, while a dramatic, automated voice-over accompanies you as you walk through the rooms, pointing out cool finds (the heating system for the private baths, the mysterious fragment of a statue, the marks left by wooden beams used to fill in the foundations of Palazzo Valentini during the Renaissance) and a WWII bunker and escape tunnel connected to the domus. If it sounds corny, hold your skepticism: it's an effective, excellent way to actually "experience" the houses as ancient Romans would have—and to learn a lot about ancient Rome in the process. A multimedia presentation halfway through also shows you the detailed battle scenes sculpted onto Trajan's Column above the site.

The multimedia tour takes about an hour. There are limited spots, so book in advance over the phone, online, or in person; make sure you book the English tour (at 2 pm). ✉ *Via Foro Traiano 85, Piazza Venezia* ☎ *06/32810* ⊕ *www.palazzovalentini.it* 🎫 *€13.50, including booking fee* 🕐 *Closed Mon.–Thurs.* Ⓜ *Colosseo.*

★ **Musei Capitolini**

ART MUSEUM | Surpassed in size and richness only by the Musei Vaticani, this immense collection was the world's first public museum. A greatest hits of Roman art through the ages, from the ancients to the baroque, it's housed in the Palazzo dei Conservatori and the Palazzo Nuovo, which mirror one another across Michelangelo's famous piazza. The collection was begun by Pope Sixtus IV (the man who built the Sistine Chapel) in 1473, when he donated a room of ancient statuary to the people of the city. This core of the collection includes the She Wolf, which is the symbol of Rome, and the piercing gaze of the Capitoline Brutus.

Buy your ticket and enter the Palazzo dei Conservatori where, in the first courtyard, you'll see the giant head, foot, elbow, and imperially raised finger of the fabled seated statue of Constantine, which once dominated the Basilica of Maxentius in the Forum. Upstairs is the resplendent Sala degli Orazi e Curiazi (Hall of the Horatii and Curatii), decorated with a magnificent gilt ceiling, carved wooden doors, and 16th-century frescoes depicting the history of Rome's legendary origins. At each end of the hall are statues of two of the most important popes of the baroque era, Urban VIII and Innocent X.

The heart of the museum is the modern Exedra of Marcus Aurelius (Esedra di Marco Aurelio), which displays the spectacular original bronze statue of the Roman emperor whose copy dominates the piazza outside. To the right, the room segues into the area of the Temple of Jupiter, with the ruins of part of its vast base rising organically into the museum space. A reconstruction of the temple and the Capitoline Hill from the Bronze Age to the present day makes for a fascinating glimpse through the ages. On the top floor, the museum's *pinacoteca*, or painting gallery, has some noted baroque masterpieces, including Caravaggio's *The Fortune Teller* and *St. John the Baptist.*

To get to the Palazzo Nuovo section of the museum, take the stairs or elevator to the basement of the Palazzo dei Conservatori, where the corridor uniting the two contains the Epigraphic Collection, a poignant assembly of ancient

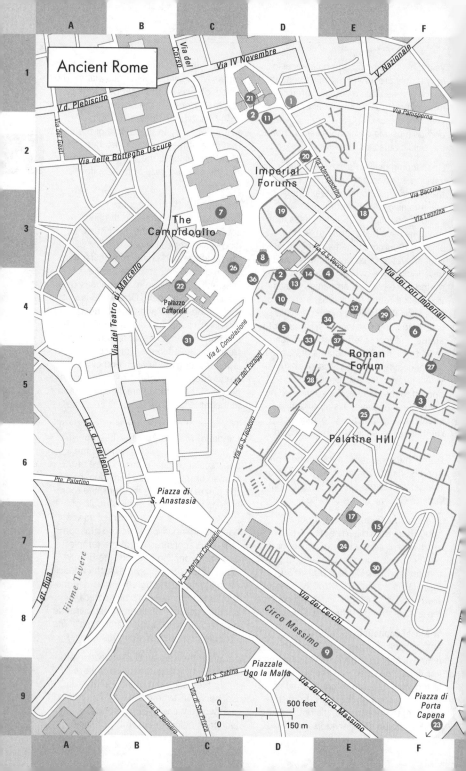

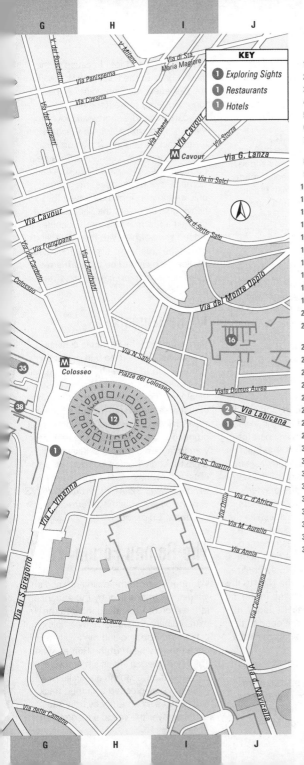

gravestones. Just over halfway along the corridor, and before going up into the Palazzo Nuovo, be sure to take the staircase to the right to the Tabularium gallery and its unparalleled view over the Forum.

On the stairs inside the Palazzo Nuovo, you'll be immediately dwarfed by Mars in full military rig and lion-topped sandals. Upstairs is the noted Sala degli Imperatori, lined with busts of Roman emperors, and the Sala dei Filosofi, where busts of philosophers sit in judgment—a fascinating who's who of the ancient world. Within these serried ranks are 48 Roman emperors, ranging from Augustus to Theodosius. Nearby are rooms filled with sculptural masterpieces, including the famed *Dying Gaul*, the *Red Faun* from Hadrian's Villa, and a *Cupid and Psyche*. ⊠ *Piazza del Campidoglio 1, Piazza Venezia* ☏ *06/0608* ⊕ *www.museicapitolini.org* ✉ *€11.50 (€22 with exhibitions); €16 with access to Centrale Montemartini; €7 audio guide* Ⓜ *Colosseo.*

Palazzo Senatorio

GOVERNMENT BUILDING | During the Middle Ages, this city hall looked like those you might see in Tuscan hill towns: part fortress and part assembly hall. The building was entirely rebuilt in the 1500s as part of Michelangelo's revamping of the Campidoglio for Pope Paul III; the master's design was adapted by later architects, who wisely left the front staircase as the focus of the facade. The ancient statue of Minerva at the center was renamed the Goddess Rome, and the river gods (the River Tigris remodeled to symbolize the Tiber, to the right, and the Nile, to the left) were hauled over from the Terme di Costantino on the Quirinal Hill. Today, it is Rome's city hall and is not open to the public. ⊠ *Piazza del Campidoglio, Piazza Venezia* Ⓜ *Colosseo.*

Tarpeian Rock

RUINS | In ancient Rome, traitors were hurled to their deaths from here. In the 18th and 19th centuries, the Tarpeian Rock became a popular stop for people making the Grand Tour because of the view it gave of the Palatine Hill. Today, the Belvedere viewing point has been long shuttered for restoration, but you can proceed a short walk down to Via di Monte Tarpeo, where the view is spectacular enough. It was on this rock that, in the 7th century BC, Tarpeia betrayed the Roman citadel to the early Romans' sworn enemies, the Sabines, only asking in return to be given the heavy gold bracelets the Sabines wore on their left arm. The scornful Sabines did indeed shower her with their gold, and added the crushing weight of their heavy shields, also carried on their left arms. ⊠ *Via del Tempio di Giove, Piazza Venezia* Ⓜ *Colosseo.*

🍴 Restaurants

Terra e Domus della Provincia di Roma

$$ | ITALIAN | It's hard to find genuinely good food in this area, but this wine bar next to Trajan's Column is an exception. Ideal for coffee, a late lunch, early supper, or just an *aperitivo* (aperitif), it's run by the Province of Rome to showcase local produce and is a great spot to rest after wandering amid the ruins. **Known for:** tourist-friendly Roman classics; daily specials; local wines. ⑤ *Average main: €14* ⊠ *Foro Traiano 82, Monti* ☏ *06/69940273* ⊕ *www.palazzovalentini.it/terre-domus* Ⓜ *Cavour, Colosseo.*

The Roman Forum

Whether it's from the main entrance on Via dei Fori Imperiali or by the entrance at the Arch of Titus, descend into the extraordinary archaeological complex that is the Foro Romano and the Palatine Hill, once the very heart of the Roman world. The Forum began life as a marshy valley between the Capitoline and Palatine Hills—a valley crossed by a mud track and used as a cemetery by Iron Age settlers. Over the years, a market center

An Emperor Cheat Sheet

OCTAVIAN, or Caesar Augustus, was Rome's first emperor (27 BC–AD 14). While it upended the republic once and for all, his rule began a period of prosperity and peace known as the Pax Romana.

The name of **NERO** (AD 54–68) lives in infamy as a violent persecutor of Christians and as the murderer of his wife, his mother, and countless others. Although it's not certain whether he actually played the fiddle (as legend has it) as Rome burned in AD 64, he was well known as an actor.

DOMITIAN (AD 81–96) declared himself "Dominus et Deus"—Lord and God. He stripped away power from the Senate, and as a result, after his death, he suffered "Damnatio Memoriae": the Senate had his name and image erased from all public records.

TRAJAN (AD 98–117), the first Roman emperor to be born outside Italy (in southern Spain), enlarged the empire's boundaries to include modern-day Romania, Armenia, and Upper Mesopotamia.

HADRIAN (AD 117–138) rebuilt the Pantheon as we know it today, possibly to his own design, constructed a majestic villa at Tivoli, and initiated myriad other constructions, including a famed namesake wall in northern Britain.

MARCUS AURELIUS (AD 161–180) is remembered as a humanitarian emperor and a Stoic philosopher whose *Meditations* are still read today. Nonetheless, he was an aggressive leader of the empire and devoted to expansion.

CONSTANTINE I (AD 306–337) made his mark by legalizing Christianity, an act that changed the course of history by legitimizing the once-banned religion and paving the way for the immense powers that would be held by the papacy in Rome.

3

Ancient Rome THE ROMAN FORUM

and some huts were established here, and after the land was drained in the 6th century BC, the site eventually became a political, religious, and commercial center: the Forum.

Hundreds of years of plunder reduced the Forum to its current desolate state. But this enormous area was once Rome's pulsating hub, filled with stately and extravagant temples, palaces, and shops and crowded with people from all corners of the empire. Adding to today's confusion is the fact that the Forum developed over many centuries; what you see today are not the ruins from just one period but from a span of almost 900 years, from about 500 BC to AD 400. Nonetheless, the enduring romance of the place, with its lonely columns and great broken fragments of sculpted marble and stone, makes for a quintessential Roman experience.

■ TIP➜ **Tickets must be purchased online in advance; they cannot be purchased in person.** A combined ticket with the Colosseum and Palatine Hill costs €16 (but must be used within 24 hours); the audio guide costs an additional €5. Your ticket is valid for one entrance to the Roman Forum and the Palatine Hill, which are part of a single continuous complex. Certain sites within the Forum require a "Full Experience" ticket. The Full Experience ticket (good for two full days) costs €22 and also includes access to the Temple of Romulus, Palatine Museum, exterior of the House of Augustus, and the Curia Giulia (open on Saturday and Sunday). Visits to the

Neronian Cryptoporticus, the Houses of Augustus and Livia, and the Aula Isiaca have been temporarily suspended. Both tickets include a single timed admission to the Colosseum and carry an additional €2 booking fee. Choose the print-at-home option (a PDF on a smartphone works, too) and avoid the line to pick up tickets. The Forum is open every day, but a few sights within it are not. Buy tickets at ⊕ *parcocolosseo.it*.

Sights

★ Arco di Settimio Severo
(*Arch of Septimius Severus*)
RUINS | One of the grandest triumphal arches erected by a Roman emperor, this richly decorated monument was built in AD 203 to celebrate Severus's victory over the Parthians. It was once topped by a bronze statuary group depicting a chariot drawn by four (or perhaps as many as six) life-size horses. Masterpieces of Roman statuary, the stone reliefs on the arch were probably based on huge painted panels depicting the event, a kind of visual report on his foreign campaigns that would have been displayed during the emperor's triumphal parade in Rome to impress his subjects (and, like much statuary then, were originally painted in florid, lifelike colors). ⊠ *West end of Foro Romano, Monti* 🚇 *€16 24-hour ticket required* Ⓜ *Colosseo.*

Arco di Tito (*Arch of Titus*)
RUINS | Standing at the northern approach to the Palatine Hill on the Via Sacra, this triumphal arch was erected in AD 81 to celebrate the sack of Jerusalem 10 years earlier, after the First Jewish–Roman War. The superb view of the Colosseum from the arch reminds us that it was the emperor Titus who helped finish the vast amphitheater, begun earlier by his father, Vespasian. Under the arch are two great sculpted reliefs, both showing scenes from Titus's triumphal parade along this very Via Sacra. You still can make out the spoils of war plundered from Herod's Temple, including a gigantic seven-branched candelabrum (menorah) and silver trumpets. During his sacking of Jerusalem, Titus killed or deported most of the Jewish population, thus initiating the Jewish diaspora—an event that would have far-reaching historical consequences. ⊠ *East end of Via Sacra, Monti* 🚇 *€16 24-hour ticket required* Ⓜ *Colosseo.*

Basilica di Massenzio
(*Basilica of Maxentius*)
RUINS | Only about one-third of the original of this gigantic basilica (in the sense of a Roman courthouse and meeting hall) remains, so you can imagine what a wonder this building was when first erected. Today, its great arched vaults still dominate the north side of the Via Sacra. Begun under the emperor Maxentius about AD 306, the edifice was a center of judicial and commercial activity, the last of its kind to be built in Rome. Over the centuries, like so many Roman monuments, it was exploited as a quarry for building materials and was stripped of its sumptuous marble and stucco decorations. Its coffered vaults, like that of the Pantheon's dome, were later copied by many Renaissance artists and architects. ⊠ *Via Sacra, Monti* 🚇 *€16 24-hour ticket required* Ⓜ *Colosseo.*

Basilica Emilia
RUINS | Once a great colonnaded hall, this served as a meeting place for merchants and as a courthouse from the 2nd century BC; it was rebuilt by Augustus in the 1st century AD. To the right as you enter the Forum from Via dei Fori Imperiali, a spot on one of the basilica's preserved pieces of floor testifies to one of Rome's more harrowing moments—and to the hall's purpose. That's where bronze coins melted, leaving behind green stains, when Rome was sacked and the basilica was burned by the Visigoths in 410 AD. The term "basilica" refers here to the particular architectural form developed by the Romans: a rectangular hall flanked

by colonnades, it could serve as a court of law or a center for business and commerce. The basilica would later become the building type adopted for the first official places of Christian worship in the city. ⊠ *Monti* ✚ *On right as you descend into Roman Forum from Via dei Fori Imperiali entrance* ⌛ *€16 24-hour ticket required* Ⓜ *Colosseo.*

Basilica Giulia

RUINS | The Basilica Giulia owes its name to Julius Caesar, who ordered its construction; it was later completed by his adopted heir Augustus. One of several such basilicas in the center of Rome, it was where the Centumviri, the hundred-or-so judges forming the civil court, met to hear cases. The open space between the Basilica Emilia and this basilica was the heart of the Forum proper—the prototype of Italy's Renaissance piazzas, and the center of civic and social activity in ancient Rome. ⊠ *Via Sacra, Monti* ⌛ *€16 24-hour ticket required* Ⓜ *Colosseo.*

Colonna di Foca (*Column of Phocas*)

RUINS | The last monument to be added to the Forum was erected in AD 608 in honor of the Byzantine emperor Phocas who had donated the Pantheon to Pope Boniface IV. It stands 44 feet high and remains in good condition. ⊠ *West end of Foro Romano, Monti* ⌛ *€16 24-hour ticket required* Ⓜ *Colosseo.*

Comitium

RUINS | The open space in front of the Curia was the political hub of ancient Rome. Julius Caesar had rearranged the Comitium, moving the Curia to its current site and transferring the imperial Rostra, the podium from which orators spoke to the people (decorated originally with the prows of captured ships, or *rostra*, the source for the term "rostrum"), to a spot just south of where the Arch of Septimius Severus would be built. It was from this location that Mark Antony delivered his funeral oration in Caesar's honor.

On the left of the Rostra stands what remains of the Tempio di Saturno, which served as ancient Rome's state treasury. The area of the Comitium has been under excavation for several years and is currently not open to visitors. ⊠ *West end of Foro Romano, Monti* ⌛ *€16 24-hour ticket required* Ⓜ *Colosseo.*

Curia Giulia

RUINS | This large brick structure next to the Arch of Septimius Severus, restored during Diocletian's reign in the late 3rd century AD, is the Forum's best-preserved building—thanks largely to having been turned into a church in the 7th century. By the time the Curia was built, the Senate, which met here, had lost practically all of the power and prestige that it had possessed during the Republican era. Still, the Curia appears much as the original Senate house would have looked. You need the "Full Experience" ticket to visit, and the Curia is open only Saturday through Monday. Definitely peek inside if it's open, and don't miss the intricately inlaid 3rd-century floor of marble and porphyry, a method called *opus sectile.* ⊠ *Via Sacra, northwest corner of Foro Romano, Monti* ⌛ *€22 Full Experience ticket required* ⊙ *Closed Tues.–Fri.* Ⓜ *Colosseo.*

Santa Francesca Romana

CHURCH | This church, a 10th-century edifice with a Renaissance facade, is dedicated to the patron saint of motorists. On her feast day, March 9, cars and taxis crowd the Via dei Fori Imperiali below for a special blessing—a cardinal and *carabinieri* (Italian military) on hand, plus a special siren to start off the ceremony. The incomparable setting continues to be a favorite for weddings. ⊠ *Piazza di Santa Francesca Romana, next to Colosseum, Monti* ⌛ *€16 24-hour ticket required* Ⓜ *Colosseo.*

Santa Maria Antiqua

RUINS | The earliest Christian site in the Forum was originally part of an imperial structure at the foot of Palatine Hill before it was converted into a church sometime in the late 5th century. Within it are some exceptional frescoes dating from the 6th to the 9th century. Buried by a 9th-century earthquake, the church was abandoned and a replacement was eventually built on top in the 17th century. This newer church was knocked down in 1900 during excavation work on the Forum, which revealed the early medieval church beneath. Santa Maria Antiqua is only accessible with the Full Experience Roman Forum ticket. ⊠ *South of Tempio di Castore and Polluce, at foot of Palatine Hill, Monti* 🖙 *€22 Full Experience ticket required* ⚲ *Online booking essential* Ⓜ *Colosseo.*

Tempio di Antonino e Faustina

RUINS | Erected by the Senate in honor of Faustina, deified wife of Emperor Antoninus Pius (AD 138–161), Hadrian's successor, this temple was rededicated to the emperor as well upon his death. Because it was transformed into a church (San Lorenzo in Miranda), it's one of the best-preserved ancient structures in the Forum. ⊠ *North of Via Sacra, Monti* 🖙 *€16 24-hour ticket required* Ⓜ *Colosseo.*

Tempio di Castore e Polluce

RUINS | The three remaining Corinthian columns of this temple beautifully evoke the former grandeur and elegance of the Forum. This temple was dedicated in 484 BC to Castor and Pollux, the twin brothers of Helen of Troy, who carried to Rome the news of victory at Lake Regillus, southeast of Rome—the definitive defeat of the deposed Tarquin dynasty. The twins flew on their fabulous white steeds 20 km (12 miles) to the city to bring the news to the people before mortal messengers could arrive. Rebuilt over the centuries before Christ, the temple suffered a major fire and was reconstructed by the future Emperor Tiberius in 12 BC, the date of the three standing columns. ⊠ *West of Casa delle Vestali, Monti* 🖙 *€16 24-hour ticket required* Ⓜ *Colosseo.*

Tempio di Cesare

RUINS | Built by Augustus, Julius Caesar's successor, what survives of the base of the temple stands over the spot where Caesar's body was cremated. A pyre was improvised by grief-crazed citizens who kept the flames going with their own possessions. ⊠ *Via Sacra, opposite the Tempio di Antonino e Faustina, Monti* 🖙 *€16 24-hour ticket required* Ⓜ *Colosseo.*

Tempio di Venere e Roma

RUINS | Once Rome's largest temple, this was in fact originally two temples back-to-back. The half dedicated to Venus, facing the Colosseum, is the section we see today, while its twin, which once faced the Forum, was dedicated to the goddess Roma, and is now the foundation of the church of Santa Maria Nova. Begun by Hadrian in AD 121, the temple is accessible from the end of the Forum near the Arch of Titus, and offers a great view of the Colosseum. ⊠ *East of Arco di Tito, Monti* 🖙 *€16 24-hour ticket required* Ⓜ *Colosseo.*

Tempio di Vespasiano

RUINS | All that remains of Vespasian's temple are three graceful Corinthian columns. They marked the site of the Forum through the centuries while the rest was hidden beneath overgrown rubble. Nearby is the ruined platform that was the Tempio di Concordia. ⊠ *West end of Foro Romano, Monti* 🖙 *€16 24-hour ticket required* Ⓜ *Colosseo.*

Tempio di Vesta

RUINS | Although it's just a fragment of the original building, the remnant of this temple conveys the sophisticated elegance architecture achieved in the later Roman Empire. Set off by florid Corinthian columns, the circular *tholos* was rebuilt by Emperor Septimius Severus when he restored this temple around AD 205. Dedicated to Vesta, the goddess of the hearth, the highly privileged vestal virgins kept the sacred flame alive. Next to the temple, the Casa delle Vestali gives you a glimpse of the splendor in which these women lived out their 30-year vows of chastity. Marble statues of the vestals and fragments of mosaic pavement line the garden courtyard, which once would have been surrounded by lofty colonnades and at least 50 rooms. Chosen when they were between six and 10 years old, the six vestal virgins dedicated the next 30 years of their lives to keeping the sacred fire burning, a tradition that dated back to the very earliest days of Rome, when guarding the community's precious fire was essential to its well-being. Their standing in Rome was considerable: among women, they were second in rank only to the Empress. Their intercession could save a condemned man, and they did, in fact, rescue Julius Caesar from the lethal vengeance of his enemy Sulla. The virgins were handsomely maintained by the state, but if they allowed the sacred fire to go out, they were scourged by the high priest, and if they broke their vows of celibacy, they were buried alive (a punishment doled out only a handful of times throughout the cult's 1,000-year history). The vestal virgins were one of the last of ancient Rome's institutions to die out, enduring until the end of the 4th century AD—even after Rome's emperors had become Christian. ⊠ *South side of Via Sacra, Monti* ⊠ *€16 24-hour ticket required* Ⓜ *Colosseo.*

Via Sacra

RUINS | The celebrated "Sacred Way," paved with local volcanic rock, runs through the Roman Forum, lined with temples and shrines. It was also the traditional route of religious and triumphal processions. Pick your way across the paving stones, some rutted with the iron-clad wheels of Roman wagons, to walk in

the footsteps of Julius Caesar and Marc Antony. ⊠ *Monti* ⊠ *€16 24-hour ticket required* Ⓜ *Colosseo.*

Hotels

NH Collection Roma Fori Imperiali

$$ | HOTEL | It would be hard to find a modern hotel closer to the Roman Forum—the ancient ruins are practically right outside the door. **Pros:** incredible views of ancient Rome; restaurant Oro Bistrot by renowned chef Natale Giunta; rooftop bar serves a great aperitivo. **Cons:** no spa or gym; not much public space; breakfast foods are pre-packaged. Ⓢ *Rooms from: €200* ⊠ *Via di Santa Eufemia 19, Piazza Venezia* ☎ *06/697689911* ⊕ *www.nh-collection. com/it/hotel/nh-collection-roma-fori-imperiali* ⇄ *42 rooms* ⦿*No Meals* Ⓜ *Cavour.*

The Palatine Hill

Just beyond the Arco di Tito, the Clivus Palatinus—the road connecting the Forum and the Palatine Hill—gently rises to the heights of the Colle Palatino (Palatine Hill), the oldest inhabited site in Rome. Now charmingly bucolic, with pines and olive trees providing shade in summer, this is where Romulus is said to have founded the city that bears his name, and despite its location overlooking the Forum's traffic and attendant noise, the Palatine was the most coveted address for ancient Rome's rich and famous. During the Roman Republic it was home to wealthy patrician families—Cicero, Catiline, Crassus, and Agrippa all had homes here—and when Augustus (who had himself been born on the hill) came to power, declaring himself to be the new Romulus, it would thereafter become the home of emperors. The Houses of Livia and Augustus (which you can visit with the S.U.P.E.R. ticket, for the same price as the Roman Forum admission) are today the hill's best-preserved structures, replete with fabulous frescoes. If you only have time for one, the House of Augustus is the more spectacular of the two. After Augustus's relatively modest residence, Tiberius extended the palace and other structures followed, notably the gigantic extravaganza constructed for Emperor Domitian which makes up much of what we see today.

A combined ticket to the Palatine Hill–Forum site and single entry to Colosseum (if used within 24 hours) costs €16 (€18 with online reservation); a Full Experience ticket costs €22 (€24 with online reservation) and includes access to the Houses of Augustus and Livia, the Palatine Museum, Aula Isiaca, Santa Maria Antiqua, and Temple of Romulus. All tickets must be booked in advance at ⊕ parcocolosseo.it.

 Sights

Circo Massimo (Circus Maximus)
RUINS | From the belvedere of the Domus Flavia on the Palatine Hill, you can see the Circus Maximus; there's also a great free view from Piazzale Ugo La Malfa on the Aventine Hill side. The giant space where once 300,000 spectators watched chariot races while the emperor looked on is ancient Rome's oldest and largest racetrack; it lies in a natural hollow between the two hills. The oval course stretches about 650 yards from end to end; on certain occasions, there were as many as 24 chariot races a day and competitions could last for 15 days. The charioteers could amass fortunes rather like the sports stars of today. (The Portuguese Diocles is said to have totted up winnings of 35 million sestertii.) The noise and the excitement of the crowd must have reached astonishing levels as the charioteers competed in teams, each with their own colors—the Reds, the Blues, etc. Betting also provided Rome's majority of unemployed with a potentially lucrative occupation. The central ridge

was the site of two Egyptian obelisks (now in Piazza del Popolo and Piazza San Giovanni in Laterano). Picture the great chariot race scene from MGM's Ben-Hur and you have an inkling of what this all looked like. ☒ Between Palatine and Aventine Hills, Aventino ☒ €16 24-hour ticket required Ⓜ Circo Massimo.

Domus Augustana
RUINS | In the imperial palace complex, this area, named in the 19th century for the "Augustuses" (a generic term used for emperors, in honor of Augustus himself), consisted of private apartments built for Emperor Domitian and his family. Here Domitian—"Dominus et Deus," as he liked to be called—would retire to dismember flies (at least, according to Suetonius), before eventually being assassinated. ☒ Southern crest of Palatine Hill, Monti ☒ €16 24-hour ticket required Ⓜ Circo Massimo.

Domus Flavia
RUINS | Domitian used this area of the imperial palace complex for official functions and ceremonies. It included a basilica where the emperor could hold judiciary hearings. There was also a large audience hall, a peristyle (a columned courtyard), and the imperial triclinium (dining room)—some of its mosaic floors and stone banquettes are still in place. According to Suetonius, Domitian had the walls and courtyards of this and the adjoining Domus Augustana covered with the shiniest marble to act as mirrors to alert him to any knife pointed at his back. They failed in their purpose: he died in a palace plot, engineered, some say, by his wife Domitia. ☒ Southern crest of Palatine Hill, Monti ☒ €16 24-hour ticket required Ⓜ Circo Massimo.

Museo Palatino
ART MUSEUM | The Palatine Museum charts the history of the hill from Archaic times, with quaint models of early villages (on the ground floor), to Roman times (on the ground and upper floors). There is a good video reconstruction of

The "Bel Air" of ancient Rome, the Palatine Hill was the address of choice of Cicero, Agrippa, and the emperors Tiberius, Caligula, and Domitian.

the hill in Room V on the ground floor, and a collection of colored stones used in the decorations of the palace, with a map showing the distant imperial regions whence they came. Upstairs, the room dedicated to Augustus houses painted terra-cotta moldings and sculptural decorations from various temples—notably the Temple of Apollo Actiacus, whose name derives from the god to whom Octavian attributed his victory at Actium (the severed heads of the Medusa in the terra-cotta panels symbolize the defeated Queen of Egypt). There is also a selection of imperial portraits on the upper floor, including a rare surviving image of Nero. The museum closes early, at 3:30 pm. ⊠ *Northwest crest of Palatine Hill, Monti* ⊕ *www.parcocolosseo.it* ✉ *€22 Full Experience ticket required* Ⓜ *Colosseo.*

Orti Farnesiani

GARDEN | Alessandro Farnese, a nephew of Pope Paul III, commissioned the 16th-century architect Vignola to lay out this archetypal Italian garden over the ruins of the Palace of Tiberius, on the northern side of the Palatine, with a spectacular view over the Forum. This was yet another example of the Renaissance renewing an ancient Roman tradition. To paraphrase the poet Martial, the statue-studded gardens of the Flavian Palace were such as to make even an Egyptian potentate turn green with envy. ⊠ *Palatine Hill, Monti* ✉ *€16 24-hour ticket required* Ⓜ *Colosseo.*

Stadio Palatino

RUINS | Built by Domitian and erroneously referred to since the 19th century as the "stadium," this was in fact a sunken garden that created a terrace on the slopes of the hill. It may also have been used to stage games (but not chariot races) and other amusements for the emperor's benefit. ⊠ *Southeast crest of Palatine Hill, Monti* ✉ *€16 24-hour ticket required* Ⓜ *Circo Massimo.*

Continued on page 94

ANCIENT ROME:

ROME WASN'T BUILT IN A DAY

by Robert I. C. Fisher

RE-CREATING THE ANCIENT CITY

Time has reduced ancient Rome to fields of silent ruins, but the powerful impact of what happened here, of the genius and power that made Rome the center of the Western world, echoes across the millennia. In this one compact area of the city, you can step back into the Rome of Cicero, Julius Caesar, and Virgil. You can walk along the streets they knew, cool off in the shade of the Colosseum that loomed over the city, and see the sculptures poised over their piazzas.

Today, this part of Rome, more than any other, is a perfect example of the layering of historic eras, the overlapping of ages, of religions, of a past that is very much a part of the present.

Although it has been the capital of the Republic of Italy only since 1946, Rome has been the capital of something for more than 2,500 years, and it shows. The magnificent ruins of the Palatine Hill, the ancient complexity of the Forum, the Renaissance harmony of the Campidoglio—all are part of Rome's identity as one of the world's most enduring seats of government.

This is not to say that it's been an easy 2½ millennia. The Vandal hordes of the 3rd century, the Goth sacks of the Middle Ages, the excavations of a modern-day Mussolini, and today's modern citizens—all played a part in transforming Rome into a city of fragments. Semi-preserved ruins of ancient forums, basilicas, stadiums, baths, and temples are strewn across the city like remnants of some Cecil B. DeMille movie set. No wonder first-time visitors feel that the only thing more intimidating than crossing a Roman intersection at rush hour is trying to make sense of the layout of ancient Rome.

The following pages detail how the new Rome overlaps the old, showing how the modern city is crammed with details of all the city's ageless walls and ancient sites, even though some of them now lie hidden underneath the earth. Written in these rocks is the story of the emperors, the city's greatest builders. Thanks in large part to their dreams of glory—combined with their architectural megalomania—Imperial Rome became the fountainhead of Western civilization.

(Left) Colosseum; (top) Head of Emperor Constantine, Musei Capitolini

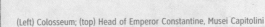

THE WAY ROME WAS

Circus Maximus (Circo Massimo): Atop the Palatine Hill, the emperor's royal box looked down on the races and games of this vast stadium—most early Christians met their untimely end here, not in the Colosseum.

Capitoline Hill (Campidoglio): Most important of Rome's original seven hills, and home to the Temple of Jupiter, the "capital" hill was strategically located high above the Tiber and became the hub of the Roman Republic.

Palatine Hill (Colle Palatino): The birthplace of Rome, settled by Romulus and Remus, the Palatine ultimately became Rome's "Beverly Hills,"

Rome in the Year 300 AD

for it was home to Cicero, Julius Caesar, and a dozen emperors.

Roman Forum (Foro Romano): Downtown ancient Rome, this was the political heart of the republic and empire—the place

for processions, tribunals, law courts, and orations, and it was here that Mark Antony buried Caesar and Cleopatra made her triumphant entry.

Colosseum (Colosseo): Gladiators fought for the chance to live another day on the floor before 50,000 spectators in this giant arena, built in a mere eight years and inaugurated in AD 80.

Domus Aurea: Nero's "Golden House," a sprawling example of the excesses of Imperial Rome, once comprised 150 rooms, some shimmering with gold.

THEY CAME, THEY SAW, THEY BUILT

Remember the triumphal scene in the 2000 film *Gladiator*? Awesome expanses of pristine marble, a cast of thousands in gold-lavished costumes, and close-ups of Joaquin Phoenix (playing Emperor Commodus) on his way to the Colosseum: Rome à la Hollywood. But behind all the marble splendor seen in the film lies an eight-century-long trail that extends back from Imperial Rome to a tiny village of mud huts along the Tiber river.

Museo della Civiltà Romana's model of Imperial Rome

ROMULUS GOES TO TOWN

Legend has it that Rome was founded by Romulus and Remus, twin sons of the god Mars. Upon being abandoned in infancy by a wicked uncle, they were taken up and suckled by a she-wolf living on a bank of the Tiber. (Ancient gossip says the wolf was actually a woman nick-named Lupa for her multiple infidelities to her shepherd husband.)

As young men, Romulus and Remus returned in 753 BC to the hallowed spot to found a city but came to blows during its building, ending in the death of Remus—which is how the city became Roma, not Rema.

Where myth ends, archaeology takes over. In 2007, Roman excavators uncovered a cavernous sanctuary dedicated to the brothers situated in the valley between the Palatine (Palatino) and Capitoline (Campidoglio) hills in central Rome. Often transformed into "islands" when

the Tiber river overflowed, these two hills soon famously expanded to include seven hills, including the Esquiline, Viminale, Celian, Quirinale, and Aventine.

SIMPLY MARBLE-LOUS

Up to 510 BC, the style of the fledging city had been set by the fun-loving, sophisticated Etruscans—Rome was to adopt their vestal virgins, household gods, and gladiatorial games. Later, when the republic took over the city (509 BC–27 BC), the austere values promulgated by its democratic Senate eventually fell to the power-mad triumvirate of Crassus, Pompey, and Julius Caesar, who waved away any detractors—including Rome's main power-players, the patrician Senators and the populist Tribunes—by invoking the godlike sovereignty of emperorship.

Republican Rome's city was badly planned, in fact not planned at all, and the great contribution of the Emperor Augustus—who took over when his stepfather Caesar was assassinated in 43 BC—was to commence serious town planning, with results far surpassing even his own claim that he "found Rome brick and left it marble." Which was only fitting, as floridly colored marbles began to flow into Rome from all of the Mediterranean provinces he had conquered (including obelisks transported from Egypt to flaunt his victory over Cleopatra).

Via Sacra in the Roman Forum, with the Temple of Saturn in the foreground and the Basilica Julia on the right.

A FUNNY THING HAPPENED ON THE WAY TO THE ROMAN FORUM

It was during Augustus's peaceful 40-year reign that Rome began its transition from glorified provincial capital into great city. While excavations have shown that the area of the Roman Forum was in use as a burial ground as far back as the 10th century BC, the importance of the Forum area as the political, commercial, and social center of Rome and, by extension, of the whole ancient world, grew immeasurably during Imperial times. The majestic ruins still extant are remnants of the massive complex of markets, civic buildings, and temples that dominated the city center in its heyday.

After Rome gained "empire" status, however, the original Forum was inadequate to handle the burden of the many trials and meetings required to run Western civilization, so Julius Caesar built a new forum. This apparently started a trend, as over the next 200-plus years (43 BC–AD 180), four different emperors—Augustus, Domitian, Vespasian, and Trajan—did the same. Oddly enough, the Roman Forum became four different Forums. They grew, in part, thanks to the Great Fire of AD 64, which Nero did not set but for which he took credit for laying waste to shabbier districts to build new ones.

For half a millennium, the Roman Forum area became the heart and soul of a worldwide empire, which eventually extended from Britain to Constantinople. Unfortunately, another thousand years of looting, sacking, and decay means you have to use your vivid imagination to see the glory that once was.

WHERE ALL ROADS LEAD

Even if you don't dig ruins, a visit to the archaeological ruins in and around the Roman Forum is a must. Rome's foundation as a world capital and crossroads of culture are to be found here, literally. Overlapped with Rome's current streets, this map shows the main monuments of the Roman Forum (in tan) as they originally stood.

Basilica Julia

Temple of Antoninus and Faustina

Temple of Castor and Pollux

Domitian's Palace

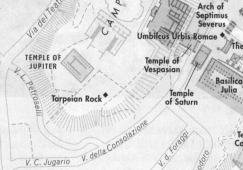

Via IV Novembre

Via C. Battisti

Trajan's Column

V. Alessandrina

TRAJAN'S FORUM

CAMPIDOGLIO

Via del Teatro di Marcello

Palazzo Senatorio

Tabularium

Carcere Mamertino

Curia

Arch of Septimus Severus

Umbilcus Urbis Romae

The Rostra

TEMPLE OF JUPITER

Temple of Vespasian

Roman Forum

V. L. Petroselli

Basilica Julia

Tarpeian Rock

Temple of Saturn

Temple of Castor and Pollux

V. C. Jugario

V. della Consolazione

V. d. Foraggi

V. d. Fienili

V. di S. Teodoro

Cloaca Maxima

TIBERIAN PALACE

MONTE

House of Livia

V. del Velabro

Circus Maximus

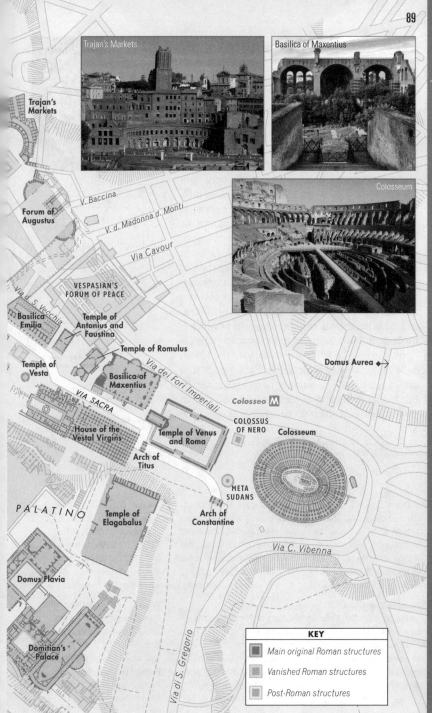

Trajan's Markets

Basilica of Maxentius

Colosseum

Trajan's Markets

V. Baccina

V. d. Madonna d. Monti

Via Cavour

Forum of Augustus

VESPASIAN'S FORUM OF PEACE

Via d. S. Vecchia

Basilica Emilia

Temple of Antonius and Faustina

Temple of Romulus

Domus Aurea ◆→

Temple of Vesta

Basilica of Maxentius

Via dei Fori Imperiali

VIA SACRA

Colosseo Ⓜ

House of the Vestal Virgins

Temple of Venus and Roma

COLOSSUS OF NERO

Colosseum

Arch of Titus

META SUDANS

PALATINO

Temple of Elagabalus

Arch of Constantine

Via C. Vibenna

Domus Flavia

Via di S. Gregorio

Domitian's Palace

KEY		
🟦		*Main original Roman structures*
🟩		*Vanished Roman structures*
🟨		*Post-Roman structures*

Pantheon

URBIS ROMÆ: THE EXPANDING CITY

Today's Campitelli district—the historic area comprising the Forums and the Colosseum—was, in fact, a relatively small part of the ancient city. From the center around the Forum, the old city dramatically grew outwards and in AD 7, the emperor Augustus organized ancient Rome into 14 regiones, administrative divisions that were the forerunners of today's historic *rioni* (districts). Rome's first city walls went up in the 6th century BC when King Servius Tullius built an 8-mile ring. As the city's borders greatly expanded, however, the outlying areas needed extra protection. This became a dire necessity in the 3rd century when Germanic tribes arrived to sack Rome while Emperor Aurelian was fighting wars on the southern border of the empire. Fueled by fear, the emperor commissioned an 11-mile bulwark to be built of brick between 271 and 275. Studding the Aurelian Walls were 380 towers and 18 main gates, the best preserved of which is the Porta di San Sebastiano, at the entrance to the Via Appia Antica. The Porta is now home to the Museo delle Mura, a small but fascinating museum that allows you to walk the ancient ramparts today; take Bus No. 118 to the Porta. From the walls' lofty perch you can see great vistas of the timeless Appian Way.

KEY

Archeological area of Rome

Hills

Mausoleum of Hadrian (Castel S. Angelo)

CAMPUS MARTIUS

Circus of Domitian (Piazza Navona)

Fiume Tevere

Theater of Pompey (Campo de' Fiori)

TRASTEVERE

Pantheon: Built in 27 BC by Augustus's general Agrippa and totally rebuilt by Hadrian in the 2nd century AD, this temple, dedicated to all the pagan gods, was topped by the largest dome ever built (until the 20th century).

Baths of Caracalla: These gigantic thermal baths, a stunning example of ancient Roman architecture, were more than just a place to bathe—they functioned somewhat like today's swank athletic clubs.

Isola Tiberina: The Temple of Aesculapius once presided over this island—which was shaped by ancient Romans to resemble a ship, complete with obelisk mast and (still visible) marble ship prow—and was Rome's shrine to medicine.

Circus of Domitian: Rome's present Piazza Navona follows the shape of this ancient oval stadium built in 96 AD—houses now stand on top of the cavea, the original stone seating, which held 30,000 spectators

Campus Borum: Today's Piazza della Bocca della Verità was ancient Rome's cattle market and the site of two beautifully preserved 2nd century BC temples, one dedicated to Fortuna Virilis, the other to Hercules.

Porta di San Sebastiano: The largest extant gate of the 3rd-century Aurelian Walls, located near the ancient aqueduct that once brought water to the nearby Baths of Caracalla, showcases the most beautiful stretch of Rome's ancient walls.

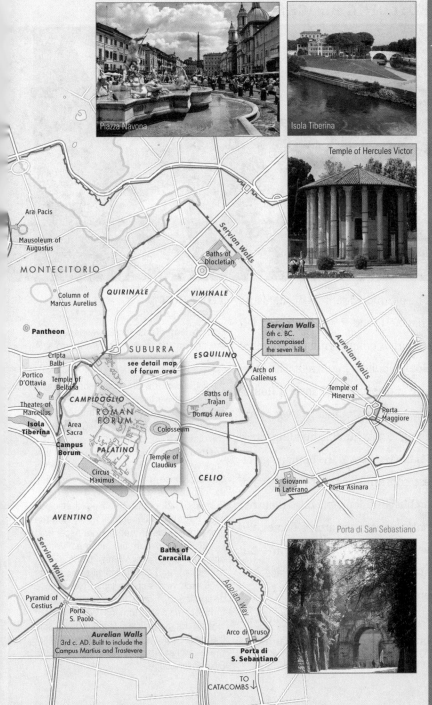

Piazza Navona

Isola Tiberina

Temple of Hercules Victor

Ara Pacis

Mausoleum of Augustus

MONTECITORIO

Column of Marcus Aurelius

QUIRINALE

Baths of Diocletian

Servian Walls

VIMINALE

Pantheon

SUBURRA

ESQUILINO

Servian Walls
6th c. BC.
Encompassed
the seven hills

Arch of Gallenus

Aurelian Walls

Cripta Balbi

see detail map of forum area

Portico D'Ottavia

Temple of Bellona

Theater of Marcellus

CAMPIDOGLIO

ROMAN FORUM

Baths of Trajan

Domus Aurea

Temple of Minerva

Porta Maggiore

Isola Tiberina

Area Sacra

Colosseum

Campus Borum

PALATINO

Temple of Claudius

Circus Maximus

CELIO

S. Giovanni in Laterano

Porta Asinara

AVENTINO

Porta di San Sebastiano

Servian Walls

Baths of Caracalla

Appian Way

Pyramid of Cestius

Porta S. Paolo

Aurelian Walls
3rd c. AD. Built to include the
Campus Martius and Trastevere

Arco di Druso

**Porta di
S. Sebastiano**

TO
CATACOMBS

BUILDING BLOCKS OF THE EMPERORS

Vespasian's Colosseum

The oft-quoted remark of Augustus, that he found Rome brick and left it marble, omits a vital ingredient of Roman building: concrete. The sheer size and spectacle of ancient Rome's most famous buildings owe everything to this humble building block. Its use was one of the Romans' greatest contributions to the history of architecture, for it enabled them not only to create vast arches, domes, and vaults—undreamed of before—but also to build at a scale and size never before attempted. The fall of the Roman Empire ultimately arrived, but great architectural monuments remain to remind us of its glory.

THE ARCH
VESPASIAN'S COLOSSEUM

Born in Riete, Titus Flavius Vespasian was the first of the new, military emperors. A down-to-earth countryman with a realistic sense of humor, his dying words "I think I am in the process of becoming a god" have lived on. Along with generally restoring the city, which had burned down under Nero, he started the Colosseum, (his son, Titus, finished it in AD 80). Erected upon the swampy marsh that once held the stagnum, or lake, of Nero's Golden House, the Colosseum was vast; its dimensions underscored how much Romans had come to value audacious size. The main architectural motif was the arch—hundreds of them in four ascending birthday tiers, each tier adorned with a different style of column: Doric, Ionic, Corinthian, and Corinthian pilaster. Inside each arch was a statue (all of which have disappeared). Under these arches, called fornices, ancient Romans were fond of looking for bedfellows (so famously said the great poet Ovid), so much so that these arches gave a new word to the English language.

omus Aurea

Hadrian's Pantheon

THE VAULT
NERO'S DOMUS AUREA

Most notorious of the emperors, but by no means the worst, Nero had domestic and foreign policies that were popular at first. However, his increasing megalomania was apparent in the size of his Domus Aurea, the "Golden House," so huge that the cry went up "All Rome has become a villa." Taking advantage of the Great Fire of AD 64, Nero wanted to re-create his seaside villa at Baia (outside Naples) right in the middle of Rome, building a vast palace of polychrome marble with a dining room with perforated ivory ceilings so that diners could be showered with flowers and perfume (designed by Fabullus, Nero's decorator). But the masterstrokes were the gigantic vaulted rooms—the Room of the Owls and the octagonal center room—designed by Nero's architects, Severus and Celer. Greek post-and-lintel architecture was banished for these highly dramatic spaces created by soaring vaults. You can still tour the ruins of Nero's "villa," but his 120-foot-high colossal bronze statue gave way to make room for the Colosseum.

THE DOME
HADRIAN'S PANTHEON

The concrete Roman dome at its most impressive can be seen in the Pantheon (around AD 125), a massive construction 141 feet across. It is a fascinating feat of both design and engineering, for it is modeled on a sphere, the height of the supporting walls being equal to the radius of the dome. Larger than Saint Peter's, this dome of domes was constructed by the greatest Imperial builder of them all, the Emperor Hadrian. Poised on top of the dome's mighty concrete ring, the five levels of trapezoid-shaped coffers represent the course of the five then-known planets and their concentric spheres. Then, ruling over them, comes the sun, represented symbolically and literally by the so-called oculus—the giant "eye" open to the sky at the top. The heavenly symmetry is further paralleled by the coffers themselves: 28 to each row, the number of lunar cycles. In the center of each would have shone a small bronze star. All of the dome's famous gilt trim was stripped away by the Barberini popes in the 17th century, who melted it down to decorate the Vatican.

The Imperial Forums

A compound of five grandly conceived complexes flanked with colonnades, the Fori Imperiali contain monuments of triumph, law courts, and temples. The complexes were tacked on to the Roman Forum, from the time of Julius Caesar in the 1st century BC until Trajan in the very early 2nd century AD, to accommodate the ever-growing need for administrative buildings as well as grand monuments.

From Piazza del Colosseo, head northwest on Via dei Fori Imperiali toward Piazza Venezia. Among the Fori Imperiali along the avenue, you can see the Foro di Cesare (Forum of Caesar) and the Foro di Augusto (Forum of Augustus). The grandest was the Foro di Traiano (Forum of Trajan), with its huge semicircular Mercati di Traiano and the Colonna Traiana (Trajan's Column). You can walk through part of Trajan's Markets on the Via Alessandrina and visit the Museo dei Fori Imperiali, which presents the Imperial Forums and shows how they would have been used through ancient fragments, artifacts, and modern multimedia.

Sights

Colonna di Traiano (*Trajan's Column*)
RUINS | The remarkable series of reliefs spiraling up this column celebrate the emperor's victories over the Dacians in today's Romania. It has stood in this spot since AD 113. The scenes on the column are an important primary source for information on the Roman army and its tactics. An inscription on the base declares that the column was erected in Trajan's honor and that its height corresponds to the height of the hill that was razed to create a level area for the grandiose Foro di Traiano. The emperor's ashes, no longer here, were kept in a golden urn in a chamber at the column's base; his statue stood atop the column until 1587, when the pope had it replaced with a statue of St. Peter. ⊠ *Via del Foro di Traiano, Monti* Ⓜ *Cavour.*

Foro di Augusto (*Forum of Augustus*)
RUINS | These ruins, along with those of the Foro di Nerva, on the northeast side of Via dei Fori Imperiali, give only a hint of what must have been impressive edifices. The three columns are all that remain of the Temple of Mars Ultor. ⊠ *Via dei Fori Imperiali, Monti* 🎫 *€22 Full Experience ticket required* Ⓜ *Colosseo.*

Foro di Cesare (*Forum of Caesar*)
RUINS | In an attempt to rival the Roman Forum, Julius Caesar had this extension built in the middle of the 1st century BC. Each year without fail, on the Ides of March, flowers are laid at the foot of Caesar's statue. ⊠ *Via dei Fori Imperiali, Monti* ☎ *06/0608* Ⓜ *Colosseo.*

Foro di Traiano (*Forum of Trajan*)
RUINS | Of all the Fori Imperiali, Trajan's was the grandest and most imposing, a veritable city unto itself. Designed by architect Apollodorus of Damascus, it comprised a vast basilica, two libraries, and a colonnade laid out around the square—all at one time covered with rich marble ornamentation. Adjoining the forum were the Mercati di Traiano (Trajan's Markets), a huge, multilevel brick complex of shops, taverns, walkways, and terraces, as well as administrative offices involved in the mammoth task of feeding the city. The Museo dei Fori Imperiali (Imperial Forums Museum) takes advantage of the Forum's soaring vaulted spaces to showcase archaeological fragments and sculptures while presenting a video re-creation of the original complex. In addition, the series of terraced rooms offers an impressive overview of the entire forum. A pedestrian walkway, the Via Alessandrina, also allows for an excellent (and free) view of Trajan's Forum.

To build a complex of this magnitude, Apollodorus and his patrons clearly had great confidence, not to mention almost unlimited means and cheap labor at their disposal (readily provided by slaves captured in Trajan's Dacian Wars). The complex also contained two semicircular lecture halls, one at either end, which are thought to have been associated with the libraries in Trajan's Forum. The markets' architectural centerpiece is the enormous curved wall, or *exedra*, that shores up the side of the Quirinal Hill excavated by Apollodorus's gangs of laborers. Covered galleries and streets were constructed at various levels, following the exedra's curves and giving the complex a strikingly modern appearance.

As you enter the markets, a large, vaulted hall stands in front of you. Two stories of shops and offices rise up on either side. Head for the flight of steps at the far end that leads down to Via Biberatica. (*Bibere* is Latin for "to drink," and the shops that open onto the street are believed to have been taverns.) Then head back to the three retail and administrative tiers that line the upper levels of the great exedra and look out over the remains of the Forum. Empty and bare today, the cubicles were once ancient Rome's busiest market stalls. Though it seems to be part of the market, the Torre delle Milizie (Tower of the Militia), the tall brick tower that is a prominent feature of Rome's skyline, was actually built in the early 1200s. ✉ *Via IV Novembre 94, Monti* ☎ *06/0608* ⊕ *www.mercatiditraiano.it* ✉ *€11.50* Ⓜ *Cavour*.

★ **Santi Cosma e Damiano**
CHURCH | Home to one of the most striking early Christian mosaics, this church was adapted in the 6th century from two ancient buildings: the library in Vespasian's Forum of Peace and a hall of the Temple of Romulus (dedicated to the son of Maxentius who had been named for Rome's founder). In the apse is the famous AD 530 mosaic of Christ in Glory. It reveals how popes at the time strove to re-create the splendor of imperial audience halls into Christian churches: Christ wears a gold, Roman-style toga, and his pose recalls that of an emperor addressing his subjects. He floats on a blue sky streaked with a flaming sunset—a miracle of tesserae mosaic work. To his side are the figures of Saint Peter and Saint Paul, who represent Cosmas and Damian (patron saints of doctors), two Syrian benefactors whose charity was such that they were branded Christians and condemned to death. Beneath this awe-inspiring work is an enchanting mosaic frieze of holy lambs. ✉ *Via dei Fori Imperiali 1, Monti* ☎ *06/6920441* ⊕ *www.cosmadamiano.com* Ⓜ *Colosseo*.

The Colosseum and Environs

Legend has it that as long as the Colosseum stands, Rome will stand—and when Rome falls, so will the world. No visit to Rome is complete without a trip to the obstinate oval that has been the iconic symbol of the city for centuries. Looming over a group of the Roman Empire's most magnificent monuments to imperial wealth and power, the Colosseum was the gigantic sports arena built by Vespasian and Titus. To its west stands the Arco di Constantino, a majestic, ornate triumphal arch, built solely as a tribute to the emperor Constantine; victorious armies purportedly marched under it on their return from war. To the east of the Colosseum, hidden under the Colle Oppio, is Nero's opulent Domus Aurea, a palace that stands as testimony to the lavish lifestyles of the emperors; it is accessible every day by joining a guided tour. Check ⊕ *parcocolosseo.it* for details and reservations.

◉ Sights

Arco di Costantino (*Arch of Constantine*)
RUINS | This majestic arch was erected in AD 315 to commemorate Constantine's victory over Maxentius at the Milvian Bridge. It was just before this battle, in AD 312, that Constantine—the emperor who converted Rome to Christianity—legendarily had a vision of a cross and heard the words, "In this sign thou shalt conquer." Many of the costly marble decorations for the arch were scavenged from earlier monuments, both saving money and placing Constantine in line with the great emperors of the past. It is easy to picture ranks of Roman centurions marching under the great barrel vault. ⊠ *Piazza del Colosseo, Monti* Ⓜ *Colosseo.*

★ **Colosseum** (*Colosseo*)
RUINS | The most spectacular extant edifice of ancient Rome, the Colosseum has a history that is half gore, half glory. Once able to house 50,000 spectators, it was built to impress Romans with its spectacles involving wild animals and fearsome gladiators from the farthest reaches of the empire. Senators had marble seats up front and the vestal virgins took the ringside position, while the plebs sat in wooden tiers at the back, then the masses above on the top tier. Looming over all was the amazing velarium, an ingenious system of sail-like awnings rigged on ropes and maneuvered by sailors from the imperial fleet, who would unfurl them to protect the arena's occupants from sun or rain.

From the second floor, you can get a bird's-eye view of the hypogeum: the subterranean passageways that were the architectural engine rooms that made the slaughter above proceed like clockwork. In a scene prefiguring something from Dante's *Inferno*, hundreds of beasts would wait to be eventually launched via a series of slave-powered hoists and lifts into the bloodthirsty sand of the arena above. Designed by order of the emperor Vespasian in AD 72, and completed by his son Titus in AD 80, the arena has a circumference of 573 yards, and its external walls were built with travertine from nearby Tivoli. Its construction was a remarkable feat of engineering, for it stands on marshy terrain reclaimed by draining an artificial lake that formed part of the vast palace of Nero. Originally known as the Flavian amphitheater (Vespasian's and Titus's family name was Flavius), it came to be known as the Colosseum thanks to a colossal gilded bronze statue which once stood nearby.

The legend made famous by the Venerable Bede says that as long as the Colosseum stands, Rome will stand; and when Rome falls, so will the world … not that the prophecy deterred medieval and Renaissance princes and popes from using the Colosseum as a quarry. In the 19th century, poets came to view the arena by moonlight; today, mellow golden spotlights make the arena a spectacular sight at night, and evening visits are possible with guided tours from May through October.

All visitors must book a combination ticket (with the Roman Forum and Palatine Hill) in advance online for a €2 surcharge. If you have a Roma Pass, you can use it. Aim for early or late slots to minimize lines, as even the preferential lanes get busy in the middle of the day. Alternatively, you can book a tour online with a company (do your research to make sure it's reputable) that lets you skip the line. Avoid the tours sold on the spot around the Colosseum; although you can skip the lines, the tour guides tend to be dry, the tour groups huge, and the tour itself rushed. If you wish to see the arena or the underground, you must purchase a special timed ticket with those features, though they do not cost extra with the Full Experience ticket. ⊠ *Piazza del Colosseo, Colosseo* ☎ *06/39967700* ⊕ *www.coopculture.it* ✉ *Requires either*

Hollywood got it wrong, historians got it right: plenty of gladiators died in the Colosseum (pictured here), but early Christians only met their tragic fate in the nearby Circus Maximus arena.

the €16 24-hour ticket or the €22 Full Experience ticket (can include the arena and underground areas for no additional fee, but they must be specified during the purchase) ⚹ Requires a timed ticket purchased in advance Ⓜ Colosseo.

Domus Aurea (*Golden House of Nero*)
RUINS | Legend has it that Nero famously fiddled while Rome burned. Fancying himself a great actor and poet, he played, as it turns out, his harp to accompany his recital of "The Destruction of Troy" while gazing at the flames of Rome's catastrophic fire of AD 64. Anti-Neronian historians propagandized that Nero, in fact, had set the Great Fire to clear out a vast tract of the city center to build his new palace. Today's historians discount this as historical folderol (going so far as to point to the fact that there was a full moon on the evening of July 19, hardly the propitious occasion to commit arson). But legend or not, Nero did get to build his new palace, the extravagant Domus Aurea (Golden House)—a vast "suburban villa" that was inspired by the emperor's

pleasure palace at Baia on the Bay of Naples. His new digs were huge and sumptuous, with a facade of pure gold; seawater piped into the baths; decorations of mother-of-pearl, fretted ivory, and other precious materials; and vast gardens. It was said that after completing this gigantic house, Nero exclaimed, "Now I can live like a human being!" Note that access to the site is exclusively via guided tours that use virtual reality headsets for part of the presentation. Booking ahead is essential. ✉ *Viale della Domus Aurea 1, Monti* ☎ *06/39967700 booking information* ⊕ *www.coopculture.it* ✇ *€14 including booking fee and guided visit* ⚹ *reservations essential* Ⓜ *Colosseo*.

Museo delle Mura
RUINS | Rome's first walls were erected in the 6th century BC, but the ancient city greatly expanded over the next few centuries, and when Rome was at its peak, it didn't need walls. But in the 3rd century AD, Emperor Aurelian commissioned a 12-mile wall to protect the city,

which was considered by many a sign of weakness. Indeed just over a century later, those walls were breached for the first time in a siege that would herald the end of the empire. The ancient walls eventually became the fortifications of the papal city, and remained in use for 16 centuries until the unification of Italy in 1870. Studding the Aurelian Walls were 18 main gates, the best preserved of which is the Porta di San Sebastiano at the entrance to the Via Appia Antica. That gate is also home to a small museum that allows visitors to walk a section of the ancient ramparts, from which there are wonderful views. Note that the museum closes relatively early at 2 pm. ✉ Via di Porta San Sebastiano 18, Via Appia Antica ☎ 06/060608 ⊕ www.museodellemuraroma.it ⊗ Closed Mon.

Restaurants

Aroma
$$$$ | MODERN ITALIAN | The panoramas from this Michelin-starred restaurant atop the Palazzo Manfredi Hotel are undeniably stunning; it's the best unobstructed view of the Colosseum in Rome, so ask for a table on the terrace. With chef Giuseppe Di Iorio's seven-course tasting menu, each dish is an innovative twist on Italy's top cuisine. **Known for:** sustainable fish and local produce; gluten-free tasting menu; intimate 28-seat restaurant. ⑤ Average main: €110 ✉ Palazzo Manfredi, Via Labicana 125, Colosseo ☎ 06/77591380 ⊕ www.aromarestaurant.it Ⓜ Colosseo.

Hotels

Palazzo Manfredi
$$$$ | HOTEL | If you dream of waking up to head-on views of the Colosseum, look no further. **Pros:** incredible views; excellent restaurant and cocktail bar; unparalleled location. **Cons:** no meals included; not pet-friendly; not all rooms have views of the Colosseum. ⑤ Rooms from: €506 ✉ Via Labicana 125, Colosseo ☎ 06/77591380 ⊕ www.palazzomanfredi.com ⇨ 20 ⑩ No Meals Ⓜ Colosseo.

Nightlife

BARS
★ The Court
COCKTAIL LOUNGES | For a winning combination of creative cocktails and incredible views of the Colosseum, this bar in Palazzo Manfredi can't be beat. Bar manager Matteo "Zed" Zamberlan cut his teeth in New York's top bars and here his creativity is on full display. The cocktails are pricey, but they come with a bounty of snacks from the hotel's acclaimed restaurant. ✉ Via Labicana 125, Colosseo ☎ 06/77591380 ⊕ www.palazzomanfredi.com Ⓜ Colosseo.

Monti

As the hill starts to slope downward from Termini station, right around Santa Maria Maggiore, the streets become cobblestone, the palazzos prettier, and the boutiques higher-end. This is the area known as Monti, the oldest rione in Rome. Gladiators, prostitutes, and even Caesar made their homes in this area that stretches from Santa Maria Maggiore down to the Forum. Today, Monti is one of the best-loved neighborhoods in Rome, known for its appealing mix of medieval streets, old-school trattorias, and hip boutiques.

Sights

Palazzo delle Esposizioni
ART MUSEUM | The late-19th-century Palazzo delle Esposizioni holds temporary exhibitions on everything from Etruscan art to Pixar movies. The complex also has a great bookshop (including some books in English), a coffee bar, and a restaurant. ✉ Via Nazionale 194, Monti ☎ 06/696271 ⊕ www.palazzoesposizioni.it ⌺ €12.50; costs vary by exhibition ⊗ Closed Mon. Ⓜ Repubblica.

★ San Pietro in Vincoli

CHURCH | Michelangelo's *Moses,* carved in the early 16th century for the never-completed tomb of Pope Julius II, has put this church on the map. The tomb was to include dozens of statues and stand nearly 40 feet tall when installed in St. Peter's Basilica. But only three statues—*Moses* and the two that flank it here, *Leah* and *Rachel*—had been completed when Julius died. Julius's successor as pope, from the rival Medici family, had other plans for Michelangelo, and the tomb was abandoned unfinished. The fierce power of this remarkable sculpture dominates its setting. People say that you can see the sculptor's profile in the lock of Moses's beard right under his lip, and that the pope's profile can also be seen. As for the rest of the church, St. Peter takes second billing to Moses. The reputed sets of chains (*vincoli*) that bound St. Peter during his imprisonment by the Romans in both Jerusalem and Rome are in a bronze and crystal urn under the main altar. Other treasures include a 7th-century mosaic of St. Sebastian, in front of the second altar to the left of the main altar, and, by the door, the tomb of the Pollaiuolo brothers, two 15th-century Florentine artists. ✉ *Piazza di San Pietro in Vincoli, Monti* ☎ *06/97844952* Ⓜ *Cavour.*

★ Santa Maria Maggiore

CHURCH | Despite its florid 18th-century facade, Santa Maria Maggiore is one of the oldest churches in Rome, built around 440 by Pope Sixtus III. One of the four great pilgrimage churches of Rome, it's also the city center's best example of an Early Christian basilica—one of the immense, hall-like structures derived from ancient Roman civic buildings and divided into thirds by two great rows of columns marching up the nave. The other three major basilicas in Rome (San Giovanni in Laterano, St. Peter's, and St. Paul Outside the Walls) have been largely rebuilt. Paradoxically, the major reason why this church is such a striking example of Early Christian design is that the same man who built the undulating exteriors circa 1740, Ferdinando Fuga, also conscientiously restored the interior, throwing out later additions and, crucially, replacing a number of the great columns.

Precious 5th-century mosaics high on the nave walls and on the triumphal arch in front of the main altar bear splendid testimony to the basilica's venerable age. Those along the nave show 36 scenes from the Old Testament (unfortunately, tough to see clearly without binoculars), and those on the arch illustrate the Annunciation and the Youth of Christ. The resplendent carved-wood ceiling dates to the early 16th century; it's supposed to have been gilded with the first gold brought from the New World. The inlaid marble pavement (called Cosmatesque, after the family of master artisans who developed the technique) in the central nave is even older, dating to the 12th century.

The Cappella Sistina (Sistine Chapel), in the right-hand transept, was created by architect Domenico Fontana for Pope Sixtus V in 1585. Elaborately decorated with precious marbles "liberated" from the monuments of ancient Rome, the chapel includes a lower-level museum in which some 13th-century sculptures by Arnolfo da Cambio are all that's left of what was the once richly endowed chapel of the *presepio* (Christmas crèche), looted during the Sack of Rome in 1527.

Directly opposite, on the church's other side, stands the Cappella Paolina (Pauline Chapel), a rich baroque setting for the tombs of the Borghese popes Paul V—who commissioned the chapel in 1611 with the declared intention of outdoing Sixtus's chapel across the nave—and Clement VIII. The Cappella Sforza (Sforza Chapel) next door was designed by Michelangelo and completed by Della Porta. Just right of the altar, next to his father, lies Gian Lorenzo Bernini; his monument is an engraved slab, as

Did You Know?

Another Capella Sistina (Sistine Chapel) exists within the basilica known as the Santa Maria Maggiore. Several sistine chapels actually exist in Rome; the word "sistine" means anything relating to a pope with the name Sixtus, Pope Sixtus V commissioned the chapel within the Santa Maria Maggiore, while the more famous one within the Vatican was commissioned by Pope Sixtus IV.

humble as the tombs of his patrons are grand. Above the loggia, the outside mosaic of Christ raising his hand in blessing is one of Rome's most beautiful sights, especially when lighted at night. ⊠ *Piazza di Santa Maria Maggiore, Monti* ☎ *06/69886802* Ⓜ *Termini.*

★ Santa Prassede

CHURCH | This small, inconspicuous 9th-century church is known above all for the exquisite Cappella di San Zenone, just to the left of the entrance. It gleams with vivid mosaics that reflect their Byzantine inspiration. Though much less classical and naturalistic than the earlier mosaics of Santa Pudenziana, they are no less splendid, and the composition of four angels hovering on the sky-blue vault is one of the masterstrokes of Byzantine art. Note the square halo over the head of Theodora, mother of St. Paschal I, the pope who built this church. It indicates that she was still alive when she was depicted by the artist. The chapel also contains one curious relic: a miniature pillar, supposedly part of the column at which Christ was flogged during the Passion. It was brought to Rome in the 13th century. Over the main altar, the magnificent mosaics on the arch and apse are also in rigid Byzantine style. In them, Pope Paschal I wears the square halo of the living and holds a model of his church. ⊠ *Via di Santa Prassede 9/a, Monti* ☎ *06/4882456* Ⓜ *Cavour.*

★ Santa Pudenziana

CHURCH | Apart from Ravenna, Rome has some of the most opulent mosaics in Italy, and this church has its earliest example. Commissioned during the papacy of Innocent I, its early 5th-century apse mosaic depicts Christ teaching the apostles and sits above a baroque altarpiece surrounded by a bevy of florid 18th-century paintings. The mosaic is remarkable for its iconography; at the center sits Christ enthroned, shown as an emperor or as a philosopher holding court, surrounded by his apostles. Each apostle faces the spectator, literally rubbing shoulders with his companion (unlike later hieratic styles in which each figure is isolated), and bears an individualized expression. Above these figures and a landscape symbolizing Heavenly Jerusalem float the signs of the four evangelists in a blue sky flecked with the orange of sunset, made from thousands of *tesserae* (mosaic tiles).

To either side of Christ, Sts. Praxedes and Pudentiana hold wreaths over the heads of Sts. Peter and Paul. These two women were actually daughters of the Roman senator Pudens (probably the one mentioned in 2 Timothy 4:21), whose family befriended both apostles. During the persecutions of Nero, both sisters collected the blood of many martyrs before suffering their fate. Pudentiana transformed her house into a church, but her namesake church was constructed over a 2nd-century bathhouse. Beyond the sheer beauty of the mosaic work, the size, rich detail, and number of figures make this both the last gasp of ancient Roman art and one of the first major works of Early Christian art. ⊠ *Via Urbana 160, Monti* ☎ *06/4814622* ⊕ *www.stpudenziana.org* ☾ *Closed Mon.* Ⓜ *Termini.*

🍴 Restaurants

Rocco Ristorante

$$ | ROMAN | This slightly vintage, slightly trendy trattoria has a timeless quality. Terrazzo floors, vaulted brick ceilings, white tablecloths, and vintage photos, sketches, and a Pink Floyd poster lend the place a hip yet easygoing vibe that attracts people of all ages. **Known for:** Italian comfort food; local favorite spot; cool, welcoming atmosphere. ⑤ *Average main: €18* ⊠ *Via Giovanni Lanza 93, Monti* ☎ *06/4870942* ☾ *Closed Sun. No dinner Sat.* Ⓜ *Vittorio Emanuele, Cavour.*

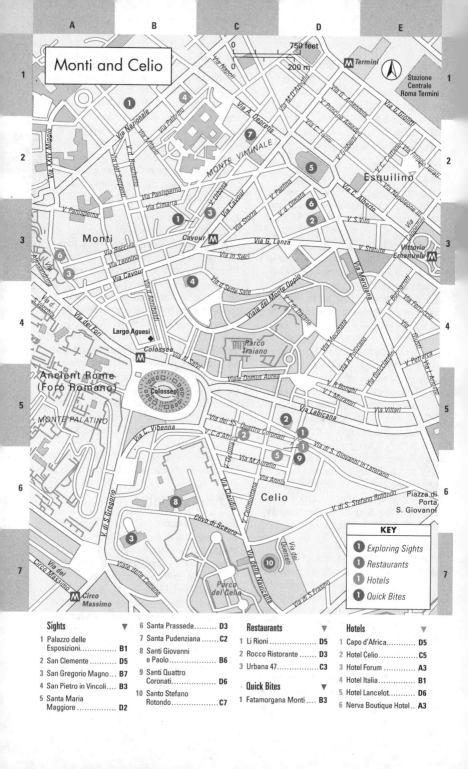

Monti and Celio

0 ——— 750 feet
0 ——— 200 m

A B C D E

Termini
Stazione
Centrale
Roma Termini

MONTE VIMINALE

Esquilino

Monti

Cavour M

Vittorio
Emanuele M

Via del Monte Oppio

Largo Aguesi

Colosseo M

Colosseo

Ancient Rome
(Foro Romano)

MONTE PALATINO

Parco
Traiano

Via Labicana

Celio

Piazza di
Porta
S. Giovanni

Parco
del Celio

Circo
Massimo M

KEY

1 Exploring Sights
1 Restaurants
1 Hotels
1 Quick Bites

★ Urbana 47

$$$ | MODERN ITALIAN | This restaurant serving lunch and dinner embodies the *kilometro zero* concept, highlighting hyper-local food from the surrounding Lazio region. The local boho crowd comes for tasty lunch and dinner options like fried calamari or cheeseburgers (with free Wi-Fi) in an industrial-chic space. **Known for:** hyper-local produce; aperitivo and tapas; industrial-chic design. $ *Average main: €30* ✉ *Via Urbana 47, Monti* ☎ *06/47884006* ⊕ *www.urbana47.it* ✹ *Closed Tues.* Ⓜ *Cavour.*

☕ Coffee and Quick Bites

★ Fatamorgana Monti

$ | ICE CREAM | The emphasis is on all-natural ingredients at this woman-owned gelateria, which has several locations in Rome. Flavors change often but might include favorites like stracciatella and hazelnut as well as more unusual flavors like matcha or carrot cake. **Known for:** gluten-free with many vegan options; unusual flavors; all natural ingredients. $ *Average main: €3* ✉ *Piazza degli Zingari 5, Monti* ☎ *06/48906955* ⊕ *www.gelateriafatamorgana.com* Ⓜ *Cavour.*

Hotels

Hotel Forum

$$ | HOTEL | A longtime favorite, this converted 18th-century convent has a truly unique setting on one side of the Fori Imperiali, with cinematic views of ancient Rome across the avenue so impressive that it has drawn celebrities and socialites. **Pros:** bird's-eye view of ancient Rome; discounted rates can be found from time to time; "American" bar on rooftop terrace. **Cons:** food and drinks are expensive; outdated decor; small rooms. $ *Rooms from: €180* ✉ *Via Tor de' Conti 25–30, Monti* ☎ *06/6792446* ⊕ *www.hotelforum.com* ✑ *80 rooms* ⑩ *No Meals* Ⓜ *Cavour, Colosseo.*

Hotel Italia

$$ | HOTEL | Just one block from bustling Via Nazionale and some of Rome's great shopping, this friendly, family-run hotel feels like a classic *pensione:* low budget with a lot of heart. **Pros:** free breakfast; great price; individual attention and personal care. **Cons:** Wi-Fi can be hit or miss; some rooms have shared baths; can be a bit noisy. $ *Rooms from: €140* ✉ *Via Venezia 18, Termini* ☎ *06/4828355* ⊕ *www.hotelitaliaroma.it* ✑ *36 rooms* ⑩ *Free Breakfast* Ⓜ *Repubblica.*

Nerva Boutique Hotel

$$ | HOTEL | Step out of this charming, clean, well-run hotel and you'll feel like you've landed in the middle of an ancient imperial stomping ground; a stone's throw from the Forum, it's surrounded by the breathtaking splendor of ancient Roman ruins. **Pros:** close to the Forum in the lovely Monti neighborhood; friendly staff; free Wi-Fi. **Cons:** single rooms are only slightly bigger than a closet; not many amenities; some showers are tiny. $ *Rooms from: €180* ✉ *Via Tor de' Conti 3/4, Monti* ☎ *06/6781835* ⊕ *www.hotel-nerva.com* ✑ *18 rooms* ⑩ *No Meals* Ⓜ *Cavour, Colosseo.*

⑨ Nightlife

Lately, Monti has been wearing the crown as the "it" neighborhood, reigning supreme as an all-ages hipster hangout with trendy bars, top-notch restaurants, and artisan shops, as well as picturesque piazze.

BARS

★ Ai Tre Scalini

WINE BARS | An ivy-covered wine bar in the center of Monti, Rome's trendiest 'hood, Ai Tre Scalini has a warm and cozy menu of delicious antipasti and light entrées to go along with its enticing wine list. After about 8 pm, if you haven't booked, be prepared to wait—this is one extremely popular spot with locals. ✉ *Via*

Panisperna 251, Monti ☎ *06/48907495* ⊕ *www.aitrescalini.org* Ⓜ *Cavour.*

★ Drink Kong

COCKTAIL LOUNGES | Irish-Italian bartender Patrick Pistolesi worked his way up the ranks at bars in Rome and New York City before opening this cocktail bar that's regarded as one of the world's best. His first solo venture, it's an expression of Pistolesi's bold aesthetic and philosophy of hospitality. Inspired by the Japanese cartoons he watched as a kid, the space is dark and dramatic with flashes of neon. The creative cocktails feature ingredients like lettuce cordial and parmesan water and arrive at your table impressively quickly. Pair them with Asian-inspired snacks like shrimp dumplings or octopus-filled bao. ⊠ *Piazza di San Martino ai Monti 8, Monti* ☎ *06/23488666* ⊕ *www. drinkkong.com* Ⓜ *Cavour.*

JAZZ CLUBS

Charity Café Jazz & Blues Club

LIVE MUSIC | An intimate jazz club with live music performances nightly, Charity hosts local and international jazz musicians in a relaxed atmosphere. It's closed on Monday. ⊠ *Via Panisperna 68, Monti* ☎ *06/47825881* ⊕ *www.charitycafe.it* Ⓜ *Cavour.*

Shopping

CLOTHING

★ Sacripante

WOMEN'S CLOTHING | This tiny Monti art gallery/boutique/bar houses some of the most sophisticated retro-inspired fashion garments around Rome. Its owner, Wilma Silvestri, cleverly combines vintage and contemporary fabrics for her label Le Gallinelle, evolving them into stylish clothing with a modern edge made for everyday wear. ⊠ *Via Panisperna 59, Monti* ☎ *06/48903495* ⊕ *www.facebook. com/sacripantegallery* Ⓜ *Cavour.*

Kokoro

WOMEN'S CLOTHING | This pared-down little boutique on one of Monti's most charming streets sells women's clothes designed by owners Benedetta Piccirilli and David Anav. Their pieces tend to be familiar silhouettes made with colorful Italian fabrics and often feature botanical or Asian-inspired prints. Each piece is one-of-a-kind, but they also make garments made to measure. ⊠ *Via del Boschetto 75, Monti* ☎ *349/7434694* ⊕ *www.kokoroshop.it* Ⓜ *Cavour.*

★ Mercato Monti

MARKET | On weekends, hip locals flock to this indoor market where vendors sell vintage clothing and accessories, designer sunglasses, hats and jewelry by local makers, and decorative objects. It's a good place to see Monti's creative spirit on display and find unique items you can't get elsewhere. ⊠ *Via Leonina 46/48, Monti* ⊕ *www.mercatomonti.com* ⊙ *Closed weekdays* Ⓜ *Cavour.*

FOOD

Grezzo Raw Chocolate

CHOCOLATE | This chocolate shop opened in 2014 claims to be the first raw pastry shop in the world. Everything is 100% organic, vegan, gluten-free, dairy-free, and made without refined sugar—and nothing is cooked above 108 degrees Fahrenheit. If you're skeptical, seeing (or, in this case, tasting) is believing. The pralines and truffles are as delicious as traditional ones, and there are also cookies, organic nut and chocolate spreads, pastries, and gelato. ⊠ *Via Urbana 130, Monti* ☎ *06/483443* ⊕ *www.grezzoraw-chocolate.com* Ⓜ *Cavour.*

JEWELRY

Art Privé

JEWELRY & WATCHES | On one of Monti's steeply sloping streets is the small jewelry shop where Tiziana Salzano makes elegant necklaces and earrings using the finest gold or silverwork and a combination of semiprecious gemstones. Each piece is unique, so if you feel something tug at your heart be sure to grab it. She and her business partner Antonio also take orders for bespoke made-to-order pieces. ⊠ *Via Panisperna 51, Monti* ☎ *06/47826347* ⊘ *Closed Sun.* Ⓜ *Cavour.*

L'Artigianaio

JEWELRY & WATCHES | "The Artisan" is the place to go for handmade watches and rare vintage timepieces. The store's expert watchmakers specialize in nostalgic mechanical watches and chronographs from the early 1900s through the 1970s. Whether you are looking for a solid gold dress watch or a World War II military pilot's chronograph, chances are you'll find what you're looking for here. Have an heirloom piece that has stopped working or that needs a little fine-tuning? Bring it to the shop, and the owners will get it ticking again in no time. ⊠ *Via Urbana 103, Monti* ☎ *06/4742284* ⊘ *Closed Sun.* Ⓜ *Cavour.*

Celio

Bordering Monti, from the Colosseum west toward Piazza San Giovanni, the Celio neighborhood is a tranquil, lovely residential area replete with medieval churches and ruins. Sights not to miss here include the Basilica of San Clemente, the church of Santi Quattro Coronati, and the church of Santo Stefano Rotondo.

 Sights

★ San Clemente

CHURCH | One of the most impressive archaeological sites in Rome, San Clemente is a historical triple-decker. A 12th-century church was built on top of a 4th-century church, which had been built over a 2nd-century pagan temple to the god Mithras and 1st-century Roman apartments. The layers were uncovered in 1857, when a curious prior, Friar

Joseph Mullooly, started excavations beneath the present basilica. Today, you can descend to explore all three.

The upper church (at street level) is a gem in its own right. In the apse, a glittering 12th-century mosaic shows Jesus on a cross that turns into a living tree. Green acanthus leaves swirl and teem with small scenes of everyday life. Early Christian symbols, including doves, vines, and fish, decorate the 4th-century marble choir screens. In the left nave, the Castiglioni chapel holds frescoes painted around 1400 by the Florentine artist Masolino da Panicale (1383–1440), a key figure in the introduction of realism and one-point perspective into Renaissance painting. Note the large Crucifixion and scenes from the lives of Saints Catherine, Ambrose, and Christopher, plus the Annunciation (over the entrance).

To the right of the sacristy (and bookshop), descend the stairs to the 4th-century church, used until 1084, when it was damaged beyond repair during a siege of the area by the Norman prince Robert Guiscard. Still intact are some vibrant 11th-century frescoes depicting stories from the life of St. Clement. Don't miss the last fresco on the left, in what used to be the central nave. It includes a particularly colorful quote—including "Go on, you sons of harlots, pull!"—that's not only unusual for a religious painting, but also one of the earliest examples of written vernacular Italian.

Descend an additional set of stairs to the Mithraeum, a shrine dedicated to the god Mithras. His cult spread from Persia and gained a foothold in Rome during the 2nd and 3rd centuries AD. Mithras was believed to have been born in a cave and was thus worshipped in cavernous, underground chambers, where initiates into the all-male cult would share a meal while reclining on stone couches, some visible here along with the altar block. Most such pagan shrines in Rome were destroyed by Christians, who often built churches over their remains, as happened here. ✉ *Via Labicana 95, Celio* ☎ *06/7740021* ⊕ *www.basilicasanclemente.com* 🖭 *Archaeological area €10* Ⓜ *Colosseo.*

San Gregorio Magno

CHURCH | Set amid the greenery of the Celian Hill, this church wears its baroque facade proudly. Dedicated to St. Gregory the Great (who served as pope 590–604), it was built about 750 by Pope Gregory II to commemorate his predecessor and namesake. The church of San Gregorio itself has the appearance of a typical baroque structure, the result of remodeling in the 17th and 18th centuries. But you can still see what's said to be the stone slab on which the pious St. Gregory the Great slept; it's in the far right-hand chapel. Outside are three chapels. The right chapel is dedicated to Gregory's mother, Saint Sylvia, and contains a Guido Reni fresco of the *Concert of Angels.* The chapel in the center, dedicated to Saint Andrew, contains two monumental frescoes showing scenes from the saint's life. They were painted at the beginning of the 17th century by Domenichino (*The Flagellation of St. Andrew*) and Guido Reni (*The Execution of St. Andrew*). It's a striking juxtaposition of the sturdy, if sometimes stiff, classicism of Domenichino with the more flamboyant and heroic baroque manner of Guido Reni. ✉ *Piazza di San Gregorio al Celio 1, Celio* ☎ *06/7008227* ⊕ *www.camaldolesiromani.com* Ⓜ *Colosseo.*

★ Santi Giovanni e Paolo

CHURCH | Perched up the incline of the Clivio di Scauro—a magical time-machine of a street, where the dial seems to be stuck somewhere in the 13th century—Santi Giovanni e Paolo is an image that would tempt most landscape painters. Marked by one of Rome's finest Romanesque bell towers, it looms over a picturesque piazza. Underneath, however, are other treasures, whose excavations can be seen in the Case

Romane del Celio museum (temporarily closed). A basilica erected on the spot was, like San Clemente, destroyed in 1084 by attacking Normans. Its half-buried columns, near the current church entrance, are visible through misty glass. The current church's origins date to the start of the 12th century, but most of the interior dates to the 17th century and later. The lovely, incongruous chandeliers are a hand-me-down from New York's Waldorf-Astoria hotel, a gift arranged by the late Cardinal Francis Spellman of New York, whose titular church this was. Spellman also initiated the excavations here in 1949. ✉ *Piazza di Santi Giovanni e Paolo 13, Celio* ☎ *06/772711* ⊕ *www.basilicassgiovanniepaolo.it* ⊙ *Closed Mon.* Ⓜ *Colosseo.*

★ Santi Quattro Coronati

CHURCH | Situated on one of those evocative cul-de-sacs in Rome where history seems to be holding its breath, this church is strongly imbued with the sanctity of the Romanesque era. Marvelously redolent of the Middle Ages, this is one of the most unusual and unexpected corners in Rome, a quiet citadel that has resisted the tides of time and traffic. The church, which dates back to the 4th century, honors the Four Crowned Saints: the four brothers Severus, Severianus, Carpophorus, and Victorinus, all Roman officials who were whipped to death for their faith by Emperor Diocletian (284–305). After its 9th-century reconstruction, the church was twice as large as it is now; the abbey was partially destroyed during the Normans' sack of Rome in 1084 but reconstructed about 30 years later. This explains the inordinate size of the apse in relation to the small nave. Don't miss the cloister, with its well-tended gardens and 12th-century fountain. The entrance is the door in the left nave; ring the bell if it's not open.

There's another medieval gem hidden away off the courtyard at the church entrance: the Chapel of San Silvestro. The chapel has remained, for the most part, as it was when consecrated in 1246. Some of the best-preserved medieval frescoes in Rome decorate the walls, telling the story of the Christian emperor Constantine's recovery from leprosy thanks to Pope Sylvester I. Note, too, the delightful *Last Judgment* fresco above the door, in which the angel on the left neatly rolls up sky and stars like a backdrop, signaling the end of the world. ⊠ *Via Santi Quattro Coronati 20, Celio* ☎ *06/70475427* ⊕ *www.monacheagostinianesantiquattrocoronati.it* Ⓜ *Colosseo.*

Santo Stefano Rotondo

CHURCH | This 5th-century church is thought to have been inspired by the design of the Church of the Holy Sepulchre in Jerusalem. Its unusual round plan and timbered ceiling set it apart from most other Roman churches. So do the frescoes, which lovingly depict 34 of the goriest martyrdoms in Catholicism—a catalog, above the names of different emperors, of every type of violent death conceivable. (You've been warned: these are not for the fainthearted.) ⊠ *Via Santo Stefano Rotondo 7, Celio* ☎ *06/421199* ⊕ *www.cgu.it* ☉ *Closed Mon.* Ⓜ *Colosseo.*

🍴 Restaurants

Li Rioni

$ | **PIZZA** | **FAMILY** | This busy pizzeria conveniently close to the Colosseum has been serving real-deal Roman-style pizza—super thin and cooked to a crisp—since the mid-1980s. The magic might be due to the fact that they let their pizza dough rise 24–48 hours before baking to guarantee an extra-light pizza, said to be more easily digested than others. **Known for:** homemade tiramisu; pizza margherita; olive ascolane (fried, breaded olives stuffed with sausage). ⑤ *Average main: €12* ⊠ *Via dei Santi Quattro 24, Celio* ☎ *06/70450605* ⊕ *www.lirioni.it* ☉ *Closed Tues. and 2 weeks in Aug. No lunch* Ⓜ *Colosseo.*

🛏 Hotels

Capo d'Africa

$ | **HOTEL** | Hotels in Rome come a dime a dozen, but the contemporary design of Capo d'Africa combined with modern amenities and outstanding customer service make your stay worth every *centesimo*. **Pros:** quiet, comfortable rooms; fitness center; great food served at the hotel. **Cons:** not a lot of restaurants in the immediate neighborhood; Wi-Fi can be spotty; hotel lacks a great view of Colosseum despite proximity. ⑤ *Rooms from: €100* ⊠ *Via Capo d'Africa 54, Celio* ☎ *06/772801* ⊕ *www.hotelcapodafrica.com* ☞ *65 rooms* ⑩ *Free Breakfast* Ⓜ *Colosseo.*

Hotel Celio

$$ | **HOTEL** | There's much more to brag about than proximity to the Colosseum at this chic boutique hotel. **Pros:** beautiful rooftop garden; comfortable beds; nice decor. **Cons:** breakfast not that substantial; service can be iffy; very small bathrooms. ⑤ *Rooms from: €180* ⊠ *Via dei Santissimi Quattro 35/c, Celio* ☎ *06/70495333* ⊕ *www.hotelcelio.com* ☞ *22 rooms* ⑩ *Free Breakfast* Ⓜ *Colosseo.*

Hotel Lancelot

$$ | **HOTEL** | **FAMILY** | This friendly home-away-from-home in a quiet residential area close to the Colosseum has been run by the same family since 1970. **Pros:** hospitable staff; secluded and quiet; very family-friendly. **Cons:** no refrigerators in the rooms; rooms are in need of redecorating; some bathrooms are on the small side. ⑤ *Rooms from: €130* ⊠ *Via Capo d'Africa 47, Celio* ☎ *06/70450615* ⊕ *www.lancelothotel.com* ☞ *60 rooms* ⑩ *Free Breakfast* Ⓜ *Colosseo.*

Chapter 4

THE VATICAN

4

Updated by
Laura Itzkowitz

⊙ Sights	🍴 Restaurants	🛏 Hotels	🛍 Shopping	🍸 Nightlife
★★★★★	★★★☆☆	★★★☆☆	★★☆☆☆	★★☆☆☆

NEIGHBORHOOD SNAPSHOT

TOP REASONS TO GO

Michelangelo's Sistine Ceiling: The most sublime example of artistry in the world, this 10,000-square-foot fresco took the artist four long, neck-craning years to finish.

St. Peter's Dome: Climb the twisting Renaissance stairs to the top for a well-earned view (the elevator to the right of the main church portico goes up to the base of the dome, but there are still a lot of stairs afterwards).

Papal Blessing: Join the singing, flag-waving throngs from around the world at the Wednesday general audience on St. Peter's Square (usually only in spring, summer, and early fall).

Musei Vaticani: Savor one of the Western world's best art collections—from the Apollo Belvedere to Raphael's *Transfiguration*. It can be overwhelming though, so don't plan to see everything in one day.

St. Peter's Basilica: Stand in awe of the largest church in the world.

GETTING HERE

Metro stops Cipro or Ottaviano will get you within about a 10-minute walk of the entrance to the Musei Vaticani. Or, from Termini station, Bus No. 40 Express or the famously crowded No. 64 will take you to Piazza San Pietro. Both routes swing past Largo Argentina, where you can also get Bus No. 492 or 46.

A leisurely meander from the *centro storico* (historic center), across the exquisite Ponte Sant'Angelo, will take about a half hour.

HOW TO BEAT THOSE LONG LINES

■ Home to the Sistine Chapel and the Raphael rooms, the Musei Vaticani are among the most congested of all Rome's attractions, drawing up to 30,000 visitors per day in high season.

■ The best way to avoid long lines is to make reservations online for an extra €4 (⊕ *tickets.museivaticani.va/home*). Although reservations do minimize your wait time, it can still be extremely busy once you're inside, though afternoons are usually less busy. The free Sunday is best avoided altogether unless you're feeling very brave and patient.

■ Another good idea is to schedule your visit during the Wednesday General Audience, held in the piazza of St. Peter's or at Aula Paolo VI, usually at 9:15 am when the pope is in town. To see the pope's calendar, visit ⊕ *papalaudience.org*.

■ Finally, you might book a tour, either with the Musei Vaticani directly or with a private agency that guarantees that you'll skip the line. The Vatican's own guided tour of the museums and Sistine Chapel, which can be booked online, costs €34 and lasts two hours.

For many, a visit to the Vatican is one of the top reasons to visit Rome, and it is a vast and majestic place, jam-packed with things to see. The Borgo and Prati are the neighborhoods immediately surrounding the Vatican, and it's worth noting that, while the Vatican may well be a priority, these neighborhoods are not the best places to choose a hotel, as they're quite far from other top sights in the city.

The Vatican

Climbing the steps to St. Peter's Basilica feels monumental, like a journey that has reached its climactic end. Suddenly, all is cool and dark … and you are dwarfed by the gargantuan nave and its magnificence. Above is a ceiling so high it must lead to heaven itself. Great, shining marble figures of saints frozen mid-whirl loom from niches and corners. And at the end, a throne for an unseen king whose greatness, it is implied, must mirror the greatness of his palace. For this basilica is a palace, the dazzling center of power for a king and a place of supplication for his subjects. Whether his kingdom is earthly or otherwise may lie in the eye of the beholder.

For good Catholics and sinners alike, the Vatican is an exercise in spirituality, requiring patience but delivering joy. Some come here for a transcendent glimpse of a heavenly Michelangelo fresco; others come in search of a direct connection with the divine. But what all visitors share, for a few hours, is an awe-inspiring landscape that offers a famous sight for every taste: rooms decorated by Raphael, antique sculptures like the *Apollo Belvedere*, famous paintings by Giotto and Bellini, and, perhaps most of all, the Sistine Chapel—for the lover of beauty, few places are as historically important as this epitome of faith and grandeur.

The story of this area's importance dates back to the 1st century, when St. Peter, the first Roman Catholic pope, was buried here. The first basilica in his honor rose on this spot some 250 years later under Emperor Constantine, who legitimized Christianity. It wasn't until the early 15th century, however, that the papacy decided to make this area not only a major spiritual center but the spot from which they would wield temporal power as well. Today, it's difficult not to be reminded of that worldly power when you take in the massive Renaissance walls surrounding Vatican City—the international boundary of an independent sovereign state, established by the Lateran Treaty of 1929 between the Holy See and Mussolini's government.

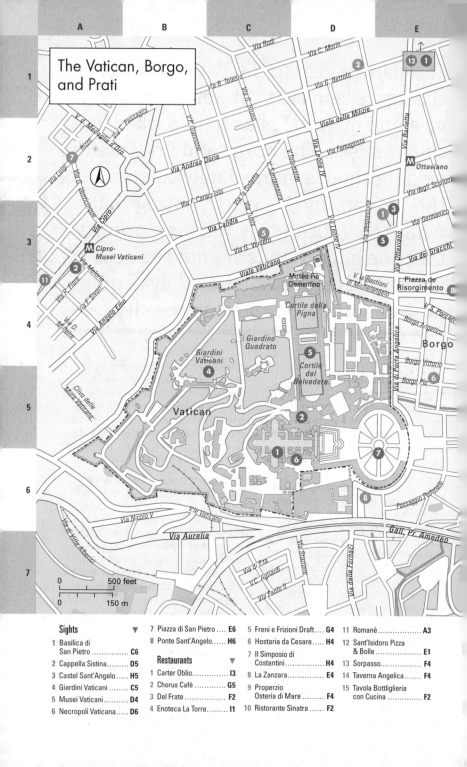

The Vatican, Borgo, and Prati

Sights ▼

1 Basilica di
San Pietro **C6**
2 Cappella Sistina......... **D5**
3 Castel Sant'Angelo..... **H5**
4 Giardini Vaticani **C5**
5 Musei Vaticani **D4**
6 Necropoli Vaticana..... **D6**
7 Piazza di San Pietro **E6**
8 Ponte Sant'Angelo...... **H6**

Restaurants ▼

1 Carter Oblio............... **I3**
2 Chorus Café **G5**
3 Del Frate **F2**
4 Enoteca La Torre......... **I1**
5 Freni e Frizioni Draft.... **G4**
6 Hostaria da Cesare...... **H4**
7 Il Simposio di
Costantini **H4**
8 La Zanzara................ **E4**
9 Properzio
Osteria di Mare **F4**
10 Ristorante Sinatra **F2**
11 Romanè **A3**
12 Sant'Isidoro Pizza
& Bolle **E1**
13 Sorpasso................. **F4**
14 Taverna Angelica....... **F4**
15 Tavola Bottiglieria
con Cucina **F2**

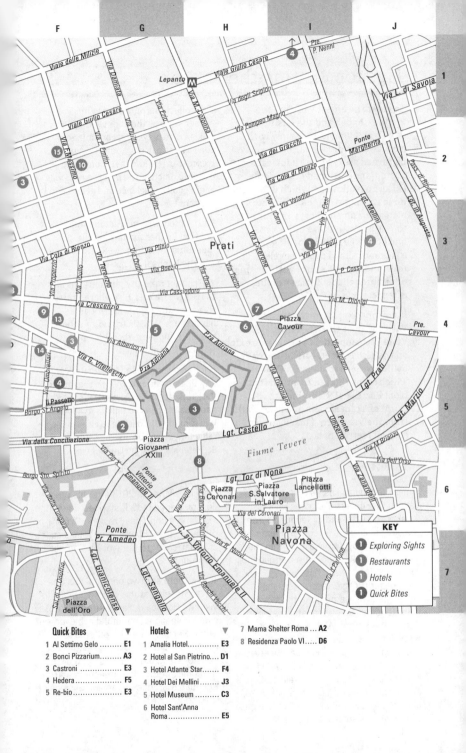

Tips for Visiting the Vatican

To enter the Musei Vaticani, the Sistine Chapel, and the Basilica di San Pietro, you must comply with the Vatican's dress code or you may be turned away by the implacable custodians stationed at the doors. (Also: no penknives, which will show up in the metal detector.) For both men and women, shorts and tank tops are taboo, as are miniskirts and other revealing clothing. Wear a jacket or shawl over sleeveless tops, and avoid T-shirts with writing or pictures that could risk giving offense.

If you opt to start at the Musei Vaticani, note that the entrance on Viale Vaticano (there's a separate exit on the same street) can be reached by Bus No. 49 from Piazza Cavour, which stops right in front; on foot from Piazza del Risorgimento (Bus No. 81 or Tram No. 19); or a brief walk from the Via Cipro–Musei Vaticani stop on Metro Linea A.

The collections of the museums are immense, covering about 7 km (4½ miles) of displays. To economize on time and effort, once you've seen the frescoes in the Raphael rooms, you can skip much of the modern religious art in good conscience and get on with your tour.

You can rent a somewhat dry audio guide in English explaining the museums, including the Sistine Chapel and the Raphael rooms.

You cannot take any photographs in the Sistine Chapel. Elsewhere, you're free to photograph what you like—barring use of flash, tripod, or other special equipment, for which permission must be obtained.

With an average of 20,000 visitors per day, lines at the entrance to the Musei Vaticani can move slowly. It is always a good idea to reserve tickets in advance. It is sometimes possible to exit the museums from the Sistine Chapel into St. Peter's, saving further legwork.

Legally recognized as its own city-state, Vatican City covers 110 acres on a hill west of the Tiber and is separated from the city on all sides, except at Piazza di San Pietro, by high walls. Within the walls, about 840 people are permanent residents. The Vatican has its own daily newspaper (*L'Osservatore Romano*), issues its own stamps, mints its own coins, and has its own postal system (run by the Swiss). Within its territory are administrative and foreign offices, a pharmacy, banks, an astronomical observatory, a print shop, a mosaic school and art restoration institute, a tiny train station, a supermarket, a small department store, and several gas stations. The sovereign of the world's smallest state is the pope,

Francis, elected in 2013 after his predecessor, Benedict XVI, stepped down (the first time a pope has "resigned" from office since 1415). His main role is as spiritual leader to the world's Catholic community.

Today, there are two principal reasons for sightseeing at the Vatican. One is to visit the Basilica di San Pietro, the most overwhelming architectural achievement of the Renaissance; the other is to visit the Musei Vaticani, which contain collections of staggering richness and diversity, from ancient Etruscan treasures and Egyptian mummies to an actual piece of the Moon.

For St. Peter's, Michelangelo originally designed a dome much higher than the one ultimately completed by his follower Giacomo della Porta.

Inside the basilica—breathtaking both for its sheer size and for its extravagant interior—are artistic masterpieces including Michelangelo's *Pietà* and Bernini's great bronze *baldacchino* (canopy) over the main altar. The Musei Vaticani, their entrance a 10-minute walk from the piazza, hold endless collections of many of the greatest works of Western art. The Laocoön, Leonardo's *St. Jerome in the Wilderness,* and Raphael's *Transfiguration* are all here. The Sistine Chapel, accessible only through these museums, is Michelangelo's magnificent artistic legacy, and his ceiling is the High Renaissance in excelsis in more ways than one.

⊙ Sights

★ Basilica di San Pietro

CHURCH | The world's largest church, built over the tomb of St. Peter, is the most imposing and breathtaking architectural achievement of the Renaissance (although much of the lavish interior dates to the baroque). No fewer than five of Italy's greatest artists—Bramante,

Raphael, Peruzzi, Antonio da Sangallo the Younger, and Michelangelo—died while striving to erect this new St. Peter's. The history of the original St. Peter's goes back to AD 326, when the emperor Constantine completed a basilica over the site of the tomb of Saint Peter, the Church's first pope. The original church stood for more than 1,000 years, undergoing a number of restorations and alterations, until, toward the middle of the 15th century, it was on the verge of collapse. In 1452, a reconstruction job began but was abandoned for lack of money. In 1503, Pope Julius II instructed the architect Bramante to raze all the existing buildings and build a new basilica, one that would surpass even Constantine's for grandeur. It wasn't until 1626 that the new basilica was completed and consecrated.

Highlights include the Loggia delle Benedizioni (Benediction Loggia), the balcony where newly elected popes are proclaimed; Michelangelo's *Pietà*; and Bernini's great bronze baldacchino,

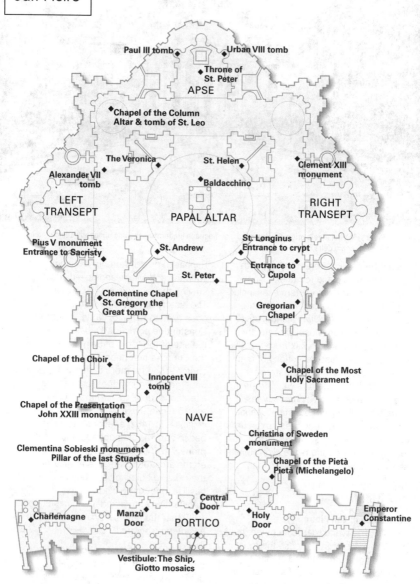

Basilica di San Pietro

a huge, spiral-columned canopy—at 100,000 pounds, perhaps the largest bronze object in the world—as well as many other Bernini masterpieces. There's also the collection of Vatican treasures in the Museo Storico-Artistico e Tesoro, and the Grotte Vaticane crypt. For views of both the dome above and the piazza below, take the elevator or stairs to the roof; those with more stamina (and without claustrophobia) can then head up more stairs to the apex of the dome. ■TIP➜ The basilica is free to visit, but a security check at the entrance can create very long lines. Arrive before 8:30 or after 5:30 to minimize the wait and avoid the crowds. ✉ Piazza San Pietro, Vatican ⊕ www.vatican.va ⊘ Closed during Papal Audience (Wed. until 1 pm) and during other ceremonies in piazza Ⓜ Ottaviano.

★ Cappella Sistina (Sistine Chapel)
ART MUSEUM | In 1508, the redoubtable Pope Julius II commissioned Michelangelo to fresco the more than 10,000 square feet of the Sistine Chapel's ceiling. (Sistine, by the way, is simply the adjective form of Sixtus, in reference to Pope Sixtus IV, who commissioned the chapel itself.) The task took four years, and it's said that, for many years afterward, Michelangelo couldn't read anything without holding it over his head. The result, however, was the greatest artwork of the Renaissance. A pair of binoculars helps greatly, as does a small mirror—hold it facing the ceiling and look down to study the reflection. More than 20 years after his work on the ceiling, Michelangelo was called on again, this time by Pope Paul III, to add to the chapel's decoration by painting the Last Judgment on the wall over the altar. By way of signature on this, his last great fresco, Michelangelo painted his own face on the flayed-off human skin in St. Bartholomew's hand. ■TIP➜ The chapel is entered through the Musei Vaticani, and lines are much shorter after 2:30 (reservations are always advisable)—except free Sundays, which are extremely busy and

when admissions close at 12:30. ✉ Musei Vaticani, Vatican ⊕ www.museivaticani. va ☎ €17 (part of the Vatican Museums) ⊘ Closed Sun. Ⓜ Ottaviano.

★ Musei Vaticani (Vatican Museums)
ART MUSEUM | Other than the pope and his papal court, the occupants of the Vatican are some of the most famous artworks in the world. The Vatican Palace, residence of the popes since 1377, consists of an estimated 1,400 rooms, chapels, and galleries. The pope and his household occupy only a small part; most of the rest is given over to the Vatican Library and Museums. Beyond the glories of the Sistine Chapel, the collection is extraordinarily rich: highlights include the great antique sculptures (including the celebrated Apollo Belvedere in the Octagonal Courtyard and the Belvedere Torso in the Hall of the Muses); the Stanze di Raffaello (Raphael Rooms), with their famous gorgeous frescoes; and the Old Master paintings, such as Leonardo da Vinci's beautiful (though unfinished) St. Jerome in the Wilderness, some of Raphael's greatest creations, and Caravaggio's gigantic Deposition in the Pinacoteca ("Picture Gallery").

For those interested in guided visits to the Vatican Museums, tours start at €34, including entrance tickets, and can also be booked online. Other offerings include a regular two-hour guided tour of the Vatican gardens; call or check online to confirm. For more information, call ☎ 06/69884676 or go to ⊕ museivaticani.va. For information on tours, call ☎ 06/69883145 or ☎ 06/69884676; visually impaired visitors can arrange tactile tours by calling ☎ 06/69884947. ✉ Viale Vaticano, near intersection with Via Leone IV, Vatican ☎ 06/69883145 ⊕ www.museivaticani.va ☎ €17 ⊘ Closed Sun. and church holidays Ⓜ Cipro–Musei Vaticani or Ottaviano–San Pietro; Bus 64 or 40.

4

The Vatican THE VATICAN

Tips on Touring the Vatican Museums

Remember that the Vatican's museum complex is humongous: only after walking through what seems like miles of galleries do you see the entrance to the Sistine Chapel (which cannot be entered from St. Peter's Basilica directly). Most people—especially those who rent an audio guide and must return it to the main desk—tour the complex, see the Sistine, then trudge back to the main museum entrance, itself a 15-minute walk from St. Peter's Square.

However, there is an "insider" exit directly from the Sistine Chapel to St. Peter's Basilica. Look for the "tour groups only" door on the right as you face the rear of the chapel and, when a group exits, go with the flow and follow them. This will deposit you on the porch of St. Peter's Basilica. While this has served as a sly trick for years, if a guard is on watch you may not be able to slip in so smoothly. Also note that if you run to the Sistine Chapel, using the "shortcut" exit into the basilica, you will have missed the rest of the Vatican Museum collection.

Another possibility is to visit in the evening. This experiment began in 2009 and has been running intermittently ever since, with the Vatican opening on Friday evening 7–11 (final entry at 9:30), April–October. While the major hits, like the Sistine Chapel, are usually open during these special evenings, many more off-the-beaten-path rooms and galleries are not. Reservations are required (and possible to secure online at ⊕ *museivaticani.va*).

Giardini Vaticani (*Vatican Gardens*)
GARDEN | Neatly trimmed lawns and flower beds extend over the hills behind St. Peter's Basilica, an area dotted with some interesting constructions and other, duller ones that serve as office buildings. The Vatican Gardens occupy almost 40 acres of land on the Vatican hill. They include a formal Italian garden, a flowering French garden, a romantic English landscape, and a small forest. There's also the little-used Vatican railroad station, which now houses a museum of coins and stamps made in the Vatican, and the Torre di San Giovanni (Tower of St. John), restored by Pope John XXIII as a retreat for work and now used as a residence for distinguished guests. To visit the gardens, join a two-hour guided walking tour or a 45-minute open-bus tour (no stops). Garden visits must be booked online. ✉ *Vatican City, Vatican* ☎ *06/69883145 tour info* ⊕ *museivaticani.*

va ✉ *€39 for two-hour walking tour, €37 for 45-minute open-bus tour (both options include admission to the Musei Vaticani)* ☉ *Closed Sun.* Ⓜ *Ottaviano.*

Necropoli Vaticana (*Vatican Necropolis*)
CEMETERY | With advance notice you can take a 1½-hour guided tour in English of the Vatican Necropolis, under the Basilica di San Pietro, which gives a rare glimpse of Early Christian Roman burial customs and a closer look at the tomb of St. Peter. Apply via the contact form online, by fax, or in person (the entrance to the office is on the left of the Bernini colonnade), specifying the number of people in the group (all must be age 15 or older), preferred language, preferred time, available dates, and your contact information in Rome. Each group will have about 12 participants. Visits are not recommended for those with mobility issues or who are claustrophobic. ✉ *Ufficio Scavi, Vatican*

Continued on page 128

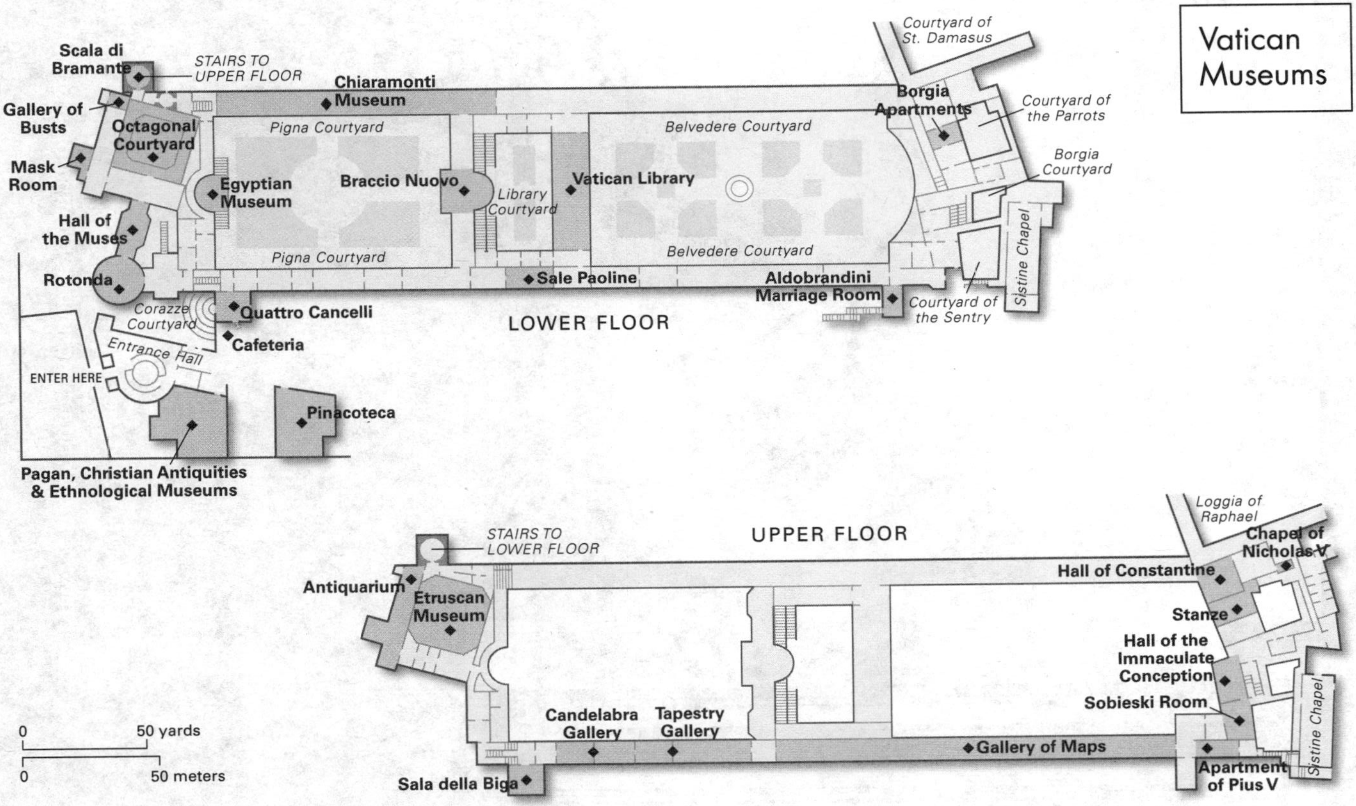

Vatican Museums

LOWER FLOOR

Courtyard of St. Damasus

Courtyard of the Parrots

Borgia Courtyard

Borgia Apartments

Sistine Chapel

Courtyard of the Sentry

Chiaramonti Museum

Belvedere Courtyard

Belvedere Courtyard

Vatican Library

Library Courtyard

Aldobrandini Marriage Room

Sale Paoline

STAIRS TO UPPER FLOOR

Pigna Courtyard

Braccio Nuovo

Pigna Courtyard

Scala di Bramante

Gallery of Busts

Octagonal Courtyard

Mask Room

Hall of the Muses

Rotonda

Egyptian Museum

Corazze Courtyard

Quattro Cancelli

Cafeteria

Entrance Hall

ENTER HERE

Pinacoteca

Pagan, Christian Antiquities & Ethnological Museums

UPPER FLOOR

Loggia of Raphael

Chapel of Nicholas V

Sistine Chapel

Hall of Constantine

Stanze

Hall of the Immaculate Conception

Sobieski Room

Apartment of Pius V

Gallery of Maps

STAIRS TO LOWER FLOOR

Candelabra Gallery

Tapestry Gallery

Antiquarium

Etruscan Museum

Sala della Biga

0   50 yards

0   50 meters

HEAVENS ABOVE:
THE SISTINE CEILING

Forming lines that are probably longer than those waiting to pass through the Pearly Gates, hordes of visitors arrive at the Sistine Chapel daily to view what may be the world's most sublime example of artistry:

Michelangelo: *The Creation of Adam*, Sistine Chapel, The Vatican, circa 1511.

Michelangelo's Sistine Ceiling. To paint this 12,000-square-foot barrel vault, it took four years, 343 frescoed figures, and a titanic battle of wits between the artist and Pope Julius II. While in its typical fashion, Hollywood focused on the element of agony, not ecstasy, involved in the saga of creation, a recently completed restoration of the ceiling has revolutionized our appreciation of the masterpiece of masterpieces.

By Martin Bennett

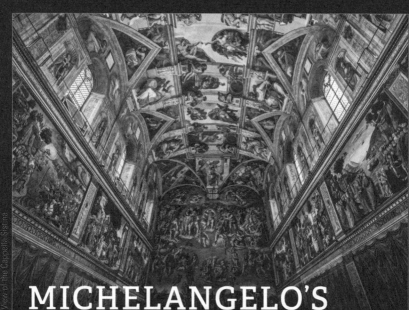

View of the Cappella Sistina

MICHELANGELO'S
MISSION IMPOSSIBLE

Designed to match the proportions of Solomon's Temple described in the Old Testament, the Sistine Chapel is named after Pope Sixtus VI, who commissioned it as a place of worship for himself and as the venue where new popes could be elected. Before Michelangelo, the barrel-vaulted ceiling was an expanse of azure fretted with golden stars. Then, in 1504, an ugly crack appeared. Bramante, the architect, managed do some patchwork using iron rods, but when signs of a fissure remained, the new Pope Julius II summoned Michelangelo to cover it with a fresco 135 feet long and 44 feet wide.

Taking in the entire span of the ceiling, the theme connecting the various participants in this painted universe could be said to be mankind's anguished waiting. The majestic panel depicting the Creation of Adam leads, through the stages of the Fall and the expulsion from Eden, to the tragedy of Noah found naked and mocked by his own sons; throughout all runs the underlying need for man's redemption. Witnessing all from the side and end walls, a chorus of ancient Prophets and Sibyls peer anxiously forward, awaiting the Redeemer who will come to save both the Jews and the Gentiles.

APOCALYPSE NOW

The sweetness and pathos of his *Pietà*, carved by Michelangelo only ten years earlier, have been left behind. The new work foretells an apocalypse, its congregation of doomed sinners facing the wrath of heaven through hanging, beheading, crucifixion, flood, and plague. Michelangelo, by nature a misanthrope, was already filled with visions of doom thanks to the fiery orations of Savonarola, whose thunderous preachments he had heard before leaving his hometown of Florence. Vasari, the 16th-century art historian, coined the word "terribilità" to describe Michelangelo's tension-ridden style, a rare case of a single word being worth a thousand pictures.

Michelangelo wound up using a Reader's Digest condensed version of the stories from Genesis, with the dramatis personae overseen by a punitive and terrifying God. In real life, poor Michelangelo answered to a flesh-and-blood taskmaster who was almost as vengeful: Pope Julius II. Less vicar of Christ than latter-day Caesar, he was intent on uniting Italy under the power of the Vatican, and was eager to do so by any means, including riding into pitched battle. Yet this "warrior pope" considered his most formidable adversary to be Michelangelo. Applying a form of blackmail, Julius threatened to wage war on Michelangelo's Florence, to which the artist had fled after Julius canceled a commission for a grand papal tomb unless Michelangelo agreed to return to Rome and take up the task of painting the Sistine Chapel ceiling.

MICHELANGELO, SCULPTOR

A sculptor first and foremost, however, Michelangelo considered painting an inferior genre—"for rascals and sissies" as he put it. Second, there was the sheer scope of the task, leading Michelangelo to suspect he'd been set up by a rival, Bramante, chief architect of the new St. Peter's Basilica. As Michelangelo was also a master architect, he regarded this fresco commission as a Renaissance mission-impossible. Pope Julius's powerful will prevailed—and six years later the work of the Sistine Ceiling was complete. Irving Stone's famous novel *The Agony and the Ecstasy*—and the granitic 1965 film that followed—chart this epic battle between artist and pope.

THINGS ARE LOOKING UP

To enhance your viewing of the ceiling, bring along opera-glasses, binoculars, or just a mirror (to prevent your neck from becoming bent like Michelangelo's). Note that no photos are permitted. Insiders know the only time to get the chapel to yourself is during the papal blessings and public audiences held in St. Peter's Square. Failing that, get there during lunch hour. Admission and entry to the Sistine Chapel is only through the Musei Vaticani (Vatican Museums).

SCHEMATIC OF THE SISTINE CEILING

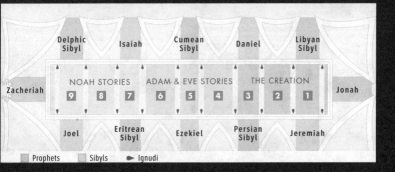

PAINTING THE BIBLE

The ceiling's biblical symbols were ideated by three Vatican theologians, Cardinal Alidosi, Egidio da Viterbo, and Giovanni Rafanelli, along with Michelangelo. As for the ceiling's

painted "framework," this quadratura alludes to Roman triumphal arches because Pope Julius II was fond of mounting "triumphal entries" into his conquered cities (in imitation of Christ's procession into Jerusalem on Palm Sunday).

THE CENTER PANELS

Prophet turned art-critic or, perhaps doubling as ourselves, the ideal viewer, Jonah the prophet (painted at the altar end) gazes up at the Creation, or Michelangelo's version of it.

1 The first of three scenes taken from the Book of Genesis: God separates Light from Darkness.

2 God creates the sun and a craterless pre-Galilean moon while the panel's other half offers an unprecedented rear view of the Almighty creating the vegetable world.

3 In the panel showing God separating the Waters from the Heavens, the Creator tumbles towards us as in a self-made whirlwind.

4 Pausing for breath, next admire probably Western Art's most famous image—God giving life to Adam.

The Creation of Eve from Adam's rib leads to the sixth panel.

6 In a sort of diptych divided by the trunk of the Tree of Knowledge of Good and Evil, Michelangelo retells the Temptation and the Fall.

Illustrating Man's fallen nature, the last three panels narrate, in un-chronological order, the Flood. In the first Noah offers a pre-Flood sacrifice of thanks.

8 Damaged by an explosion in 1794, next comes Michelangelo's version of Flood itself.

Finally, above the monumental Jonah, you can just make out the small, wretched figure of Noah, lying drunk—in pose, the shrunken anti-type of the majestic Adam five panels down the wall.

THE CREATION OF ADAM

Michelangelo's Adam was partly inspired by the Creation scenes Michelangelo had studied in the sculpted doors of Jacopo della Quercia in Bologna and Lorenzo Ghiberti's Doors of Paradise in Florence. Yet in Michelangelo's version Adam's hand hangs limp, waiting God's touch to impart the spark of life. Facing his Creation, the Creator—looking a bit like the pagan god Jupiter—is for the first time ever depicted as horizontal, mirroring the Biblical "in his own likeness." Decades after its completion, a crack began to appear, amputating Adam's fingertips. Believe it or not, the most famous fingers in Western art are the handiwork, at least in part, of one Domenico Carnevale.

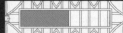

Meet the Pope

Piazza di San Pietro is the scene of large papal audiences, as well as special commemorations, masses, and beatification ceremonies. When he's in Rome, the pope makes an appearance every Sunday at noon at the window of the Vatican Palace. He addresses the crowd and blesses all present, a ceremony that lasts about 10 to 15 minutes. The pope also holds general audiences in the square on Wednesday morning at about 9:15 am; a ticket is usually necessary for a seat, but even with a ticket you will have to arrive early, as about 40,000 people attend every week, sometimes many more for special occasions. The general audience lasts between an hour and an hour and a half. In the winter and inclement weather, the audience is held in a hall adjacent to the basilica (Aula Paolo Sesto), which houses far fewer people than the square.

For admission to an audience, apply for free tickets by fax, in advance, indicating your preferred date, preferred language, and your contact information during your stay in Rome. You can also apply for tickets at the Prefettura della Casa Pontifice, either by fax (☎ 06/69885863), or by going to the office Tuesday 3–6 pm (7 pm in summer), or on the morning of the audience, 7–10 am. You can reach the office through the Portone di Bronzo (Bronze Door) at the end of the right-hand colonnade. Or arrange your tickets for free for a Wednesday general audience only (not for the papal Mass) through the Mission of the Catholic American Community of St. Patrick's Church (✉ *Via Boncompagni 31* ☎ *06/88818727)*; but the best way is to fill out a booking form directly online at ⊕ *www. stpatricksamericanrome.org.* You can pick up your tickets Tuesday from 4:30 to 6:15 pm only. Note that in August no official tickets are issued; you just have to show up early and hope to get a seat.

☎ *06/69885318, 06/69873017 reservations* ⊕ *www.scavi.va* ✉ *€13* ⊙ *Closed Sun. and Roman Catholic holidays* ⚲ *Reservations required* Ⓜ *Ottaviano.*

★ Piazza di San Pietro

PLAZA/SQUARE | Mostly enclosed within high walls that recall the papacy's stormy history, the Vatican opens the spectacular arms of Bernini's colonnade to embrace the world only at St. Peter's Square, scene of the pope's public appearances. One of Bernini's most spectacular masterpieces, the elliptical Piazza di San Pietro was completed in 1667 after only 11 years' work and holds about 100,000 people. Surrounded by a pair of quadruple colonnades, it is gloriously studded with 140 statues of saints and martyrs. At the piazza's center, the 85-foot-high Egyptian obelisk was brought to Rome by Caligula in AD 37 and moved here in 1586 by Pope Sixtus V. The Vatican post offices can be found on both sides of St. Peter's Square and inside the Vatican Museums complex and are open to the public. ■ TIP→ **The main information office is just left of the basilica as you face it.** ✉ *Piazza di San Pietro, Vatican* ⊕ *www. vaticanstate.va* Ⓜ *Ottaviano.*

Borgo

Between the Vatican and the once-moated bulk of Castel Sant'Angelo—erstwhile mausoleum of Emperor Hadrian and now an imposing relic of medieval Rome—is the old Borgo neighborhood, whose workaday charm has largely succumbed to gentrification. Be wary of the tourist-trap lunch spots and souvenir shops right outside the Vatican walls.

◉ Sights

Castel Sant'Angelo

CASTLE/PALACE | FAMILY | Standing between the Tiber and the Vatican, this circular castle has long been one of Rome's most distinctive landmarks. Opera lovers know it well as the setting for the final scene of Puccini's *Tosca*. Started in AD 135, the structure began as a mausoleum for the emperor Hadrian and was completed by his successor, Antoninus Pius. From the mid-6th century the building became a fortress, a place of refuge for popes during wars and sieges. Its name dates to AD 590, when Pope Gregory the Great, during a procession to plead for the end of a plague, saw an angel standing on the summit of the castle, sheathing his sword. Taking this as a sign that the plague was at an end, the pope built a small chapel at the top, placing a statue next to it to celebrate his vision—thus the name, Castel Sant'Angelo.

In the rooms off the Cortile dell'Angelo, look for the Cappella di Papa Leone X (Chapel of Pope Leo X), with a facade by Michelangelo. In the Pope Alexander VI courtyard, a wellhead bears the Borgia coat of arms. The stairs at the far end of the courtyard lead to the open terrace for a view of the Passetto, the fortified corridor connecting Castel Sant'Angelo with the Vatican. In the *appartamento papale* (papal apartment), the Sala Paolina (Pauline Room) was decorated in the 16th century by Perino del Vaga and assistants with lavish frescoes of scenes from the Old Testament and the lives of Saint Paul and Alexander the Great. ✉ *Lungotevere Castello 50, Prati* ☎ *06/6819111 central line, 06/6896003 tickets* ⊕ *castelsan-tangelo.beniculturali.it* ⊠ *€13* ⊗ *Closed Mon.* ⚐ *Online reservations recommended* Ⓜ *Lepanto.*

Ponte Sant'Angelo

BRIDGE | Angels designed by baroque master Bernini line the most beautiful of central Rome's 20-odd bridges. Bernini himself carved only two of the angels (those with the scroll and the crown of thorns), both of which were moved to the church of Sant'Andrea delle Fratte shortly afterward at the behest of the Bernini family. Though copies, the angels on the bridge today convey forcefully the grace and characteristic sense of movement—a key element of baroque sculpture—of Bernini's best work. Originally built in AD 133–134, the Ponte Elio, as it was originally called, was a bridge over the Tiber to Hadrian's Mausoleum. Pope Gregory changed the bridge's name after he had a vision of an angel sheathing its sword to signal the ending of the plague of 590. In medieval times, continuing its sacral function, the bridge became an important element in funneling pilgrims toward St. Peter's. As such, in 1667 Pope Clement IX commissioned Bernini to design 10 angels bearing the symbols of the Passion, turning the bridge into a sort of Via Crucis. ✉ *Between Lungotevere Castello and Lungotevere Altoviti, Borgo* Ⓜ *Ottaviano.*

🍴 Restaurants

Many tourists think the area around the Vatican is rip-off central when it comes to drinking and dining. Although there are an overwhelming number of tourist "trap-torias," the Borgo area, just outside the Vatican walls, is home to some genuinely good restaurants off the usual tourist radar.

Did You Know?

Designed to be Hadrian's tomb, the Castel Sant'Angelo was originally topped by a marble-sheathed tumulus and crowned by a gigantic bronze of the emperor in his chariot.

★ Chorus Café

$$ | MODERN ITALIAN | Tucked away above the Auditorium della Conciliazione, this glamorous restaurant/lounge with sky-high ceilings, marble walls, and plush seating feels like something out of Paolo Sorrentino's award-winning film *La Grande Bellezza*. Renowned bartender Massimo d'Addezio shakes up creative cocktails like a twist on a French 75 made with yuzu while lauded chef Arcangelo Dandini has taken the reins in the kitchen. **Known for:** creative cuisine by a renowned chef; DJ sets on the weekends; top-notch cocktails. ⑤ *Average main: €23* ✉ *Auditorium della Conciliazione, Via della Conciliazione 4, Borgo* ☎ *06/68892774* ⊕ *www.choruscafe.it* ☽ *Closed Sun. and Mon.* Ⓜ *Ottaviano.*

Taverna Angelica

$$ | MODERN ITALIAN | The Borgo area near St. Peter's Basilica hasn't been known for culinary excellence, but this is starting to change, and Taverna Angelica was one of the first refined restaurants in this part of town. The dining room is small, which allows the chef to create a menu that's inventive without being pretentious. **Known for:** ravioli with salt cod in arrabbiata oil spiced with red chile; elegant surroundings; eclectic Italian dishes. ⑤ *Average main: €22* ✉ *Piazza Amerigo Capponi 6, Borgo* ☎ *06/6874514* ⊕ *www.tavernaangelica.com* ☽ *Closed Mon.* Ⓜ *Ottaviano.*

☕ Coffee and Quick Bites

Hedera

$ | ICE CREAM | This gelato shop is charming in its historic ivy-covered building in the Piazza del Catalone with its famous fountain for pilgrims. The products here are made according to tradition with just the essentials: milk, cream, sugar, and eggs, usually all from organic farms. **Known for:** Calabrian truffles, hazelnut gelato balls with a liquid chocolate center; seasonal fruit gelato; soft brioche with mocha coffee granita. ⑤ *Average main: €4* ✉ *Borgo Pio 179, Borgo* ☎ *06/6832971* ⊕ *www.hederaroma.it.*

Hotels

Just east of the Vatican, the Borgo area has a certain medieval charm but can be overwhelming with tourists (and the tourist traps that love them). That said, there are a few appealing and atmospheric hotels here, and you can't beat the location for soaking up the Vatican sights.

Hotel Atlante Star

$$ | HOTEL | The lush rooftop-garden terrace with a center-stage view of St. Peter's Basilica is just one reason to stay here; you'll also enjoy the proximity to the Vatican and superb shopping nearby. **Pros:** all rooms come with robes and amenity kits; panoramic roof garden and terrace is open from morning to night; restaurant serves sophisticated cuisine with beautiful views. **Cons:** elevators are on the small side and a bit slow; bathrooms in some rooms are a little outdated; some rooms are nicer than others. ⑤ *Rooms from: €180* ✉ *Via Vitelleschi 34, Borgo* ☎ *06/686386* ⊕ *www.atlantehotels.com* ⟿ *65 rooms* ⑪ *Free Breakfast* Ⓜ *Ottaviano.*

Hotel Sant'Anna Roma

$ | HOTEL | In the picturesque, medieval Borgo neighborhood in the shadow of St. Peter's, this small, fashionable hotel is a good value. **Pros:** street is a pedestrian-only zone during the day; beds are comfy; staff are friendly. **Cons:** the neighborhood is dead at night; they can charge extra for a late checkout; no on-site bar or restaurant, and many nearby restaurants are tourist traps. ⑤ *Rooms from: €120* ✉ *Borgo Pio 133, Borgo* ☎ *06/68801602* ⊕ *www.santannahotel.net* ⟿ *20 rooms* ⑪ *Free Breakfast* Ⓜ *Ottaviano.*

Residenza Paolo VI

$$ | HOTEL | Set in a former monastery—still an extraterritorial part of the Vatican—magnificently abutting Bernini's colonnade of St. Peter's Square, the Paolo VI (pronounced "Sesto," a reference to Pope Paul VI) is unbeatably close to St. Peter's, with comfortable and amazingly quiet guest rooms. **Pros:** direct views of St. Peter's from the rooftop terrace; lovely staff and service; quiet rooms. **Cons:** far away from Rome's historical attractions; bathrooms are a tight space; some rooms are really small. $ *Rooms from: €139* ✉ *Via Paolo VI 29, Borgo* ☎ *06/684870* ⊕ *www.residenzapaolovi.com* ⇆ *35 rooms* ⦿ *Free Breakfast* Ⓜ *Ottaviano.*

Nightlife

Bukowski's Bar

COCKTAIL LOUNGES | This cozy spot outside the Vatican is furnished like a familiar living room with a giant leather sofa and armchairs, making it easy to meet the people sitting next to you. In addition to a strong cocktail and wine menu, the owners regularly host art, theater, and shopping events. *Aperitivo* (Italian happy hour) is served every evening, with a selection of drinks and the option of adding a small plate for €5. ✉ *Via Degli Ombrellari 25, Borgo* ☎ *351/7139892* Ⓜ *Ottaviano.*

Shopping

Borgo is your destination for religious relics.

Savelli Arte e Tradizione

CRAFTS | Here you'll find a fully stocked selection of religious gifts: everything from rosaries and crosses to religious artwork and Pope Francis memorabilia. Founded in 1898, this family business provides a place for pilgrims to pick up a souvenir from the Holy See and also specializes in mosaics. The store has another location at the Self-Service Restaurant in

Piazza del Sant'Uffizio 6/7. It's closed on Sunday afternoon. ✉ *Via Paolo VI 27–29, Borgo* ☎ *06/68307017* ⊕ *www.savellireligious.com* Ⓜ *Ottaviano.*

Prati

Outside the Vatican walls, but slightly upriver from the Borgo neighborhood, Prati is coming into its own as a foodie destination.

 Restaurants

Carter Oblio

$$ | MODERN ITALIAN | This restaurant's name is an anagram of the name of its chef, Ciro Alberto Cucciniello, whose creativity is on full display in the menu. Having studied economics, he pivoted to cooking and cut his teeth at renowned restaurants in Italy and abroad before opening this intimate restaurant with a Nordic-inspired design. **Known for:** beautifully presented and creative dishes; sleek Nordic design; reasonably priced tasting menus. $ *Average main: €20* ✉ *Via Giuseppe Gioachino Belli 21, Prati* ☎ *391/4649097* ⊗ *Closed Mon.* Ⓜ *Lepanto.*

Del Frate

$$ | MODERN ITALIAN | This impressive wine bar matches sleek, modern decor with creative cuisine and three-dozen wines available by the glass. The house specialty is marinated meat and fish, but you can also get cheeses, smoked meats, and composed salads. **Known for:** wide selection of after-dinner drinks, including mezcal (smoky agave liquor) and *amari* (bitter cordial); daily aperitivo with a nice selection of wines by the glass; adjacent to one of Rome's noted wine shops. $ *Average main: €23* ✉ *Via degli Scipioni 118, Prati* ☎ *06/3236437* ⊕ *www.enotecadelfrate.it* ⊗ *Closed Sun. and Aug.* Ⓜ *Ottaviano.*

★ Enoteca La Torre

$$$$ | MODERN ITALIAN | In the Villa Laetitia, a boutique hotel owned by the Fendi family, this gorgeous restaurant has soaring ceilings, a crystal chandelier, and art nouveau motifs. The elegant setting provides the perfect backdrop for creative, flavorful dishes by Domenico Stile, one of Rome's youngest Michelin-starred chefs. **Known for:** one of the most beautiful restaurants in Rome; out-of-the-box wine pairings; flavorful, creative cuisine. $ *Average main: €35* ✉ *Villa Laetitia, Lungotevere delle Armi 23, Prati* ☎ *06/45668304* ⊕ *www.enotecalatorreroma.com* ☉ *Closed Mon. and Tues.* Ⓜ *Lepanto.*

Freni e Frizioni Draft

$ | PIZZA | Fancy a cocktail with your pizza? This hip new pizzeria by the team behind award-winning bar Freni & Frizioni in Trastevere is outfitted with 18 taps, but only six of them are used for beer. **Known for:** cocktails on draft; sleek, minimalist design; Roman-style pizza. $ *Average main: €12* ✉ *Via Sforza Pallavicini 12, Prati* ☎ *388/1832577* ⊕ *www.freniefrizioni.com* Ⓜ *Ottaviano.*

Hostaria da Cesare

$$ | TUSCAN | An old standby in Prati, Hostaria da Cesare is dedicated to Roman culinary tradition. The general menu's tendency toward hearty, stick-to-your-ribs comfort food makes this a popular spot in the autumn and winter. **Known for:** saltimbocca (thinly sliced veal with prosciutto and sage); speciality pasta with white truffles; fresh, local ingredients. $ *Average main: €20* ✉ *Via Crescenzio 13, Prati* ☎ *06/6861227* ⊕ *www.ristorantecesare.com* ☉ *Closed 3 weeks in Aug.* Ⓜ *Lepanto.*

Il Simposio di Costantini

$$$ | MODERN ITALIAN | At the most upscale wine bar in town, you come for the wine but return for the food. Everything here is appropriately *raffinato* (refined): marinated and smoked fish, salads, and top-quality *salumi* (salted

meat) and other cured meats and pâtés. **Known for:** artichokes prepared three ways; roughly 80 cheeses to savor with your dessert wine; favorite among locals. $ *Average main: €30* ✉ *Piazza Cavour 16, Prati* ☎ *06/3241489* ⊕ *www.ilsimposioroma.it* ☉ *Closed Sun. and 2 weeks in Aug.* Ⓜ *Lepanto.*

La Zanzara

$$ | INTERNATIONAL | This bright and modern restaurant functions as a bar, caffè, and restaurant all in one, with plenty of indoor and outdoor seating. The menu runs the international gamut, with salads, pasta, steak, and seafood—standouts include the beef burger. **Known for:** artisan Italian beers; large grill for freshly cooked meats; bacon cheeseburger. $ *Average main: €20* ✉ *Via Crescenzio 84, Prati* ☎ *06/68392227* ⊕ *www.lazanzararoma.com* Ⓜ *Ottaviano.*

Properzio Osteria di Mare

$$ | SEAFOOD | A bit of a local secret, this new osteria has a romantic atmosphere that's perfect for a date night, with stone walls, a wooden ceiling, chairs painted seafoam green, gilded mirrors, and fresh flowers. The menu focuses on seafood, with deliciously straightforward dishes like roasted octopus with broccoli rabe, linguine with raw and cooked shrimp, and seabass meunière. **Known for:** romantic atmosphere; affordable tasting menus; fresh seafood. $ *Average main: €18* ✉ *Via Properzio 20-24, Prati* ☎ *06/68308471* ⊕ *www.osteriaproperzio.it* ☉ *Closed Mon.* Ⓜ *Ottaviano.*

Ristorante Sinatra

$$ | MODERN ITALIAN | Named in homage to the Italian-American crooner, this intimate restaurant has a refined yet casual atmosphere, with wine bottles lining the walls, black-and-white photographs of jazz musicians, and vintage touches like rotary telephones. The menu hews toward Italian classics with a few surprises, including focaccia with Spanish pata negra ham; lime and raw shrimp in the *cacio e pepe* (pasta prepared with

a pecorino-cheese sauce and black pepper); and a selection of sushi rolls. **Known for:** charming vintage setting; live music; eclectic menu. $ *Average main: €18* ⊠ *Via Fabio Massimo 68, Prati* ☎ *06/3219657* ⊕ *ristorante-sinatra.business.site* ⊗ *Closed Sun.* Ⓜ *Lepanto.*

Romanè

$$ | **ROMAN** | This casual spot on the edge of Prati is Trapizzino impresario Stefano Callegari's first restaurant where diners sit and eat with forks and knives. Like Trapizzino, it excels at conjuring nostalgic flavors and presenting them in new ways. **Known for:** fettuccine al tortellino; laid-back, homey vibe; Roman culinary traditions, including quinto quarto. $ *Average main: €15* ⊠ *Via Cipro 106, Prati* ☎ *340/7845281* Ⓜ *Cipro.*

Sant'Isidoro Pizza & Bolle

$ | **PIZZA** | Taking the traditional pairing of pizza and beer up a notch, this modern pizzeria on a quiet street pairs its pies with an extensive selection of sparkling wines. More upscale than a typical pizzeria but casual enough for a weeknight, this place serves classic flavor combinations as well as some creative options, like a pizza topped with stracciatella, raw shrimp, lemon peel, and mint. **Known for:** chic modern design; creative pizzas; wide selection of sparkling wines. $ *Average main: €12* ⊠ *Via Oslavia 41, Prati* ☎ *06/89822607* ⊕ *www.pizzaebolle.it* ⊗ *No lunch Sat.* Ⓜ *Lepanto.*

★ Sorpasso

$$ | **MODERN ITALIAN** | The focus at this happening spot, open from early morning until late in the evening, is on using excellently sourced products to make simple but wonderful food. In the morning and afternoon, this is the perfect place to stop in for freshly baked sweet treats, while evenings are popular for aperitivo or hearty meals when people spill out into the street, cocktail in hand. **Known for:** *strozzapretti* (a short pasta) served with eggplant, pistachio, and chili bread crumbs; juicy steaks; meat and

cheese board. $ *Average main: €15* ⊠ *Via Properzio 31-33, Prati* ☎ *06/89024554* ⊕ *www.sorpasso.info* ⊗ *Closed Sun., and Aug.* Ⓜ *Ottaviano.*

Tavola Bottiglieria con Cucina

$$ | **MODERN ITALIAN** | This industrial-chic bistro was started by two surfer brothers with a passion for convivial dining. With the exception of *primi* (starters) and burgers, all of the dishes can be ordered as full-size or small portions so you can satisfy your curiosity and taste your way through the menu. **Known for:** convivial atmosphere; creative takes on Italian classics; choice of full-size or tapas-style portions. $ *Average main: €18* ⊠ *Via Fabio Massimo 91, Prati* ☎ *06/3211178* ⊕ *www.tavolaristorante.com* Ⓜ *Ottaviano.*

☕ Coffee and Quick Bites

Al Settimo Gelo

$ | **ICE CREAM** | The unusual flavors of gelato scooped up here include cinnamon and ginger and fig with cardamom and walnut, but the classics also get rave reviews. Ask for a taste of the *passito* flavor, if it's available; it's inspired by the popular sweet Italian dessert wine. **Known for:** completely gluten-free shop; homemade whipped cream; organic Sicilian lemon sorbetto. $ *Average main: €5* ⊠ *Via Vodice 21/a, Prati* ☎ *06/3725567* ⊕ *www.alsettimogelo.it* ⊗ *Closed Mon., and 1 wk in Aug.* Ⓜ *Lepanto.*

Bonci Pizzarium

$ | **PIZZA** | This tiny storefront by famed pizzaiolo Gabriele Bonci is the city's most famous place for pizza *al taglio* (by the slice). It serves more than a dozen flavors, from the standard margherita to slices piled high with prosciutto and other tasty ingredients. **Known for:** long lines; over a dozen flavors; Rome's best pizza al taglio. $ *Average main: €5* ⊠ *Via della Meloria 43, Prati* ☎ *06/39745416* ⊕ *www.bonci.it* ⊗ *Closed Mon.* Ⓜ *Cipro.*

Castroni

$ | **SANDWICHES** | There are the usual
range of pastries and sandwiches at this
old-school coffee shop; sit outside, or
do as the Romans do and stand at the
bar. The attached store sells all sorts of
gourmet goodies (and, of course, fresh
coffee)—ideal for souvenirs. **Known for:**
gourmet shop; old-school style; espresso
roasted in-house. ⑤ *Average main: €5*
✉ *Via Ottaviano 55, Prati* ☎ *06/39723279*
⊕ *www.castroni.it* Ⓜ *Ottaviano.*

Re-bio

$ | **CAFÉ** | This friendly shop, a stone's
throw from the Musei Vaticani, spe-
cializes in super-fresh, made-to-order
sandwiches using organic ingredients.
It also serves poke bowls, salads, and
great fresh juices and smoothies but has
limited seating. **Known for:** smoothies
and fresh juices; poke bowls; vege-
tarian and vegan options. ⑤ *Average
main: €9* ✉ *Via Germanico 59, Prati*
☎ *06/39746510* ⊕ *www.rebio.it* ⊘ *Closed
Sun.* Ⓜ *Ottaviano.*

Hotels

Here you'll find small, friendly hotels that
don't break the bank.

Amalia Hotel

$$ | **HOTEL** | Convenient to St. Peter's,
the Vatican, and Prati's Cola di Rienzo
shopping district (and just a block from
the Ottaviano stop of Metro Line A),
this small, family-run hotel situated in a
19th-century palazzo is crisp and smart.
Pros: good location for both visiting the
Vatican and shopping; helpful staff; large
beds. **Cons:** bedding could use a revamp;
limited breakfast buffet; showers can be
small. ⑤ *Rooms from: €150* ✉ *Via Ger-
manico 66, Prati* ☎ *06/39723356* ⊕ *www.
hotelamalia.com* ⊲ *34 rooms* ⦿ *Free
Breakfast* Ⓜ *Ottaviano.*

Hotel al San Pietrino

$ | **HOTEL** | This simple budget hotel on
the third floor of a 19th-century palazzo
offers rock-bottom rates at a five-minute
walk from the Vatican. **Pros:** heavenly
rates near the Vatican; free parking
nearby; air-conditioning and Wi-Fi. **Cons:**
no bar; flat pillows and basic bedding; a
couple of Metro stops from the centro
storico. ⑤ *Rooms from: €40* ✉ *Via
Giovanni Bettolo 43, Prati* ☎ *328/3416714
WhatsApp, 06/3700132* ⊕ *www.hotelsan-
pietrino.it* ⊲ *11 rooms* ⦿ *Free Breakfast*
Ⓜ *Ottaviano.*

Hotel Dei Mellini

$$ | **HOTEL** | On the west bank of the
Tiber between the Spanish Steps and
St. Peter's Basilica (a five-minute stroll
from Piazza del Popolo), this modern
luxury hotel is tucked away from the
chaos of the centro storico but still close
enough for convenient sightseeing. **Pros:**
spacious and spotless rooms; breakfast
served until 11 am; free bicycles to use
based on availability. **Cons:** few dining
options right nearby; rooms facing
courtyard can be dark; not for those
who want to be in the center of the
action. ⑤ *Rooms from: €149* ✉ *Via Muzio
Clementi 81, Prati* ☎ *06/324771* ⊕ *www.
hotelmellini.com* ⊲ *80 rooms* ⦿ *Free
Breakfast* Ⓜ *Lepanto.*

Hotel Museum

$ | **HOTEL** | A stone's throw from the
Musei Vaticani, this family-run hotel offers
good service and rates. **Pros:** friendly
staff; rooftop terrace; good-sized rooms.
Cons: room decor is outdated; not much
of interest besides the Vatican nearby;
breakfast is tasty but goes quickly.
⑤ *Rooms from: €60* ✉ *Via Tunisi 8, Prati*
☎ *06/97276695* ⊕ *www.hotelmuseum.it*
⊲ *31 rooms* ⦿ *Free Breakfast* Ⓜ *Ottaviano, Cipro.*

⭐ Mama Shelter Roma

$$ | HOTEL | FAMILY | This hip hotel is the first Italian outpost of the French brand Mama Shelter, and it feels right at home in Rome, including a wide variety of useful room amenities and two good restaurants. **Pros:** programming like beer tastings and weekend brunch; spa area with a pool, sauna, and gym; sex-positive and LGBTQ+ friendly. **Cons:** a bit far from most of the major sites; breakfast is nothing special and costs extra; €25 cleaning fee for pets. ⑤ *Rooms from: €129* ✉ *Via Luigi Rizzo 20, Prati* ☎ *06/94538900* ⊕ *www.mamashelter. com/roma* 🛏 *217 rooms* ⦿ *No Meals* Ⓜ *Cipro.*

Nightlife

BARS

Emerald's Bar

COCKTAIL LOUNGES | This classy cocktail bar a few blocks from the Vatican makes you feel transported to a cozy salon in New York or London. The bartenders shake up reliably good classics, including an excellent dirty martini, and also some original creations. ✉ *Via Crescenzio 91C, Prati* ☎ *06/88654275* 🕙 *Closed Mon.* Ⓜ *Ottaviano.*

LIVE MUSIC

Alexanderplatz Jazz Club

LIVE MUSIC | The black-and-white-checker floors of Alexanderplatz, Rome's most important live jazz and blues club, are reminiscent of Harlem's 1930s jazz halls, and Alexanderplatz loves to promote this image with excellent jazz programming featuring both Italian and international performers. The bar and restaurant are always busy, so reservations are suggested. ✉ *Via Ostia 9, Prati* ☎ *349/9770309 WhatsApp* ⊕ *www.alexanderplatzjazz. com* Ⓜ *Ottaviano.*

Fonclea

LIVE MUSIC | Conveniently just around the corner from Castel Sant'Angelo, Fonclea jams with live music every night of the week—from jazz and Latin American to R&B and '60s cover bands. Entry is free. ✉ *Via Crescenzio 82/a, Prati* ☎ *06/6896302* ⊕ *www.fonclea.it* Ⓜ *Ottaviano.*

Shopping

Just a hop, skip, and jump from the Vatican, you'll find an array of religious relic shops, department stores, and gourmet food and wine shops.

DEPARTMENT STORES

Coin

DEPARTMENT STORE | FAMILY | Department stores aren't the norm in Italy, but Coin comes close with its large selection of upscale merchandise including accessories, handbags, cosmetics, and clothing for men, women, and children. Searching for a pressure-driven espresso machine, a simpler stove-top Bialetti model, or a mezzaluna? You can find these and other high-quality, stylish cookware items that are difficult to find back home. There's a smaller version at Termini station, and ten total around Rome. ✉ *Via Cola di Rienzo 173, Prati* ☎ *06/36004298* ⊕ *www.coin.it* Ⓜ *Lepanto, Ottaviano.*

FOOD AND WINE

⭐ Castroni

FOOD | Opening its flagship shop near the Vatican in 1932, this gastronomic paradise has long been Rome's port of call for decadent delicacies from around the globe; there are now 13 locations throughout the city. Jonesing expats and study-abroad students pop in for local sweets, 300 types of tea, and even some good old-fashioned Kraft Macaroni & Cheese. If you're just doing a little window-shopping, be sure to try their in-house roasted espresso, some of the best coffee in Rome. ✉ *Via Cola di Rienzo 196/198, Prati* ☎ *06/6874383* ⊕ *www. castronicoladirienzo.com* Ⓜ *Lepanto, Ottaviano.*

SHOES AND ACCESSORIES
Il Sellaio di Serafini

LEATHER GOODS | For more than 70 years, artisan Ferruccio Serafini has been churning out some of the best handmade leather bags, shoes, and belts in Rome. Only a handful of these true saddler artisans still exist today. Marlon Brando, Elizabeth Taylor, and the Kennedy brothers were all faithful followers of Serafini's design and work in the 1960s. Today, the family business is run by Francesca, Ferruccio Serafini's youngest daughter. Choose from their premade stock or select your own style and accompanying leathers. They also repair vintage leather bags and accessories. ⊠ *Via Caio Mario 14, Prati* ☎ *06/3211719* ⊕ *www.serafinipelletteria.it* ☾ *Closed Sun.* Ⓜ *Ottaviano.*

PIAZZA NAVONA, CAMPO DE' FIORI, AND THE JEWISH GHETTO

Updated by
Natalie Kennedy

⊙ Sights
★★★★★

🍴 Restaurants
★★★☆☆

🛏 Hotels
★★★★★

🛍 Shopping
★★★★☆

🍸 Nightlife
★★★★☆

NEIGHBORHOOD SNAPSHOT

MAKING THE MOST OF YOUR TIME

Start at Campo de' Fiori, where the popular market takes place every morning, Monday through Saturday. The cobblestone streets that stretch out from the square are still lined with artisans' workshops. Wind your way west through the Jewish Ghetto, the historic home of Rome's once-vibrant Jewish community (and a good place for lunch); don't miss the area around the Portico d'Ottavia, with some of the city's most atmospheric ruins. Heading north will take you across busy Corso Vittorio Emanuele toward the Pantheon. Duck into the piazza of Santa Maria Sopra Minerva, which contains Rome's most delightful baroque conceit, the 17th-century elephant obelisk memorial designed by Bernini, and pop into the church, which has the only Gothic interior in Rome. Straight ahead is one of the wonders of the world, the ancient Pantheon, with that postcard icon, Piazza Navona, just a few blocks to the west. You could spend about five hours exploring, not counting breaks—but taking breaks is what this area is all about.

GETTING HERE

■ Piazza Navona and Campo de' Fiori are an easy walk from the Vatican or Trastevere, or a half-hour stroll from the Spanish Steps. From Termini or the Vatican, take Bus No. 40 Express or the No. 64 to Largo Torre Argentina; then walk 10 minutes to either piazza. Bus No. 116 winds from Via Veneto past the Spanish Steps to Campo de' Fiori.

■ From the Vatican or the Spanish Steps, it's a 30-minute walk to the Jewish Ghetto, or take the No. 40 Express or the No. 64 bus from Termini station to Largo Torre Argentina.

TOP REASONS TO GO

Piazza Navona: This is the city's most glorious piazza—the showcase for Rome's exuberant baroque style. Savor Bernini's fantastic fountain, set off by the curves and steeples of Borromini's church of Sant'Agnese.

Caravaggio: Marvel at the play of light and dark in three of the finest paintings by 17th-century Rome's rebel artist at the church of San Luigi dei Francesi.

The Pantheon: Gaze up to the heavens through the dome of Rome's best-preserved ancient temple—could this be the world's only architecturally perfect building?

Campo de' Fiori: Stroll through the morning market for a taste of the sweet life.

Portico d'Ottavia: This famed ancient Roman landmark casts a spell over Rome's time-honored Jewish Ghetto.

OFF THE BEATEN PATH

■ The market at Campo de' Fiori attracts the most visitors, but on the weekends Romans head to the Mercato Campagna Amica on Via di San Teodoro. One of the only true farmers' markets in the city brings producers from around the Lazio region to sell local cheese like the hard-to-find *marzolino* cheese, fresh produce, bread made from stone-ground wheat, and *salumi* (cured meats) galore. A small kitchen near the back door whips up lunch with seasonal ingredients for about €8, and there is ample outdoor seating.

The area around Piazza Navona, Campo de' Fiori, and the Jewish Ghetto, also known as the Campo Marzio (Field of Mars) for its martial past, is one of the city's most beautiful, most atmospheric, and liveliest neighborhoods. More than almost anywhere else in Rome, this is an area worth getting lost in, with cobblestone side streets and artisans' shops just around the corner from the piazze and sights that crowd with tourists (and the establishments that cater to them).

Piazza Navona

In terms of sheer sensual enjoyment—from a mouthwatering range of restaurants and cozy bars to the ornate baroque settings—it's tough to top this area of Rome. Just a few blocks (and some 1,200 years) separate the two main showstoppers: Piazza Navona and the Pantheon. The first is the most beautiful baroque piazza in the world, and it serves as the open-air salon for this quarter of Rome. As if this is not grandeur enough, across Corso di Rinascimento—and more than a millennium away—is the Pantheon, the grandest extant building still standing from ancient Rome, topped by the world's largest unreinforced concrete dome. Near the same massive hub, Bernini's delightful elephant obelisk proves that small can also be beautiful.

And beautiful is the word to describe this entire area, one that is packed with baroque wonders, charming stores, and very happy sightseers.

 Sights

Museo Napoleonico
OTHER MUSEUM | Housed in an opulent collection of velvet-and-crystal salons that hauntingly capture the fragile charm of early-19th-century Rome, this small museum in the Palazzo Primoli contains a specialized and rich collection of Napoléon memorabilia, including a bust by Canova of the general's sister, Pauline Borghese (as well as a plaster cast of her left bust). You may well ask why this outpost of Napoléon is in Rome, but in 1798 the French emperor sent his troops to Rome, kidnapping Pope Pius VII and proclaiming his young son the

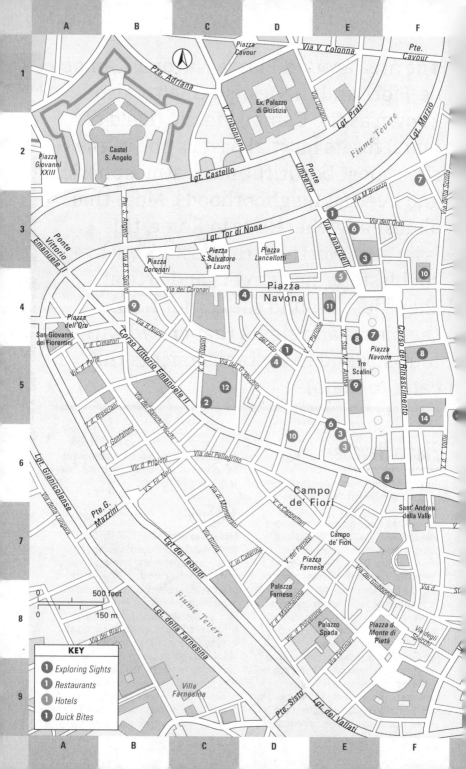

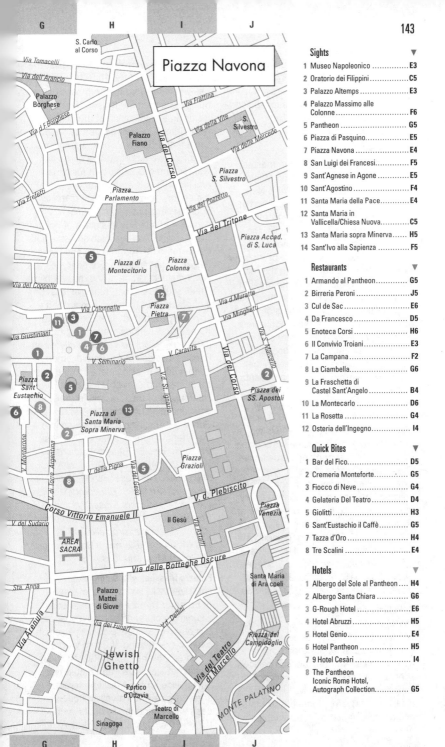

Piazza Navona

Sights ▼

1 Museo Napoleonico E3
2 Oratorio dei Filippini C5
3 Palazzo Altemps E3
4 Palazzo Massimo alle
   Colonne F6
5 Pantheon G5
6 Piazza di Pasquino E5
7 Piazza Navona E4
8 San Luigi dei Francesi F5
9 Sant'Agnese in Agone E5
10 Sant'Agostino F4
11 Santa Maria della Pace E4
12 Santa Maria in
   Vallicella/Chiesa Nuova C5
13 Santa Maria sopra Minerva H5
14 Sant'Ivo alla Sapienza F5

Restaurants ▼

1 Armando al Pantheon G5
2 Birreria Peroni J5
3 Cul de Sac E6
4 Da Francesco D5
5 Enoteca Corsi H6
6 Il Convivio Troiani E3
7 La Campana F2
8 La Ciambella G6
9 La Fraschetta di
   Castel Sant'Angelo B4
10 La Montecarlo D6
11 La Rosetta G4
12 Osteria dell'Ingegno I4

Quick Bites ▼

1 Bar del Fico D5
2 Cremeria Monteforte G5
3 Fiocco di Neve G4
4 Gelateria Del Teatro D4
5 Giolitti H3
6 Sant'Eustachio il Caffè G5
7 Tazza d'Oro H4
8 Tre Scalini E4

Hotels ▼

1 Albergo del Sole al Pantheon H4
2 Albergo Santa Chiara G6
3 G-Rough Hotel E6
4 Hotel Abruzzi H5
5 Hotel Genio E4
6 Hotel Pantheon H5
7 9 Hotel Cesàri I4
8 The Pantheon
   Iconic Rome Hotel,
   Autograph Collection G5

King of Rome—though it all ultimately came to naught. ✉ *Palazzo Primoli, Piazza di Ponte Umberto I, Piazza Navona* ☎ *06/68806286* ⊕ *www.museonapoleonico.it* ⊗ *Closed Mon.* Ⓜ *Bus Nos. 70, 30, 81, 628, and 492.*

Oratorio dei Filippini

LIBRARY | Housed in a baroque masterwork by Borromini, this former religious residence named for Saint Philip Neri, founder in 1551 of the Congregation of the Oratorians, now contains Rome's Archivio Storico. Like the Jesuits, the Oratorians—or Filippini, as they were commonly known—were one of the new religious orders established in the mid-16th century as part of the Counter-Reformation. Neri, a man of rare charm and wit, insisted that the members of the order—most of them young noblemen whom he had recruited personally—not only renounce their worldly goods, but also work as common laborers in the building of Neri's great church of Santa Maria in Vallicella. The Oratory itself, once headquarters of the order, was built by Borromini between 1637 and 1662. Its gently curving facade is typical of Borromini's insistence on introducing movement into everything he designed. The inspiration here is that of arms extended in welcome to the poor. The building houses the Vallicelliana Library founded by Philip Neri, and the courtyard is usually accessible during the library's opening hours. Otherwise, guided visits can be booked by email. ✉ *Piazza della Chiesa Nuova (Corso Vittorio Emanuele), Piazza Navona* ☎ *06/6892537* ✉ *b-vall. didattica@beniculturali.it* ⊗ *Closed Sun.*

★ Palazzo Altemps

CASTLE/PALACE | Containing some of the finest ancient Roman statues in the world, Palazzo Altemps is part of the Museo Nazionale Romano. The palace's sober exterior belies a magnificence that appears as soon as you walk into the majestic courtyard, studded with statues and covered in part by a retractable awning. The restored interior hints at the Roman lifestyle of the 16th–18th centuries while showcasing the most illustrious pieces from the Museo Nazionale, including the collection of the Ludovisi noble family. In the frescoed salons you can see the *Galata Suicida*, a poignant sculptural work portraying a barbarian warrior who chooses death for himself and his wife, rather than humiliation by the enemy. Another highlight is the large Ludovisi sarcophagus, magnificently carved from marble. In a place of honor is the *Ludovisi Throne*, which shows a goddess emerging from the sea and being helped by her acolytes. For centuries this was heralded as one of the most sublime Greek sculptures, but, today, at least one authoritative art historian considers it a colossally overrated fake. Look for the framed explanations of the exhibits that detail (in English) how and exactly where Renaissance sculptors, Bernini among them, added missing pieces to the classical works. In the lavishly frescoed loggia stand busts of the Caesars. In the wing once occupied by early-20th-century poet Gabriele d'Annunzio (who married into the Altemps family), three rooms host the museum's Egyptian collection. ✉ *Piazza di Sant'Apollinare 46, Piazza Navona* ☎ *06/684851* ⊕ *museonazionaleromano. beniculturali.it* ✉ *€8; €12 combined ticket includes three other Museo Nazionale Romano sites over one week (Crypta Balbi, Palazzo Massimo alle Terme, and Museo delle Terme di Diocleziano)* ⊗ *Closed Mon. and Tues.*

Palazzo Massimo alle Colonne

CASTLE/PALACE | Following the shape of Emperor Domitian's Odeon arena, a curving, columned portico identifies this otherwise inconspicuous palace on a traffic-swept bend of Corso Vittorio Emanuele. In the 1530s, Renaissance architect Baldassare Peruzzi built this new palace for the Massimo family, after their previous dwelling had been destroyed during the Sack of Rome. (High in the papal aristocracy, they claimed an ancestor who had been responsible for the defeat of Hannibal.) If you visit on March 16, you'll be able to go upstairs to visit the family chapel in commemoration of a miracle performed here in 1583 by St. Philip Neri, who is said to have recalled a young member of the family, one Paolo Massimo, from the dead (expect a line). Any other day of the year, though, you'll only be able to view the building from the outside. The palazzo's name comes from the columns of the ancient Odeon; one is still visible in the square at the back of the palazzo. ⊠ *Corso Vittorio Emanuele II 141, Piazza Navona.*

★ Pantheon

RELIGIOUS BUILDING | The best-preserved ancient building in the city, this former Roman temple is a marvel of architectural harmony and proportion. It was entirely rebuilt by the emperor Hadrian around AD 120 on the site of an earlier Pantheon (from the Greek: *pan,* all, and *theon,* gods) erected in 27 BC by Augustus's right-hand man and son-in-law, Agrippa.

The most striking thing about the Pantheon is not its size, immense though it is, nor even the phenomenal technical difficulties posed by so massive a construction; rather, it's the remarkable unity of the building. The diameter described by the dome is exactly equal to its height. It's the use of such simple mathematical balance that gives classical architecture its characteristic sense of proportion and its nobility. The opening at the apex of the dome, the *oculus,* is nearly 30 feet in diameter and was intended to symbolize the "all-seeing eye of the heavens." On a practical note, this means when it rains, it rains inside: look out for the drainage holes in the floor.

Although little is known for sure about the Pantheon's origins or purpose, it's worth noting that the five levels of

trapezoidal coffers (sunken panels in the ceiling) represent the course of the five then-known planets and their concentric spheres. Ruling over them is the sun, represented symbolically and literally by the 30-foot-wide eye at the top. The heavenly symmetry is further paralleled by the coffers: 28 to each row, the number of lunar cycles. In the center of each would have shone a small bronze star. Down below, the seven large niches were occupied not by saints, but, it's thought, by statues of Mars, Venus, the deified Caesar, and the other "astral deities," including the moon and sun, the "sol invictus." (Academics still argue, however, about which gods were most probably worshipped here.)

One of the reasons the Pantheon is so well preserved is the result of it being consecrated as a church in AD 608. (It's still a working church today.) No building, church or not, though, escaped some degree of plundering through the turbulent centuries of Rome's history after the fall of the empire. In 655, for example, the gilded bronze covering the dome was stripped. The Pantheon is also one of the city's important burial places. Its most famous tomb is that of Raphael (between the second and third chapels on the left as you enter). Mass takes place on Sunday and on religious holidays at 10:30; it's open to the public, but you are expected to arrive before the beginning and stay until the end. General access usually resumes at about 11:30.

On weekends and public holidays, you must register in advance (only for the next upcoming weekend or holiday) for a free timed entry slot. Each guest can register up to six people at ⊕ *pantheon. cultura.gov.it.* ⊠ *Piazza della Rotonda, Piazza Navona* ☎ *06/68300230* ⊕ *www. pantheonroma.com* 🎫 *Free; audio guide €8.50.*

Piazza di Pasquino

PLAZA/SQUARE | This tiny piazza takes its name from the figure in the corner, the remnant of an old Roman statue depicting Menelaus. The statue underwent a name change in the 16th century when Pasquino, a cobbler or barber (and part-time satirist), started writing comments around the base. The habit caught on; soon everyone was doing it. The most loquacious of Rome's "talking statues," its lack of arms or face is more than made up for with commentary of any topic of the day. ⊠ *Piazza di Pasquino, Piazza Navona.*

★ Piazza Navona

PLAZA/SQUARE | Always camera-ready, the beautiful baroque plaza known as Piazza Navona has Bernini sculptures, three gorgeous fountains, and a magnificently baroque church (Sant'Agnese in Agone), all built atop the remains of a Roman athletics track. Pieces of the arena are still visible near the adjacent Piazza Sant'Apollinare, and the ancient spirit of entertainment lives on in the buskers and artists who populate the piazza today.

The piazza took on its current look during the 17th century, after Pope Innocent X of the Pamphilj family decided to make over his family palace (now the Brazilian embassy and an ultra-luxe hotel) and the rest of the piazza. Center stage is the Fontana dei Quattro Fiumi, created for Innocent by Bernini in 1651. Bernini's powerful figures of the four rivers represent the longest rivers of the four known continents at the time: the Nile (his head covered because the source was unknown); the Ganges; the Danube; and the Plata (the length of the Amazon was then unknown). Popular legend has it that the figure of the Plata—the figure closest to Sant'Agnese in Agone—raises his hand before his eyes because he can't bear to look upon the church's "inferior" facade designed by Francesco Borromini, Bernini's rival.

If you want a café with one of the most beautiful, if pricey, views in Rome, grab a seat at Piazza Navona. Just be aware that all the restaurants here are heavily geared toward tourists, so while it's a beautiful place for a coffee, you can find cheaper, more authentic, and far better meals elsewhere. ⊠ *Piazza Navona.*

★ San Luigi dei Francesi

CHURCH | A pilgrimage spot for art lovers, San Luigi's Contarelli Chapel (the fifth and last chapel on the left, toward the main altar) is adorned with three stunningly dramatic works by Caravaggio (1571–1610), the baroque master of the heightened approach to light and dark. They were commissioned for the tomb of Mattheiu Cointerel in one of Rome's French churches (San Luigi is St. Louis, patron saint of France). The inevitable coin machine will light up his *Calling of Saint Matthew, Saint Matthew and the Angel,* and *Martyrdom of Saint Matthew* (seen from left to right), and Caravaggio's mastery of light takes it from there. When painted, they caused considerable consternation among the clergy of San Luigi, who thought the artist's dramatically realistic approach was scandalously disrespectful. A first version of the altarpiece was rejected; the priests were not particularly happy with the other two, either. Time has fully vindicated Caravaggio's patron, Cardinal Francesco del Monte, who secured the commission for these works and stoutly defended them. ⊠ *Piazza di San Luigi dei Francesi, Piazza Navona* ☎ *06/688271* ⊕ *www.saintlouis-rome.net.*

Sant'Agnese in Agone

CHURCH | The quintessence of baroque architecture, this church has a facade that is a wonderfully rich mélange of bell towers, concave spaces, and dovetailed stone and marble. It's the creation of Francesco Borromini (1599–1667), a contemporary and rival of Bernini. Next to his new Pamphilj family palace, Pope Innocent X had the adjacent chapel expanded into this full-fledged church. The work was first assigned to the architect Rainaldi. However, Donna Olimpia, the pope's famously domineering sister-in-law, became increasingly impatient with how the work was going and brought in Borromini, whose wonderful concave entrance has the magical effect of making the dome appear much larger than it actually is. The name of this church comes from the Greek *agones,* the source of the word *navona* and a reference to the agonistic competitions held here in Roman times. The saint associated with the church is Agnes, who was martyred here in the piazza's forerunner, the Stadium of Domitian. As she was stripped nude before the crowd, her hair miraculously grew to maintain her modesty before she was killed. The interior is a marvel of modular baroque space and is ornamented by giant marble reliefs sculpted by Raggi and Ferrata. ⊠ *Via di Santa Maria dell'Anima, 30/A, Piazza Navona* ☎ *06/68192134* ⊕ *www. santagneseinagone.org* ⊗ *Closed Mon.* Ⓜ *Bus Nos. 87, 40, and 64.*

Sant'Agostino

CHURCH | Caravaggio's celebrated *Madonna of the Pilgrims*—which scandalized all of Rome for depicting a kneeling pilgrim all too realistically for the era's tastes, with dirt on the soles of his feet, and the Madonna standing in a less-than-majestic pose in a dilapidated doorway—is in the first chapel on the left. Pause at the third column on the left of the nave to admire Raphael's blue-robed *Isaiah,* said to be inspired by Michelangelo's prophets on the Sistine ceiling (Raphael, with the help of Bramante, had taken the odd peek at the master's original against strict orders of secrecy). Directly below is Sansovino's Leonardo-influenced sculpture, *St. Anne and the Madonna with Child.* As you leave, in a niche just inside the door, is

the sculpted *Madonna and Child,* known to the Romans as the "Madonna del Parto" (of Childbirth) and piled high with ex-voto offerings giving thanks for the safe deliveries of children. The artist is Jacopo Tatti, also sometimes confusingly known as Sansovino after his master. ⊠ *Piazza Sant'Agostino, Piazza Navona* ☎ *06/68801962.*

Santa Maria della Pace

CHURCH | In 1656, Pietro da Cortona (1596–1669) was commissioned by Pope Alexander VII to enlarge the tiny Piazza della Pace in front of the 15th-century church of Santa Maria, to accommodate the carriages of its wealthy parishioners. His architectural solution was to design a new church facade complete with semicircular portico, demolish a few buildings here and there to create a more spacious approach to the church, add arches to give architectural unity to the piazza, and then complete it with a series of bijou-size palaces. The result was one of Rome's most delightful little architectural set pieces. Within are several great Renaissance treasures. Raphael's fresco above the first altar on your right depicts the *Four Sibyls*—almost exact replicas of Michelangelo's, if more relaxed. The fine decorations of the Cesi Chapel, second on the right, were designed in the mid-16th century by Sangallo. Opposite is Peruzzi's wonderful fresco of the *Madonna and Child.* Meanwhile, the octagon below the dome is something of an art gallery in itself, with works by Cavalliere Arpino, Orazio Gentileschi, and others as Cozzo's *Eternity* fills the lantern above. Behind the church is its cloister, designed by Bramante (architect of St. Peter's) as the very first expression of High Renaissance style in Rome. The cloister has an exhibition space and a lovely coffee bar on the upper level. ⊠ *Via Arco della Pace 5, Piazza Navona* ☎ *06/68804038* ⊗ *Closed Thurs., Fri., Sun., and Tues.* Ⓜ *Bus Nos. 87, 40, and 64.*

Santa Maria in Vallicella/Chiesa Nuova

CHURCH | This church, sometimes known as Chiesa Nuova (New Church), was built toward the end of the 16th century at the urging of Philip Neri and, like Il Gesù, is a product of the fervor of the Counter-Reformation. It has a sturdy baroque interior, all white and gold, with ceiling frescoes by Pietro da Cortona depicting a miracle reputed to have occurred during the church's construction: the Virgin and strong-armed angels hold up the broken roof to prevent it from crashing down upon the congregation below. The church is most famous for its three magnificent altarpieces by Rubens. ⊠ *Piazza della Chiesa Nuova, Corso Vittorio Emanuele II, Piazza Navona* ☎ *06/6875289* ⊕ *www.vallicella.org.*

★ **Santa Maria sopra Minerva**

CHURCH | The name of the church reveals that it was built *sopra* (over) the ruins of a temple of Minerva, the ancient goddess of wisdom. Erected in 1280 by Dominicans along severe Italian Gothic lines, it has undergone a number of more or less happy restorations to the interior. Certainly, as the city's major Gothic church, it provides a refreshing contrast to baroque flamboyance. Have a €1 coin handy to illuminate the Cappella Carafa in the right transept, where Filippino Lippi's (1457–1504) glowing frescoes are well worth the small investment, opening up the deepest azure expanse of sky where musical angels hover around the Virgin. Under the main altar is the tomb of St. Catherine of Siena, one of Italy's patron saints. Left of the altar you'll find Michelangelo's *Risen Christ* and the tomb of the gentle artist Fra Angelico. Bernini's unusual and little-known monument to the Blessed Maria Raggi is on the fifth pier of the left-hand aisle. In front of the church, Bernini's *Elephant and Obelisk* is perhaps the city's most charming sculpture. An inscription on the base references the church's ancient patroness, reading something to the effect that it takes a strong mind to sustain solid wisdom. ⊠ *Piazza della Minerva, Piazza Navona* ☎ *06/792257* ⊕ *www.santamariasopraminerva.it.*

Sant'Ivo alla Sapienza

CHURCH | The main facade of this eccentric baroque church, probably Borromini's best, is on the stately courtyard of an austere building that once housed Rome's university. Sant'Ivo has what must surely be one of the most delightful "domes" in all of Rome—a dizzying spiral said to have been inspired by a bee's stinger. The apian symbol is a reminder that Borromini built the church on commission from the Barberini pope Urban VIII (a swarm of bees figure on the Barberini family crest), although it was completed by Alexander VII. The interior, open only for three hours on Sunday morning, is worth a look, especially if you share Borromini's taste for complex mathematical architectural idiosyncrasies. "I didn't take up architecture solely to be a copyist," he once said. Sant'Ivo is certainly the proof. ⊠ *Corso del Rinascimento 40, Piazza Navona* ☎ *06/6864987* ⊘ *Closed Mon.–Sat. and Aug.*

🍴 Restaurants

The narrow, cobblestone *vicoli* (alleys) around Piazza Navona are home to a vast range of dining options. You'll find everything from casual pizzerie, where hurried waiters scribble your bill on a paper tablecloth, to several of the city's most revered gourmet temples, featuring star chefs and inventive cuisine, with decidedly higher bills placed on the finest high-thread-count damask tablecloths. The area around the Pantheon is full of classic, old-school trattorias and mid-range to upscale restaurants, including many with tables set in gorgeous piazze that could double as opera sets. You'll feel the grandeur of Rome here, sometimes with prices to match.

★ Armando al Pantheon

$$ | ROMAN | In the shadow of the Pantheon, this small family-run trattoria, open since 1961, delights tourists and locals alike. There's an air of authenticity to the Roman staples here, and the quality of the ingredients and the cooking mean booking ahead is a must. **Known for:** good wine list; spaghetti *alla gricia* (with guanciale, pecorino cheese, and black pepper); beautifully executed traditional Roman cooking. ⑤ *Average main: €16* ✉ *Salita dei Crescenzi 31, Piazza Navona* ☎ *06/68803034* ⊕ *www.armandoalpantheon.it* ⊘ *Closed Sun. and Aug.*

Birreria Peroni

$ | NORTHERN ITALIAN | With its long wooden tables, hard-back booths, and free-flowing beer, this casual restaurant in a 16th-century palazzo might seem more like a Munich beer hall than a popular Roman hangout (around since 1906). But remember that in the far northern reaches of Italy, locals speak as much German as they do Italian, and that's where Birreria Peroni draws its inspiration. **Known for:** convivial atmosphere; great location close to the Trevi Fountain; hearty German fare. ⑤ *Average main: €10* ✉ *Via di San Marcello 19, Piazza Navona* ☎ *06/6795310* ⊕ *www.anticabirreriaperoni.it* ⊘ *Closed Sun. and 1 wk in Aug.*

★ Cul de Sac

$$ | WINE BAR | This popular wine bar near Piazza Navona is among the city's oldest and offers a book-length selection of wines from Italy, France, the Americas, and elsewhere. Offering great value and pleasant service a stone's throw from Piazza Navona, it's open all afternoon, making it a lovely spot for a late lunch or an early dinner when most restaurants aren't open yet. **Known for:** relaxed atmosphere and outside tables; eclectic Italian and Mediterranean fare; great wine list (and wine bottle–lined interior). ⑤ *Average main: €14* ✉ *Piazza di Pasquino 73, Piazza Navona* ☎ *06/68801094* ⊕ *www.enotecaculdesacroma.it.*

Da Francesco

$ | ROMAN | FAMILY | For good, hearty, Roman cuisine in an area filled with mediocre touristy restaurants, head to this authentic trattoria that's been on the scene since the late 1950s. Food-wise, stick to the classics: start off with a mixed salumi plate (with Parma ham and buffalo mozzarella cheese), then hit the *primi* (first course)—the gricia and the *amatriciana* (the famous Roman pasta with tomato sauce, guanciale, and pecorino cheese) are usually the standouts. **Known for:** outside tables in summer; traditional Roman cooking; informal atmosphere. ⑤ *Average main: €13* ✉ *Piazza del Fico 29, Piazza Navona* ☎ *06/6864009* ⊕ *www.dafrancesco.it.*

Enoteca Corsi

$ | ITALIAN | Very convenient for a good-value lunch in the *centro storico* (historic center), this trattoria is undeniably old-school—it's been renovated, but you wouldn't know it—and that's all part of the charm. It's packed at lunch with a mix of civil servants from the nearby government offices, construction workers, and in-the-know tourists, when a few specials—classic pastas, a delicious octopus salad, and some *secondi* (second course) like roast veal with peas—are offered. **Known for:** brusque but friendly service; Roman specialities; casual atmosphere. ⑤ *Average main: €12* ✉ *Via del Gesù 88, Piazza Navona* ☎ *06/6790821* ⊕ *www.enotecacorsi.com* ⊘ *Closed Sun., and 3 wks in Aug. No dinner Sat. and Mon.*

★ Il Convivio Troiani

$$$$ | MODERN ITALIAN | In a tiny, nondescript alley north of Piazza Navona, the three Troiani brothers—Angèlo in the kitchen, and brothers Giuseppe and Massimo presiding over the dining room and wine cellar—have been quietly redefining the experience of Italian *alta cucina* (haute cuisine) since 1990 at this well-regarded establishment. Service is attentive without being overbearing, and the wine list

An alimentari is a specialty food shop. Visit one to stock up on lunch or picnic fixings; some will give you samples to taste.

is exceptional. **Known for:** amazing wine cellar and a great sommelier; inventive modern Italian cooking with exotic touches; fine dining in elegant surroundings. ⑤ *Average main: €38* ⊠ *Vicolo dei Soldati 31, Piazza Navona* ☎ *06/6869432* ⊕ *www. ilconviviotroiani.it* ⊗ *Closed Sun., and 1 wk in Aug. No lunch.*

La Campana
$$ | ITALIAN | FAMILY | Thought to be the oldest restaurant in Rome (a document dates it back to 1518), La Campana remains a favorite of both locals and visitors. It's well-liked for its honest Roman cuisine and its old-school, slightly upmarket feel—think white tablecloths and unflappable waiters in black tie who have been there since the beginning of time. **Known for:** traditional Roman cooking; fantastic oxtail stew; old-school elegance. ⑤ *Average main: €18* ⊠ *Vicolo della Campana 18, Piazza Navona* ☎ *06/6875273, 347/1098632* ⊗ *Closed Mon.* Ⓜ *Spagna.*

La Ciambella
$$ | ITALIAN | A large glass wall to the kitchen and massive skylight in the dining room hint at the contemporary leanings of this restaurant built atop the ruins of the Baths of Agrippa behind the Pantheon. The emphasis here is on high-quality ingredients and classic Italian culinary traditions interpreted for modern diners. **Known for:** great location near the Pantheon; sophisticated Italian cuisine; elegant setting. ⑤ *Average main: €17* ⊠ *Via dell'Arco della Ciambella 20, Piazza Navona* ☎ *06/6832930* ⊕ *www.la-ciambella.it* ⊗ *Closed Mon.*

La Fraschetta di Castel Sant'Angelo
$ | ROMAN | A *fraschetta* is the name given to one of the casual, boisterous countryside spots just outside Rome, where the menu focuses on *porchetta*, the Italian version of roast pork. This is a city-styled version of the same, and the atmosphere is typical, with waiters yelling across the room and frequently breaking into song. **Known for:** great value; excellent porchetta, of course; jovial

informal atmosphere. $ *Average main: €12* ✉ *Via del Banco di Santo Spirito 20, Piazza Navona* ☎ *06/68307661* ⊕ *www. facebook.com/lafraschettadicastelsantangelo* ⊗ *Closed Sun. No lunch Aug.*

La Montecarlo

$ | PIZZA | FAMILY | The crusts on the pizza at this casual, perennially popular spot just off the Piazza Navona are super-thin and charred around the edges a little— the sign of a good wood-burning oven. This is one of a few pizzerie open for both lunch and dinner, and it's busy day and night. **Known for:** outside tables; great value; thin-crust pizza. $ *Average main: €12* ✉ *Vicolo Savelli 13, Piazza Navona* ☎ *06/6861877* ⊕ *www.lamontecarlo.it* ⊗ *Closed Mon., and 3 wks in Aug.*

La Rosetta

$$$$ | SEAFOOD | Chef-owner Massimo Riccioli may have taken the nets and fishing gear off the walls of the trattoria he inherited from his parents, but this is still widely known as *the* place to go in Rome for first-rate seafood. The experience here includes friendly staff and undeniably high-quality fish, but be prepared for simple preparations and high prices. **Known for:** first-rate fish and seafood; outside seating; elegant restaurant (jackets required for men). $ *Average main: €50* ✉ *Via della Rosetta 9, Piazza Navona* ☎ *06/6861002* ⊕ *www.larosetta.com* ⊗ *No lunch Mon., closed 2 wks in Aug.* ⚱ *Jacket required.*

Osteria dell'Ingegno

$$ | MODERN ITALIAN | This casual, trendy place is a great spot to enjoy a glass of wine or a gourmet meal in an ancient piazza in the city center, but the modern interior—vibrant with colorful paintings by local artists—brings you back to the present day. The simple but innovative menu includes dishes like Roman artichokes with *baccalà* (salt cod), beef *tagliata* (sliced grilled steak) with a red-wine reduction, and a perfectly cooked duck breast with red fruit sauce. **Known for:** outdoor seating with views

of ancient ruins; a great spot both for aperitifs and/or a meal; beautiful location on a pedestrian square. $ *Average main: €22* ✉ *Piazza di Pietra 45, Piazza Navona* ☎ *06/6780662* ⊕ *www.osteriadellingegno.com* ⊗ *Closed Mon.*

☕ Coffee and Quick Bites

Bar del Fico

$ | ITALIAN | FAMILY | Everyone in Rome knows Bar del Fico, located right behind Piazza Navona, so if you're looking to hang out with the locals, this is the place to come for a drink or something to eat at any time of day or night. In the mornings, chess players sit at tables outside playing under the shade of the fig tree that gives the bar its name. **Known for:** buzzy atmosphere; Italian-style brunch; outside tables in a pretty square. $ *Average main: €10* ✉ *Piazza del Fico 26, Piazza Navona* ☎ *06/68891373* ⊕ *www. bardelfico.com.*

Cremeria Monteforte

$ | ICE CREAM | Immediately beside the Pantheon is this gelateria, which is well known for its flavors, like mango, pistachio, and chocolate chip. The chocolate *sorbetto*—an icier version of gelato, made without the dairy—is also excellent, and even better with a dollop of whipped cream on top. **Known for:** location right next to the Pantheon; large scoops for a fair price; artisan gelato. $ *Average main: €3* ✉ *Via della Rotonda 22, Piazza Navona* ☎ *06/6867720* ⊗ *Closed Mon. and mid-Dec.–mid-Jan.*

★ Gelateria Del Teatro

$ | ICE CREAM | FAMILY | In a window next to the entrance of this renowned gelateria, you can see the fresh fruit being used in the laboratory to create the flavors of the day, which highlight the best of Italy, from Amalfi lemons to hazelnuts from Alba. In addition to traditional flavors, they serve a few interesting combinations, like raspberry and sage or white chocolate with basil. **Known for:** charming location on a cobblestone street; seasonal, all natural ingredients; sublime gelato. $ *Average main: €3 ✉ Via dei Coronari 65/66, Piazza Navona ☎ 06/45474880 ⊕ www.gelateriadelteatro.it.*

Fiocco di Neve

$ | ICE CREAM | FAMILY | The gelato is certainly excellent—the chocolate chip and After Eight (mint chocolate chip) flavors are delicious—but this small spot is also known for its Affogato di Zabaione (hot espresso poured over a small scoop of creamy marsala wine ice cream). Look for intriguing seasonal gelato flavors like pear-cinnamon. **Known for:** interesting seasonal flavors; great location near the Pantheon; delicious gelato. $ *Average main: €4 ✉ Via del Pantheon 51, Piazza Navona ☎ 06/96006762.*

★ Giolitti

$ | ICE CREAM | FAMILY | Open since 1900, Giolitti near the Pantheon is Rome's old-school gelateria par excellence. Pay in advance at the register by the door and take your receipt to the counter, where you can choose from dozens of flavors, including chocolate, cinnamon, and pistachio. **Known for:** wide selection of flavors; old-school setting; excellent gelato. $ *Average main: €3 ✉ Via degli Uffici del Vicario 40, Piazza Navona ☎ 06/6991243 ⊕ www.giolitti.it.*

Sant'Eustachio il Caffè

$ | CAFÉ | Frequented by tourists and government officials from the nearby Senate alike, this café is considered by many to make Rome's best coffee. Take it at the counter Roman-style: servers are hidden behind a huge espresso machine, where they vigorously mix the sugar and coffee to protect their "secret method" for the perfectly prepared cup (if you want your caffè without sugar here, ask for it *senza zucchero*). **Known for:** 1930s interior; old-school Roman coffee bar vibe; *gran caffè* (large sugared espresso). $ *Average main: €2 ✉ Piazza Sant'Eustachio 82, Piazza Navona ☎ 06/68802048 ⊕ caffe-santeustachio.com.*

Tazza d'Oro

$ | CAFÉ | On the east corner of the piazza in front of the Pantheon, the Tazza d'Oro coffee bar is the place for serious coffee drinkers—there are no tables, no frills. Indulge in their *granita di caffè con panna* (coffee ice with whipped cream). **Known for:** coffee roasted on-site; gleaming retro interior; granita di caffè con panna. $ *Average main: €3 ✉ Via degli Orfani 86, Piazza Navona ☎ 06/6789792 ⊕ www.tazzadorocoffeeshop.com ▭ No credit cards.*

Tre Scalini

$ | ICE CREAM | The sidewalk tables of the caffè, along with its restaurant annex, offer a grandstand view of all the action of the Piazza Navona. This is the place that invented the *tartufo*, a luscious chocolate ice-cream specialty. **Known for:** decadent ice cream covered with a chocolate shell and whipped cream; sticker shock prices for table service; tables on the square with unmatched views of the fountain. $ *Average main: €8 ✉ Piazza Navona 30, Piazza Navona ☎ 06/6879148 ⊕ www.ristorante-3scalini.com.*

Hotels

Thanks to its baroque palazzi, Bernini fountains, and outdoor caffè, Piazza Navona is one of Rome's most popular squares. The nearby Pantheon area, equally as beautiful but not as lively, offers great restaurants and shops. Hotels in this area offer postcard views of Rome and personalized service.

Albergo del Sole al Pantheon

$$$ | HOTEL | The granddaddy of Roman hotels and one of the oldest in the world—the doors first opened in 1467—this charming hotel is adjacent to the Pantheon and right in the middle of the lovely Piazza della Rotonda. **Pros:** complimentary newspaper delivered to your room daily; rich breakfast buffet; fabulous location. **Cons:** despite the double-glazed windows, street noise can be an issue;

some rooms in need of updating; rooms are a bit small. $ *Rooms from: €220* ✉ *Piazza della Rotonda 63, Piazza Navona* ☎ *06/6780441* ⊕ *www.hotelsolealpantheon.com* ⊅ *27 rooms* ⦿| *Free Breakfast.*

Albergo Santa Chiara
$$$ | HOTEL | If you're looking for a good location and top-notch service at great rates—not to mention comfortable beds and a quiet stay—look no further than this historic hotel, run by the same family for some 200 years. **Pros:** great location near the Pantheon; lovely sitting area in front, overlooking the piazza; free Wi-Fi. **Cons:** street-side rooms can be noisy; Wi-Fi can be slow; some rooms are on the small side and need updating. $ *Rooms from: €210* ✉ *Via Santa Chiara 21, Piazza Navona* ☎ *06/6872979* ⊕ *www.albergosantachiara.com* ⊅ *96 rooms* ⦿| *Free Breakfast.*

G-Rough Hotel
$$$$ | HOTEL | This consciously cool hotel is strategically located around the corner from the lively Piazza Navona, inside a 17th-century palazzo. **Pros:** organic continental breakfast; free Wi-Fi; free soft minibar that includes soda, juice, and water. **Cons:** no real reception desk area; hip decor might be too overdone for some; rooms facing Piazza Pasquino can be noisy. $ *Rooms from: €350* ✉ *Piazza Pasquino 69, Piazza Navona* ☎ *06/68801085* ⊕ *www.g-rough.com* ⊅ *10 rooms* ⦿| *Free Breakfast.*

Hotel Abruzzi
$$$ | HOTEL | This friendly, comfortable, family-run hotel has magnificent views of the Pantheon at relatively gentle rates, given the location. **Pros:** views of the Pantheon; sizable bathrooms; the piazza is a hot spot. **Cons:** about a 15-minute walk from the Spagna Metro stop; elevator doesn't go to ground floor; area can be somewhat noisy. $ *Rooms from: €245* ✉ *Piazza della Rotonda 69, Piazza Navona* ☎ *06/97841351* ⊕ *www.hotelabruzzi.it* ⊅ *26 rooms* ⦿| *Free Breakfast* Ⓜ *Spagna.*

Hotel Genio
$$ | HOTEL | Just off one of Rome's most beautiful piazzas—Piazza Navona—this pleasant hotel has a lovely rooftop terrace perfect for enjoying a cappuccino or a glass of wine while taking in the view. **Pros:** breakfast buffet is abundant; spacious, elegant bathrooms; free Wi-Fi. **Cons:** beds can be too firm for some; spotty Internet; rooms facing the street can be noisy. $ *Rooms from: €160* ✉ *Via Giuseppe Zanardelli 28, Piazza Navona* ☎ *06/6833781* ⊕ *www.hotelgenioroma.it* ⊅ *60 rooms* ⦿| *Free Breakfast.*

Hotel Pantheon
$$$ | HOTEL | On a quiet street around the corner from the Pantheon, this little hotel is warm and inviting, with trompe-l'oeil frescoes, a Liberty-style staircase, and terra-cotta floors. **Pros:** proximity to the Pantheon; big, clean bathrooms; comfortable beds. **Cons:** credit-card machine isn't always reliable; decor could use some restyling; some rooms are on the small side. $ *Rooms from: €280* ✉ *Via dei Pastini 131, Piazza Navona* ☎ *06/6787746* ⊕ *www.hotelpantheon.com* ⊅ *13 rooms* ⦿| *Free Breakfast.*

9 Hotel Cesàri
$$$ | HOTEL | On a pedestrian-only street near the Pantheon, this lovely little hotel has an air of warmth and serenity, and a rooftop bar with great views. **Pros:** prime location; free Wi-Fi throughout the hotel; beautiful rooftop bar. **Cons:** the area can be a bit noisy; rooftop bar not open in winter; some rooms need a little updating. $ *Rooms from: €270* ✉ *Via di Pietra 89/a, Piazza Navona* ☎ *06/6749701* ⊕ *www.9-hotel-cesari-rome.it* ⊅ *51 rooms* ⦿| *Free Breakfast* Ⓜ *Barberini.*

The Pantheon Iconic Rome Hotel, Autograph Collection
$$$ | HOTEL | A member of Marriott's Autograph Collection, this boutique hotel is a sleek retreat in the center of the action. **Pros:** modern design and amenities; Marriott Bonvoy members

can use and redeem points; restaurant by one of the city's best chefs. **Cons:** design might be considered a bit cold and corporate; no spa or gym; some rooms lack external views. $ *Rooms from: €250 ⊠ Via di Santa Chiara 4A, Piazza Navona ☎ 06/87807070 ⊕ www. thepantheonhotel.com ↻ 79 rooms* ⊙| *No Meals.*

Nightlife

Piazza Navona is where you can find just about anything, from sophisticated caffè life and flirty cocktail bars to dance clubs and outdoor chess games. Expect to be easily understood, as there is a high concentration of English-speaking establishments.

BARS

★ Bar del Fico

CAFÉS | Bar del Fico looks a lot different from the days of yore when raucous outdoor chess matches accompanied cocktails at the once-bare-bones local hangout. Though the chess tables are still sitting in the shade of the historic fig tree, Bar del Fico is now a happening bar, restaurant, evening cocktail spot, and late-night hangout. ⊠ *Piazza del Fico 26, Piazza Navona ☎ 06/68891373 ⊕ www. bardelfico.com/en/bar.*

Enoteca al Parlamento Achilli

WINE BARS | The proximity of this traditional *enoteca* (wine bar) to Montecitorio, the Italian Parliament building, makes it a favorite with journalists and politicos, who often stop in for a glass of wine after work. But it's the tantalizing smell of truffles from the snack counter, where a sommelier waits to organize your tasting, that will probably lure you inside. There's also a celebrated restaurant where you can book a table and enjoy a parade of elegant Italian plates. Don't forget to check out their wine shop to take home a bottle of your favorite wine. ⊠ *Via dei Prefetti 15, Piazza Navona ☎ 06/6873446 ⊕ www.achilli.restaurant ↻ Closed Sun.*

Jerry Thomas Project

COCKTAIL LOUNGES | One of just a handful of hidden bars in Rome, this intimate bar looks like a Prohibition-era haunt and serves the kind of classic cocktails you find in New York speakeasies. It's seating room only, so reservations must be made in advance. Upon booking, you'll receive a password via email. Serious cocktail aficionados can also purchase specialty bitters and mixology tools at the Emporium across the alley from the drinks spot. ⊠ *Vicolo Cellini 30, Piazza Navona ☎ 370/1146287 ⊕ www.thejerrythomasproject.it ↻ Closed Mon. and Tues.*

Shari Vari

DANCE CLUBS | Shari Vari has reinvented itself as a sumptuous supper club, lounge, and disco. Its bistro and champagnerie are stocked with delicious delicacies and sought-after vintages. Its nightclub covers every genre of music from electronic and underground, to hip-hop, lounge, and international. ⊠ *Via di Torre Argentina 78, Piazza Navona ☎ 06/68806936 ⊕ www.sharivari.it.*

Terrace Bar of the Hotel Raphaël

CAFÉS | Want to sneak a peek at Rome's rooftops? Head to the small terrace bar at the Hotel Raphaël, noted for its bird's-eye view of the campaniles and palazzi of Piazza Navona. This is one of Rome's most romantic spots, so booking a table is advised. ⊠ *Hotel Raphaël, Largo Febo 2, Piazza Navona ☎ 06/682831 ⊕ www. raphaelhotel.com.*

Vinoteca Novecento

WINE BARS | A lovely, tiny enoteca with a very old-fashioned vibe, Vinoteca Novecento has a seemingly unlimited selection of wines, proseccos, vini santi, and grappe, along with salami-and-cheese tasting menus. Inside is standing-room only; in good weather, sit outside on one of the oak barriques on a quiet cobblestone street leading to one of Rome's prettiest small squares. ⊠ *Piazza delle Coppelle 47, Piazza Navona ☎ 06/6833078.*

La Grande Bellezza Rooftop at Eitch Borromini

COCKTAIL LOUNGES | Rome has no shortage of gorgeous rooftop terrace bars, but this one atop the Eitch Borromini hotel is exceptional. Nestled directly among cupolas and bell towers, the seats along the edge are poised atop Piazza Navona, looking down on Bernini's famed fountain. The chic white couches are almost always filled with well-heeled Romans, making sunset reservations essential. ⊠ *Eitch Borromini, Via di Santa Maria dell'Anima, 30, Piazza Navona* ☎ *06/68215459* ⊕ *www.eitchborromini. com* ⊗ *Closed Nov.–Mar.*

 # Performing Arts

FILM

Nuovo Olimpia

FILM | Just off Rome's Via del Corso in the center of the city, two-screen Nuovo Olimpia is *the* cinema for Rome's international community, showing new-release films in original language with Italian subtitles. ⊠ *Via in Lucina 16/b, Piazza Navona* ☎ *06/88801283* ⊕ *www. circuitocinema.com.*

THEATER

English Theatre of Rome

THEATER | The oldest English-language theater group in town, English Theatre of Rome has a repertoire of original and celebrated plays. Performances are usually held at Teatro Arciliuto. ⊠ *Piazza Montevecchio 5, Piazza Navona* ☎ *346/3612209* ⊕ *www. rometheatre.com* ⊗ *Closed Sun.–Tues.*

 # Shopping

The area around Piazza Navona is filled with vintage boutiques and tiny artisan shops; unique gifts such as delicate Florentine stationery or hand-blown Murano glass can be found here. Near the Pantheon, you'll also find some classic Italian toys like wooden Pinocchios and cuckoo clocks.

ANTIQUES

Galleria Biagiarelli

ANTIQUES & COLLECTIBLES | Rome's leading antiques dealer of 18th- and 19th-century Russian icons and religious artifacts resides in a superb setting in the former chapel of the Pre-Renaissance Palazzo Capranica. The shop also features an exquisite array of English watercolors, Eastern European antique china figurines, and a vast collection of Soviet-era artwork. ⊠ *Piazza Capranica 97, Piazza Navona* ☎ *06/69940728* ⊕ *biagiarelli.com* ⊗ *Closed Sun. and Mon.*

BEAUTY

Antica Erboristeria Romana

OTHER HEALTH & BEAUTY | Complete with hand-labeled wooden drawers holding more than 200 varieties of herbs, flowers, and tinctures, Antica Erboristeria Romana has maintained its old-world apothecary feel (it's the oldest shop of its kind in Rome, dating back to 1752). The shop stocks an impressive array of teas and herbal infusions, more than 700 essential oils, bud derivatives, and powdered extracts. ⊠ *Via Torre Argentina 15, Piazza Navona* ☎ *06/6879493* ⊕ *www.anticaerboristeriaromana.it.*

CERAMICS AND DECORATIVE ARTS

★ **IN.OR. dal 1952**

CRAFTS | For more than 50 years, IN.OR. dal 1952 has served as a trusty friend for Romans in desperate need of an exclusive wedding gift or those oh-so-perfect china place settings for a fancy Sunday dinner. Entrance is via a secluded 15th-century courtyard and up a flight of stairs. The store specializes in work handcrafted by the silversmiths of Pampaloni and Bastianelli in Florence. ⊠ *Via della Stelletta 23, Piazza Navona* ☎ *06/6878579* ⊕ *www.inor.it* ⊗ *Closed Sun.*

Murano Più

GLASSWARE | If you can't make it to Venice during your visit to the "Bel Paese," your next best option is to visit Murano Più for famous handblown Venetian glass pieces, including Murano jewelry (necklaces and pendants), tableware, vases, and extravagant chandeliers. Each individual piece is handcrafted from the furnaces of master glassblowers using ancient techniques kept alive by the island's artisans since 1291. ⊠ *Corso Rinascimento 53/55, Piazza Navona* ☎ *06/68808038* ⊕ *www.murano-roma.com/en.*

CLOTHING

Davide Cenci

MIXED CLOTHING | Thanks to immaculate tailoring and custom-designed clothing, Davide Cenci is an Italian fashion powerhouse. The store features high-quality men's and women's clothing for every occasion. Cenci's clothiers will tailor most anything to fit your body like a glove and have it delivered to your hotel within three days. The label is famous for its opulent cashmere, sailing sportswear, and trench coats, and you will appreciate their customer service and attention to detail. ⊠ *Via Campo Marzio 1–7, Piazza Navona* ☎ *06/6990681* ⊕ *www.davidecenci.com* ⊗ *Closed Sun. and Mon. morning.*

Le Tartarughe

WOMEN'S CLOTHING | A familiar face on the catwalks of Rome's fashion shows, designer Susanna Liso, a Rome native, adds suggestive elements of playful experimentation to her haute couture and ready-to-wear lines, which are much loved by Rome's aristocracy and intelligentsia. With intense, enveloping designs, she mixes raw silks or cashmere and fine merino wool together to form captivating garments that combine seduction and linear form. ⊠ *Via Piè di Marmo 17, Piazza Navona* ☎ *06/6792240* ⊗ *Closed Sun.*

Morgana

WOMEN'S CLOTHING | When strolling down Via del Governo Vecchio, a street popular for funky and edgy clothing boutiques, you can't help but stop and stare inside this shop's windows where the family-run business displays some of their best hippie-chick and bridal-chic gowns. Designer Luciana Iannace creates these highly original and highly sought-after clothes and accessories that many of Rome's ladies are desperate to get their hands on. In addition to her own designs, she also sources inventive items from Paris and Florence. ⊠ *Via del Governo Vecchio 27, Piazza Navona* ☎ *06/6879995.*

Replay

MIXED CLOTHING | A typical example of young Italians' passion for American trends, Replay has jeans and T-shirts with American sports teams emblazoned on them—with that little extra Italian kiss that transforms sloppy hip into fashionable casual-chic. Styles range from punk to hip-hop, as well as more traditionally cut jeans. ⊠ *Via della Rotonda 24, Piazza Navona* ☎ *06/68301212* ⊕ *www.replay.it.*

SBU

MEN'S CLOTHING | SBU stands for Strategic Business Unit, a hip menswear fashion label created by the Perfetti brothers in 1993. Just as their last name suggests, the jeans, casual clothing, shoes, and other sportswear sold here are just plain *perfetti*. In a 19th-century former draper's workshop, it's the place where Rome's VIPs buy their soft and supple vintage low-cut Japanese denim. The label also does well among A-listers in Paris, London, and Los Angeles. ⊠ *Via di San Pantaleo 68–69, Piazza Navona* ☎ *06/68802547* ⊕ *www.sbu.it.*

Vestiti Usati Cinzia

MIXED CLOTHING | Vintage-clothes hunters, costume designers, and stylists alike love browsing through the racks at Vestiti Usati Cinzia. The shop is fun and very inviting and stocked with wall-to-wall funky 1960s and '70s apparel and loads of goofy sunglasses. There's definitely no shortage of flower-power bell-bottoms and hippie shirts, embroidered tops, trippy and psychedelic boots, and other awesome accessories that will take you back to the days of peace and love. ✉ *Via del Governo Vecchio 45, Piazza Navona* ☎ *06/6832945.*

FOOD AND WINE

Moriondo e Gariglio

CANDY | Not exactly Willy Wonka (but in the same vein), Moriondo e Gariglio is a chocolate lover's paradise, churning out some of the finest chocolate delicacies in town. The shop dates back to 1850 and adheres strictly to family recipes passed on from generation to generation. Whether you favor marrons glacés or dark-chocolate truffles, you'll delight in choosing from more than 80 delicacies. ✉ *Via Piè di Marmo 21, Piazza Navona* ☎ *06/6990856* ⊕ *www.moriondoegariglio.com.*

HOME DECOR

Society

HOUSEWARES | Have decorator envy? Everything you need for do-it-yourself Italian home couture can be found at Society, the flagship store for Limonta, one of the most prestigious and historic textile brands made in Italy. Centering on the rarest and most sought-after fabrics, their designs give the appearance they come from a different era (the 18th, 19th, and 20th centuries). You'll find everything from plush striped duvet covers and fancy table linens to comfy robes and other clothing perfect for lounging around the house. ✉ *Piazza di Pasquino 4, Piazza Navona* ☎ *06/6832480* ⊕ *www.societylimonta.com* ☉ *Closed Sun. and Mon.*

Tebro

OTHER SPECIALTY STORE | First opened in 1867 and listed with the Associazione Negozi Storici di Roma (Association of Historic Shops of Rome), Tebro is a classic Roman department store that epitomizes quality. It specializes in household linens and sleepwear, and you can even find those 100-percent cotton, Italian waffle-weave bath sheets that are synonymous with Italian hotels. ✉ *Via dei Prefetti 48, Piazza Navona* ☎ *06/6873441* ⊕ *www.tebro.it.*

JEWELRY

Massimo Maria Melis

JEWELRY & WATCHES | Drawing heavily on ancient Roman and Etruscan designs, Massimo Maria Melis jewelry will carry you back in time. Working with 21-carat gold, he often incorporates antique coins in many of his exquisite bracelets and necklaces. Some of his pieces are done with an ancient technique, much-loved by the Etruscans, in which tiny gold droplets are fused together to create intricately patterned designs. ✉ *Via dell'Orso 57, Piazza Navona* ☎ *06/6869188* ⊕ *www.massimomariamelis.com* ☉ *Closed Sun.*

Quattrocolo

JEWELRY & WATCHES | This historic shop dating to 1938 showcases exquisite antique micro-mosaic jewelry painstakingly crafted in the style perfected by the masters at the Vatican mosaic studio. You'll also find 18th- and 19th-century cameos and beautiful engraved stones as well as contemporary jewelry handmade in the studio. The small works were beloved by cosmopolitan clientele of the Grand Tour age and offer modern-day shoppers a taste of yesteryear's grandeur. ✉ *Via della Scrofa 48, Piazza Navona* ☎ *06/68801367* ⊕ *www.quattrocolo.com* ☉ *Closed Sun. and Mon.*

SHOES AND ACCESSORIES

Superga

SHOES | In business for more than 100 years, Superga sells those timeless sneakers that every Italian wears at some point, in classic white or a rainbow of colors. Their 2750 model has been worn by everyone from Kelly Brook to the Duchess of Cambridge. If you are a sneakerhead stuck on Converse, give these Italian brethren a look. ✉ *Via delle Vite 86, Piazza di Spagna* ☎ *06/6787654* ⊕ *www.superga.com* Ⓜ *Spagna.*

STATIONERY
★ Cartoleria Pantheon dal 1910

STATIONERY | Instead of sending a post-card home, head to the simply sumptuous Cartoleria Pantheon dal 1910 for fine handmade paper to write that special letter. In addition to simple, stock paper and sheets of handcrafted Amalfi paper, there are hand-bound leather journals in an extraordinary array of colors and sizes. The store has two locations in the neighborhood. ⊠ *Via della Maddalena 41, Piazza Navona* ☎ *06/6795633* ⊕ *www.cartoleriapantheon.it.*

Manufactus

OTHER SPECIALTY STORE | One of Rome's preferred shops for those who appreciate exquisite writing materials, particularly handbound leather journals. They also carry a fine selection of wax seals, presses for paper embossing, Venetian glass pens, and ink stamps. There are two other locations on Via della Rotonda and Piazza Navona. ⊠ *Via del Pantheon 50, Piazza Navona* ☎ *06/6875313.*

TOYS
Al Sogno

TOYS | FAMILY | If you're looking for quality toys that encourage imaginative play and learning, look no further than Al Sogno. With an emphasis on the artistic as well as the multisensory, the shop has a selection of toys that are both discerning and individual, making them perfect for children of all ages. Carrying an exquisite collection of fanciful puppets, collectible dolls, masks, stuffed animals, and illustrated books, this Navona jewel, around since 1945, is crammed top to bottom with beautiful, well-crafted playthings. If you believe that children's toys don't have to be high-tech, you will adore reliving some of your best childhood memories here. ⊠ *Piazza Navona 53, corner of Via Agonale, Piazza Navona* ☎ *06/6864198* ⊕ *www.alsogno.com.*

★ Bartolucci

TOYS | FAMILY | This shop opened in the '90s, but the Bartolucci family has been making whimsical, handmade curiosities out of pine, including clocks, bookends, bedside lamps, and wall hangings, since 1936. You can even buy a child-size motorbike entirely made of wood (wheels, too). Don't miss the life-size Pinocchio pedaling furiously on a wooden bike. ⊠ *Via dei Pastini 98, Piazza Navona* ☎ *06/69190894* ⊕ *www.bartolucci.com.*

La Città del Sole

TOYS | FAMILY | Chock-full of fair-trade and eco-friendly toys that share shelf space with retro and vintage favorites, La Città del Sole is the perfect place for parents looking to stock up on educational toys. The store, which arranges toys by age group, is a child-friendly browser's delight crammed with puzzles, gadgets, books, and toys in safe plastics and sustainable wood. The knowledgeable sales staff can help you choose the perfect age-appropriate gift. ⊠ *Via della Scrofa 65, Piazza Navona* ☎ *06/68803805* ⊕ *www.cittadelsole.it.*

Campo de' Fiori

In the mornings, Campo de' Fiori, an evocative piazza ringed by medieval palazzi, is one of the city's most popular markets. The market, like the square, is no longer a mainly local haunt—some stalls now hawk souvenirs and T-shirts, and tour groups are as common as bag-toting nonnas—it remains one of the most beloved, and bustling, institutions in the centro storico. In the evening until past midnight, outdoor bars and restaurants transform this humble square into a hot spot.

👁 Sights

Chiesa del Gesù

CHURCH | The mother church of the Jesuits in Rome is the prototype of all Counter-Reformation churches, and its spectacular interior tells a great deal about an era of religious triumph and turmoil. Its architecture influenced ecclesiastical buildings in Rome for more than a century (the overall design was by Vignola, the facade by della Porta) and was exported by the Jesuits throughout the rest of Europe. Though consecrated in 1584, the interior of the church wasn't fully decorated for another 100 years. It was originally intended that the interior be left plain to the point of austerity—but, when it was finally embellished, the mood had changed and no expense was spared. Its interior drips with gold and lapis lazuli, gold and precious marbles, gold and more gold, all covered by a fantastically painted ceiling. Unfortunately, the church is also one of Rome's most crepuscular, so its visual magnificence is considerably dulled by lack of light.

The architectural significance of Il Gesù extends far beyond the splendid interior. As the first of the great Counter-Reformation churches, it was put up after the Council of Trent (1545–63) had signaled the determination of the Roman Catholic Church to fight back against the Reformed Protestant heretics of northern Europe. The church decided to do so through the use of overwhelming pomp and majesty, in an effort to woo believers. As a harbinger of ecclesiastical spectacle, Il Gesù spawned imitations throughout Italy and the other Catholic countries of Europe as well as the Americas.

The most striking element is the ceiling, which is covered with frescoes that swirl down from on high to merge with painted stucco figures at the base, the illusion of space in the two-dimensional painting becoming the reality of three dimensions in the sculpted figures. Baciccia, their painter, achieved extraordinary effects in these frescoes, especially in the *Triumph of the Holy Name of Jesus*, over the nave. Here, the figures representing evil are cast out of heaven and seem to be hurtling down onto the observer. To appreciate in detail, the spectacle is best viewed through a specially tilted mirror in the nave.

The founder of the Jesuit order himself is buried in the Chapel of St. Ignatius, in the left-hand transept. This is surely the most sumptuous baroque altar in Rome; as is typical, the enormous globe of lapis lazuli that crowns it is really only a shell of lapis over a stucco base—after all, baroque decoration prides itself on achieving stunning effects and illusions. The heavy, bronze altar rail by architect Carlo Fontana is in keeping with the surrounding opulence. ✉ *Via degli Astalli 16, Campo de' Fiori* ☎ *06/697001* ⊕ *www.chiesadelgesu.org.*

Galleria Spada

ART MUSEUM | In this neighborhood of huge, austere palaces, Palazzo Spada strikes an almost frivolous note, with its pretty ornament-encrusted courtyard and its upper stories covered with stuccoes and statues. While the palazzo houses an impressive collection of Old Master paintings, it's most famous for its trompe-l'oeil garden gallery, a delightful example of the sort of architectural games rich Romans of the 17th century found irresistible. Even if you don't go into the gallery, step into the courtyard and look through the glass window of the library to the colonnaded corridor in the adjacent courtyard. See—or seem to see—a 26-foot-long gallery quadrupled in depth, a sort of optical telescope taking the Renaissance's art of perspective to another level, as it stretches out for a great distance with a large statue at the end. In fact the distance is an illusion: the

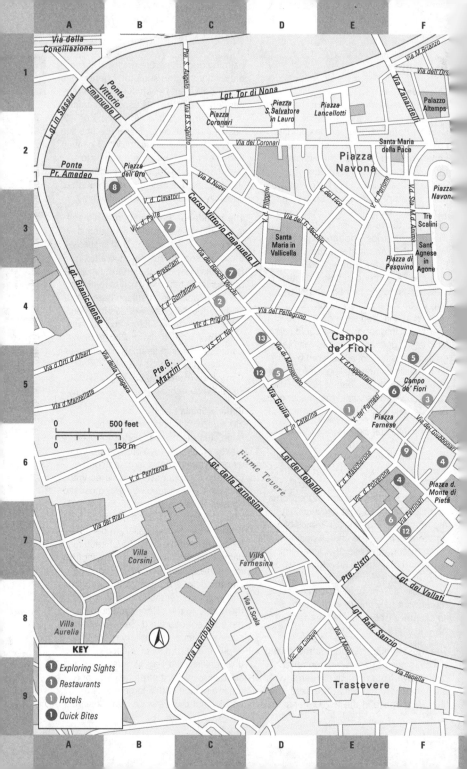

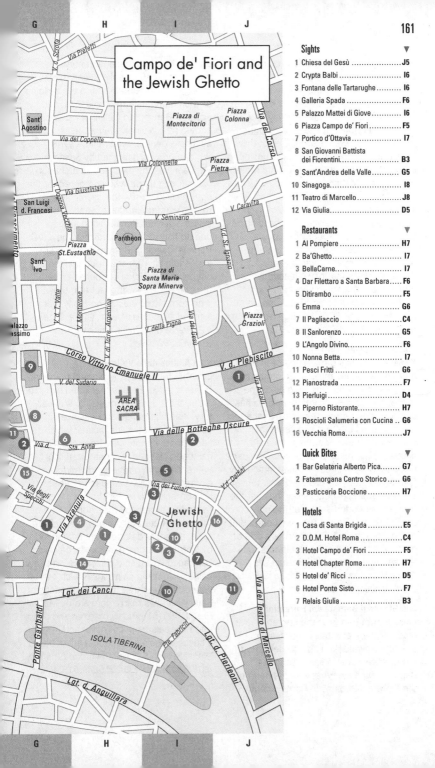

Campo de' Fiori and the Jewish Ghetto

corridor grows progressively narrower and the columns progressively smaller as they near the statue, which is just two feet tall. The baroque period is known for special effects, and this is rightly one of the most famous. It was long thought that Borromini was responsible for this ruse; it's now known that it was designed by an Augustinian priest, Giovanni Maria da Bitonto. Upstairs is a seignorial picture gallery with the paintings shown as they would have been, piled on top of each other clear to the ceiling. Outstanding works include Brueghel's *Landscape with Windmills*, Titian's *Musician*, and Andrea del Sarto's *Visitation*. Look for the fact sheets that have descriptive notes about the objects in each room. ✉ *Piazza Capo di Ferro 13, Campo de' Fiori* ☎ *06/6874896* ⊕ *www.galleriaspada. beniculturali.it* ⌂ *€5* ⊙ *Closed Tues.*

Piazza Campo de' Fiori

MARKET | A bustling marketplace in the morning (Monday through Saturday from 8 to 2) and a trendy meeting place the rest of the day and night, this piazza has plenty of down-to-earth charm. Just after lunchtime, all the fruit and vegetable vendors disappear, and this so-called *piazza trasformista* takes on another identity, becoming a circus of bars particularly favored by study-abroad students, tourists, and young expats. Brooding over the piazza is a hooded statue of the philosopher Giordano Bruno, who was burned at the stake here in 1600 for heresy, one of many victims of the Roman Inquisition. ✉ *Intersection of Via dei Baullari, Via Giubbonari, Via del Pellegrino, and Piazza della Cancelleria, Campo de' Fiori.*

San Giovanni Battista dei Fiorentini

CHURCH | Imbued with the supreme grace of the Florentine Renaissance, this often-overlooked church dedicated to Florence's patron saint, John the Baptist, stands in what was the heart of the Florentine colony in Rome's centro

storico. Many of these Florentines were goldsmiths, bankers, and money changers who contributed to the building of the church. Talented goldsmith and sculptor Benvenuto Cellini of Florence, known for his vindictive nature as much as for his genius, lived nearby. While the church was designed by Sansovino, Raphael (yes, he was also an architect) was among those who competed for this commission. Today, the church interior makes you feel you have wandered inside a perfect Renaissance space, one so harmonious it seems to be a 3-D Raphael painting. Borromini executed a splendid altar for the Falconieri family chapel in the choir. He's buried under the dome, despite the fact that those who committed suicide normally were refused a Christian burial. ✉ *Via Acciaioli 2, Piazza dell'Oro, Campo de' Fiori* ☎ *06/68892059.*

Sant'Andrea della Valle

CHURCH | Topped by the highest dome in Rome after St. Peter's (designed by Maderno), this huge and imposing 17th-century church is remarkably balanced in design. Fortunately, its facade, which had turned a sooty gray from pollution, has been cleaned to a near-sparkling white. Use one of the handy mirrors to examine the early-17th-century frescoes by Domenichino in the choir vault and those by Lanfranco in the dome. One of the earliest ceilings done in full baroque style, its upward vortex was influenced by Correggio's dome in Parma, of which Lanfranco was also a citizen. (Bring a few coins to light the paintings, which can be very dim.) The three massive paintings of Saint Andrew's martyrdom are by Mattia Preti (1650–51). Richly marbled and decorated chapels flank the nave, and in such a space, Puccini set the first act of *Tosca*. ✉ *Piazza Vidoni 6, Corso Vittorio Emanuele II, Campo de' Fiori* ☎ *06/6861339.*

★ Via Giulia

STREET | Still a Renaissance-era diorama and one of Rome's most exclusive addresses, Via Giulia was the first street in Rome since ancient times to be deliberately planned. Straight as a die, it was named for Pope Julius II (of Sistine Chapel fame), who commissioned it in the early 1500s as part of a scheme to open up a grandiose approach to St. Peter's Basilica, and it is flanked with elegant churches and palaces. Although the pope's plans to change the face of the city were only partially completed, Via Giulia became an important thoroughfare in Renaissance Rome. Today, after more than four centuries, it remains the "salon of Rome," address of choice for Roman aristocrats, although controversy has arisen about a recent change—the decision to add a large parking lot along one side of the street—that meant steamrolling through ancient and medieval ruins underneath. A stroll will reveal elegant palaces and churches (one, San Eligio, on the little side street Via di Sant'Eligio, was designed by Raphael himself). The area around Via Giulia is wonderful to wander through and get the feel of daily life as carried on in a centuries-old setting. Among the buildings that merit your attention are Palazzo Sacchetti (Via Giulia 66), with an imposing stone portal (inside are some of Rome's grandest staterooms, still, after 300 years, the private quarters of the Marchesi Sacchetti), and the forbidding brick building that housed the Carceri Nuove (New Prison; Via Giulia 52), Rome's prison for more than two centuries and now the offices of Direzione Nazionale Antimafia. Near the bridge that arches over the southern end of Via Giulia is the church of Santa Maria dell'Orazione e Morte (Holy Mary of Prayer and Death), with stone skulls on its door. These are a symbol of a confraternity that was charged with burying the bodies of the unidentified dead found in the city streets. Home since 1927 to the Hungarian Academy, the Palazzo Falconieri (✉ *Via Giulia 1* ☎ *06/68896700*) was designed by Borromini—note the architect's rooftop belvedere adorned with statues of the family "falcons," best viewed from around the block along the Tiber embankment. (The Borromini-designed salons and loggia are sporadically open as part of a guided tour; call the Hungarian Academy for information.) Remnant of a master plan by Michelangelo, the arch over the street was meant to link massive Palazzo Farnese, on the east side of Via Giulia, with the building across the street and a bridge to the Villa Farnesina, directly across the river. Finally, on the right and rather green with age, dribbles that star of many a postcard, the Fontana del Mascherone. ✉ *Via Giulia, between Piazza dell'Oro and Piazza San Vincenzo Palloti, Campo de' Fiori.*

🍴 Restaurants

Campo de' Fiori is home to one of Rome's largest open-air produce markets, and is historically the secular crossroads of the city: even in ancient Rome, pilgrims gathered here to eat, drink, and be merry. Today's shoppers at the market include local chefs who head here to concoct menus based on what looks good.

Dar Filettaro a Santa Barbara

$ | **ITALIAN** | The window reads "Filetti di Baccalà," but the official name of this small restaurant that specializes in one thing—deliciously battered and deep-fried fillets of salt cod—is Dar Filettaro a Santa Barbara. The location, down the street from Campo de' Fiori in a little piazza in front of the beautiful Santa Barbara church, practically begs you to eat at one of the outdoor tables, where service is brusque. **Known for:** tables outside on the pretty square; functional "hole-in-the-wall" interior; filetti di baccalà. $ *Average main: €6* ✉ *Largo dei Librari 88, Campo de' Fiori* ☎ *06/6864018* 🕐 *Closed Sun. and Aug.*

Continued on page 169

Life in the Campo de' Fiori

A small square with two personalities as different as day and night, the Campo de' Fiori is Rome's mecca for people with a picky purpose—whether it is picking out food or picking out that night's amorous adventure.

You can explore the Colosseum until your ears ring with roars of wild beasts, and make the rounds of churches until visions of angels dance in your head. But you won't know Rome until you have paused to appreciate the loveliness and vibrancy of the cityscape, perhaps from a table on one of Rome's beautiful squares. The Campo de' Fiori is particularly well endowed with such ringside seats, for here you can enjoy the show 24/7.

The Campo is heavily foot trafficked at any given hour, whether for its sunlit market stalls or its moon-shadowed cobblestones. If you only have 24 hours in Rome (and especially if the past 20 have been dedicated to sightseeing), take a breather here and inhale a truly Roman social scene, no matter what time of day or night.

In the daytime, the piazza is a buzzing produce market where vendors shout out the day's specialties and caffè-goers gossip behind newspapers while enjoying the morning's cappuccino. In the late afternoon, the Campo de' Fiori transforms into the ultimate hangout with overflowing bars, caffès, and restaurants filled with locals and tourists all vying for the perfect seat to check out passersby.

Campo life is decidedly without pause. The only moment of repose happens in the very wee hours of the morning when the remaining stragglers start the stumble home and just before the produce-filled mini-trucks begin their magnificent march in to the square. At any given hour, you will always find something going on in Campo, the "living room" of today's Rome.

By Erica Firpo

24 HOURS IN THE CAMPO DE' FIORI

5–6 am The Flight of the Bumble-Bees: Ape ("bee" in Italian) trucks file into the Campo to unload the day's goods. These mini-trucks are very cute, no? "Ao, Claudia! Che sta a fa?!" (Hey, Claudia! How ya doin'?), Daniele yells across to Claudia as market guys and gals joke around. Good lessons in Roman slang.

7–8 am The Calm before the Storm: The only time the Campo seems a bit sluggish, as stands have just opened, shoppers have yet to arrive, and everyone is just waking up. Market locals gather before heading off to work and school.

9–10 am The Herd: Tourists arrive. The locals take their "Pausa" coffee break while shops and late-opening caffès set up.

11–12 am The Eye of the Storm: Everyone is taking photos—photos of food, market-goers, vendors, models, caffè-goers.

1–2 pm Pranzo: Lunchtime in the Campo. Everyone is looking for an outdoor table. Meanwhile, the vendors start to pack up.

3–4 pm The Denoument: The Campo is officially shutting down, marked by the notable odor of Campo refuse and the loud din of the cleaning trucks. This is perhaps the absolute worst time to be in Campo. When the trucks depart, they leave the square to parents and toddlers.

5–6 pm Gelato Time: Shoppers and strollers replace replace market-goers. The first of the Campo's many musicians begin warming up for the evening's concert. Favorites always include: "Guantanamera," "My Way," and "Volare."

1PM

3PM

7–8 pm Happy Hours:
The pre-aperitivi people enjoy the cocktail before the cocktails. Always good for the punctual. By 6 aperitivi have been served. Are you "in" or "out"? Outside means picking any of the umbrella tavoli that line the piazza. If you prefer to be on the sly, try an indoor enoteca. Late-comers arrive for a last sip of wine before deciding where to dine.

9–10 pm Dining Hour:
Dining in Rome is an all-evening experience. It's common custom to argue for a half-hour about the perfect restaurant.

11 pm–12 am After-dinner Drinks: Everyone moves back to the Campo for a drink (or many). Drunkenness can include catcalls, stiletto falls, volleyed soccer balls, and the cops (polizia or carabinieri, take your pick).

1–2 am Time to Go Home:
Bars begin to shut down, with lingering kisses and hugs ("Dude, I love you!"). Clean-up crews come back. The din returns, this time as trucks clean up broken bottles and plastic cups.

3–4 am Some stragglers are still hanging around. For the first time, Campo de' Fiori is silent, to the delight of the residents around it. They have to hurry . . . because the Ape (see 5 am) are pressing to get back in.

Via del Baullari

Piazza Campo de' Fiori

To Via del Giubbonari

CAMPO DE FIORI

11PM

7PM

THE COGNOSCENTI'S CAMPO

WHAT TO KNOW

No longer a simple flower market, from Monday through Saturday mornings the Campo de' Fiori is Rome's most famous produce market. This is where you'll find standard Italian favorites (like Pacchino tomatoes, peppers, and eggplant), as well as seasonal delicacies such as puntarelle (a variety of chicory) and Roman artichokes. There are also meat, regional cheese, and homegrown honey vendors. The bancarelle (tchotchke stands) sell T-shirts, purses, bangles, and cookware; sometimes they're good for souvenir shopping.

This is one of the best places for people-watching in Rome, so hang out for a while. The many bars and caffès may look different but all have very similar menus and similar food. Mornings mean cappuccinos and pastries; in the evening there is wine, beer, and mixed drinks. Most also have Wi-Fi.

A word of advice: leave the high heels at home—the uneven cobblestones can be treacherous.

It's worth noting that the Campo de' Fiori and the adjacent Piazza Farnese have two of the best newspaper kiosks for international publications; so if you want something to read while you sip your caffè, stop by.

Ditirambo

$$ | ITALIAN | Don't let the country-kitchen setting fool you: at this little spot off Campo de' Fiori, the constantly changing selection of offbeat takes on Italian classics makes this a step beyond the ordinary. There are several good options for vegetarians. **Known for:** good vegetarian options; hearty meat and pasta dishes; cozy and casual atmosphere. $ *Average main: €16* ✉ *Piazza della Cancelleria 74, Campo de' Fiori* ☎ *06/6871626* ⊕ *www.ristoranteditirambo. it* ⊗ *Closed Aug.*

★ Emma

$$$ | ROMAN | FAMILY | With dough by Rome's renowned family of bakers, the Rosciolis, this large, sleek, modern pizzeria is smack in the middle of the city, with the freshest produce right outside the door. The wine list features many local Lazio options. **Known for:** tasty *fritti* (classic fried Roman pizzeria appetizers); thin-crust Roman pizza; light and airy, casual atmosphere. $ *Average main: €25* ✉ *Via Monte della Farina 28–29, Campo de' Fiori* ☎ *06/64760475* ⊕ *www. emmapizzeria.com.*

Il Pagliaccio

$$$$ | MODERN ITALIAN | Some of the most innovative interpretations of Roman fine dining can be found in this starkly chic restaurant on a backstreet between upscale Via Giulia and the popular Campo de' Fiori. Chef Anthony Genovese was born in France to Calabrese parents, and spent time cooking in Japan and Thailand, so it's no surprise that the food he turns out makes use of nontraditional spices, ingredients, and preparations—all of which have gained him a loyal following and multiple accolades. **Known for:** discreet location close to Piazza Navona; elegant surroundings; fine dining, including elaborate tasting menus. $ *Average main: €55* ✉ *Via dei Banchi Vecchi 129a, Piazza Navona* ☎ *06/68809595* ⊕ *www. ristoranteilpagliaccio.com* ⊗ *Closed Sun., Mon., and Aug. No lunch Tues. and Wed.*

Il Sanlorenzo

$$$$ | SEAFOOD | This gorgeous space, with its chandeliers and soaring original brickwork ceilings, houses one of the best seafood restaurants in the Eternal City. Order à la carte, or if you're hungry, the eight-course tasting menu is extremely tempting—it might include the likes of cuttlefish-ink tagliatelle with mint, artichokes, and roe, or shrimp from the island of Ponza with rosemary, bitter herbs, and porcini mushrooms—and, given the quality of the fish, a relative bargain at €90. **Known for:** elegant surroundings; spaghetti *con ricci* (sea urchins); top-quality fish and seafood. $ *Average main: €36* ✉ *Via dei Chiavari 4/5, Campo de' Fiori* ☎ *06/6865097* ⊕ *www.ilsanlorenzo.it* ⊗ *Closed Sun. and 2 wks in Aug. No lunch Sat. and Mon.*

L'Angolo Divino

$ | WINE BAR | There's something about this cozy wine bar that feels as if it's in a small university town instead of a bustling metropolis. The walls are lined with a tempting array of bottles from around the Italian peninsula, and the counter is stocked with cheese and salumi that can be sliced and piled on plates to order. **Known for:** late-night snacks; cozy atmosphere; excellent wine selection and advice. $ *Average main: €13* ✉ *Via dei Balestrari 12, Campo de' Fiori* ☎ *06/6864413* ⊕ *www.angolodivino. it* ⊗ *Closed 2 wks in Aug.*

Pesci Fritti

$$ | SOUTHERN ITALIAN | This cute jewel box of a restaurant sits on the seating of the ancient Theatre of Pompey just behind Campo de' Fiori (note the curve of the street). Step inside, and the whitewashed walls with touches of pale sea blue will make you feel like you've escaped to the Mediterranean for seafood favorites. **Known for:** cozy setting; spaghetti with clams; fried fish and seafood choices. $ *Average main: €18* ✉ *Via di Grottapinta 8, Campo de'*

Fiori ☎ 06/68806170 ⊕ www.pescifritti.it ⊗ Closed Mon. and Aug.

★ Pianostrada

$$ | MODERN ITALIAN | This gourmet restaurant has an open kitchen, where you can watch the talented women owners cook up a storm of inventive delights—this is a "kitchen lab," after all, where top local ingredients are whipped into delicious plates. The spaghetti with tomato sauce, smoked ricotta, parmigiano, basil, and lemon peel is one of the signature dishes, and the amped up traditional recipe is a delicious indication of how interesting the food can get. **Known for:** secret garden seating; creative burgers and salads; freshly baked focaccia with various toppings. ⑤ Average main: €20 ✉ Via delle Zoccolette 22, Campo de' Fiori ☎ 06/89572296 ⊗ Closed Mon. No lunch Tues.

★ Pierluigi

$$$ | ITALIAN | This popular seafood restaurant is a fun spot on balmy summer evenings, with tables out on the pretty Piazza de' Ricci. As at most Italian restaurants, fresh fish is sold per hectogram (100 grams, or about 3.5 ounces), so you may want to double-check the cost after it's been weighed. **Known for:** elegant atmosphere with great service; tables on the pretty pedestrianized piazza; top-quality fish and seafood. ⑤ Average main: €30 ✉ Piazza de' Ricci 144, Campo de' Fiori ☎ 06/6861302 ⊕ www.pierluigi.it ⊗ Closed Mon.

★ Roscioli Salumeria con Cucina

$$ | WINE BAR | The shop in front of this wine bar will beckon you in with top-quality comestibles like hand-sliced cured ham from Italy and Spain, more than 300 cheeses, and a dizzying array of wines—but venture farther inside to try an extensive selection of unusual dishes and interesting takes on the classics.

There are tables in the cozy wine cellar downstairs, but try and bag a table at the back on the ground floor (reserve well ahead; Roscioli is very popular). **Known for:** best prosciutto in town; arguably Rome's best spaghetti alla carbonara; extensive wine list. ⑤ Average main: €22 ✉ Via dei Giubbonari 21, Campo de' Fiori ☎ 06/6875287 ⊕ www.salumeriaroscioli. com ⊗ Closed 1 wk in Aug.

☕ Coffee and Quick Bites

Bar Gelateria Alberto Pica

$ | ICE CREAM | FAMILY | Beloved owner Alberto Pica sadly died in 2015, but his name lives on in the gelato shop he ran close to the river. Gelato production is artisanal, and the selection of seasonal sorbetti and cremolate (the latter is similar to sorbetto but made with the fruit pulp, rather than just fruit juice) is diverse. **Known for:** brusque owners who keep the lines moving; riso a cannella gelato (cinnamon rice pudding); sleek bar without losing its old-school attitude. ⑤ Average main: €4 ✉ Via della Seggiola 12, Campo de' Fiori ☎ 06/6868405 ⊗ Closed Sun. and 2 wks in Aug. No lunch in summer.

Fatamorgana Centro Storico

$ | ICE CREAM | FAMILY | There are plenty of ordinary gelaterie around the Campo de' Fiori but it's worth searching out this branch of small Roman chain Fatamorgana. The highest-quality ingredients go into the gelato here and the flavors range from the traditional to the wonderfully unique (think Gorgonzola or tobacco and chocolate). **Known for:** seasonal fruit flavors; beloved local brand; quality gelato. ⑤ Average main: €4 ✉ Via dei Chiavari 37, Campo de' Fiori ☎ 06/88818437 ⊕ www. gelateriafatamorgana.it ⊗ Closed 1 wk in Aug.

🛏 Hotels

If you're looking to be in the *cuore of Roma vecchia* (or "heart of Old Rome"), there's no better place than Campo de' Fiori, a gorgeous piazza with lively merchants, outdoor caffè, and bars. The hotels here are not generally as lovely as their surroundings, however: many are cramped and could use updating.

Casa di Santa Brigida

$ | B&B/INN | The friendly sisters of Santa Brigida oversee simple, straightforward, and centrally located accommodations in one of Rome's loveliest convents, with a rooftop terrace overlooking Palazzo Farnese. **Pros:** insider papal tickets; free Wi-Fi; large library and sunroof. **Cons:** far from a Metro stop; no TVs in the rooms (though there is a common TV room); weak air-conditioning. $ *Rooms from: €50* ✉ *Piazza Farnese 96, Campo de' Fiori* ☎ *06/68892596* 🌐 *www.brigidine. org* ⬏ *20 rooms* ⏐❀⏐ *Free Breakfast.*

D.O.M Hotel Roma

$$$$ | HOTEL | In an old convent on Via Giulia, one of Rome's romantic ivy-covered streets, the D.O.M (Deo Optimo Maximo) is an ultrachic luxury hotel that resembles an aristocratic *casa nobile*. **Pros:** complimentary Acqua di Parma toiletries; hip decor; heated towel racks. **Cons:** standard rooms are small for a five-star hotel; delicious but expensive cocktails; an armed guard at the anti-terrorism headquarters opposite the hotel may be off-putting for some. $ *Rooms from: €390* ✉ *Via Giulia 131, Campo de' Fiori* ☎ *06/6832144* 🌐 *www.domhotelroma. com* ⬏ *18 rooms* ⏐❀⏐ *Free Breakfast.*

Hotel Campo de' Fiori

$$$ | HOTEL | This handsome, ivy-draped hotel is a romantic refuge located right in the heart of Campo de' Fiori. **Pros:** free Wi-Fi; rooftop terrace; well-stocked library where one can relax and read. **Cons:** some apartments are too close to the area's noisy bar scene; can get pricey in high season; rooms are on the small side. $ *Rooms from: €250* ✉ *Via del Biscione 6, Campo de' Fiori* ☎ *06/68806865* 🌐 *www.hotelcampo-defiori.com/en* ⬏ *25 rooms* ⏐❀⏐ *Free Breakfast.*

Hotel de' Ricci

$$$$ | HOTEL | This intimate boutique hotel from the team behind Pierluigi is a top spot for wine lovers. **Pros:** excellent wine cellar and wine tastings; perks include complimentary aperitivo and priority reservations at Pierluigi; great location on a quiet street. **Cons:** there's no spa or gym; there is a weekend crowd for the brunch; there's a charge of 50 euros per day to bring pets. $ *Rooms from: €350* ✉ *Via della Barchetta 14, Campo de' Fiori* ☎ *06/6874775* 🌐 *www.hoteldericci.com* ⬏ *8 rooms* ⏐❀⏐ *No Meals.*

Hotel Ponte Sisto

$$$ | HOTEL | Situated in a remodeled Renaissance palazzo with one of the prettiest patio-courtyards in Rome, this hotel is a relaxing retreat close to Trastevere and Campo de' Fiori. **Pros:** rooms with views (and some with balconies and terraces); beautiful courtyard garden; luxury bathrooms. **Cons:** carpets starting to show signs of wear; some upgraded rooms are small and not worth the price difference; street-side rooms can be a bit noisy. $ *Rooms from: €250* ✉ *Via dei Pettinari 64, Campo de' Fiori* ☎ *06/6863100* 🌐 *www.hotelpontesisto.it* ⬏ *106 rooms* ⏐❀⏐ *Free Breakfast.*

Relais Giulia

$$$ | HOTEL | In a 15th-century palazzo on one of Rome's oldest streets, Relais Giulia is a classic Roman Renaissance boutique hotel with sophisticated modern furnishings and fixtures. **Pros:** quiet area; great location in between Campo de' Fiori and Trastevere; thoughtful amenities. **Cons:** some rooms and facilities could use updating; keyless entry system takes getting used to; Wi-Fi can be patchy. $ *Rooms from: €220* ✉ *Via Giulia 93, Campo de' Fiori* ☎ *06/95581300* 🌐 *www.relaisgiuliahotel.it* ⬏ *13 rooms* ⏐❀⏐ *Free Breakfast.*

Nightlife

With plenty of college bars, Campo de' Fiori is Rome's magnet for the study-abroad scene.

BARS
Il Goccetto
CAFÉS | A historic wine bar with a copious amount of elusive vintages, Il Goccetto specializes in wines from smaller vineyards from Sicily to Venice. Stay for a snack—its carefully chosen menu of Italian delicacies (meats and cheeses) represents the entire Italian peninsula. The burrata with sun-dried tomatoes is a perennial favorite. The tiny bar is well designed but is always busy and never accepts reservations. ⊠ *Via dei Banchi Vecchi 14, Campo de' Fiori* ☎ *06/6864268* ⊕ *www.ilgoccetto.com.*

L'Angolo Divino
WINE BARS | Nestled on a quiet side street around the corner from the ever-vivacious Campo de' Fiori, this wood-paneled enoteca is a hidden treasure of wines. Its extensive selection lists more than 1,000 labels to go along quite nicely with its quaint menu of delicious homemade pastas and local *antipasti* (appetizers). And because it's open every night until 1:30 am, it's the ideal place for a late-night tipple. ⊠ *Via dei Balestrari 12, Campo de' Fiori* ☎ *06/6864413* ⊕ *www.angolodivino.it.*

The Sofa Bar & Roof Terrace Restaurant
BARS | The romantic rooftop terrace at Sofa has a 360-degree view of the Eternal City, so it's no surprise that it's a prime spot for a late-afternoon cocktail (weather permitting). Head downstairs in the cooler months for a wide selection of craft beers on tap inside the Hotel Indigo. ⊠ *Hotel Indigo Rome—St. George, Via Giulia 62, Campo de' Fiori* ☎ *06/686611* ⊕ *www.hotelindigorome.com.*

 Performing Arts

THEATER
★ Teatro Argentina
THEATER | A gorgeous 18th-century theater, the Teatro Argentina evokes glamour and sophistication with its velvet upholstery, large crystal chandeliers, and beautifully dressed theatergoers, who come to see international productions of stage and dance performances. ⊠ *Largo di Torre Argentina 52, Campo de' Fiori* ☎ *06/684000314* ⊕ *www.teatrodiroma.net.*

Shopping

Campo de' Fiori, one of Rome's most captivating piazzas, comes to life early in the morning, when merchants theatrically sell their best tomatoes, salumi, artichokes, blood oranges, herbs, and spices. Around the piazza, labyrinthine streets are crowded with small shops to suit any budget.

ANTIQUES
Nardecchia
ANTIQUES & COLLECTIBLES | Since the 1950s, the Nardecchia family has been in the business of selling beautiful 19th-century prints, old photographs, and watercolors that depict Rome in centuries past. Can't afford an 18th-century etching? They have beautiful postcards, too. ⊠ *Via del Monserrato 106, Campo de' Fiori* ☎ *06/6869318* ◷ *Closed Sun. and Mon. morning.*

CHILDREN'S CLOTHING
Rachele
CHILDREN'S CLOTHING | FAMILY | Rachele is a small, charming shop near the Piazza Campo de' Fiori that sells original and whimsical handmade children's clothing. If you're looking for something truly unique, Rachele (the Swedish owner and designer) makes only two of everything for tykes up to age 12. Your children can make a statement with any of her cute pants, skirts, or rainbow-color tops.

✉ *Vicolo del Bollo 6–7, Campo de' Fiori* ☎ *329/6481004* 🕙 *Closed Sun. and Mon.*

CLOTHING
★ L'Archivio di Monserrato
WOMEN'S CLOTHING | This airy, spacious boutique curated by Soledad Twombly (daughter-in-law of painter Cy Twombly) showcases her original designs as well as a sophisticated mix of antique Turkish and Indian textiles, jewelry, shoes, and small homewares picked up on her travels. Tailored jackets trimmed with exotic fabrics, dresses in eclectic prints and bold colors, and smart linen suits are some of Twombly's signatures. ✉ *Via di Monserrato 150, Campo de' Fiori* ☎ *06/45654157* 🌐 *www.soledadtwombly. com* 🕙 *Closed Sun.*

JEWELRY
Delfina Delettrez
JEWELRY & WATCHES | When your great-grandmother is Adele Fendi, it's not surprising that creativity runs in your genes. Young Roman designer Delfina Delettrez creates edgy, glam-rock accessories using human body–inspired pieces that blend skulls, wild animals, and botanical elements in her jewelry. Delettrez also daringly merges gold, silver, bone and glass, crystals, and diamonds to create gothic styles worthy of Fritz Lang's *Metropolis,* or *Blade Runner.* ✉ *Via di Monserrato, 24A, Campo de' Fiori* ☎ *06/68134105* 🌐 *www.delfinadelettrez. com* 🕙 *Closed Sun.*

SHOES, HANDBAGS, AND LEATHER GOODS
★ Chez Dede
OTHER SPECIALTY STORE | Husband-and-wife duo Andrea Ferolla and Daria Reina (he's a fashion illustrator, she's a photographer) curate an edited selection of clothes, bags, vintage jewelry, books, home decor, and anything else you might need in this cult favorite lifestyle-concept shop. Their signature bags are designed to go from the plane straight to the beach, and they regularly release collectible items featuring Ferolla's whimsical illustrations.

✉ *Via di Monserrato 35, Campo de' Fiori* ☎ *06/83772934* 🌐 *www.chezdede.com* 🕙 *Closed Sun.*

Ibiz
LEATHER GOODS | In business since 1972, this family team creates colorful, stylish leather handbags, belts, and sandals near Piazza Campo de' Fiori. Choose from the premade collection or order something in the color of your choice; their workshop is visible in the boutique. ✉ *Via dei Chiavari 39, Campo de' Fiori* ☎ *06/68307297* 🌐 *www.ibizroma.it* 🕙 *Closed Sun.*

★ Maison Halaby
HANDBAGS | Lebanese designer and artist Gilbert Halaby was featured in fashion magazines like *Vogue* and created jewelry for Lady Gaga before giving up the rat race and opening his own shop, where the ethos is all about slow fashion. He designs boldly colored leather handbags incorporating suede, python, fringe, raffia, or jeweled handles, as well as silk scarves printed with his original watercolors, which he sells in this small boutique that feels like an extension of his home, with a velvet sofa, plenty of books and plants, and his own paintings on the walls. The shop is mainly open by appointment, but if Gilbert is there when you pass by, ring the bell and he'll invite you in for coffee or Campari. ✉ *Via di Monserrato 21, Campo de' Fiori* ☎ *06/96521585* 🌐 *www.maisonhalaby. com* 🕙 *Open by appointment.*

Jewish Ghetto

Although today most of Rome's Jews live outside the Ghetto, the area remains the spiritual and cultural home of Jewish Rome, and that heritage permeates its small commercial area of Judaica shops, kosher bakeries, and restaurants. The Jewish Ghetto was established by papal decree in the 16th century. It was by definition a closed community, where Roman Jews lived under lock and key until Italian unification in 1870. In 1943–44, the already small Jewish population there was decimated by deportations.

The turn-of-the-20th-century synagogue, with its museum dedicated to the history of Jewish Rome, is a must for understanding the Ghetto. Tight, teeming alleys lead from there up to Giacomo della Porta's unmistakable Fontana delle Tartarughe (Turtle Fountain); nearby is the adorned courtyard of Palazzo Mattei. Via Portico d'Ottavia is a walk through the olden days. Most businesses in the Ghetto observe the Jewish Sabbath, so it's a ghost town on Saturday. At its east end, the street leads down to a path past the 1st-century Teatro di Marcello. The Tiber River separates the Ghetto and Trastevere, with the lovely Isola Tiberina (Tiber Island) in the middle. Cross the river via the Ponte Fabricio, the oldest bridge in Rome.

 ## Sights

Crypta Balbi
RUINS | The fourth component of the magnificent collections of the Museo Nazionale Romano, this museum is unusual because it represents several periods of Roman history. The crypt is part of the Balbus Theater complex (13 BC), and other parts of the complex are from the medieval period, up through the 20th century. The written explanations accompanying the well-lit exhibits are excellent, and this museum is a popular field trip for teachers and school groups. ⊠ *Via delle Botteghe Oscure 31, Jewish Ghetto* ☎ *06/39967701* ⊕ *www.coopculture. it* ⊠ *€10 Crypta Balbi only; €14 includes three other Museo Nazionale Romano sites over a one-week period (Palazzo Altemps, Palazzo Massimo, Museo Diocleziano)* ⊘ *Closed Mon.* Ⓜ *Bus Nos. 64 and 40, Tram No. 8.*

Fontana delle Tartarughe
FOUNTAIN | Designed by Giacomo della Porta in 1581 and sculpted by Taddeo Landini, this fountain, set in pretty Piazza Mattei, is one of Rome's most charming. The focus of the fountain is four bronze boys, each grasping a dolphin spouting water into a marble shell. Bronze turtles held in the boys' hands drink from the upper basin. The turtles were added in the 17th century by Bernini. ⊠ *Piazza Mattei, Jewish Ghetto.*

★ Palazzo Mattei di Giove
CASTLE/PALACE | Graceful and opulent, the arcaded, multistory courtyard of this palazzo is a masterpiece of turn-of-the-17th-century style. Designed by Carlo Maderno, it is a veritable panoply of sculpted busts, heroic statues, sculpted reliefs, and Paleo-Christian epigrams, all collected by Marchese Asdrubale Mattei. Inside are various scholarly institutes, including the Centro Studi Americani (Center for American Studies), which also contains a library of American books. Salons in the palace (not usually open to visitors) are decorated with frescoes by Cortona, Lanfranco, and Domenichino. It's publicly accessible Monday through Friday. ⊠ *Via Michelangelo Caetani 32, other entrance in Via dei Funari, Jewish Ghetto* ☎ *06/68801613 Centro Studi Americani* ⊘ *Closed weekends.*

Portico d'Ottavia
RUINS | Looming over the Jewish Ghetto, this huge portico, with a few surviving columns, is one of the area's most picturesque set pieces, with the church of Sant'Angelo in Pescheria built right into its ruins. Named by Augustus in honor of his sister Octavia, it was originally 390 feet wide and 433 feet long, encompassed two temples, a meeting hall, and a library, and served as a kind of grandiose entrance foyer for the adjacent Teatro di Marcello. The ruins of the portico

At the center of the Jewish Ghetto you'll find Portico d'Ottavia, which was Rome's fish market in the Middle Ages.

became Rome's *pescheria* (fish market) during the Middle Ages. A stone plaque on a pillar (a copy; the original is in the Musei Capitolini) states in Latin that the head of any fish surpassing the length of the plaque was to be cut off "up to the first fin" and given to the city fathers, or else the vendor was to pay a fine of 10 gold florins. The heads were used to make fish soup and were considered a great delicacy. ✉ *Via Portico d'Ottavia 29, Jewish Ghetto.*

Sinagoga

RELIGIOUS BUILDING | This synagogue has been the city's largest Jewish temple, and a Roman landmark with its aluminum dome, since its construction in 1904. The building also houses the Jewish Museum, with its precious ritual objects and other exhibits, which document the uninterrupted presence of a Jewish community in the city for nearly 22 centuries.

Until the 16th century, Jews were esteemed citizens of Rome. Among them were bankers and physicians to the popes, who had themselves given permission for the construction of synagogues. But in 1555, during the Counter-Reformation, Pope Paul IV decreed the building of the walls of the Ghetto, confining the Jews to this small area and imposing a series of restrictions, some of which continued to be enforced until 1870. For security reasons, entrance is via guided visit only, and tours in English are available twice a day but should be booked online ahead of time; entrance to the synagogue is through the museum located in Via Catalana (✉ *Largo 16 Ottobre 1943*). ✉ *Lungotevere de' Cenci 15, Jewish Ghetto* ☎ *06/68400661* ⊕ *www.museoebraico.roma.it* 🎫 *€11* ☉ *Museum closed Sat. and Jewish holidays.*

Teatro di Marcello

RUINS | Begun by Julius Caesar and completed by the emperor Augustus in 13 BC, this theater could house around 14,000 spectators. Like other Roman monuments, it was transformed into a fortress during the Middle Ages. During the Renaissance, it was converted into a residence by the Savelli, one of the city's noble families. Today, the archaeological park around the theater is used as a summer venue for open-air classical music concerts. ✉ *Via del Teatro di Marcello, Jewish Ghetto* ☎ *06/87131590 concert info* ⊕ *www.tempietto.it.*

Restaurants

Across Via Arenula from the Campo de' Fiori, the Ghetto is home to Europe's oldest Jewish population, who have lived in Rome uninterrupted for more than 2,000 years. There are excellent restaurants not just along its main drag, Via del Portico d'Ottavia, but also hidden in the narrow backstreets that wind between the river, Via Arenula, and Piazza Venezia.

Al Pompiere

$$$ | ROMAN | The nondescript entrance on a narrow side street leads upstairs to the main dining room of this neighborhood favorite, where those in the know enjoy dining on classic Roman fare under arched ceilings. Fried zucchini flowers, battered salt cod, and gnocchi are all consistently excellent, and the menu has some nice, historic touches, like a beef-and-citron stew from an ancient Roman recipe of Apicius. **Known for:** high-quality Roman cuisine; excellent porchetta; traditional elegant setting. $ *Average main: €25* ✉ *Via Santa Maria dei Calderari 38, Jewish Ghetto* ☎ *06/6868377* ⊕ *www.*

Roman Jewish Cuisine

Variations on cured pork, such as guanciale, prosciutto, and pancetta, are signature flavorings for Roman dishes. When Jewish culinary culture started intermingling with Roman, it was discovered that Jewish cooks used *alici* (anchovies) to flavor dishes the way Romans used cured pork. For excellent-quality anchovies, check out the Jewish *alimentari* (food shops) in the Ghetto.

alpompiereroma.com ⊙ *Closed Tues. and Aug. No dinner Sun.*

★ Ba'Ghetto

$$ | ITALIAN | FAMILY | This hot spot on the main promenade in the Jewish Ghetto has been going strong for years, with pleasant indoor and outdoor seating. The kitchen is kosher (many places featuring Roman Jewish fare are not) and serves meat dishes (so no dairy) from the Roman Jewish tradition as well as from elsewhere in the Mediterranean; down the street is Ba'Ghetto Milky (✉ *Via del Portico d'Ottavia 2/a*), the kosher dairy version of the original. **Known for:** outside tables on the pedestrianized street; casual family atmosphere; carciofi alla giudia (deep-fried artichokes) and other Roman Jewish specialities. $ *Average main: €22* ✉ *Via del Portico d'Ottavia 57, Jewish Ghetto* ☎ *06/68892868* ⊕ *www.baghetto.com* ⊙ *Dinner Fri. and lunch Sat. are strictly for those who observe Shabbat with advance payment.*

BellaCarne

$$ | ROMAN | *Bellacarne* means "beautiful meat," and that's the focus of the menu here, though the double entendre is that it's also what a Jewish Italian grandmother might say while pinching her grandchild's cheek. The kosher kitchen makes its own pastrami, though the setting is definitely more fine dining than deli. **Known for:** outside seating; deep-fried artichokes; homemade pastrami. ⑤ *Average main: €17* ✉ *Via Portico d'Ottavia 51, Jewish Ghetto* ☎ *06/6833104* ⊕ *www.bellacarne. it* ⊗ *No dinner Fri. No lunch Sat.*

Nonna Betta

$ | ROMAN | Right on the main street of the Jewish Ghetto, Nonna Betta is an institution in the neighborhood. All the Roman Jewish classics are on the menu here, and the *carciofi alla giudia* (Jewish-style artichokes) are outstanding, as are most of the fried starters. **Known for:** vegetarian carbonara with zucchini; outside seating; casual and busy atmosphere. ⑤ *Average main: €12* ✉ *Via del Portico d'Ottavia 16, Jewish Ghetto* ☎ *06/68806263* ⊕ *www.nonnabetta.it* ⊗ *Closed Tues.*

Piperno Ristorante

$$ | ROMAN | The place to go for Rome's extraordinary carciofi alla giudia, Piperno has been in business since 1860. The location, up a tiny hill in a piazza tucked away behind the palazzi of the Jewish Ghetto, lends the restaurant a rarefied air. **Known for:** great fish dishes; fried stuffed zucchini flowers; old-school elegance. ⑤ *Average main: €20* ✉ *Monte dei Cenci 9, Jewish Ghetto* ☎ *06/68806629* ⊕ *www.ristorantepiperno.it* ⊗ *Closed Mon. and Aug. No dinner Sun.*

Vecchia Roma

$$ | SEAFOOD | Though the frescoed dining rooms are lovely, when the weather is good the choice place to dine is outside on the piazza, under the big white umbrellas, in the shadow of Santa Maria in Campitelli. Seafood is the specialty, and simple southern Italian preparations, such as grilled calamari with Sicilian tomatoes, are excellent no-fail choices. **Known for:** fruit desserts; some of the best outdoor seating in the city; large portions. ⑤ *Average main: €22* ✉ *Piazza Campitelli 18, Jewish Ghetto* ☎ *06/6864604* ⊕ *www.ristorantevecchiaroma.com* ⊗ *Closed Wed. and 1 wk in Aug.*

Coffee and Quick Bites

Pasticceria Boccione

$ | BAKERY | This tiny, old-school bakery is an institution in the Ghetto area and is famed for its Roman-Jewish sweet specialties. Service is brusque, choices are few, what's available depends on the season, and when it's sold out, it's sold out. **Known for:** old-school bakery, so no frills and no seats; pizza ebraica ("Jewish pizza," a dense baked sweet rich in nuts and raisins); ricotta and cherry tarts. ⑤ *Average main: €4* ✉ *Via del Portico d'Ottavia 1, Jewish Ghetto* ☎ *06/6878637* ⊗ *Closed Sat.*

📖 Hotels

Hotel Chapter Roma

$$$ | HOTEL | This hip new member of Design Hotels has an edgy, of-the-moment design that juxtaposes plush midcentury Italian furnishings with street art murals and industrial touches. **Pros:** trendy design; lively rooftop bar in summer; coworking space available. **Cons:** service can be a bit spotty; no spa; no gym. ⑤ *Rooms from: €230* ✉ *Via di Santa Maria de' Calderari 47, Jewish Ghetto* ☎ *06/89935351* ⊕ *www.chapter-roma.com* ⟿ *47 rooms* ⦿ *Free Breakfast.*

 Performing Arts

CLASSICAL MUSIC

Il Tempietto

FESTIVALS | Music festivals and intimate concerts are organized throughout the year in otherwise inaccessible sites, such as the Teatro di Marcello, the Church of San Nicola in Carcere, and Villa Torlonia. Music covers the entire scope from classical to contemporary. ✉ *Piazza Campitelli 9, Jewish Ghetto* ☎ *06/45615180* ⊕ *www.tempietto.it.*

Chapter 6

PIAZZA DI SPAGNA

Updated by
Natalie Kennedy

⦿ Sights	🍴 Restaurants	🛏 Hotels	🛍 Shopping	🍸 Nightlife
★★★★★	★★★★★	★★★★★	★★★★★	★☆☆☆☆

NEIGHBORHOOD SNAPSHOT

MAKING THE MOST OF YOUR TIME

This neighborhood is chock-full of postcard-worthy sights, including the Spanish Steps, the Trevi Fountain, and the Victor Emanuel monument (Il Vittoriano), which means a long, rewarding walk alongside plenty of tourists. Consider starting early or taking an evening stroll, when many of the area's must-sees (including the Trevi Fountain) are lighted. Shoppers flock to Via del Corso, though in recent years the street has been given over mostly to multinational chains. Poke through backstreets instead; Rome's swankiest boutiques and designers are on Via del Babuino and the surrounding streets.

GETTING HERE

■ The Piazza di Spagna is a short walk from Piazza del Popolo, the Pantheon, and the Trevi Fountain. One of Rome's handiest subway stations, Spagna, is tucked just left of the steps. Buses No. 117 (from the Colosseum) and No. 119 (from Piazza del Popolo) hum through the area; the latter tootles up Via del Babuino, famed for its shopping.

TOP REASONS TO GO

Trevi Fountain: Iconic would be an understatement—this is the Elvis of waterworks: overblown, flashy, and reliably thronged by legions of fans.

The Spanish Steps: Saunter seductively up the world's most celebrated stairway—everyone's doing it.

The Ceiling of San Ignazio: Stand beneath the stupendous ceiling of San Ignazio—Rome's most splendiferous baroque church—and, courtesy of painter-priest Fra Andrea Pozzo, prepare to be transported heavenward.

Fabulous Palazzos: Visit the Palazzo Doria Pamphilj and the Palazzo Colonna for an intimate look at the homes of Rome's 17th-century grandees.

Luxe Shopping on Via Condotti: You can flit from Bulgari to Gucci to Valentino to Ferragamo with no effort at all.

PAUSE HERE

■ Buzzing Piazza di Spagna is characterized by its thoroughfares packed with shoppers. Slip away from the crowds by strolling down Via Margutta, a street that has long been synonymous with artists and is still full of galleries and studios. Film buffs who prefer cinema to paintings can pay homage at house number 51, where Gregory Peck's character lived in the film *Roman Holiday*.

In spirit, and in fact, this area of Rome is grandiose. The overblown Vittoriano monument, the labyrinthine treasure-chest palaces of Rome's surviving aristocracy—even the diamond-draped denizens of Via Condotti—all embody the exuberant ego of a city at the center of its own universe. Here's where you'll see ladies in fur as you walk through a thousand snapshots while climbing the famous Spanish Steps.

At the top of everyone's sightseeing list is that great baroque confection, the Trevi Fountain. Since pickpockets favor this tourist-heavy spot, be particularly aware as you withdraw that wallet. Once you've chucked your change in the fountain, follow the crowds and get ready to take some serious time to explore this neighborhood.

If Rome has a Main Street, it's Via del Corso, which is often jammed with swarms of Roman teenagers, in from the city's outlying districts for a ritual stroll that resembles a strutting migra-tion of lemmings in blue jeans. Along this thoroughfare it's easy to forget that the gray and stolid atmosphere comes partially from the enormous palaces lin-ing both sides of the street. Many were built over the past 300 years by princely families who wanted to secure front-row seats for the frantic antics of Carnevale, which once sent horses racing down the street from Piazza del Popolo to Piazza Venezia. But once you make it past their chaste entrances, you'll discover some of Rome's grandest 17th- and 18th-cen-tury treasures, including golden baroque ballrooms, glittering churches, and great Old Master paintings.

Via del Corso begins at noisy, chaotic Piazza Venezia, the imperial-size hub of all this ostentation, presided over by Il Vittoriano, also known as the Altare della Patria (Altar of the Nation)—or, less piously, "the typewriter," "the wedding cake," or "the Eighth Hill of Rome." Sitting grandly off the avenue are the Palazzo Doria Pamphilj and the Palaz-zo Colonna, two of the city's great art collections housed in magnificent family palaces.

Extending just east of Via del Corso, but miles away in style, Piazza di Spagna and its surrounding streets are where Rome's elite congregate for shopping sprees and gallery hopping. The piazza's main draw remains the 18th-century Spanish Steps, which connect the ritzy shops at the bot-tom of the hill with the ritzy hotels (and one lovely church) at the top. The reward for climbing the *scalinata* (staircase) is a dizzying view of central Rome. Because the steps face west, the views are especially good around sunset.

 Sights

★ Ara Pacis Augustae
(*Altar of Augustan Peace*)
MONUMENT | In a city better known for its terra-cotta–colored palazzi, this pristine monument sits inside one of Rome's newer architectural landmarks: a gleaming, rectangular glass-and-travertine structure designed by American architect Richard Meier. Overlooking the Tiber on one side and the ruins of the marble-clad Mausoleo di Augusto (Mausoleum of Augustus) on the other, the result is a serene, luminous oasis right in the center of Rome. The altar itself dates back to 13 BC; it was commissioned to celebrate the Pax Romana, the era of peace ushered in by Augustus's military victories. Like all ancient Roman monuments of this kind, you have to imagine its spectacular and moving relief sculptures painted in vibrant colors, now long gone. The reliefs on the short sides portray myths associated with Rome's founding and glory; the long sides display a procession of the imperial family. It's fun to try to play "who's who"—although half of his body is missing, Augustus is identifiable as the first full figure at the procession's head on the south-side frieze—but academics still argue over exact identifications of most of the figures. This one splendid altar is the star of the small museum downstairs, which hosts rotating exhibits on Italian culture, with themes ranging from design to film. ⊠ *Lungotevere in Augusta, at the corner of Via Tomacelli, Piazza di Spagna* ☎ *06/0608* ⊕ *www.arapacis.it* ☜ *€10.50, €13 when there's an exhibit* Ⓜ *Flaminio.*

Colonna di Marco Aurelio
MONUMENT | Inspired by Trajan's Column, this 2nd-century-AD column is composed of 27 blocks of marble covered in reliefs recounting Marcus Aurelius's victory over the Germanic tribes. A bronze statue of St. Paul, which replaced the original effigy of the emperor and his wife Faustina in the 16th century, stands at the top. The column is the centerpiece of Piazza Colonna. ⊠ *Piazza Colonna, Piazza di Spagna.*

Fontana della Barcaccia
(*Leaky Boat Fountain*)
FOUNTAIN | At the foot of the Spanish Steps, this curious, leaky boat fountain in Piazza di Spagna is fed by Rome's only surviving ancient aqueduct, the Acqua Vergine. The sinking ship design is a clever solution to low water pressure and was created by fountain genius Gian Lorenzo Bernini, together with his father Pietro. The project was commissioned by Barberini Pope Urban VIII, and the bees and suns on the boat are symbols of the Barberini family. Looking for more symbolism, some insist that the Berninis intended the fountain to be a reminder that this part of town was often flooded by the Tiber; others claim that it represents the Ship of the Church; and still others think that it marks the presumed site of the emperor Domitian's water stadium in which sea battles were reenacted in the glory days of the Roman Empire. ⊠ *Piazza di Spagna, Piazza di Spagna* Ⓜ *Spagna.*

Gagosian Gallery
ART GALLERY | One of the most prestigious contemporary galleries in the world opened its Rome branch in 2007 in a former bank. The always highly anticipated temporary exhibitions have included megastars such as Cy Twombly, Damien Hirst, and Jeff Koons. ⊠ *Via Francesco Crispi 16, Piazza di Spagna* ☎ *06/42086498* ⊕ *www.gagosian.com* ⊗ *Closed Sun. and Mon.* Ⓜ *Spagna.*

Rome's Fountains

Anyone who has thrown a coin backward over their shoulder into the Fontana di Trevi to ensure a return to Rome appreciates the magic of the city's fountains. From the magnificence of the Fontana dei Quattro Fiumi in Piazza Navona to the graceful caprice of the Fontana delle Tartarughe in the Jewish Ghetto, the water-spouting sculptures seem as essential to their piazzas as the cobblestones and ocher buildings that surround them.

Rome's original fountains date back to ancient times, when they were part of the city's remarkable aqueduct system. But from AD 537 to 1562, the waterworks were in disrepair, and the city's fountains lay dry and crumbling. Romans were left to draw their water from the Tiber and from wells. During the Renaissance, the popes brought running water back to the city as a means of currying political favor. To mark the restoration of the Virgin Aqueduct, architect Giacomo della Porta designed 18 unassuming, functional fountains. Each consisted of a large basin with two or three levels of smaller basins in the center, which were built and placed throughout the city at points along the water line.

Although nearly all of della Porta's fountains remain, their spare Renaissance design is virtually unrecognizable. With the baroque era, most were elaborately redecorated with dolphins, obelisks, and sea monsters.

Of this next generation of baroque fountaineers, the most famous is Gian Lorenzo Bernini. Bernini's writhing, muscular creatures of myth adorn most of Rome's most visible fountains, including the Fontana di Trevi (perhaps named for the three streets, or "tre vie," that converge at its piazza); the Fontana del Nettuno, with its tritons, in Piazza Barberini; and, in Piazza Navona, the Fontana dei Quattro Fiumi, whose hulking figures represented the four great rivers of the known world: the Nile, the Ganges, the Danube, and the Plata.

The most common type of fountain in Rome, however, is a kind rarely noted by visitors: the small, inconspicuous drinking fountains that burble away from side-street walls, old stone niches, and fire hydrant–like installations on street corners. You can drink this water, and many of these *fontanelle* even have pipes fitted with a little hole from which water shoots up when you press your hand under the main spout.

To combine the glorious Roman fountain with a drink of water, head to Piazza di Spagna, where the Barcaccia fountain is outfitted with spouts from which you can wet your whistle—but be sure to stay outside the rim. In a bid to better protect its fantastic fountains, the mayor of Rome has recently instituted steep fines for anyone who dares to step into the water.

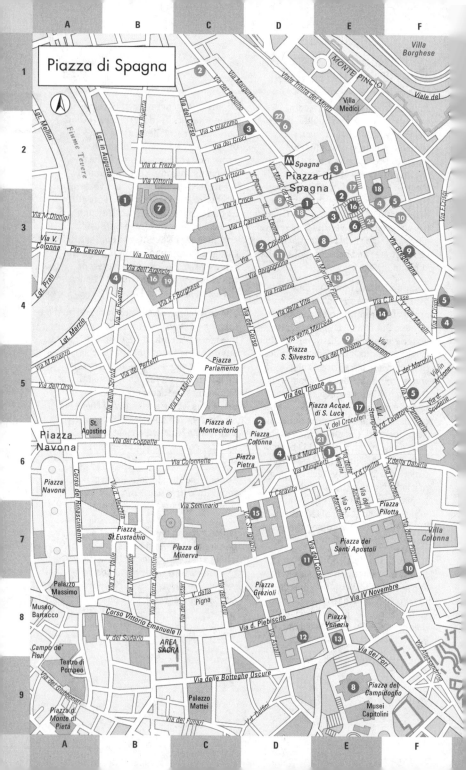

Sights ▼

1 Ara Pacis Augustae **B3**
2 Colonna di Marco Aurelio **D5**
3 Fontana della Barcaccia **E3**
4 Gagosian Gallery **F4**
5 Galleria d'Arte Moderna **F4**
6 Keats-Shelley Memorial House **E3**
7 Mausoleo di Augusto **B3**
8 Monumento a Vittorio Emanuele II, or Altare della Patria **E9**
9 Palazzetto Zuccari **F3**
10 Palazzo Colonna **F7**
11 Palazzo Doria Pamphilj **D7**
12 Palazzo Venezia **D8**
13 Piazza Venezia **E8**
14 Sant'Andrea delle Fratte **E4**
15 Sant'Ignazio **D7**
16 The Spanish Steps **E3**
17 Trevi Fountain **E5**
18 Trinità dei Monti **E2**

Restaurants ▼

1 Baccano **E6**
2 Caffè Romano **D3**
3 GiNa **E2**
4 Il Marchese **B4**
5 Imàgo **F3**
6 Mirabelle **G2**
7 Moma **I3**
8 Ristorante Nino **E3**
9 Settimo **G2**

Quick Bites ▼

1 Antico Caffè Greco **D3**
2 Babington's Tea Rooms **E3**
3 Caffè Canova-Tadolini **D2**
4 Gelateria Venchi **D6**
5 Il Gelato di San Crispino **F5**

Hotels ▼

1 Aleph Rome Hotel **H3**
2 Babuino 181 .... **C1**
3 Baglioni Hotel Regina .. **H2**
4 The Hassler **E3**
5 Hotel Alexandra **G3**
6 Hotel Art **D2**
7 Hotel Barberini **H5**
8 Hotel Condotti **D3**
9 Hotel dei Borgognoni **E4**
10 Hotel de la Ville **F3**
11 Hotel d'Inghilterra **D3**
12 Hotel Eden **G2**
13 Hotel Homs **E4**
14 Hotel Julia **G5**
15 Hotel Tritone **E5**
16 Hotel Vilòn **B4**
17 Il Palazzetto **E2**
18 Inn at the Spanish Steps **D3**
19 J.K. Place Roma **B4**
20 La Residenza **H2**
21 Maalot Roma **E6**
22 Margutta 19 .... **D2**
23 Marriott Grand Hotel Flora **H1**
24 Scalinata di Spagna **E3**
25 The Westin Excelsior, Rome **H2**
26 W Rome **H2**

KEY

1 *Exploring Sights*
1 *Restaurants*
1 *Hotels*
1 *Quick Bites*

★ Galleria d'Arte Moderna

ART MUSEUM | The city of Rome's modern art gallery is housed in a former convent on the opposite side of Villa Borghese, from the entrance above the Spanish Steps. The 18th-century building in this quiet corner of Rome is the perfect spot for more than 3,000 19th- and 20th-century paintings, drawings, prints, and sculptures by artists including Giorgio de Chirico, Gino Severini, Scipione, Antonio Donghi, and Giacomo Manzù. In fact, the permanent collection is too large to be displayed at once, so exhibits rotate. A trip out to the museum offers a look at modern Roman art as well as at another side of the city—one where, in the near-empty halls, tranquility and contemplation reign. ⊠ *Via Francesco Crispi 24, Piazza di Spagna* ☎ *06/0608* ⊕ *www. galleriaartemodernaroma.it* ☒ *€7.50* ⊗ *Closed Mon.* Ⓜ *Spagna.*

Keats-Shelley Memorial House

HISTORIC HOME | Sent to Rome in a last-ditch attempt to treat his consumptive condition, English Romantic poet John Keats lived—and died—in this house at the foot of the Spanish Steps. At the time, this was the heart of the colorful bohemian quarter of Rome that was especially favored by English expats. He took his last breath here on February 23, 1821, and is now buried in the Non-Catholic Cemetery in Testaccio. Even before his death, Keats was celebrated for such poems as "Ode to a Nightingale" and "Endymion." In this "Casina di Keats," you can visit his final home and see his death mask, though all his furnishings were burned after his death as a sanitary measure by the local authorities. You'll also find a rather quaint collection of memorabilia of English literary figures of the period—Lord Byron, Percy Bysshe Shelley, Joseph Severn, and Leigh Hunt, as well as Keats—and an exhaustive library of works on the Romantics. ⊠ *Piazza di Spagna 26, Piazza di Spagna* ☎ *06/6784235* ⊕ *www.*

keats-shelley-house.org ☒ *€6* ⊗ *Closed Sun.* Ⓜ *Spagna.*

Mausoleo di Augusto

TOMB | The largest circular tomb in the world, the mausoleum certainly made a statement about the glory of Augustus, Julius Caesar's successor. He was only 35 years old when he commissioned it following his victory over Marc Antony and Cleopatra. Though the ruins we see now are brick and stone, it was originally covered in marble and travertine, with evergreen trees planted on top, a colossal statue of the emperor at the summit, and a pair of bronze pillars inscribed with his achievements at the entrance. The mausoleum's innermost sepulchral chamber housed the ashes of several members of the Augustan dynasty, but it was subsequently raided and the urns were never found. Between the 13th and 20th centuries, it lived several other lives as a garden, an amphitheater that hosted jousting tournaments, and a concert hall, which Mussolini tore down in 1936 in a bid to restore the monument to its imperial glory. His plans were interrupted by World War II, after which the mausoleum was all but abandoned until a recent restoration reopened it to the public. Booking online as far in advance as possible is recommended because of the limited number of visitors allowed inside at any one time. A new public piazza is currently being constructed around it. ⊠ *Piazza Augusto Imperatore, Piazza di Spagna* ☎ *06/0608* ⊕ *www.mausoleodiaugusto.it* ☒ *€4* Ⓜ *Spagna.*

Monumento a Vittorio Emanuele II, or Altare della Patria (*Victor Emmanuel II Monument, or Altar of the Nation*)

MONUMENT | The huge white mass known as the "Vittoriano" is an inescapable landmark that has been likened to a huge wedding cake or an immense typewriter. Present-day Romans joke that you can only avoid looking at it if you are standing on it, but it was the source of great civic pride at the time of its construction at the turn of the 20th century. To create this elaborate marble monster and the vast piazza on which it stands, its architects blithely destroyed many ancient and medieval buildings and altered the slope of the Campidoglio (Capitoline Hill), which abuts it. Built to honor the unification of Italy and the nation's first king, Victor Emmanuel II, it also shelters the eternal flame at the tomb of Italy's Unknown Soldier, killed during World War I. You can't miss the Monumento, so enjoy neo-imperial grandiosity at its most bombastic.

The underwhelming exhibit inside the building tells the history of the country's unification, but the truly enticing feature of the Vittoriano is its rooftop terrace, which offers some of the best panoramic views of Rome. The only way up is by elevator (the entrance is located several flights of stairs up on the right as you face the monument). ✉ *Entrances on Piazza Venezia, Piazza del Campidoglio, and Via di San Pietro in Carcere, Piazza di Spagna* ☎ *06/0608* ⊕ *vittoriano.benicul-turali.it* 🖾 *Free main building, €10 for the terrace* Ⓜ *Colosseo.*

★ Palazzo Colonna

HISTORIC HOME | Rome's grandest family built themselves Rome's grandest private palace, a fusion of 17th- and 18th-century buildings that has been occupied by the Colonna family for more than 20 generations. The immense palatial residence faces Piazza dei Santi Apostoli on one side and the Quirinale (Quirinal Hill) on the other (with a little bridge over Via della Pilotta linking to the gardens on the hill). The palazzo is still home to some Colonna patricians, but it also holds an exquisite art gallery, which is open to the public on Saturday morning (or by guided tour on Friday morning). The gallery is itself a setting of aristocratic grandeur; you might recognize the Sala Grande as the site where Audrey Hepburn meets

the press in *Roman Holiday.* An ancient red marble column (*colonna* in Italian), which is the family's emblem, looms at one end, but the most spectacular feature is the ceiling fresco of the Battle of Lepanto painted by Giovanni Coli and Filippo Gherardi beginning in 1675. Adding to the opulence are works by Poussin, Tintoretto, and Veronese, and a number of portraits of illustrious members of the family, such as Vittoria Colonna, Michelangelo's muse and longtime friend. There are guided tours in English included in the entrance fee and can help you to navigate through the array of madonnas, saints, goddesses, popes, and cardinals to see Annibale Carracci's lonely *Beaneater,* spoon at the ready and front teeth missing. The gallery also has a caffè with a pleasant terrace. ✉ *Via della Pilotta 17, Piazza di Spagna* ☎ *06/6784350* ⊕ *www.galleriacolonna. it* 🖾 *€15 for gallery and gardens, €25 to also visit the Princess Isabelle Apartment* ⊙ *Closed Sun.–Fri.* Ⓜ *Barberini.*

★ Palazzo Doria Pamphilj

HISTORIC HOME | Along with the Palazzo Colonna and the Galleria Borghese, this dazzling family palace provides the best glimpse of aristocratic Rome. The main attractions in the gilded galleries are the legendary Old Master paintings, including treasures by Velázquez and Caravaggio; the splendor of the halls themselves; and a unique suite of private family apartments. The understated beauty of the graceful facade, designed by Gabriele Valvassori in 1730, is best admired by crossing to the opposite side of the street for a good view, but it barely hints at the opulence that awaits inside. The palace passed through several hands before becoming the property of the Pamphilj family, who married into the famous seafaring Doria family of Genoa in the 18th century. The family still lives in part of the palace.

The gallery contains 550 paintings, including three by Caravaggio—a young *St. John the Baptist, Mary Magdalene,* and the breathtaking *Rest on the Flight to Egypt.* Off the eye-popping Galleria degli Specchi (Gallery of Mirrors)—a smaller version of the one at Versailles—are the famous Velázquez *Pope Innocent X,* considered by some historians to be the greatest portrait ever painted, and the Bernini bust of the same Pamphilj pope. The delightful audio guide is included in the ticket price and narrated by the current heir, Prince Jonathan Doria Pamphilj, who divulges an intimate family history. ⊠ *Via del Corso 305, Piazza di Spagna* ☎ *06/6797323* ⊕ *www.doriapamphilj.it* 🎫 *€14* ⊗ *Closed the third Wed. of the month* ♿ *Reservations required* Ⓜ *Barberini.*

Palazzo Venezia

CASTLE/PALACE | The centerpiece of the eponymous piazza, this was Rome's first great Renaissance palace. It was originally built for Venetian cardinal Pietro Barbo (who eventually became Pope Paul II), but it was repurposed in the 20th century by Mussolini, who used it to harangue crowds with speeches from the balcony over the finely carved door. Lights were left on through the night during his reign to suggest that the Fascist leader worked without pause. The palace is now open to the public and rooms include frescoes by Giorgio Vasari and an Algardi sculpture of Pope Innocent X. There are many decorative art exhibits inside and the loggia has a pleasant view over the tranquil garden courtyard, a million miles away from the chaos of Piazza Venezia on the other side of the building. The ticket price includes an audio guide. ⊠ *Via del Plebiscito 118, Piazza di Spagna* ☎ *06/69994388* ⊕ *www.museopalazzovenezia.beniculturali.it* 🎫 *€12.*

Palazzetto Zuccari

CASTLE/PALACE | This amusing palazzo was designed in 1591 by noted painter Federico Zuccari (1540–1609), who frescoed the first floor of his custom-built home. Typical of the outré mannerist style of the period, the two windows and the main door are designed to look like monsters with mouths gaping wide. Zuccari—whose frescoes adorn many Roman churches, including Trinità dei Monti just up the block—sank all his money into his new home, dying in debt before his curious memorial, as it turned out to be, was completed. Today, it is home to the German state-run Bibliotheca Hertziana, a prestigious fine-arts library. Access is reserved for scholars, but the pristine facade can be admired for free. Leading up to the quaint Piazza della Trinità del Monti, the nearby Via Gregoriana is quite charming and has long been one of Rome's most elegant addresses, home to such residents as 19th-century French painter Ingres and Valentino's first couture salon. ⊠ *Via Gregoriana 30, Piazza di Spagna* ☎ *06/69993242 Bibliotheca Hertziana* Ⓜ *Spagna.*

Piazza Venezia

PLAZA/SQUARE | The geographic heart of the city, this is the spot from which all distances from Rome are calculated and the main center of city traffic. It was transformed in the late 19th century when much older ruins were destroyed to make room for a modern capital city (and a massive monument to unified Italy's first king). Piazza Venezia stands at what was the beginning of Via Flaminia, the ancient Roman road leading northeast across Italy to Fano on the Adriatic Sea. The Via Flaminia was, and remains, a vital artery, and the part which leads from Piazza Venezia to Piazza del Popolo is now known as Via del Corso, after the horse races (*corse*) that were run here during the wild Roman

Did You Know?

One of Rome's most popular shopping streets, the Via Condotti—seen here from the Spanish Steps—gets its name from the conduits that carried water to the Baths of Agrippa.

carnival celebrations of the 17th and 18th centuries. It also happens to be one of Rome's busiest shopping streets. The massive female bust near the church of San Marco in the corner of the piazza, a fragment of a statue of Isis, is known to the Romans as Madama Lucrezia. This was one of the "talking statues" on which anonymous poets hung verses pungent with political satire, a practice that has not entirely disappeared. ⊠ *Piazza Venezia, Piazza di Spagna*.

Sant'Andrea delle Fratte

CHURCH | Copies have now replaced Bernini's original angels on the Ponte Sant'Angelo, but two of the originals can be found here, placed on either side of the high altar. The door in the right aisle leads into one of Rome's hidden gardens, where orange trees bloom in the cloister. Borromini's fantastic contributions—the dome and a curious bell tower with its droop-winged angels looking out over the city—are best seen from Via di Capo le Case, across Via dei Due Macelli. ⊠ *Via di Sant'Andrea delle Fratte 1, at Via della Mercede, Piazza di Spagna* ☎ *06/6793191* ⊕ *www.madonnadelmiracolo.it* Ⓜ *Spagna*.

★ Sant'Ignazio

CHURCH | Rome's second Jesuit church, this 17th-century landmark set on a rococo piazza harbors some of the city's most magnificent trompe l'oeils. To get the full effect of the marvelous illusionistic ceiling by priest-artist Andrea Pozzo, stand on the small yellow disk set into the floor of the nave. The heavenly vision above you, seemingly extending upward almost indefinitely, represents the *Allegory of the Missionary Work of the Jesuits* and is part of Pozzo's cycle of works in this church exalting the early history of the Jesuit order, whose founder was the reformer Ignatius of Loyola. The saint soars heavenward, supported by a cast of thousands, creating a jaw-dropping effect that was fully intended to rival the glorious ceiling produced by Baciccia in the nearby mother church of Il Gesù. Be sure to have coins handy for the machine that switches on the lights so you can marvel at the false dome, which is actually a flat canvas—a trompe l'oeil trick Pozzo used when the architectural budget drained dry. The dazzling church hardly stops there: scattered around the nave are several awe-inspiring altars; their soaring columns, gold-on-gold decoration, and gilded statues are pure splendor. The church is often host to concerts of sacred music performed by choirs from all over the world. Look for posters by the main doors or check the website for more information. ⊠ *Via del Caravita 8A, Piazza Navona* ☎ *06/6794406* ⊕ *www.chiesasantignazio.it*.

★ The Spanish Steps

NOTABLE BUILDING | **FAMILY** | The iconic Spanish Steps (often called simply *la scalinata,* or "the staircase," by Italians) and the Piazza di Spagna from which they ascend both get their names from the Spanish Embassy to the Vatican on the piazza—even though the staircase was built with French funds by an Italian in 1723. In honor of a diplomatic visit by the King of Spain, the hillside was transformed by architect Francesco de Sanctis with a spectacular piece of urban planning to link the church of Trinità dei Monti at the top with the Via Condotti below. In an allusion to the church, the staircase is divided by three landings (beautifully lined by potted azaleas mid-April–mid-May). Bookending the bottom of the steps are two beloved holdovers from the 18th century, when the area was known as the "English Ghetto": to the right, the Keats-Shelley House, and to the left, Babington's Tea Rooms—both beautifully redolent of the era of the Grand Tour. For weary sightseers who find the 135 steps too daunting, there is an elevator at Vicolo del Bottino 8, next to the Metro entrance. (Those with mobility problems should be aware that there is still a small flight of stairs after, however, and that the elevator is sporadically closed for repair.) At the bottom of the steps, Bernini's splendid "Barcaccia" (sinking ship) fountain dates to the early 17th century and still spouts drinking water from the ancient Aqua Vergine aqueduct. ⊠ *Piazza di Spagna, Piazza di Spagna* Ⓜ *Spagna.*

★ Trevi Fountain

FOUNTAIN | Alive with rushing waters commanded by an imperious sculpture of Oceanus, the Fontana di Trevi has been all about theatrical effects from the start; it is an aquatic marvel in a city filled with them. The fountain's unique drama is largely due to its location: its vast basin is squeezed into the tight confluence of three little streets (the *tre vie,* which may give the fountain its name), with cascades emerging as if from the wall of Palazzo Poli. The dream of a fountain emerging full-force from a palace was first envisioned by Bernini and Pietro da Cortona from Pope Urban VIII's plan to rebuild an older fountain, which had earlier marked the end-point of the ancient Acqua Vergine aqueduct, created in 18 BC by Agrippa. Three popes later, under Pope Clement XIII, Nicola Salvi finally broke ground with his winning design. Unfortunately, Salvi did not live to see his masterpiece of sculpted seashells, roaring sea beasts, and diva-like mermaids completed; he caught a cold and died while working in the culverts of the aqueduct 11 years before the fountain was finally finished in 1762.

Everyone knows the famous legend that if you throw a coin into the Trevi Fountain you will ensure a return trip to the Eternal City, but not everyone knows how to do it the right way. You must toss a coin with your right hand over your left shoulder, with your back to the fountain. One coin means you'll return to Rome; two, you'll return *and* fall in love; three, you'll return, find love, and marry. The fountain grosses some €600,000 a year, with every cent going to the Italian Red Cross, which is why Fendi was willing to foot the bill and

fully funded the Trevi's marvelous recent restoration.

Tucked away in a little alley nearby (⊠ *Vicolo del Puttarello, 25*), visitors can pay €8 for a tour that descends into a newly uncovered subterranean area that gives a glimpse at the underground water source that keeps the fountain running. ⊠ *Piazza di Trevi, Piazza di Spagna* Ⓜ *Barberini.*

Trinità dei Monti

CHURCH | Standing high above the Spanish Steps, this 16th-century church has a rare double-tower facade, suggestive of late–French Gothic style; in fact, the French crown paid for the church's construction. Today, it is beautiful primarily for its dramatic location and magnificent views. The obelisk in front was moved here in 1789, but dates back to the early years of the Roman Empire. It opens late on Wednesday. ⊠ *Piazza della Trinità dei Monti, Piazza di Spagna* ☎ *06/6794179* ⊕ *www.trinitadeimonti.net* Ⓜ *Spagna.*

Restaurants

During the day, the area around the Spanish Steps is a hotbed of tourists, shoppers, and office workers. It gets significantly quieter at night and, as a result, it's easy to fall into tourist traps and overpriced hotel dining. Stick to recommended restaurants.

Baccano

$$$ | **BRASSERIE** | There are plenty of options for good food at reasonable prices around the Trevi Fountain, but this large brasserie is a good bet, and is open for lunch and dinner and everything in between. The extensive menu with a focus on seafood has something for everyone, from salads to pasta and entrées. **Known for:** champagne menu; tasty burgers; oyster bar. Ⓢ *Average main: €28* ⊠ *Via delle Muratte 23, Piazza di Spagna* ☎ *06/69941166* ⊕ *www.baccanoroma.com* Ⓜ *Barberini.*

Caffè Romano

$$$ | ECLECTIC | With *orario continuato,* or nonstop operating hours (noon till late at night), this sleek spot in the Hotel d'Inghilterra caters to jet-setters and hotel guests. The creative global menu can mean international misfires, so it's best to select from among the authentic Northern Italian meat and Southern Italian seafood dishes such as boar with polenta, seafood soup, or classic pastas. **Known for:** truffle pasta; signature Caesar salad with prawns; enviable outdoor seating. $ *Average main: €28* ✉ *Hotel d'Inghilterra, Via Borgongna 4M, Piazza di Spagna* ☎ *06/69981500* ⊕ *collezione. starhotels.com* Ⓜ *Spagna.*

GiNa

$ | CAFÉ | "Homey minimalism" isn't a contradiction at this multilevel whitewashed caffè with a modern edge. The menu offers various bruschette, mixed salads, and sandwiches, making this a great spot for a light lunch or *aperitivo* (happy hour) at a reasonable price (considering the high-end neighborhood); and the sweets are top-notch, whether you're in the mood for gelato, pastries, fruit with yogurt, or even cheesecake. **Known for:** light, fresh sandwiches; popular hot chocolate; packed picnic baskets. $ *Average main: €10* ✉ *Via San Sebastianello 7A, Piazza di Spagna* ☎ *06/6780251* ⊙ *Closed Mon. No dinner* Ⓜ *Spagna.*

★ Il Marchese

$$ | ITALIAN | This rustic-meets-glamorous bistro attracts locals for its flawless execution of Roman classics (many served photogenically in metal cooking pans) as well as original dishes. Its bar is known among amaro connoisseurs for having the largest selection in Rome, and the bitter liquors are the stars of the expertly crafted cocktail menu. **Known for:** extensive selection of amaros and great cocktails; well-executed classics; beautiful design. $ *Average main: €18* ✉ *Via di Ripetta 162, Piazza di Spagna* ☎ *06/90218872* ⊕ *www. ilmarcheseroma.it* Ⓜ *Spagna.*

Imàgo

$$$$ | MODERN ITALIAN | Excellence is at the forefront of everything at Imàgo, the Michelin-starred restaurant inside the legendary Hotel Hassler, now headed by young star chef Andrea Antonini. You can order à la carte, but this is the place to splurge on a tasting menu. **Known for:** innovative creations inspired by all of Italy; sweeping city views from rooftop terrace; tempting tasting menus. $ *Average main: €50* ✉ *Hotel Hassler, Piazza Trinità dei Monti 6, Piazza di Spagna* ☎ *06/69934726* ⊕ *www.hotelhasslerroma.com* ⊙ *No lunch* Ⓜ *Spagna.*

Mirabelle

$$$$ | MODERN ITALIAN | Old-world elegance is the name of the game here—think white-jacketed waiters who attend to your every need, classic decor, and impeccable dishes, which are the most modern thing about this restaurant on the seventh floor of the Hotel Splendide Royal. Be sure to request a table on the terrace, which boasts panoramic views of leafy Villa Borghese and the center of Rome. **Known for:** top-notch food and service; panoramic terrace; romantic atmosphere. $ *Average main: €54* ✉ *Hotel Splendide Royal, Via di Porta Pinciana 14, Piazza di Spagna* ☎ *06/42168838* ⊕ *www.mirabelle.it* 🏛 *business casual* Ⓜ *Spagna, Barberini.*

★ Moma

$$$ | MODERN ITALIAN | In front of the American embassy, a favorite of the design *trendoisie,* modern, Michelin-starred Moma attracts well-heeled businessmen at lunch but turns into a more intimate affair for dinner. The kitchen turns out hits as it creates *alta cucina* (haute cuisine) made using Italian ingredients sourced from small producers. **Known for:** affordable fine dining; creative presentation; pasta with a twist. $ *Average main: €25* ✉ *Via San Basilio 42/43, Piazza di Spagna* ☎ *06/42011798* ⊕ *www.ristorantemoma.it* ⊙ *Closed Sun.* Ⓜ *Barberini.*

Ristorante Nino

$$$ | ITALIAN | Almost more of a landmark than an eatery, Nino has been a favorite among international journalists and the rich and famous since the 1930s and does not seem to have changed at all over the decades. The interior is Tuscan country rustic , and the menu, accordingly, sticks to the classics. **Known for:** *ribollita* (Tuscan bean soup); upscale old-school Italian vibe; warm crostini spread with pâté. $ *Average main: €26* ✉ *Via Borgognona 11, Piazza di Spagna* ☎ *06/6786752* ⊕ *www.ristorantenino.it* ⊘ *Closed Sun. and Aug.* Ⓜ *Spagna.*

Settimo

$$$ | ITALIAN | Crowning the Sofitel Rome Villa Borghese hotel, this chic restaurant serves fancified takes on Rome's *cucina povera* (peasant cooking) in a chic space with graphic punches of color. The terrace offers fantastic views that stretch from Villa Borghese to the dome of St. Peter's, but the interior dining room, with its floor-to-ceiling windows and terrazzo-inspired floors, is lovely too. **Known for:** terrace with great views; colorful, modern design; amped up version of classic Roman recipes. $ *Average main: €26* ✉ *Sofitel Rome Villa Borghese, Via Lombardia 47, Piazza di Spagna* ☎ *06/478021* ⊕ *www.settimoristorante.it* Ⓜ *Barberini.*

☕ Coffee and Quick Bites

Antico Caffè Greco

$ | CAFÉ | Pricey Antico Caffè Greco is a national landmark and Rome's oldest caffè; its red-velvet chairs, marble tables, and marble busts have seen the likes of Byron, Shelley, Keats, Goethe, and Casanova. Add to this the fact that it's in the middle of the shopping madness on the upscale Via Condotti, and you won't be surprised that the place is often filled with tourists. **Known for:** crystal goblets and high prices to match; perfect espresso; lavish historic design. $ *Average main: €12* ✉ *Via dei Condotti 86, Piazza di Spagna* ☎ *06/6791700* ⊕ *www.caffegreco.shop* Ⓜ *Spagna.*

Babington's Tea Rooms

$$ | BRITISH | At the left foot of the Spanish Steps is Babington's Tea Rooms, which has catered to the refined tea and scone cravings of travelers since opening in 1893. The blends are carefully designed and can be brought to the homey tables in this historic restaurant alongside a tower of tiny sandwiches or as an accompaniment to risotto and fully loaded salads. **Known for:** homemade scones; cozy, historic atmosphere; unique loose leaf teas. $ *Average main: €20* ✉ *Piazza di Spagna 23, Piazza di Spagna* ☎ *06/6786027* ⊕ *www.babingtons.com* Ⓜ *Spagna.*

Caffè Canova-Tadolini

$ | CAFÉ | On chic Via del Babuino, the former studio of neoclassical sculptor Antonio Canova and his student Adamo Tadolini is now a wonderfully atmospheric spot for coffee or a snack. Either go for the budget option and take your coffee at the bar while admiring the enormous plaster copies of the maestros' work, or pay for table service and sit amid vast sculptures in this eccentric spot. **Known for:** museum-like setting; respectable aperitivo snacks for the price; slow and serious service. $ *Average main: €5* ✉ *Via del Babuino 150/A, Piazza di Spagna* ☎ *06/32110702* ⊕ *www.canovatadolini.com* Ⓜ *Spagna.*

Gelateria Venchi

$ | ITALIAN | Established in 1878, Venchi is one of Italy's premier chocolate and confectionery makers, and you'll see the brand all over the country. At this brick-and-mortar shop, you can buy chocolate as well as gelato, made fresh daily. **Known for:** creamy gelato flavors; packaged candies; free-flowing melted chocolate. $ *Average main: €5* ✉ *Via del Corso 335, Piazza di Spagna* ☎ *06/69797790* Ⓜ *Spagna.*

Il Gelato di San Crispino

$ | ICE CREAM | Many people say this is the best gelato in Rome, and though it's hard to pick just one, this is definitely the place to go if you want a delicious iced treat around the corner from the Trevi Fountain. The shop even had a cameo in the movie *Eat, Pray, Love* and is known for keeping its gelato hidden under metal covers in order to best preserve the quality. **Known for:** offerings only cups and no cones; wine-based gelato; seasonal fruit flavors. $ *Average main: €4* ✉ *Via della Panetteria 42, Piazza di Spagna* ☎ *06/6793924* ⊕ *www.ilgelatodisancrispino.it* Ⓜ *Barberini.*

Hotels

If being right in the heart of Rome's shopping district and within walking distance of major sights is a priority, this is the place to stay. You'll find a wide range of accommodations here—exclusive boutique hotels with over-the-top amenities as well as moderately priced urban bed-and-breakfasts and *pensioni* (guesthouses) with clean, comfortable rooms.

Aleph Rome Hotel
$$$$ | **HOTEL** | Fashionable couples tend to favor the Aleph, a former bank–turned–luxury Rome hotel, where the motto seems to be "more marble, everywhere." Now part of Hilton's Curio Collection, the hotel has ample facilities that include two pools (one in the spa and one on the roof), a cigar lounge, a cocktail bar, and two restaurants, one on the ground floor and one on the rooftop. **Pros:** free access to the spa for hotel guests; terrace with pool; award-winning design. **Cons:** buffet breakfast not included; rooftop views don't showcase Rome's most flattering side; rooms are too petite for the price. $ *Rooms from: €380* ✉ *Via San Basilio 15, Piazza di Spagna* ☎ *06/4229001* ⊕ *alephrome.com* ⇆ *88 rooms* ♔ *No Meals* Ⓜ *Barberini.*

Babuino 181
$$$ | **HOTEL** | On chic Via del Babuino, known for its high-end boutiques, jewelry stores, and antiques shops, this discreet and stylish hotel is an ideal Roman pied à terre that has spacious rooms spread over two historic buildings. **Pros:** spacious suites; iPhone docks and other handy in-room amenities; luxury Frette linens. **Cons:** annex rooms feel removed from service staff; breakfast is nothing special; rooms can be a bit noisy. $ *Rooms from: €250* ✉ *Via del Babuino 181, Piazza di Spagna* ☎ *06/32295295* ⊕ *www.rome-luxurysuites.com/babuino* ⇆ *24 rooms* ♔ *Free Breakfast* Ⓜ *Flaminio, Spagna.*

Baglioni Hotel Regina
$$$$ | **HOTEL** | The former home of Queen Margherita of Savoy, the Baglioni Hotel Regina, which enjoys a prime spot on the Via Veneto, is still a favorite among today's international jet-setters. **Pros:** nice decor; excellent on-site restaurant and bar; luxury on-site spa. **Cons:** location isn't as prestigious as it once was; service is hit-or-miss; some rooms are noisy. $ *Rooms from: €319* ✉ *Via Veneto 72, Piazza di Spagna* ☎ *06/421111* ⊕ *www.baglionihotels.com/rome* ⇆ *114 rooms* ♔ *No Meals* Ⓜ *Barberini.*

★ The Hassler
$$$$ | **HOTEL** | When it comes to million-dollar views, the best place to stay in the whole city is the Hassler, so it's no surprise many rich and famous (Tom Cruise, Jennifer Lopez, and the Beckhams among them) are willing to pay top dollar for a room at this exclusive hotel atop the Spanish Steps. **Pros:** prime location and panoramic views; sauna access included with each reservation; private rooftop with bar service upon request. **Cons:** rooms are updated on a rolling basis, leaving some feeling dated; gym and wellness area is tiny; VIP rates (10% VAT not included). $ *Rooms from: €1010* ✉ *Piazza Trinità dei Monti 6, Piazza*

di Spagna ☎ *06/699340, 800/223–6800 in U.S.* ⊕ *www.hotelhasslerroma.com* ⇥ *87 rooms* ⦿ *Free Breakfast* Ⓜ *Spagna.*

Hotel Alexandra

$$$ | **HOTEL** | For nearly a century the Hotel Alexandra has been a family affair, and distinguished style and moderate prices have allowed it to hold its own against its flashier big brothers and sisters on the upscale Via Veneto. **Pros:** great location near Piazza Barberini for sightseeing, restaurants, and transportation; decorated with authentic antiques; free Wi-Fi. **Cons:** breakfast is standard fare; not all rooms have undergone updates; mostly tiny rooms and tinier bathrooms. ⑤ *Rooms from: €280* ⊠ *Via Veneto 18, Piazza di Spagna* ☎ *06/4881943* ⊕ *www.hotelalexandraroma.com* ⇥ *57 rooms* ⦿ *Free Breakfast* Ⓜ *Barberini.*

Hotel Art

$$$ | **HOTEL** | High-fashion Rome meets chic contemporary art gallery at this hotel that sits on Via Margutta, "the street of painters." As you glide through the stylish lobby, the smart furnishings and unique fixtures in the public spaces of the hotel feel positively eclectic, but the color-coordinated guest rooms have been done in a more standard contemporary style (sleek wood headboards accented with handmade Florentine leather, puffy white comforters, bathrobes, and high-speed Internet). **Pros:** hotel has an ultrahip art-gallery feel; free access to the fitness center with sauna and Turkish baths; comfortable beds. **Cons:** courtyard bar crowd may keep you awake; sometimes more about form over function, and the air-conditioning can be iffy; glass floors are noisy at night. ⑤ *Rooms from: €260* ⊠ *Via Margutta 56, Piazza di Spagna* ☎ *06/328711* ⊕ *www.hotelart.it* ⇥ *46 rooms* ⦿ *Free Breakfast* Ⓜ *Spagna.*

Hotel Barberini

$$$ | **HOTEL** | This elegant four-star hotel, housed in a 19th-century palazzo near Piazza Barberini, has old-world luxury and charm an easy distance from the Metro, the Trevi Fountain, and sophisticated Via Veneto. **Pros:** beautiful views from the rooftop terrace; located on a quiet side street close to several important attractions; great value for the area. **Cons:** not all rooms have bathtubs; beds are a bit hard; some rooms are on the small side. ⑤ *Rooms from: €250* ⊠ *Via Rasella 3, Piazza di Spagna* ☎ *06/4814993* ⊕ *www.hotelbarberini.com* ⇥ *35 rooms* ⦿ *Free Breakfast* Ⓜ *Barberini.*

Hotel Condotti

$$ | **B&B/INN** | Near the most expensive shopping street in Rome, Via Condotti, and one block from the Spanish Steps, this delightful little hotel is all about peace, comfort, and location. **Pros:** soundproof rooms with terraces; individual climate control; gorgeous decor. **Cons:** tiny elevator; annex rooms on a different street; small rooms. ⑤ *Rooms from: €200* ⊠ *Via Mario de' Fiori 37, Piazza di Spagna* ☎ *06/6794661* ⊕ *www.hotelcondotti.com* ⇥ *21 rooms* ⦿ *Free Breakfast* Ⓜ *Spagna.*

Hotel dei Borgognoni

$$$ | **HOTEL** | Travelers who love peace and tranquility appreciate the position of this quietly chic hotel set in a prestigious palazzo from the 1800s. **Pros:** free in-room Wi-Fi; some rooms have private balconies or terraces; small pets (6 kg [13 pounds]) are permitted. **Cons:** cramped bathrooms; breakfast lacks variety; some rooms are small for the price. ⑤ *Rooms from: €280* ⊠ *Via del Bufalo 126, Piazza di Spagna* ☎ *06/69941505* ⊕ *www.hotelborgognoni.com* ⇥ *51 rooms* ⦿ *Free Breakfast* Ⓜ *Barberini.*

6

Piazza di Spagna

★ Hotel de la Ville

$$$$ | HOTEL | Occupying a prime position at the top of the Spanish Steps, the sister property to the beloved Hotel de Russie is the most glamorous new hotel in town. **Pros:** must-visit rooftop bar with panoramic views; pampering spa uses signature made-in-Italy organic products; prestigious location atop the Spanish Steps. **Cons:** no pets allowed; service can be a bit slow at the bar; some rooms are a bit small. $ *Rooms from: €594* ✉ *Via Sistina 69, Piazza di Spagna* ☎ *06/977931* ⊕ *www.roccofortehotels.com* ✈ *104 rooms* ⫙ *No Meals* Ⓜ *Spagna.*

Hotel d'Inghilterra

$$$$ | HOTEL | Situated in a stately 16th-century building and founded in 1845, Hotel d'Inghilterra has a long, storied history: it has been used as a guesthouse for aristocratic travelers visiting a noble family who once lived across the cobblestone street and has been the home away from home for various monarchs and movie stars, like Elizabeth Taylor, not to mention some of the greatest writers of all time—Lord Byron, John Keats, Mark Twain, and Ernest Hemingway among them. **Pros:** distinct character and opulence; excellent in-house restaurant; turndown service (with chocolates). **Cons:** some rooms badly in need of renovations and maintenance; the location, despite soundproofing, is still noisy; elevator is small. $ *Rooms from: €400* ✉ *Via Bocca di Leone 14, Piazza di Spagna* ☎ *06/699811* ⊕ *www.starhotelscollezione.com/en/our-hotels/hotel-d-inghilterra-rome* ✈ *84 rooms* ⫙ *Free Breakfast* Ⓜ *Spagna.*

★ Hotel Eden

$$$$ | HOTEL | Once a favorite haunt of Ingrid Bergman, Ginger Rogers, and Fellini, this superlative hotel combines dashing elegance, exquisitely lush decor, and stunning vistas of Rome with true Italian hospitality to create one of the city's top luxury lodgings. **Pros:** gorgeous rooftop terrace restaurant; 24-hour room service; tranquil spa facilities. **Cons:** some rooms overlook an unremarkable courtyard; gym is standard but small; breakfast not included (and very expensive, at €45). $ *Rooms from: €780* ✉ *Via Ludovisi 49, Piazza di Spagna* ☎ *06/478121* ⊕ *www.dorchestercollection.com* ✈ *98 rooms* ⫙ *No Meals* Ⓜ *Spagna.*

Hotel Homs

$$ | HOTEL | Tucked away on a quiet street near the Spanish Steps, this midsize hotel is convenient to great caffè, serious shopping, and all the sights. **Pros:** walking distance to Piazza di Spagna; steps away from a big bus hub and close to the Metro; helpful staff. **Cons:** small rooms and bathrooms; rickety old elevator; breakfast not included. $ *Rooms from: €170* ✉ *Via della Vite 71–72, Piazza di Spagna* ☎ *06/6792976* ⊕ *www.hotelhoms.it* ✈ *58 rooms* ⫙ *No Meals* Ⓜ *Barberini, Spagna.*

Hotel Julia

$$ | HOTEL | This small three-star hotel, situated on a small cobblestone street just behind Piazza Barberini and a short walk to the Trevi Fountain, offers clean, comfortable rooms in the center of Rome that won't break the bank. **Pros:** safe neighborhood; convenient to sights and transportation; moderate prices for a central area. **Cons:** very basic accommodations; some of the rooms are dark and cramped; some street noise at night. $ *Rooms from: €180* ✉ *Via Rasella 29, Piazza di Spagna* ☎ *06/4881637* ⊕ *www.hoteljulia.it* ✈ *33 rooms* ⫙ *Free Breakfast* Ⓜ *Barberini.*

Hotel Tritone

$$ | HOTEL | This trusty hotel offers modern accommodations in a great location, steps from Rome's majestic Trevi Fountain. **Pros:** walking distance to major attractions; modern rustic decor; friendly staff. **Cons:** breakfast isn't very exciting; spotty Wi-Fi; rooms can be noisy despite soundproofing. $ *Rooms from: €160* ✉ *Via del Tritone 210, Piazza di Spagna* ☎ *06/69922575* ⊕ *www.tritonehotel.com* ✈ *43 rooms* ⫙ *Free Breakfast* Ⓜ *Barberini.*

★ Hotel Vilòn

$$$$ | **HOTEL** | This intimate hotel in the 16th-century mansion annexed to Palazzo Borghese might be Rome's best-kept secret. **Pros:** gorgeous design; fantastic location; attentive staff. **Cons:** not much communal space; some rooms are a bit small; no spa or gym. *$ Rooms from: €460* ✉ *Via dell'Arancio 69, Piazza di Spagna* ☎ *06/878187* ⊕ *www.hotelvilon.com* ⮑ *18 rooms* ⦿ *Free Breakfast* Ⓜ *Spagna.*

Il Palazzetto

$$$ | **B&B/INN** | Once a retreat for one of Rome's richest noble families, this 15th-century house is one of the most intimate and luxurious hotels in Rome, with gorgeous terraces and a rooftop bar where you can watch the never-ending theater of the Spanish Steps. **Pros:** location and view; guests have full access to the Hassler's services; free Wi-Fi. **Cons:** breakfast is served in the main building at the Hassler; bedrooms do not access communal terraces; often books up far in advance, particularly in high season. *$ Rooms from: €290* ✉ *Vicolo del Bottino 8, Piazza di Spagna* ☎ *06/69934560* ⊕ *www.ilpalazzettoroma.com* ⮑ *4 rooms* ⦿ *Free Breakfast* Ⓜ *Spagna.*

Inn at the Spanish Steps

$$$$ | **B&B/INN** | Occupying the upper floors of a centuries-old town house it shares with Antico Caffè Greco, this elegant setting was once the Roman home of fairy tale writer Hans Christian Andersen. **Pros:** rooms with superb views of the Spanish Steps; afternoon snacks and outstanding breakfast buffet; impressive design. **Cons:** area can be noisy due to crowds at the Spanish Steps; rooms located in the annex don't always receive the same attention as those directly in the hotel; hefty charges for extras like early check-in. *$ Rooms from: €420* ✉ *Via dei Condotti 85, Piazza di Spagna* ☎ *06/69925657* ⊕ *www.theinnatthespanishsteps.com* ⮑ *27 rooms* ⦿ *Free Breakfast* Ⓜ *Spagna.*

J.K. Place Roma

$$$$ | **HOTEL** | Following in the footsteps of its sister hotels in Capri and Florence, this intimate boutique hotel is located a stone's throw from the mausoleum of Augustus, not far from the Spanish Steps and Piazza del Popolo. **Pros:** staff are eager to please; excellent meals at rooftop lounge; complimentary mini-bar. **Cons:** not all rooms have a balcony; some rooms are on the small side; no fitness center. *$ Rooms from: €700* ✉ *Via Monte d'Oro 30, Piazza di Spagna* ☎ *06/982634* ⊕ *www.jkroma.com* ⮑ *30 rooms* ⦿ *Free Breakfast* Ⓜ *Spagna.*

La Residenza

$$ | **HOTEL** | This cozy hotel in a converted town house near Via Veneto is widely popular among American travelers thanks to its location close to the embassy, American-style breakfast, and helpful staff. **Pros:** free breakfast buffet; spacious rooms with balconies; charming decor. **Cons:** disappointing views out windows; rooms are in need of restyling; the building's exterior doesn't compare to its interior. *$ Rooms from: €180* ✉ *Via Emilia 22/24, Piazza di Spagna* ☎ *06/4880789* ⊕ *www.laresidenzaroma.com* ⮑ *27 rooms* ⦿ *Free Breakfast* Ⓜ *Spagna.*

Maalot Roma

$$$ | **HOTEL** | This new boutique hotel inside the former residence of opera composer Gaetano Donizetto aims to be a restaurant with rooms above rather than a hotel with a restaurant. **Pros:** great food at Don Pasquale restaurant; central location just steps from the Trevi Fountain; chic design with original art. **Cons:** no spa; service can be a bit slow; some rooms look directly onto the McDonald's across the street. *$ Rooms from: €280* ✉ *Via delle Murate 78, Piazza di Spagna* ☎ *06/878087* ⊕ *www.hotelmaalot.com* ⮑ *30 rooms* ⦿ *Free Breakfast* Ⓜ *Barberini.*

Margutta 19

$$$$ | **HOTEL** | Tucked away on a quiet, leafy street known for its art galleries, this 22-suite property is like your very own hip, New York–style loft in the center of old-world Rome, with top-drawer amenities, contemporary design, and a restaurant with a verdant terrace. **Pros:** studio-loft feel in center of town; deluxe furnishings; complete privacy. **Cons:** no elevator in the annex to reach rooms on higher floors; entry-level rooms lack views; no spa or gym. ⓢ *Rooms from: €520* ✉ *Via Margutta 19, Piazza di Spagna* ☎ *06/97797979* ⊕ *www.romeluxurysuites.com* ⇥ *22 suites* Ⓞ *Free Breakfast* Ⓜ *Spagna.*

Marriott Grand Hotel Flora

$$$$ | **HOTEL** | This handsome hotel at the top of Via Veneto next to the Villa Borghese park is something of a beacon on the Rome landscape. **Pros:** convenient location and pleasant staff; spectacular view from the terrace; fitness center and spa. **Cons:** crowded with businessmen and big tour groups; free Internet only for Marriott loyalty members; sometimes the noise from Via Veneto drifts in. ⓢ *Rooms from: €465* ✉ *Via Veneto 191, Piazza di Spagna* ☎ *06/489929* ⊕ *www.hotelfloraroma.com* ⇥ *155 rooms* Ⓞ *No Meals* Ⓜ *Barberini, Spagna.*

Scalinata di Spagna

$ | **B&B/INN** | Perched atop the Spanish Steps, this charming boutique hotel makes guests fall in love over and over again—so popular, in fact, it's often booked far in advance. **Pros:** friendly and helpful concierge; free Wi-Fi throughout; fresh fruit in guest rooms. **Cons:** no porter and no elevator; small rooms; hike up the hill to the hotel. ⓢ *Rooms from: €116* ✉ *Piazza Trinità dei Monti 17, Piazza di Spagna* ☎ *06/45686150* ⊕ *www.hotelscalinata.com* ⇥ *30 rooms* Ⓞ *Free Breakfast* Ⓜ *Spagna.*

The Westin Excelsior, Rome

$$$$ | **HOTEL** | **FAMILY** | Ablaze with lights at night, this seven-layer-cake hotel—topped off by its famous cupola—is popular with visiting diplomats (who might be headed to the U.S. Embassy across the street), celebrities, and American conference groups. **Pros:** elegant period furnishings and decor; health club and indoor pool; excellent historic restaurant. **Cons:** decor is grand but in need of updating; expensive Wi-Fi; worn floors distract from nice furnishings. ⓢ *Rooms from: €435* ✉ *Via Veneto 125, Piazza di Spagna* ☎ *06/47081* ⊕ *www.westinrome.com* ⇥ *316 rooms* Ⓞ *No Meals* Ⓜ *Barberini, Spagna.*

W Rome

$$$$ | **HOTEL** | On a quiet street between Via Veneto and the Spanish Steps, the new W Rome brings a calculated cool to the old-world upscale area. **Pros:** thoughtful modern comforts, including craft cocktails in the mini-bar; live music and a popular brunch add to the buzz; great design. **Cons:** no on-site spa; rooftop pool is rare in Rome but this one is small; 24/7 energy not for everyone. ⓢ *Rooms from: €660* ✉ *Via Liguria, 23, Piazza di Spagna* ☎ *06/894121* ⊕ *www.marriott.com* ⇥ *162 rooms* Ⓞ *Free Breakfast* Ⓜ *Barberini.*

Nightlife

After 9 pm, Piazza di Spagna holds the title for being the quietest area in the *centro storico* (historic center). Don't expect a party here, but do come to seek out some lovely *enotecas*, or wine bars.

BARS

Antica Enoteca

WINE BARS | Piazza di Spagna's staple wine bar literally corners the market on prime people-watching. Cozy up to the counter to sip a drink under the charming frescoes or snag a coveted outdoor table. In addition to a vast selection of wine, Antica Enoteca has delectable *antipasti* (appetizers), perfect for a snack or a light lunch, as well as a full menu of pastas and pizzas. ⊠ *Via della Croce 76/b, Piazza di Spagna* ☎ *06/6790896* ⊕ *www.anticaenoteca.com* Ⓜ *Spagna.*

Café Doney at the Westin Excelsior

CAFÉS | Nattily dressed businesspeople and harried tourists enjoy signature martinis at the street-side Café Doney, Via Veneto's grand dame, in front of the Westin Excelsior. The outdoor tables offer prime people-watching, while the seats inside are set under impossibly sparkly chandeliers amongst impeccable Italian design. The café also offers fresh fruit juices and smoothies for a healthy option. ⊠ *Westin Excelsior, Via Vittorio Veneto 125, Piazza di Spagna* ☎ *06/47082783* ⊕ *www.westinrome.com/en/cafe-doney.*

Il Marchese

COCKTAIL LOUNGES | With high bar stools and midnight blue accents, Il Marchese feels every bit the sophisticated nightcap stop for trendy Romans. The hot spot is the first amaro bar in Europe, stocking more than 500 labels of the bitter, herbal liqueur which can be served straight or mixed into creative cocktails. Pop in for a tapas-style aperitivo or stay for dinner and watch the chef "shop" from his market of gourmet Italian ingredients that takes up part of the space in this swanky restaurant-bar. ⊠ *Via di Ripetta 162, Piazza di Spagna* ☎ *06/90218872* ⊕ *www.ilmarcheseroma.it* Ⓜ *Spagna.*

Wine Bar at the Palazzetto

WINE BARS | The prize for perfect aperitivo spot goes to the Palazzetto, with excellent drinks and appetizers, as well as a breathtaking view of Rome's domes and rooftops—all from its fifth-floor rooftop overlooking the comings and goings on the Spanish Steps. Reach it by climbing the monumental staircase that it overlooks, or getting a lift from the elevator inside the Spagna Metro station. ⊠ *Vicolo del Bottino 8, Piazza di Spagna* ✚ *The main entrance is a small gate at the top of the Spanish Steps* ☎ *06/69934560* ⊕ *www.ilpalazzettoroma.com* Ⓜ *Spagna.*

 Shopping

The Piazza di Spagna area is considered to be the heart and soul of shopping in Rome, with all the international chains, as well as independent shops. If your budget isn't big enough to binge at the high-end fashion houses along Via Condotti, try the more moderate shops down Via del Corso, where young Romans come to shop for jeans and inexpensive, trendy clothes. As you move toward Piazza del Popolo, at one end of Via del Corso, you'll find more antique shops, while most galleries are tucked away on Via Margutta.

ANTIQUES

Galleria Benucci

ANTIQUES & COLLECTIBLES | With carved and gilded late baroque and Empire period furniture and paintings culled from the noble houses of Italy's past, Galleria Benucci is a literal treasure trove. An establishment favored by professionals from Europe and abroad, this conservative gallery next to a former sculpture studio has an astonishing selection of objects in a hushed atmosphere where connoisseurs will find the proprietors only too happy to discuss their latest finds. ⊠ *Via del Babuino 150/C, Piazza di Spagna* ☎ *06/36002190* Ⓜ *Spagna.*

BEAUTY

Antica Farmacia Pesci dal 1552

COSMETICS | In business since 1552, the Antica Farmacia—likely Rome's oldest pharmacy—is run by a family of pharmacists and produces its own line of skincare products and dietary supplements. The shop's 18th-century furnishings, herbs, and vases evoke Harry Potter's Diagon Alley; and while they don't carry potions, the pharmacists can whip up a just-for-you batch of composite powders, syrups, capsules, gels, and creams to soothe modern ailments. ⊠ *Piazza di Trevi 89, Piazza di Spagna* ☎ *06/6792210 www.anticafarmaciapesci.it* ⊘ *Closed Sat. afternoon and Sun.* Ⓜ *Barberini.*

Castelli Profumerie
PERFUME | This straightforward Italian perfume shop has been in the business of heavenly scents for more than 50 years. Besides being a perfumed paradise offering an array of labels like Acqua di Parma, Bois 1920, Bond No. 9, and Comme des Garçons, their precise and courteous staff speak multiple languages and know their merchandise, making the experience a lot more pleasant than a dash through duty-free. There are three locations around the city: two on Via Frattina and one on Via Oslavia in the Prati neighborhood. ⊠ *Via Frattina 18 and 54, Piazza di Spagna* ☎ *06/6790339* ⊕ *www.profumeriecastelli.com* Ⓜ *Spagna.*

Pro Fvmvm
PERFUME | Started in 1996, Pro Fvmvm is fast on its way to becoming a new cult classic in Italian fragrance design. Each of the 35 scents is designed to be unisex and comes complete with a poem that describes the intention of the artisans. Pricey but worth it, their philosophy is that smell can trigger memories more powerfully than any photo so the scents are designed to evoke experiences like walking through a forest or listening to a thundering Roman fountain. Some of their top-selling perfumes are Acqva e Zvcchero, Fiore d'Ambra, Thvndra, Volo Az 686 (named after a direct flight from Rome to the Caribbean), and Ichnvsa. ⊠ *Via Ripetta 248, Piazza di Spagna* ☎ *06/3200306* ⊕ *www.profumum.com* Ⓜ *Spagna.*

BOOKS AND STATIONERY
Anglo-American Book Co
BOOKS | FAMILY | A large and friendly bookstore with more than 40,000 books in English, Anglo-American Book has been a mecca for English-language reading material in Rome for more than 60 years. Whether you are a study-abroad student in need of an art history or archaeology textbook, or a visitor searching for a light

read for the train, there is something for everyone here. Among shelves stuffed from floor-to-ceiling and sometimes several rows deep, book lovers can find both British and American editions and easily spend hours just browsing. The bilingual staff always go the extra mile to find what you need. ⊠ *Via della Vite 102, Piazza di Spagna* ☎ *06/6795222* ⊘ *Closed Sun.* Ⓜ *Spagna.*

Ex Libris
ANTIQUES & COLLECTIBLES | Founded in 1931 and one of the oldest and largest antiquarian bookshops in Rome, Ex Libris has a distinctive selection of scholarly and collectible books from the 16th to 20th century that will make bookworms drool. The selection includes rare and early editions on art and architecture, music and theater, and literature and humanities as well as maps and prints. ⊠ *Via dell' Umiltà 77/a, Piazza di Spagna* ☎ *06/6791540* ⊕ *www.exlibrisroma.it* ⊘ *Closed Sun. and Mon.* Ⓜ *Barberini.*

★ Pineider
STATIONERY | This shop, near Piazza di Spagna, has been making exclusive stationery in Italy since 1774. The first Rome shop opened at the request of the royal household, and this is where the city's aristocratic families still come for engraved wedding invitations and timeless visiting cards. They also use the best Florentine leather for their wallets, briefcases, and other desk accessories. ⊠ *Via del Leoncino 25, Piazza di Spagna* ☎ *06/6878369* ⊕ *www.pineider.com* ⊘ *Closed Sun.* Ⓜ *Spagna.*

CERAMICS AND DECORATIVE ARTS
Le IV Stagioni
CRAFTS | If you're looking to purchase some traditional Italian pottery, Le IV Stagioni has a colorful selection of glazed pots, vases, and charming ceramic-flower wall ornaments made by well-known manufacturers such as Faenza, Capodimonte, Vietri, and Deruta. All can be shipped internationally if you

can't quite fit the gorgeous bowls and platters in your suitcase. ✉ *Via dell'Umiltà 30/b, Piazza di Spagna* ☎ *06/69941029* Ⓜ *Barberini.*

CHILDREN'S CLOTHING
Mettimi Giù
CHILDREN'S CLOTHING | For over three decades, Mettimi Giù (which is inspired by the common childhood demand "put me down!") has been styling the littlest Romans. The shop is stocked with European brands to outfit children from head to toe, plus all the toys, bags, and adorable accessories a tiny tot can tote. There are two neighboring storefronts: one for 0-3 years, and the other for children 4-14 years old. ✉ *Via Dei Due Macelli 56/59, Piazza di Spagna* ☎ *06/6991483* ⊕ *www. mettimigiu.it/en-gb* ⊙ *Closed Sun.* Ⓜ *Spagna.*

CLOTHING
★ Brioni
MEN'S CLOTHING | Founded in 1945, Brioni is hailed for its impeccable craftsmanship in creating made-to-measure menswear. The classic brand hires the best men's tailors in Italy, who design bespoke suits to exacting standards, measured to the millimeter and completely personalized from a selection of more than 5,000 spectacular fabrics. A single made-to-measure wool suit will take a minimum of 32 hours to create. Their prêt-à-porter line is also praised for peerless cutting and stitching. Past and present clients include Clark Gable, Barack Obama, and, of course, James Bond. ✉ *Via Condotti 21A, Piazza di Spagna* ☎ *06/6783428* ⊕ *www.brioni.com* Ⓜ *Spagna.*

Dolce & Gabbana
MIXED CLOTHING | Dolce and Gabbana met in 1980 when both were assistants at a Milan fashion atelier, and they opened their first store in 1982. With a modern aesthetic that screams sex appeal, the brand has always thrived on excess and is known for its bold, creative designs.

The Rome store has a glass ceiling above a sparkling chandelier to allow natural light to spill in, illuminating the marble floors, antique brass accents, and (of course) the latest lines for men, women, and even children, plus an expansive accessories area. ✉ *Via Condotti 49–51, Piazza di Spagna* ☎ *06/69924999* ⊕ *www.dolcegabbana.com* Ⓜ *Spagna.*

Eddy Monetti
MEN'S CLOTHING | Eddy Monetti began as a hat shop in Naples more than 130 years ago, and is still known for classic, upscale men's clothing such as jackets, sweaters, slacks, and ties made out of wool, cotton, and cashmere. Sophisticated and pricey, the store carries a range of stylish British- and Italian-made pieces. ✉ *Via Borgognona 36, Piazza di Spagna* ☎ *06/6794117* ⊕ *www.eddymonetti.com* Ⓜ *Spagna.*

Elena Mirò
WOMEN'S CLOTHING | Elena Mirò is a high-end brand that specializes in sophisticated, beautifully feminine clothes for curvy, European-styled women size 46 (U.S. size 12, U.K. size 14) and up. There are several locations in Rome, including one on Via Nazionale. ✉ *Via Frattina 11, Piazza di Spagna* ☎ *06/6784367* ⊕ *www. elenamiro.com* Ⓜ *Spagna.*

Ermenegildo Zegna
MEN'S CLOTHING | For more than 100 years, Ermenegildo Zegna has been a powerhouse of men's clothing. Believing that construction and fabric are the key, Zegna is the master of both, and prefers to produce all the wool fabric they use in order to ensure the high standard of quality. Suits here start from €1,500, with the top of the line, known as "couture," costing considerably more. There is also a line of sportswear and accessories, but this is the place to splurge on a formal, tailored suit. ✉ *Via Borgognona, 7E, Piazza di Spagna* ☎ *06/69940678* ⊕ *www. zegna.com* Ⓜ *Spagna.*

Fendi

MIXED CLOTHING | Fendi has been a fixture of the Roman fashion landscape since "Mamma" Fendi first opened shop with her husband in 1925. With an eye for crazy genius, she hired Karl Lagerfeld, who began working with the group at the start of his career. His furs and runway antics made him one of the most influential designers of the 20th century and brought international acclaim to Fendi along the way. The atelier, now owned by the Louis Vuitton group, continues to symbolize Italian glamour at its finest, though the difference in ownership is noticeable. It's also gotten new life in the Italian press for its "Fendi for Fountains" campaign, which included funding the restoration of Rome's Trevi Fountain, and for moving its global headquarters to a striking Mussolini-era building known as the "square Colosseum" in the city's EUR neighborhood. The flagship store in Rome can be found on the ground floor of Palazzo Fendi. The upper floors are home to the brand's seven private suites (the first ever Fendi hotel), and the rooftop hosts Zuma, a modern Japanese restaurant with an oh-so-cool bar that has sweeping views across Rome. ☒ *Largo Carlo Goldoni 420, Piazza di Spagna* ☎ *06/33450896* ⊕ *www.fendi.com* Ⓜ *Spagna.*

Galassia

WOMEN'S CLOTHING | Classy, avant-garde women's styles by A-list designers including Gaultier, Westwood, Issey Miyake, and Yamamoto can be found at Galassia. If you're the type who dares to be different, prefers funky statement accessories, and are in need of some closet therapy, you will love the edgy selection, which gives the store a look that cannot be found elsewhere. ☒ *Via Frattina 20, Piazza di Spagna* ☎ *06/6797896* ⊕ *www.galassiaroma.com* ☉ *Closed Sun.* Ⓜ *Spagna.*

Giorgio Armani

MIXED CLOTHING | One of the most influential designers of Italian haute couture, Giorgio Armani creates fluid silhouettes and dazzling evening gowns with sexy peek-a-boo cutouts; his signature cuts are made with the clever-handedness and flawless technique achievable only by working with tracing paper and Italy's finest fabrics over the course of a lifetime. His menswear collection uses traditional textiles like wide-ribbed corduroy and stretch jersey in nontraditional ways while staying true to a clean, masculine aesthetic. The iconic Italian brand has an Emporio Armani shop on Via del Babuino, but the flagship store is the best place to find pieces that range from exotic runway-worthy masterpieces to more wearable collections emphasizing casual Italian elegance with just the right touch of whimsy and sexiness. ☒ *Via dei Condotti 77, Piazza di Spagna* ☎ *06/6991460* ⊕ *www.armani.com* Ⓜ *Spagna.*

Gucci

MIXED CLOTHING | Guccio Gucci opened his first leather shop selling luggage in Florence in 1921, and as the glamorous fashion label celebrates its centennial, the success of the double-G trademark is unquestionable. Tom Ford joined as creative director in 1994, helping the fashion house move into a new era that continues today, maintaining the label's trendiness while bringing in a breath of fresh air, thanks to old-school favorites like reinterpreted horsebit styles and Jackie Kennedy scarves. Now helmed by Alessandro Michele, Gucci remains a fashion must for virtually every A-list celebrity, and their designs have moved from heart-stopping sexy rock star to something classically subdued and retrospectively feminine, making the handbags and accessories more covetable than ever. ☒ *Via Condotti 6–8, Piazza di Spagna* ☎ *06/6790405* ⊕ *www.gucci.com* Ⓜ *Spagna.*

★ Laura Biagiotti

WOMEN'S CLOTHING | Until her death in 2017, Laura Biagiotti was a worldwide ambassador of Italian fashion. Considered the Queen of Cashmere, her soft-as-velvet pullovers have been worn by Sophia Loren, and her snow-white cardigans were said to be a favorite of the late pope John Paul II. Princess Diana even sported one of Biagiotti's cashmere maternity dresses. In addition to stocking the luxe clothing line, the flagship store has a bold red lounge where shoppers can indulge in sampling her line of his-and-her perfumes or sip a Campari cocktail while purchases are customized with Swarovski crystals. ✉ *Via Belsiana 57, Piazza di Spagna* ☎ *06/6791205* ⊕ *www.laurabiagiotti.it* ⊗ *Closed Sun.* Ⓜ *Spagna.*

★ Patrizia Pepe

WOMEN'S CLOTHING | One of Florence's best-kept secrets for up-and-coming designs, Patrizia Pepe first emerged on the scene in 1993 with an aesthetic that's both minimalist and bold, combining classic styles with low-slung jeans and jackets with oversize lapels that are bound to draw attention. Her line of shoes is hot-hot-hot for those who can walk on stilts. As a relative newcomer to the crowded Italian fashion scene, the brand's stand-alone fame is still under the radar, but take a look at this shop before the line becomes the next fast-tracked craze. ✉ *Via Frattina 44, Piazza di Spagna* ☎ *06/6781851* ⊕ *www.patrizia-pepe.com* Ⓜ *Spagna.*

Prada

MIXED CLOTHING | Besides the devil, plenty of serious shoppers wear Prada season after season, especially those willing to sell their souls for one of their ubiquitous handbags. If you are looking for that blend of old-world luxury with a touch of fashion-forward finesse, you'll hit it big here. Mario Prada first founded the Italian luggage brand in 1913, but it has been his granddaughter, Miuccia, who updated the designs into the timeless investment pieces of today. You'll find the Rome store more service-oriented than the New York City branches—a roomy elevator delivers you to a series of thickly carpeted salons where a flock of discreet assistants will help you pick out dresses, shoes, lingerie, and fashion accessories. The men's store is located at Via Condotti 88/90, while the women's is down the street at 92/95. ✉ *Via dei Condotti 88/90 and 92/95, Piazza di Spagna* ☎ *06/6790897* ⊕ *www.prada.com* Ⓜ *Spagna.*

Salvatore Ferragamo

SHOES | A major fashion player when it comes to footwear, Hollywood's gliteratti and social butterflies trust their pretty little feet with one brand: Salvatore Ferragamo. With pretty shoes and handbags displayed on pillars like jewels, fans of the brand will think they have died and followed the white light when they enter this store. The Florentine design house also specializes in small leather goods, men's and women's ready-to-wear, and scarves and ties. Men's styles are found at Via Condotti 65, women's at 73/74. Want to sleep in Ferragamo-style? Their splendid luxury Portrait Suites Hotel is on the upper floors. ✉ *Via dei Condotti 65 and 73/74, Piazza di Spagna* ☎ *06/6781130* ⊕ *www.ferragamo.com* Ⓜ *Spagna.*

Schostal

MIXED CLOTHING | A Piazza di Spagna fixture since 1870, the shop was once the go-to place for women looking to stock up on corsets, bonnets, stockings, and petticoats. Today, it's the place to stop for those essential basics that are increasingly difficult to find, like fine-quality shirts, underwear, and handkerchiefs made of wool and pure cashmere at affordable prices. ✉ *Via della Fontanella di Borghese 29, Piazza di Spagna* ☎ *06/6791240* ⊕ *www.schostalroma1870.com* ⊗ *Closed Sun.* Ⓜ *Spagna.*

Trussardi

MIXED CLOTHING | Known for its leather-working, this classic design house creates coveted bags with contemporary lines but old-world craftsmanship. Newer ventures include ready-to-wear men's and women's collections and a line of jeans. The next steps for the brand, which was originally founded in Bergamo in 1911, remain to be seen after Gaia Trussardi's recent departure following four generations of keeping the role of creative director inside the family, but it seems to be moving in a more youthful direction. A smaller shop dedicated to accessories in Termini station offers a last chance to pick up a luxury purse or belt before hopping on a train. ✉ *Via Frattina 130, Piazza di Spagna* ☎ *06/69380939* ⊕ *www.trussardi.com* Ⓜ *Spagna.*

Valentino

MIXED CLOTHING | Since taking the Valentino reins, creative director Pierpaolo Piccioli has faced numerous challenges, the most basic of which is keeping Valentino true to Valentino after the designer's retirement in 2008. He served as accessories designer under Valentino for more than a decade and understands exactly how to make the next generation of Hollywood stars swoon. Valentino has taken over most of Piazza di Spagna, where he lived for decades in a lovely palazzo next to one of the multiple boutiques showcasing his eponymous designs with a romantic edginess; think studded heels or a showstopping prêt-à-porter evening gown worthy of the Oscars. Rock stars and other music lovers can also have their Valentino guitar straps personalized when they buy one at this enormous boutique. ✉ *Piazza di Spagna 38, Piazza di Spagna* ☎ *06/94515710* ⊕ *www. valentino.com* Ⓜ *Spagna.*

Versace

MIXED CLOTHING | Versace's Rome flagship is a gem of architecture and design, with Byzantine-inspired mosaic floors and futuristic interiors with transparent walls, not to mention, of course, fashion: here shoppers will find apparel, jewelry, watches, fragrances, cosmetics, and home furnishings in designs every bit as flamboyant as Donatella and Allegra (Gianni's niece), drawing heavily on the sexy rocker gothic underground vibe. ✉ *Piazza di Spagna 12, Piazza di Spagna* ☎ *06/6784600* ⊕ *www.versace.com* Ⓜ *Spagna.*

DEPARTMENT STORES

★ La Rinascente

DEPARTMENT STORE | Italy's best-known department store is located in a dazzling space that has seven stories packed with the best luxury goods the world has to offer. Here, one can find oodles of cosmetics on the ground floor, as well as a phalanx of ready-to-wear designer sportswear and blockbuster handbags and accessories, and kitchen and homeware in the basement. Even if you're not planning on buying anything, the basement excavations of a Roman aqueduct and the roof terrace bar with its splendid view are well worth a visit. There's also a location at Piazza Fiume. ✉ *Via del Tritone 61, Piazza di Spagna* ☎ *02/91387388* ⊕ *www.rinascente.it* Ⓜ *Barberini.*

FOOD AND WINE

Buccone

WINE/SPIRITS | A landmark wineshop inside the former coach house of a noble Roman family, Buccone has 10 layers of shelves stretching impressively from floor to ceiling that are packed with quality wines and spirits ranging in price from a few euros to several hundred for rare vintages. The old atmosphere has been preserved in the original wood-beam ceiling, long marble counter, and an antique till. You can also buy jams, pasta, and packaged candy perfect for inexpensive gifts. A simple lunch is available daily, as are aperitivo and dinner (though reservations are required for dinner). However, it is the atmosphere and wine list rather than the food that makes the old shop noteworthy. For that reason, book a week in advance, and they can also give you a guided wine tasting, with highlights from many of Italy's important wine-producing regions. ✉ *Via di Ripetta 19/20, Piazza di Spagna* ☎ *06/3612154* ⊕ *www.enoteca-buccone.com* Ⓜ *Piazza del Popolo.*

HATS

Borsalino Boutique

HATS & GLOVES | Considered by many to be the Cadillac of fedoras, the dashing Borsalino fedora has been a staple of the fashionable Italian man since 1857. Adorning the heads of many silver-screen icons, including Humphrey Bogart (who donned one in *Casablanca*) and Harrison Ford (as Indiana Jones), Borsalino retains its unmistakable class, style, and elegance. Few hats are made with such exacting care and attention, and the company's milliners still use machines that are more than 100 years old. Borsalino also has boutiques near the Pantheon and Piazza di Spagna. ✉ *Piazza del Popolo 20, Piazza di Spagna* ☎ *06/3233353* ⊕ *www.borsalino.it* Ⓜ *Flaminio.*

HOME DECOR

Frette

HOUSEWARES | Classic, luxurious, colorful, timeless, and fun, there is nothing like Frette's bed collections. A leader in luxurious linens and towels for the home and hotel industry since 1860, sinking into their sophisticated cotton, satin, percale, or silk sheets is the perfect way to end the day. To create the full bedroom experience, they also offer pajamas and gorgeous silk robes. ✉ *Piazza di Spagna 11, Piazza di Spagna* ☎ *06/6790673* ⊕ *www.frette.com* Ⓜ *Spagna.*

JEWELRY

Bulgari

JEWELRY & WATCHES | Every capital city has its famous jeweler, and Bulgari is to Rome what Tiffany is to New York and Cartier to Paris. The jewelry giant has developed a reputation for meticulous craftsmanship melding noble metals with precious gems. In the middle of the 19th century, the great-grandfather of the current Bulgari brothers began working as a silver jeweler in his native Greece and is said to have moved to Rome with less than 1,000 lire in his pocket. The recent makeover of the store's temple-inspired interior pays homage to the brand's ties to both places. Today the mega-brand emphasizes colorful and playful jewelry as the principal cornerstone of its aesthetic. Popular collections include Bulgari-Bulgari and B.zero1. ✉ *Via dei Condotti 10, Piazza di Spagna* ☎ *06/6792487* ⊕ *www.bulgari.com* Ⓜ *Spagna.*

LINGERIE

Brighenti

LINGERIE | Brighenti looks like what it is: a traditional Roman shop from a gentler era, replete with a marble floor and a huge crystal chandelier suspended overhead. Silk nightgowns and classic sleepwear are available, as are lacy undergarments and sumptuous vintage-inspired swimsuits to bring out your inner pinup model. ✉ *Via Frattina 7/8, Piazza di Spagna* ☎ *06/6791484* ⊕ *www.brighentiroma.it* ⊗ *Closed Sun.* Ⓜ *Barberini, Spagna.*

La Perla

LINGERIE | La Perla was founded in Bologna in 1954 and is now the global go-to for beautifully crafted lingerie and glamorous underwear for that special night, a bridal trousseau, or just to spoil yourself on your Roman holiday. If you like decadent finery that is both stylish and romantic, with plenty of well-placed frills, you will find something here to make you feel like a goddess. There are silk boxers for gents here, too. ☒ *Via Bocca di Leone 28, Piazza di Spagna* ☎ *06/69941934* ⊕ *www.laperla.com* ◷ *Closed Sun.* Ⓜ *Spagna.*

Marisa Padovan

SWIMWEAR | The place to go for exclusive, made-to-order bathing suits, Marisa Padovan has been sewing for Holly-wood starlets like Audrey Hepburn and the well-heeled women of Rome for more than 50 years. The cheery bou-tique has ready-made styles trimmed with Swarovski crystals and polished turquoise stones, colorful cover-ups, and even offers a service where you can design your own bespoke bikini or one-piece. Each piece of this unique beachwear is carefully handmade right in Rome. The chic shop also hosts daughter Flavia's line of velvet trousers, knit pon-chos, silk dresses, and cashmere cov-erups to transition a day at the seaside to an evening of cocktail lounges and fine dining. ☒ *Via delle Carrozze 81–82, Piazza di Spagna* ☎ *06/6793946* ⊕ *www.marisapadovan.it* Ⓜ *Spagna.*

MALLS

Galleria Alberto Sordi

MALL | This gorgeous covered shopping arcade on the Piazza Colonna was envisioned in the late 19th century but not built until the 20th, and finally opened to the public in 1922. It's worth a visit as much to marvel at the unique building with its brilliant stained-glass ceiling as for its selection of classy shops. In recent years, space has opened up for some younger-focused chain shops to move in, but this is still the place to find some of Italy's most interesting brands in separate storefronts under a single art nouveau roof. ☒ *Via del Corso 79, Piazza di Spagna* ⊕ *www.galleriaalbertosordi.it* Ⓜ *Barberini.*

MARKETS

La Soffitta Sotto i Portici

MARKET | For an interesting jumble of stalls hawking antique jewelry, furniture, artwork, and other collectibles, check out this colorful vintage flea market held on the first and third Sunday of every month (except for August). It's open from 9 am until sunset. ☒ *Piazza Augusto Impera-tore, Piazza di Spagna* Ⓜ *Spagna.*

SHOES, HANDBAGS, AND LEATHER GOODS

A. Testoni

SHOES | Amedeo Testoni, the brand's found-er and original designer, was born in 1905 in Bologna, the heart of Italy's shoe-making territory. In 1929, he opened his first shop and began producing shoes as artistic as the cubist and art deco artwork of the period. His shoes have adorned the feet of Fred Astaire, proving that lightweight footwear can be comfortable and luxurious and still turn heads. Today the Testoni brand includes a line of enviable handbags and classically cool leather jackets, plus dreamy calfskin sneakers and chic messenger bags—all found at this Roman boutique. ☒ *Via Borgognona 21, Piazza di Spagna* ☎ *06/6787718* ⊕ *www.testoni.com* Ⓜ *Spagna.*

★ Braccialini

HANDBAGS | Founded in 1954 by Floren-tine stylist Carla Braccialini and her hus-band, Robert, Braccialini makes bags that are authentic works of art in bright colors and delightful shapes, such as London black cabs or mountain chalets. The ador-ably quirky tote bags have picture-post-card scenes of luxury destinations made of brightly colored appliquéd leather. Be sure to check out their eccentric Temi (Theme) creature bags; the snail-shaped handbag made out of python skin makes an unforgettable fashion statement. ☒ *Via Frattina, 117, Piazza di Spagna* ☎ *06/62286871* ⊕ *www.braccialini.it* Ⓜ *Spagna.*

Fausto Santini

SHOES | Shoe lovers with a passion for minimalist design flock to Fausto Santini to get their hands on his nerdy-chic shoes with their statement-making lines. Santini has been in business since 1970 and caters to a sophisticated, avant-garde clientele looking for elegant, classic shoes with a kick and a rainbow color palette. An outlet at Via Cavour 106, named for Fausto's father, Giacomo, sells last season's shoes at a big discount. ⌧ *Via Frattina 120, Piazza di Spagna* ☎ *06/6784114* ⊕ *www.faustosantini.com* Ⓜ *Spagna.*

Fratelli Rossetti

SHOES | An old-world company with modern aspirations, Fratelli Rossetti is the epitome of sophisticated men's and women's leather shoes, creating tasteful pumps and tasseled loafers named for the Milan neighborhood where the brand originated. While their focus has always revolved around sheer classic elegance with an emphasis on quality and luxurious craftsmanship, their new line also has a bit of playfulness, incorporating silk, velvet, and brocade. ⌧ *Via Borgognona 5/a, Piazza di Spagna* ☎ *06/6782676* ⊕ *www.fratellirossetti.com* Ⓜ *Spagna.*

Furla

HANDBAGS | Furla very well might be the best deal in Italian leather, selling high-end quality handbags and purses at affordable prices. There are multiple locations throughout the Eternal City (including one at Fiumicino Airport), but its flagship store can be found in the heart of Piazza di Spagna. Be prepared to fight your way through crowds of passionate handbag lovers, all anxious to possess one of the delectable bags, wallets, or whimsical key chains in trendy sherbet hues or timeless bold color combos. ⌧ *Piazza di Spagna 22, Piazza di Spagna* ☎ *06/6797159* ⊕ *www.furla.com* Ⓜ *Spagna.*

Sermoneta

HATS & GLOVES | Whether you're looking for some fancy gloves to wear to the opera or for a fashionable pair of warm leather gloves to get you through the winter, Sermoneta has a vast selection to choose from. Browse through stacks of nappa leather, deerskin, and cashmere-lined capybara hand-stitched gloves in all colors. You can also head upstairs for a custom fitting, and then have your gloves personalized with your own initials, logos, or other designs. ⌧ *Piazza di Spagna 61, Piazza di Spagna* ☎ *06/6791960* ⊕ *www. sermonetagloves.com* Ⓜ *Spagna.*

★ Tod's

SHOES | First founded in the 1920s, Tod's has grown from a small family brand into a global powerhouse so wealthy that its owner Diego Della Valle donated €20 million to the Colosseum restoration project. The shoe baron's trademark is his simple, classic, understated designs and butter-soft leather. Sure to please are his light and flexible slip-on Gommino driving shoes with rubber-bottomed soles for extra driving-pedal grip. There is also a location on Via Condotti. ⌧ *Via della Fontanella di Borghese 56a–57, Piazza di Spagna* ☎ *06/68210066* ⊕ *www.tods. com* Ⓜ *Spagna.*

Chapter 7

REPUBBLICA AND THE QUIRINALE

Updated by
Laura Itzkowitz

👁 Sights	🍴 Restaurants	🛏 Hotels	🛍 Shopping	🍸 Nightlife
★★★★☆	★★★☆☆	★★★★☆	★★★☆☆	★★☆☆☆

NEIGHBORHOOD SNAPSHOT

MAKING THE MOST OF YOUR TIME

While slightly off Rome's bustling tourist path, this central (and well-connected) area has a number of intriguing sights, from the stunning sweep of Piazza della Repubblica and the excellent ancient art collection of the Palazzo Massimo alle Terme to the bones of the Capuchin Crypt and Bernini's breathtaking sculpture, the *Ecstasy of St. Teresa*. It's possible to walk the whole area, but this part of town is so well connected by bus and Metro that it's usually quicker to take public transport. When choosing a time of day to visit, remember that many churches (like Santa Maria della Vittoria, home of Bernini's Saint Teresa sculpture) close at midday, reopening around 3 or 4.

TOP REASONS TO GO

Bernini's Ecstasy of St. Teresa: Admire the worldly realism of Teresa's allegedly spiritual rapture. The star of the Cappella Cornaro, Santa Maria della Vittoria, Bernini's theatrical masterpiece is a cornerstone of the high Roman baroque period.

Palazzo Barberini: Take in five centuries of art at one of Rome's greatest family palaces, where you can gape at Rome's biggest ballroom and Raphael's *La Fornarina*.

Palazzo Massimo alle Terme: Admire the spectacular Hellenistic *Boxer at Rest,* get your emperors straight in the portrait gallery, and marvel at breathtaking 2,000-year-old frescoes on the top floor.

Capuchin Crypt: Contemplate eternity in the creepy-yet-creative crypt under Santa Maria della Concezione, "decorated" with the skeletons of 4,000 monks, replete with fluted arches made of collarbones and arabesques of shoulder blades.

Piazza del Quirinale: Crowning the Quirinale—the loftiest of Rome's seven hills—is the Piazza del Quirinale, with spectacular views over the city, its horizon marked by "Il Cupolino," the dome of St. Peter's. Framing the vista are enormous ancient statues of Castor and Pollux, the Dioscuri (Horse-Tamers).

GETTING HERE

■ Located between Termini station and the Spanish Steps, this area is about a 15-minute walk from either. Bus No. 40 will get you from Termini to the Quirinale in two stops; from the Vatican take Bus No. 64. The very central Repubblica Metro stop is on the piazza of the same name.

PAUSE HERE

■ The small, verdant park across the street from the Piazza del Quirinale is a good spot to stop and take a break. In the center sits an equestrian statue of King Carlo Alberto, the king of Piedmont-Sardinia during the turbulent period of the Reunification of Italy. There are benches to sit and kids often play on the grass. If you happen to be in the area at sunset, cross the street to see the spectacular sunset over Piazza del Quirinale and the rooftops of Rome.

Just north of the modern Termini station, this area offers an extraordinary Roman blend of old and new. The stretch from Piazza della Repubblica to Piazza Barberini swarms with professionals going in and out of office buildings, as the Quirinale, home to the president of Italy, buzzes with political activity. More than just a workaday area, though, you will also find plenty of attractions for travelers, from the bizarre Capuchin Crypt to great Bernini sculptures.

Repubblica

As a gateway, Piazza della Repubblica was laid out to serve as a monumental foyer between the Termini rail station and the rest of the city. The piazza's main landmark, the vast ruins of the Terme di Diocleziano (Baths of Diocletian) were subsequently transformed into a Renaissance monastery and then, by Michelangelo's design, to the church of Santa Maria degli Angeli. The ancient treasures at Palazzo Massimo delle Terme, Bernini's spectacular Capella Cornaro, and, farther afield, the modern Museo d'Arte Contemporanea (MACRO) will always be vying for your attention.

Sights

MACRO
ART MUSEUM | Formerly known as Rome's Modern and Contemporary Art Gallery, and before that as the Peroni beer factory, this redesigned industrial space has brought new life to the gallery and museum scene of a city hitherto hailed for its "then," not its "now." The collection here covers Italian contemporary artists from the 1960s through today. The goal is to bring current art to the public in innovative spaces and, not incidentally, to give support and bring recognition to Rome's contemporary art scene, which labors in the shadow of the city's artistic heritage. After a few days—or millennia—of dusty marble, it's a breath of fresh air. ■ TIP→ **Check the website for occasional late-night openings and events.** ⊠ Via Nizza 138, Repubblica ☎ 06/696271 ⊕ www.museomacro.it ⊠ Free ⊗ Closed Mon. Ⓜ Castro Pretorio.

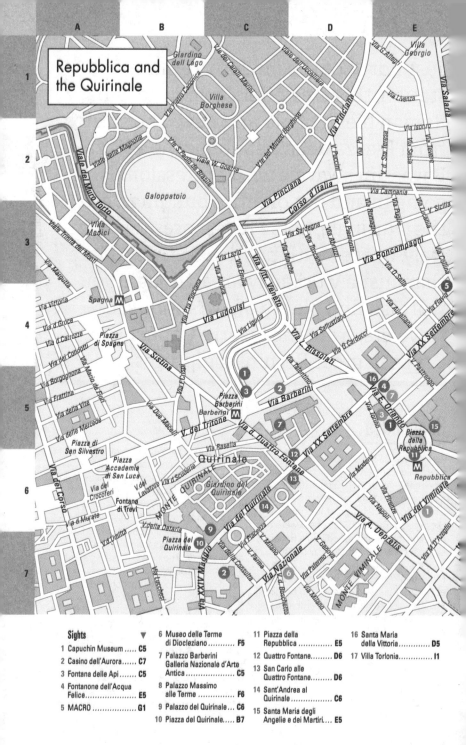

Repubblica and the Quirinale

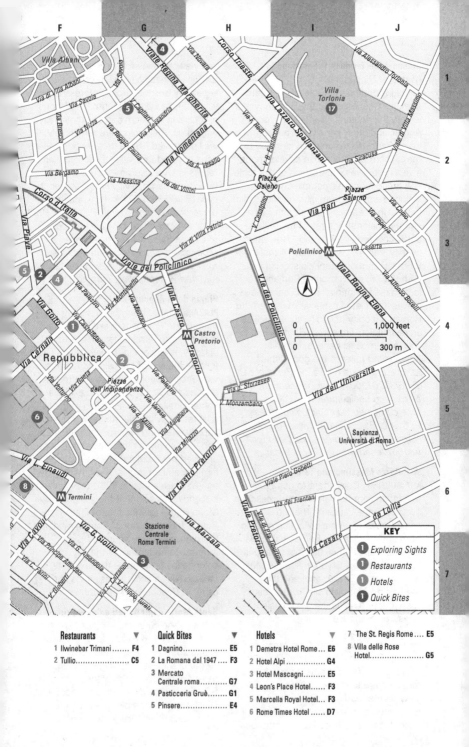

KEY

- **1** Exploring Sights
- **1** Restaurants
- **1** Hotels
- **1** Quick Bites

Restaurants ▼	Quick Bites ▼	Hotels ▼
1 Ilwinebar Trimani **F4**	1 Dagnino.................. **E5**	1 Demetra Hotel Rome ... **E6**
2 Tullio...................... **C5**	2 La Romana dal 1947 .... **F3**	2 Hotel Alpi **G4**
	3 Mercato Centrale roma........... **G7**	3 Hotel Mascagni......... **E5**
	4 Pasticceria Gruè........ **G1**	4 Leon's Place Hotel...... **F3**
	5 Pinsere.................. **E4**	5 Marcella Royal Hotel... **F3**
		6 Rome Times Hotel **D7**

7 The St. Regis Rome **E5**
8 Villa delle Rose Hotel...................... **G5**

Museo delle Terme di Diocleziano
(*Baths of Diocletian*)
RUINS | Though part of this ancient bath complex (the largest in the Roman world) is now the church of Santa Maria degli Angeli, and other parts were transformed into a Carthusian monastery or razed to make room for later urban development, a visit here gives you a sense of the scale and grandeur of this complex, which included a gymnasium, library, and public baths. Upon entering the church, you see the major structures of the baths, partly covered by 16th- and 17th-century overlay, some of which is by Michelangelo. The calm monastery cloister is filled with the Museo Nazionale Romano's collection of inscriptions; other rooms have pieces associated especially with remote Roman antiquity (think: huts), as well as archaeological finds from Rome's Republican and imperial periods, including a rare painted relief of the god Mithras. ⊠ *Viale Enrico de Nicola 78, Repubblica* ☎ *06/39967700* ⊕ *www.museonazionaleromano.beniculturali.it* 🎫 *€10, or €12 for a combined ticket including access to Crypta Balbi, Palazzo Massimo alle Terme, and Palazzo Altemps (valid for 1 wk)* ⊘ *Closed Mon.* Ⓜ *Repubblica.*

★ Palazzo Massimo alle Terme
ART MUSEUM | Come here to get a real feel for ancient Roman art—the collection rivals even the Vatican's. The Museo Nazionale Romano, with a collection ranging from striking classical Roman paintings to marble bric-a-brac, has four locations: Palazzo Altemps, Crypta Balbi, the Museo delle Terme di Diocleziano, and this, the Palazzo Massimo alle Terme. This vast structure holds the great ancient treasures of the archaeological collection and also the coin collection. Highlights include the *Dying Niobid*, the famous bronze *Boxer at Rest*, and the *Discobolus Lancellotti*. But the best part of the museum are the ancient frescoes on view on the top floor, stunningly set up to "re-create" the look of the homes they once decorated. These include stuccoes

and wall paintings found in the area of the Villa Farnesina (in Trastevere) and the legendary frescoes from Empress Livia's villa at Prima Porta, delightful depictions of a garden in bloom and an orchard alive with birds. Their colors are remarkably well preserved. These delicate decorations covered the walls of cool, sunken rooms in Livia's summerhouse outside the city. ⊠ *Largo di Villa Peretti 2, Repubblica* ☎ *06/39967700* ⊕ *www.museonazioneromano.beniculturali.it* 🎫 *€8, or €12 for a combined ticket including access to Crypta Balbi, Museo delle Terme di Diocleziano, and Palazzo Altemps (valid for 1 wk)* ⊘ *Closed Mon.* 🔒 *Reservations required* Ⓜ *Repubblica, Termini.*

Piazza della Repubblica
PLAZA/SQUARE | Often the first view that spells "Rome" to weary travelers walking from Termini station, this round piazza was laid out in the late 1800s and follows the line of the caldarium of the vast ancient public baths, the Terme di Diocleziano. At its center, the exuberant Fontana delle Naiadi (Fountain of the Naiads) teems with voluptuous bronze ladies happily wrestling with marine monsters. The nudes weren't there when the pope unveiled the fountain in 1888—sparing him any embarrassment—but when the figures were added in 1901, they caused a scandal. It's said that the sculptor, Mario Rutelli (grandfather of Francesco Rutelli, former mayor of Rome), modeled them on the ample figures of two musical-comedy stars of the day. The colonnades now house the luxe hotel Palazzo Naiadi and various shops and caffè. ⊠ *Repubblica* Ⓜ *Repubblica.*

Santa Maria degli Angeli e dei Martiri
CHURCH | The curving brick facade on the northeast side of Piazza della Repubblica is one small remnant of the colossal Terme di Diocleziano, the largest and most impressive of the baths of ancient Rome. A gift to the city from Emperor Diocletian, the complex was completed in AD 306. In 1561 Michelangelo

The Rivalry of Bernini and Borromini

Consider the famous feuding duos of Mozart vs. Salieri, Michelangelo vs. Raphael. None match the rivalry of Gian Lorenzo Bernini versus Francesco Borromini. In a pitched battle of anything-you-can-do-I-can-do-better, these two great geniuses of the baroque style transformed 17th-century Rome into a city of spectacle, the "theater of the entire world." While it was Bernini who triumphed and Borromini who wound up taking his own life, the real winner was Rome itself—a banquet for the eyes cooked up by these two baroque masters.

United in genius, the two could not have been more different in fortune and character. Born within a year of each other at the turn of the 1600s, they spent decades laying out majestic squares, building precedent-shattering churches, all the while outdoing each other in baroque bravado.

Compared and contrasted, the pair form the ultimate odd couple: Bernini, perhaps the greatest master showman of all time, exulted in Technicolor-hued theatricality; Borromini, the purist and reclusive genius, pursued the pure light of geometry, although with an artisan's hankering after detail. Bernini grew into the famed lover and solid family man; Borromini seems not to have had any love life at all. Bernini became a smooth mingler with society's great and worthy ranks; Borromini remained the quirky outsider. Bernini triumphed as the all-rounder, he of the so-called "bel composto," as in the Cornaro Chapel where his talents as sculptor/architect/dramatist come stunningly together. Borromini was an architect, pure and simple. Throughout their lives, they had tried to turn the tables—psychologically as well as architecturally—on each other, a struggle that ended with Borromini's tragic suicide.

Both, however, fervently believed in the baroque style and its mission to amaze, as well as edify. Thanks to the Counter-Reformation, the Catholic church discovered, and exploited, the effects on its congregants of such overtly baroque tricks of the trade as chiaroscuro (light and dark) and trompe l'oeil (fool-the-eye) techniques. Using emotion and motion, Bernini and Borromini learned how to give stone wing. In Bernini's famed *Pluto and Persephone*, the solid stone seems transmuted into living flesh—sculpted effects previously thought possible only in paint. Together transforming the city into a "giant theater," the rivals thus became the principal dramaturges and stage managers of baroque Rome.

was commissioned to convert the vast *frigidarium*, the central hall of the baths, into a church. His work was later altered by Vanvitelli in the 18th century, but the huge transept, which formed the nave in Michelangelo's plan, has remained. The eight enormous monolithic columns of red granite that support the great beams are the original columns of the tepidarium, 45 feet high and more than 5 feet in diameter. The great hall is 92 feet high. ✉ *Piazza della Repubblica, Repubblica* ☎ *06/4880812* ⊕ *www.santamariadegliangeliroma.it* Ⓜ *Repubblica*.

Did You Know?

To increase the hallucinatory impact of the *Ecstasy of St. Teresa*, Bernini hid a window of yellow glass above the pediment to add iridescence to the gilded rays of "divine light."

★ Santa Maria della Vittoria

CHURCH | Designed by Carlo Maderno, this church is best known for Bernini's sumptuous baroque decoration of the Cappella Cornaro (Cornaro Chapel, the last on the left as you face the altar), which houses his interpretation of divine love, the *Ecstasy of St. Teresa*. Bernini's masterly fusion of sculpture, light, architecture, painting, and relief is a multimedia extravaganza, with the chapel modeled as a theater, and one of the key examples of the Roman high baroque. The members of the Cornaro family meditate on the communal vision of the great moment of divine love before them: the swooning saint's robes appear to be on fire, quivering with life, and the white marble group seems suspended in the heavens as golden rays illuminate the scene. An angel assists at the moment of Teresa's vision as the saint abandons herself to the joys of heavenly love. Bernini represented this mystical experience in what, to modern eyes, may seem very earthly terms. Or, as the visiting French dignitary Charles de Brosses put it in the 18th century, "If this is divine love, I know all about it." ⊠ *Via XX Settembre 17, Largo Santa Susanna, Repubblica* ☎ *06/42740571* Ⓜ *Repubblica.*

Villa Torlonia

CASTLE/PALACE | FAMILY | Built for aristocrats-come-lately, the Torlonia family—the Italian Rockefellers of the 19th century—this villa became Mussolini's residence and now serves as a public park. Long neglected, the park's vegetation and buildings have recently been refurbished. The Casino Nobile, the main palace designed by the great architect Giuseppe Valadier is a grand, neoclassical edifice, replete with a gigantic ballroom, frescoed salons, and soaring temple-like facade. While denuded of nearly all their furnishings and art treasures, some salons have important remnants of decor, including the reliefs once fashioned by the father of Italian neoclassical sculpture, Antonio Canova. In the park, a complete contrast is offered by the Casina delle Civette (Little House of Owls), a hyper-charming example of the Liberty (art nouveau) style of the early 1900s: the gabled, fairy tale–like cottage-palace now displays majolica and stained-glass decorations, including windows with owl motifs—a stunning, oft-overlooked find for lovers of 19th-century decorative arts. Temporary exhibits are held in the small and elegant Il Casino dei Principi (The House of Princes), designed in part by Valadier. ⊠ *Villa Torlonia, Via Nomentana 70, Repubblica* ☎ *06/0608* ⊕ *www.museivillatorlonia.it* 🎟 *€6 Casina delle Civette with exhibit, €9 Casino Nobile, Casino dei Principe and Casina delle Civette; €11, includes Casina delle Civette, Casino dei Principi and Casino Nobile, with exhibit* ☺ *Closed Mon.* Ⓜ *Policlinico.*

🍴 Restaurants

The areas around Piazza della Repubblica and Termini station aren't known as gastronomic hot spots, but there are some classic Roman wine bars.

Ilwinebar Trimani

$$$ | WINE BAR | This wine bar is run by the Trimani family of wine merchants, whose shop next door has been in business for nearly two centuries. Hot food is served at lunch and dinner in the minimalist interior, and it is also perfect for an aperitif or an early supper (it opens for evening service at 6 pm). **Known for:** 5,000 wines from around the world; *torte salate* (savory tarts); candlelit second floor for sipping. Ⓢ *Average main: €30* ⊠ *Via Cernaia 37/b, Repubblica* ☎ *06/4469630* ⊕ *www.trimani.com* ☺ *Closed Sun. and 3 wks in Aug.* Ⓜ *Castro Pretorio, Repubblica.*

Bernini vs. Borromini: A Mini-Walk

In Rome, you may become lost looking for the work of one rival, then suddenly find yourself gazing at the work of the other. As though an eerily twinned path was destined for the two giants, several of their greatest works are just a few blocks from each other.

A short street away (Via Orlando) from mammoth Piazza Repubblica stands Santa Maria della Vittoria, famed for Bernini's Cornaro Chapel. Out of favor with new anti-Barberini Pope Innocent X, Bernini was rescued by a commission from Cardinal Cornaro to build a chapel for his family. Here, as if in a "theater," sculpted figures of family members look down from two marble balconies on the so-called "transverberation" of Carmelite Saint Theresa of Avila being pierced by the arrow of the Angel of Divine Love, eyes shut in agony, mouth open in rapture.

Leave the church and head down Via Barberini to Piazza Barberini where perch three of the largest bees you'll ever see. The Fountain of the Bees is Bernini's tribute to his arch-patron from the Barberini family, Pope Urban VIII. The bees were family emblems. Another Bernini masterstroke is the Triton Fountain in the center of Piazza Barberini. Turn left up Via delle Quattro Fontane. On your left is spectacular Palazzo Barberini, where Bernini and Borromini worked together in an uneasy partnership. The wonderful winding staircase off to the right is the work of Borromini, while the other more conventionally angled staircase on the left is by Bernini, who also has a self-portrait hanging in the art gallery upstairs.

Borromini's prospects soon took a turn for the better thanks to the Barefoot Spanish Trinitarians, who commissioned him to design San Carlo alle Quattro Fontane, set at the crossroads up the road. One of the marvels of architecture, its dome—not much bigger than a down-turned bathtub—is packed immaculately throughout with hexagons, octagons, and crosses. In the adjoining cloister, revel in Borromini's rearrangement of columns, which transform what would be a conventional rectangle into an energetic octagon. Don't forget to stop and admire the church's facade.

On the same Via del Quirinale stands a famous Bernini landmark, the Jesuits' Sant'Andrea al Quirinale. With steps flowing out into the street, it could be viewed as Bernini's response to his rival's nearby masterpiece. Ironically, the commission for the Jesuit church was originally earmarked for Borromini (but transferred when Pope Alexander VII took over).

☕ Coffee and Quick Bites

Dagnino

$ | BAKERY | Hidden inside a covered arcade, this Sicilian pasticceria, which opened in 1955 and proudly wears its midcentury modern design, boasts pastry cases filled with sweets like cannoli, cassata, cakes, and marzipan. Go for breakfast and try the cornetto filled with ricotta and chocolate chips—this is one of the few places in Rome where you can find it. **Known for:** cornetti filled with ricotta and chocolate chips; midcentury modern design; Sicilian desserts. ⑤ *Average main: €3 ✉ Via Vittorio Emanuele Orlando 75, Repubblica ☎ 06/4818660 ⊕ www. pasticceriadagnino.com Ⓜ Repubblica.*

La Romana dal 1947

$ | ICE CREAM | In summertime, the line at this gelateria stretches out the door and around the corner. Though it's a franchise that originated in Rimini, La Romana is loved by Romans for its rich, creamy gelato made with organic milk, fresh fruit, nuts, and chocolate. **Known for:** big portions; reasonably priced; modern decor. $ *Average main: €3* ⊠ *Via XX Settembre 60, Repubblica* ☎ *06/42020828* ⊕ *www.gelateriaromana.com* Ⓜ *Repubblica.*

Mercato Centrale Roma

$ | ITALIAN | This gourmet food hall is in the last place you'd expect: inside Termini station. It's great for a quick bite even if you're not catching a train. **Known for:** Sicilian specialties; trapizzino (stuffed triangle-shaped pizza dough) outpost; gourmet food hall. $ *Average main: €5* ⊠ *Termini Station, Via Giovanni Giolitti 36, Repubblica* ☎ *06/46202900* ⊕ *www.mercatocentrale.it* Ⓜ *Termini.*

Pasticceria Gruè

$ | CAFÉ | This chic, modern pasticceria and caffè is the perfect place to stop for a quick lunch or something sweet near MACRO and Villa Torlonia. Run by a husband-and-wife team, their panettone (available year-round) is award-winning, but it's far from the only thing worth trying. **Known for:** award-winning panettone; light lunch fare; French-inspired sweets. $ *Average main: €8* ⊠ *Viale Regina Margherita 95/99, Repubblica* ☎ *06/8412220* ⊕ *www.gruepasticceria.it* ⊘ *Closed Mon.*

Pinsere

$ | PIZZA | FAMILY | In Rome, you'll usually find either pizza *tonda* (round) or pizza *al taglio* (by the slice), but there's also pizza *pinsa*: it's an oval-shaped individual pie, and a little thicker than the classic Roman pizza. Pinsere is mostly a take-out shop, with people eating on the street for their lunch break, so it's the perfect quick

meal. **Known for:** mortadella and pistachio pizzas; seasonal toppings; budget-friendly options. $ *Average main: €6* ⊠ *Via Flavia 98, Repubblica* ☎ *06/42020924* ⊘ *Closed weekends and 2 wks in Aug.* Ⓜ *Castro Pretorio.*

Hotels

With its beautiful piazza and fountain, Repubblica is the place to stay if you want to be near but not *too* near Termini station, Rome's central train hub. You'll find lodging here in all price ranges, and rooms tend to be a better value in this part of town.

Demetra Hotel Rome

$$ | HOTEL | This hotel near the glorious Santa Maria Maggiore Basilica is also close to Termini station, and has modern comforts and a great concierge—all at moderate rates. **Pros:** free Wi-Fi; excellent central location; soundproof rooms. **Cons:** rooms can be on the small side; not a picturesque area, so views can be drab; basic breakfast buffet. $ *Rooms from: €180* ⊠ *Via del Viminale 8, Repubblica* ☎ *06/45494943* ⊕ *www.demetrahotel-rome.com* ⇥ *27 rooms* ⚬ *Free Breakfast* Ⓜ *Repubblica.*

Hotel Alpi

$ | HOTEL | You'll feel right at home from the moment you waltz into Hotel Alpi, where high ceilings with elegant chandeliers, white walls, and marble floors lend it both elegance and warmth—right around the corner from Termini station. **Pros:** clean and comfortable; lovely terraces and restaurant for dining and relaxing; boutique design and service. **Cons:** location is not very picturesque; you'll need to take transportation to most sights; not all rooms are created equal. $ *Rooms from: €67* ⊠ *Via Castelfidardo 84, Repubblica* ☎ *06/4441235* ⊕ *www.hotelalpi.com* ⇥ *48 rooms* ⚬ *No Meals* Ⓜ *Castro Pretorio, Termini.*

Hotel Mascagni

$$ | HOTEL | FAMILY | Situated on a side street around the corner from one of Rome's most impressive piazzas, this friendly hotel has staff that go out of their way to make you feel at home, public spaces cleverly styled with contemporary art pieces, and wood fixtures and furnishings accentuated by warm colors and handsome fabrics in the guest rooms. **Pros:** cozy library-style lobby; evening lounge serves light fare; special programs include a "Family Perfect" room option. **Cons:** breakfast options are basic; some bathrooms are smallish; elevator is too small and takes a while. ⑤ *Rooms from: €200 ⊠ Via Vittorio Emanuele Orlando 90, Repubblica ☎ 06/48904040 ⊕ www.mascagnihotelrome.it ⇗ 40 rooms ⦿ Free Breakfast Ⓜ Repubblica.*

Leon's Place Hotel

$$ | HOTEL | Located just around the corner from Piazza Repubblica, this extremely Instagrammable hotel has a lobby lounge with surrealist design elements, like lip-shaped sofas, and an interior courtyard done up in millennial pink. **Pros:** gourmet minibar; eye-catching design; top-quality toiletries. **Cons:** some rooms face the courtyard; some rooms lack windows; hotel bar is pricey. ⑤ *Rooms from: €170 ⊠ Via XX Settembre 90/94, Repubblica ☎ 06/890871 ⊕ www.leonsplacehotel.it ⇗ 56 rooms ⦿ No Meals Ⓜ Repubblica.*

Marcella Royal Hotel

$$ | HOTEL | You can do your sightseeing from the rooftop terrace of the Marcella, a midsize hotel with the feel of a smaller, more intimate establishment, where staff go the extra mile to make your stay pleasant. **Pros:** all-day dining in the rooftop garden; *aperitivo* (aperitif) or nightcap at the piano bar; large bathrooms with excellent water pressure. **Cons:** spotty Internet; closet storage is minimal; some

of the rooms are in need of restyling. ⑤ *Rooms from: €200 ⊠ Via Flavia 106, Repubblica ☎ 06/42014591 ⊕ www.marcellaroyalhotel.com ⇗ 92 rooms ⦿ Free Breakfast Ⓜ Repubblica.*

The St. Regis Rome

$$$$ | HOTEL | Originally opened by César Ritz in 1894, this grand dame is looking fabulous thanks to a $40 million renovation completed in 2018. **Pros:** recently underwent a complete renovation; the library lounge serves a lovely afternoon tea; every room comes with 24/7 butler service. **Cons:** the restaurant feels more like a lounge than a proper restaurant; breakfast is not included; food and drinks are pricey. ⑤ *Rooms from: €650 ⊠ Via Vittorio E. Orlando 3, Repubblica ☎ 06/47091 ⊕ www.stregisrome.com ⇗ 161 rooms ⦿ No Meals Ⓜ Repubblica.*

Villa delle Rose Hotel

$ | HOTEL | When the Eternal City becomes too chaotic for you, head to this relaxing 19th-century palazzo retreat in a charming Roman villa just minutes from Termini station. **Pros:** delightful garden with blooming roses and bougainvillea; delicious local breakfast; free Wi-Fi. **Cons:** elevator is cramped; decor could use revamping; some of the rooms are small (ask for a larger one). ⑤ *Rooms from: €70 ⊠ Via Vicenza 5, Repubblica ☎ 06/4451788 ⊕ www.villadellerose.it ⇗ 37 rooms ⦿ Free Breakfast Ⓜ Termini.*

 **Performing Arts**

OPERA

★ Teatro dell'Opera

OPERA | Long considered a far younger sibling of La Scala in Milan and La Fenice in Venice, the company commands an audience during its mid-November–May season. In the hot summer months, they move to the Terme di Caracalla for its outdoor opera series. As can be expected, the oft-preferred performance is *Aida,* for its spectacle, which once included real elephants. The company has lately taken a new direction, using projections atop the ancient ruins to create cutting-edge sets. ⊠ *Piazza Beniamino Gigli 1, Repubblica* ☎ *06/481601, 06/4817003 tickets* ⊕ *www.operaroma.it* Ⓜ *Repubblica.*

🛍 Shopping

In this neighborhood you'll find bookstores and souvenir shops, as well as various European clothing chains.

BOOKS AND STATIONERY

Libraccio

BOOKS | One of the best parts of Libraccio (part of the IBS chain of bookstores) is the wide variety of European cinema and music selections. Another perk is the discount the store dishes out on its stock of remainders and secondhand books. The shop also has a modest selection of English-language paperbacks and hardcovers. ⊠ *Via Nazionale 254–255, Repubblica* ☎ *06/4885405* ⊕ *www.ibs.it* Ⓜ *Repubblica.*

FOOD AND WINE

Trimani Vinai a Roma dal 1821

WINE/SPIRITS | In business since 1821, Trimani Vinai a Roma occupies an entire block near Termini station with one of the city's largest selection of wines from all over the world, plus champagne, spumante, grappa, and sundry liqueurs. With thousands of bottles to choose from and knowledgeable wine stewards to consult, Trimani will give you the opportunity to explore Italy's diverse wine regions without leaving the city. They also offer gift boxes and will ship almost anywhere in the world. ⊠ *Via Goito 20, Repubblica* ☎ *06/4469661* ⊕ *www.trimani.com* ⊗ *Closed Sun.* Ⓜ *Castro Pretorio, Repubblica.*

The Quirinale

Rome's highest hill, the Quirinale, has housed ancient Roman senators, 17th- and 18th-century popes, and, with the end of papal rule, Italy's kings. West from Via Nazionale, the hill is set with various jewels of the baroque era, including masterpieces by Bernini and Borromini. Nearby stands Palazzo Barberini, a grand and gorgeous 16th-century palace holding five centuries of masterworks.

Crowning the Piazza del Quirinale is the enormous Palazzo del Quirinale, built in the 16th century as a summer residence for the popes; it became the presidential palace in 1946. Today, you can tour its reception rooms, which are as splendid as you might imagine. The changing of the guard outside on the piazza (Sundays at 4 pm, 6 pm in summer months) is an old-fashioned exercise in pomp and circumstance.

While Bernini's work feels omnipresent in much of the city center, the vast range of his work is particularly notable here and in Repubblica. The artist as architect considered the church of Sant'Andrea al Quirinale one of his best; Bernini the urban designer and water worker wrought the muscle-bound sea gods who wrestle in the fountain at the center of Piazza Barberini; and Bernini the master sculptor gives religious passion corporeal treatment in what is perhaps his greatest work, the *Ecstasy of St. Teresa,* in the church of Santa Maria della Vittoria, in Repubblica.

Sights

Capuchin Museum

RELIGIOUS BUILDING | Devoted to teaching visitors about the Capuchin order, this museum is mainly notable for a crypt visitable at the end of the museum circuit. Not for the easily spooked, the crypt under the church of Santa Maria della Concezione holds the bones of some 4,000 dead Capuchin monks. With bones arranged in odd decorative designs around the shriveled and decayed remains of their kinsmen, a macabre reminder of the impermanence of earthly life, the crypt is strangely touching and beautiful. As one sign proclaims: "What you are, we once were. What we are, you someday will be." Upstairs in the church, the first chapel on the right contains Guido Reni's mid-17th-century *Archangel St. Michael Trampling the Devil.* The painting caused great scandal after an astute contemporary observer remarked that the face of the devil bore a surprising resemblance to Pope Innocent X, archenemy of Reni's Barberini patrons. Compare the devil with the bust of the pope that you saw in the Palazzo Doria Pamphilj and judge for yourself. ⊠ *Via Veneto 27, Quirinale* ☎ *06/88803695* ⊕ *www.cappucciniviaveneto.it* ⛾ *€8.50* Ⓜ *Barberini.*

Casino dell'Aurora

CASTLE/PALACE | Set just off the Piazza del Quirinale is the Palazzo Pallavicini-Rospigliosi, and within its grounds you'll find the *Casino dell'Aurora*, originally built for Cardinal Scipione Borghese. The *casino* (a summer pavilion) has a fabulous ceiling fresco of Aurora (the personification of the Dawn) painted by baroque artist Guido Reni—a painting once thought to be the last word in 17th-century style. The casino is only open to the public on the first day of every month, in the morning and afternoon, except January. ⊠ *Via XXIV Maggio 43, Quirinale* ☎ *06/83467000* ⊕ *www.casinoaurorapalavicini.it* ⛾ *Free* Ⓜ *Repubblica.*

Fontana delle Api (*Fountain of the Bees*)
FOUNTAIN | Decorated with the famous heraldic bees of the Barberini family, the upper shell and the inscription are from a fountain that Bernini designed for Pope Urban VIII; the rest was lost when the fountain was moved to make way for a new street. The inscription was the cause of a considerable uproar when the fountain was first built in 1644. It said that the fountain had been erected in the 22nd year of the pontiff's reign, although in fact the 21st anniversary of Urban's election to the papacy was still some weeks away. The last numeral was hurriedly erased, but to no avail—Urban died eight days before the beginning of his 22nd year as pope. The superstitious Romans, who had immediately recognized the inscription as a foolhardy tempting of fate, were vindicated. ⊠ *Piazza Barberini, Quirinale* Ⓜ *Barberini.*

Fontanone dell'Acqua Felice

(*Fountain of Moses*)
FOUNTAIN | When Pope Sixtus V (Felice Peretti) completed the restoration of the Acqua Felice aqueduct toward the end of the 16th century, Domenico Fontana was commissioned to design its monumental fountain. Sculptors Leonardo Sormani and Prospero da Brescia had the unhappy task of executing the central figure of Moses; the comparison with Michelangelo's magnificent *Moses* in the church of San Pietro in Vincoli was inevitable, and the giant sculpture was widely criticized. But the new fountain served to position the formerly rustic Quirinale neighborhood as a thriving urban center. ⊠ *Piazza di San Bernardo, Quirinale* Ⓜ *Repubblica.*

★ Palazzo Barberini Galleria Nazionale d'Arte Antica

ART MUSEUM | One of Rome's most splendid 17th-century buildings, the Palazzo Barberini is a landmark of the Roman baroque style. The grand facade was designed by Carlo Maderno (aided by his nephew, Francesco Borromini), but when Maderno died, Borromini was passed over in favor of his great rival, Gian Lorenzo Bernini. Now home to the Galleria Nazionale d'Arte Antica, the palazzo holds a splendid collection that includes Raphael's *La Fornarina*, a luminous portrait of the artist's lover (a resident of Trastevere, she was reputedly a baker's daughter). Also noteworthy are Guido Reni's portrait of the doomed *Beatrice Cenci* (beheaded in Rome for patricide in 1599)—Hawthorne called it "the saddest picture ever painted" in his Rome-based novel, *The Marble Faun*—and Caravaggio's dramatic *Judith Beheading Holofernes*.

The showstopper here is the palace's Gran Salone, a vast ballroom with a ceiling painted in 1630 by the third (and too-often-neglected) master of the Roman baroque, Pietro da Cortona. It depicts the *Glorification of Urban VIII's Reign* and has the spectacular conceit of glorifying Urban VIII as the agent of Divine Providence, escorted by a "bomber squadron" (to quote art historian Sir Michael Levey) of huge Barberini bees, the heraldic symbol of the family. ✉ *Via delle Quattro Fontane 13, Quirinale* ☎ *06/4814591* ⊕ *www.barberinicorsini. org* 🎫 *€12, includes Galleria Corsini* ⊙ *Closed Mon.* Ⓜ *Barberini.*

Palazzo del Quirinale

CASTLE/PALACE | Pope Gregory XIII started building this spectacular palace, now the official residence of Italy's president, in 1574. He planned to use it as a summer home, but less than 20 years later, Pope Clement VIII decided to make the palace—safely elevated above the malarial miasmas shrouding the low-lying location of the Vatican— the permanent residence of the papacy, which it remained until 1870. The palace underwent various expansions and alterations over time. When Italian troops under Garibaldi stormed Rome in 1870, making it the capital of the newly united Italy, the popes moved back to the Vatican, and the Palazzo del Quirinale became the official residence of the kings of Italy. After the Italian people voted out the monarchy in 1946, the palazzo passed to the presidency of the Italian Republic. The palace is now open to visitors, but you need to prebook a guided tour (in Italian only, although materials in English can be purchased). You will need your ID to enter the building. Outside the gates, you can see the changing of the military guard at 4 pm on Sunday (at 6 pm June through August), and occasionally you can glimpse the impressive presidential guard. ✉ *Piazza del Quirinale, Quirinale* ☎ *06/46991* ⊕ *www.quirinale. it* 🎫 *By tour only: Itinerary No. 1 free (€1.50 booking fee), Itinerary No. 2 €10* ⊙ *Closed Mon.–Thurs.* Ⓜ *Barberini.*

The dome of San Carlo alle Quattro Fontane was designed by Borromini and is the centerpiece of the small church.

Piazza del Quirinale

PLAZA/SQUARE | This strategic location atop the Quirinale has long been of great importance. It served as home of the Sabines in the 7th century BC—at that time, deadly enemies of the Romans, who lived on the Campidoglio and Palatino (all of 1 km [½ mile] away). Today, it's the foreground for the presidential residence, Palazzo del Quirinale, and home to the Palazzo della Consulta, where Italy's Constitutional Court sits. The open side of the piazza has an impressive vista over the rooftops and domes of central Rome and St. Peter's. The Fontana di Montecavallo, or Fontana dei Dioscuri, comprises a huge Roman statuary group and an obelisk from the tomb of the emperor Augustus. The group of the Dioscuri trying to tame two massive marble steeds was found in the Baths of Constantine, which occupied part of the summit of the Quirinale. Unlike just about every other ancient statue in Rome, this group survived the Dark Ages intact and accordingly became one of the city's great sights, especially during the Middle Ages. Next to the figures, the ancient obelisk from the Mausoleo di Augusto (Tomb of Augustus) was put here by Pope Pius VI at the end of the 18th century. ✉ *Piazza del Quirinale, Quirinale* Ⓜ *Barberini.*

Quattro Fontane (*Four Fountains*)

FOUNTAIN | The intersection takes its name from its four baroque fountains, which represent the Tiber (on the San Carlo corner), the Arno, Juno, and Diana. Despite the nearby traffic and the tightness of the sidewalk, it's worthwhile taking in the views from this point in all four directions: to the southwest, as far as the obelisk in Piazza del Quirinale; to the northeast, along Via XX Settembre to the Porta Pia; to the northwest, across Piazza Barberini to the obelisk of Trinità dei Monti; and to the southeast, as far as the obelisk and apse of Santa Maria

Maggiore. The prospect is a highlight of Pope Sixtus V's campaign of urban beautification and an example of baroque influence on city planning. ⊠ *Intersection of Via Quattro Fontane, Via XX Settembre, and Via del Quirinale, Quirinale* Ⓜ *Barberini.*

San Carlo alle Quattro Fontane

CHURCH | Sometimes known as San Carlino because of its tiny size, this is one of Borromini's masterpieces. In a space no larger than the base of one of the piers of St. Peter's Basilica, he created a church that is an intricate exercise in geometric perfection, with a coffered dome that seems to float above the curves of the walls. Borromini's work is often bizarre, definitely intellectual, and intensely concerned with pure form. In San Carlo, he invented an original treatment of space that creates an effect of rippling movement, especially evident in the double-S curves of the facade. Characteristically, the interior decoration is subdued, in white stucco with no more than a few touches of gilding, so as not to distract from the form. Don't miss the cloister: a tiny, understated baroque jewel, with a graceful portico and loggia above, echoing the lines of the church. ⊠ *Via del Quirinale 23, Quirinale* 🕾 *06/48907729* Ⓜ *Barberini.*

Sant'Andrea al Quirinale

CHURCH | Designed by Bernini, this small church is one of the triumphs of the Roman baroque period. His son wrote that Bernini considered it his best work and that he used to come here occasionally, just to sit and contemplate. Bernini's simple oval plan, a classic form in baroque architecture, is given drama and movement by the church's decoration, which carries the story of St. Andrew's martyrdom and ascension into heaven, starting with the painting over the high altar, up past the figure of the saint above, to the angels at the

base of the lantern and the dove of the Holy Spirit that awaits on high. ⊠ *Via del Quirinale 30, Quirinale* 🕾 *06/4819399* ⊕ *santandrea.gesuiti.it* 🕑 *Closed Mon.* Ⓜ *Barberini.*

Restaurants

This area has lots of government offices, hotels, and museums, and the tourist traps and expense-account stalwarts that go with them. There are some reasonable standouts though.

Tullio

$$$ | TUSCAN | Just off Piazza Barberini, this upscale trattoria has been serving Tuscan classics since 1950. They specialize in high-quality meat dishes including prime cuts of beef, lamb, and veal. **Known for:** *tagliolini* (ribbon pasta) with truffles; old-school style and brusque waiters; *bistecca alla fiorentina* (Tuscan porterhouse). Ⓢ *Average main: €32* ⊠ *Via San Nicola da Tolentino 26, Quirinale* 🕾 *06/4745560* ⊕ *www.tullioristorante.it* 🕑 *Closed Sun. and Aug.* Ⓜ *Barberini.*

Hotels

Rome Times Hotel

$$ | HOTEL | This modern hotel has large, soundproofed rooms with contemporary furnishings, hardwood floors, and huge fluffy beds. **Pros:** free minibar on arrival and late checkout if booked through site; large bright bathrooms; free use of Samsung smartphone for calls and Internet during your stay. **Cons:** lighting in rooms is not optimal; rooms in the annex don't come with all the benefits of the main hotel; lower floors can be noisy. Ⓢ *Rooms from: €180* ⊠ *Via Milano 42, Quirinale* 🕾 *06/99345101* ⊕ *www.rometimeshotel.com* 🛏 *81 rooms* ⦿ *No Meals* Ⓜ *Repubblica.*

Chapter 8

VILLA BORGHESE AND ENVIRONS

8

Updated by
Laura Itzkowitz

⊙ Sights	🍴 Restaurants	🛏 Hotels	🛍 Shopping	🍸 Nightlife
★★★★☆	★★☆☆☆	★★☆☆☆	★☆☆☆☆	★☆☆☆☆

NEIGHBORHOOD SNAPSHOT

MAKING THE MOST OF YOUR TIME

Explore this area on a clear day: the Villa Borghese park is at its best (and most bustling with strolling Italian families) on beautiful days, while the view from the top of the Pincio provides a stunning panorama over Rome's pastel rooftops. The Galleria Borghese, one of several museums within the Villa Borghese, is a Roman gem and a must-see for art lovers; just remember to book your tickets in advance (you can do so online), as walk-ins are rarely accommodated. After your "walk in the park," head down to Piazza del Popolo, one of Rome's loveliest piazzas, and duck into Santa Maria del Popolo for its gorgeous paintings by baroque master Caravaggio—keeping in mind that, like many of Rome's churches, it closes in the middle of the day.

GETTING HERE

■ The Metro stop for Piazza del Popolo is Flaminio on Line A. The Villa Giulia, the Galleria Nazionale d'Arte Moderna e Contemporanea, and the Bioparco in Villa Borghese are accessible from Via Flaminia, 1 km (½ mile) from Piazza del Popolo. Tram No. 19 stops at each.

■ Bus No. 160 and No. 628 connects Piazza del Popolo to Piazza Venezia. Bus No. 61 goes into Villa Borghese.

TOP REASONS TO GO

Piazza del Popolo: At the end of three of the *centro storico*'s (historic center) most important streets—Via del Babuino, Via del Corso, and Via di Ripetta—the "People's Square" provides a front-row seat for some of Rome's best people-watching.

Villa Borghese: Drink in the fresh air in central Rome's largest park—stretches of green and plenty of leafy pathways encourage wandering, biking, or just chilling out.

The Pincio: Stroll through formal gardens in the footsteps of aristocrats out of a 19th-century fashion plate.

Santa Maria del Popolo: Marvel at the incredible realism of Caravaggio's gritty paintings in the Cerasi Chapel, then savor Raphael's Chigi Chapel.

Galleria Borghese: Appreciate the extravagant interior decor in one of Rome's most opulent—and pleasant—museums.

OFF THE BEATEN PATH

■ **Foro Italico.** Just across the river from the northernmost reaches of Flaminio lies the Foro Italico sports complex. A pet project of Mussolini, it's a classic example of Rationalist architecture. The impressive Stadio dei Marmi features a track dotted with 60 larger-than-life statues of athletes. There's also the tennis stadium, two pools, and the olympic stadium, where soccer matches take place. Via del Foro Italico. *Take Tram 2 to* Ⓜ *Mancini.*

While it may not feel like it amid the dense warren of cobblestone streets in the centro storico, Rome is actually a very green city. All around the immediate city center are a number of vast public parks, the most central of which is the city's giant green lung: the Villa Borghese park, where residents love to escape for some serious R&R. But don't think you can completely avoid sightseeing—three of Rome's most important museums are inside the park, and Piazza del Popolo, which has more than one art-crammed church, is close by.

Villa Borghese

Rome's Central Park, the Villa Borghese was originally laid out as a recreational garden in the early 17th century by Cardinal Scipione Borghese. The word "villa" was used to mean suburban estate, of the type developed by the ancient Romans and adopted by Renaissance nobles. Today's gardens cover a much smaller area—by 1630, the perimeter wall was almost 5 km (3 miles) long. At the end of the 18th century, Scottish painter Jacob More remodeled the gardens into the English style popular at the time. In addition to the gloriously restored Galleria Borghese, the highlights of the park are Piazza di Siena, a graceful amphitheater, and the botanical garden on Via Canonica, where there is a pretty little lake as well as the neoclassical faux–Temple of Aesculapius, the Biopark zoo, Rome's own replica of London's Globe Theatre, and the Villa Giulia museum.

The Carlo Bilotti Museum (⊕ *www. museocarlobilotti.it*) is particularly attractive for Giorgio de Chirico fans, and there is more modern art in the nearby Galleria Nazionale d'Arte Moderna e Contemporanea. The 63-seat children's movie theater, Cinema dei Piccoli, shows films for adults in the evening. There's also Casa del Cinema, where film buffs can screen films or sit at the sleek, cherry-red, indoor-outdoor caffè (you can find a schedule of events at ⊕ *www. casadelcinema.it*).

Sights

Bioparco

ZOO | FAMILY | Especially good for a day out with the children, this zoo has been remodeled along eco-friendly lines: there is now more space for the animals, most of which were brought from other zoos or born from animals already in captivity (rather than those snatched from the wild). There aren't any koalas, pandas, or polar bears, but there are big cats, elephants, chimpanzees, and local brown bears from Abruzzo among others. Other features include the Reptilarium, the Bioparco train, a picnic area next to the flamingos, and a farm. ✉ *Piazzale del Giardino Zoologico 1, Villa Borghese* ☎ *06/3608211* ⊕ *www.bioparco.it* ✉ *€17; €1.50 for Bioparco Train.*

★ Galleria Borghese

ART MUSEUM | It's a real toss-up as to which is more magnificent: the museum built for Cardinal Scipione Borghese in 1612 or the art that lies within it. The luxury-loving cardinal had the museum custom built as a showcase for his fabulous collection of both antiquities and more "modern" works, including those he commissioned from the masters Caravaggio and Bernini. Today, it's a monument to Roman interior decoration at its most extravagant.

One of the most famous works in the collection is Canova's neoclassical sculpture *Pauline Borghese as Venus Victorious*. The next three rooms hold three key early baroque sculptures: Bernini's *David*, *Apollo and Daphne*, and *The Rape of Persephone*. All were done when the artist was in his twenties, and all illustrate Bernini's extraordinary skill. *Apollo and Daphne* shows the moment when, to aid her escape from the pursuing Apollo, Daphne is turned into a laurel tree. Leaves and twigs sprout from her fingertips as she stretches agonizingly away from Apollo. In *The Rape of Persephone*, Pluto has just plucked Persephone (or Proserpina)

from her flower-picking, or perhaps he's returning to Hades with his prize. (Don't miss the realistic way his grip causes dimples in Persephone's flesh.) This is the stuff that makes the baroque exciting—and moving. Other Berninis on view in the collection include a large, unfinished figure called *Verità*, or Truth.

Room 8 contains six paintings by Caravaggio, the hotheaded genius who died at age 37. All of his paintings, even the charming *Boy with a Basket of Fruit*, seethe with an undercurrent of darkness. The disquieting *Sick Bacchus* is a self-portrait of the artist who, like the god, had a fondness for wine. *David and Goliath*, painted in the last year of Caravaggio's life—while he was on the run, murder charges hanging over his head—includes his self-portrait in the head of Goliath. Upstairs, the Pinacoteca (Picture Gallery) boasts paintings by Raphael (including his moving *Deposition*), Pinturicchio, Perugino, Bellini, and Rubens. Probably the gallery's most famous painting is Titian's allegorical *Sacred and Profane Love*, a mysterious and yet-unsolved image with two female figures, one nude, one clothed. ■**TIP**➔ **Admission to the Galleria is by reservation only. Visitors are admitted in two-hour shifts 9–5. Prime-time slots usually sell out days in advance, so reserve directly through the museum's website.** ✉ *Piazzale Scipione Borghese 5, off Via Pinciana, Villa Borghese* ☎ *06/32810 reservations, 06/8413979 info* ⊕ *www.galleriaborghese.it* ✉ *€15, including €2 reservation fee; increased fee during temporary exhibitions* ⊘ *Closed Mon.* ♿ *Reservations required.*

Galleria Nazionale d'Arte Moderna e Contemporanea

(*National Gallery of Modern Art*)
ART MUSEUM | This massive white Beaux-Arts building, built for the 1911 World Exposition in Rome, contains one of Italy's leading collections of 19th- and 20th-century works. It's primarily

Principessa Pauline Borghese, Napoléon's sister, scandalized Europe by posing as a half-naked Venus for Canova; the statue is on view at the Galleria Borghese.

dedicated to the history of Italian modernism, examining the movement's development over the last two centuries, but crowd-pleasers Degas, Monet, Courbet, van Gogh, and Cézanne put in appearances, along with an outstanding Dadaist collection. You can mix coffee and culture at the art nouveau Caffè delle Arti in the columned alcove of the museum. ⊠ *Viale delle Belle Arti 131, Villa Borghese* ☎ *06/32298221* ⊕ *www. lagallerianazionale.com* ✉ *€10* ⊗ *Closed Mon.* Ⓜ *Flaminio.*

★ **Museo Nazionale Etrusco di Villa Giulia**
(*National Etruscan Museum*)
HISTORY MUSEUM | The world's most outstanding collection of Etruscan art and artifacts is housed in Villa Giulia, built around 1551 for Pope Julius III. Among the team called in to plan and construct the villa were Michelangelo and fellow Florentine Vasari. Most of the actual work, however, was done by Vignola and Ammannati. The villa's *nymphaeum*—or sunken sculpture garden—is a superb

example of a refined late-Renaissance setting for princely pleasures. No one knows precisely where the Etruscans originated, but many scholars maintain they came from Asia Minor, appearing in Italy about 2000 BC, and creating a civilization that was a dazzling prelude to the ancient Romans. Among the most striking pieces are the terra-cotta statues, such as the *Apollo of Veii* and the serenely beautiful *Sarcophagus of the Spouses*. Dating to 530–500 BC, this couple (or *Sposi*) look at the viewer with almond eyes and archaic smiles, suggesting an openness and joie de vivre rare in Roman art. Also look for the cinematic frieze from a later temple (480 BC) in Pyrgi, resembling a sort of Etruscan Elgin marbles in terra-cotta. The exhibition of Etruscan jewelry, as well as the beautiful gardens, definitely make it worth a visit. ⊠ *Piazzale di Villa Giulia 9, Villa Borghese* ☎ *06/3226571* ⊕ *villagiulia.beniculturali.it* ✉ *€10* ⊗ *Closed Mon.* Ⓜ *Tram No. 19.*

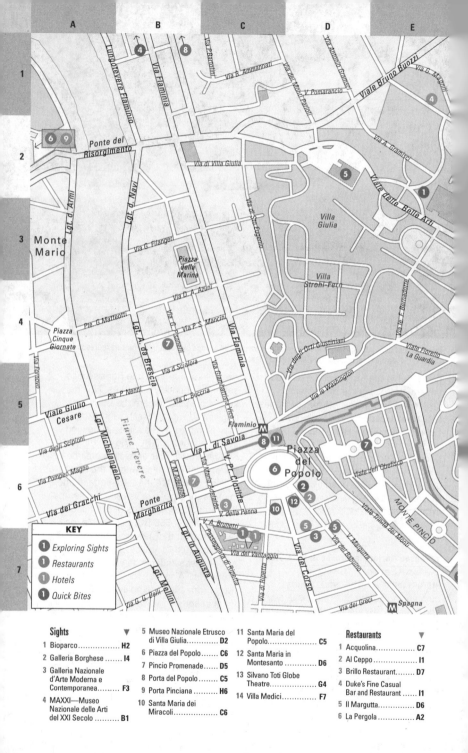

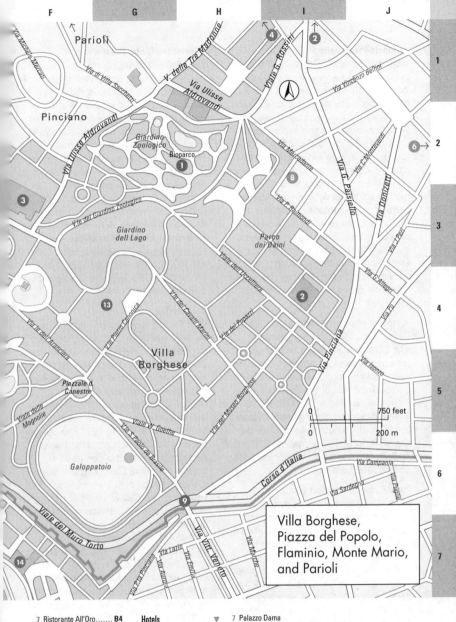

F G H I J

Parioli

Pinciano

Giardino
Zoologico
Bioparco

Giardino
dell Lago

Parco
dei Daini

Villa
Borghese

Piazzale d.
Canestre

Galoppatoio

0   750 feet
0   200 m

Via Michele Mercati
Via di Villa Sacchetti
Via Ulisse Aldrovandi
V. delle Tre Madonne
Via Ulisse Aldrovandi
Viale G. Rossini
Via Vincenzo Bellini
Via Mercadante
Via G. Paisiello
Via L. Montevardi
Via Donizetti
Via P. Raimondi
Via I Peri
Viale dell'Uccelliera
Via G. Allegri
Viale dei Cavalli Marini
Viale dei Pupazzi
Via Po
Viale del Giardino Zoologico
Viale Pietro Canonica
V.le Fiorello La Guardia
Via Teodoro Lalli
Viale del Aranciera
Viale P. Canonica
V.le Pietro Canonica
Via S. Paolo del Brasile
Viale delle Magnolie
Viale W. Goethe
V.le del Museo Borghese
Via Pinciana
Via Isonzo
Corso d'Italia
Via Campania
Via Sardegna
Via Puglie
Via Marche
Viale del Muro Torto
Via Pra Pinciana
Via Lazio
Via Emilia
Via Aurora
Via Vitt. Veneto

1

2

3

4

5

6

7

Villa Borghese,
Piazza del Popolo,
Flaminio, Monte Mario,
and Parioli

7 Ristorante All'Oro....... **B4**
8 Tree Bar.................. **B1**

Quick Bites ▼
1 Caffè delle Arti **E2**
2 Canova.................. **D6**

Hotels ▼
1 The First Roma Arte **C7**
2 Hotel de Russie **D6**
3 Hotel Locarno **C6**
4 Hotel Lord Byron........ **E1**
5 Hotel Valadier **D6**
6 The Hoxton, Rome **J2**

7 Palazzo Dama
   Hotel..................... **B6**
8 Parco dei Principi
   Grand Hotel & Spa....... **I2**
9 Rome Cavalieri,
   A Waldorf
   Astoria Hotel **A2**

★ Pincio Promenade

VIEWPOINT | FAMILY | Redolent of the bygone era of Henry James and Edith Wharton, the Pincian gardens have long been a classic setting for a walk. Grand Tourists—and even a pope or two—would head here to see and be seen among the beau monde of Rome. Today, the Pincian terrace remains a favorite spot for locals taking a springtime Sunday stroll. The rather formal, early-19th-century style contrasts with the far more elaborate terraced gardens of Lucullus, the Roman gourmand who held legendary banquets here. Today, off-white marble busts of Italian Risorgimento heroes and artists line the pathways. Along with similar busts on the Gianicolo (Janiculum Hill), their noses have been targets of vandalism.

A stretch of ancient walls separates the Pincio from the southwest corner of Villa Borghese. From the balustraded terrace, you can look down at Piazza del Popolo and beyond, surveying much of Rome. Southeast of the Pincian terrace is the Casina Valadier (☎ 06/69922090), a magnificently decorated neoclassical building, which houses an upscale bar and bistro with glorious views. ✉ Piazzale Napoleone I and Viale dell'Obelisco, Villa Borghese Ⓜ Flaminio.

Porta Pinciana (Pincian Gate)

NOTABLE BUILDING | Framed by two squat, circular towers, this gate was constructed at the beginning of the 5th century during a renovation of the 3rd century Aurelian Walls. Here you can see just how well the walls have been preserved and imagine hordes of Visigoths trying to break through them. Sturdy as they look, these walls couldn't always keep out the barbarians: Rome was sacked three times during the 5th century alone. ✉ Piazzale Brasile, corner of Via Veneto and Corso d'Italia, Villa Borghese.

Silvano Toti Globe Theatre

PERFORMANCE VENUE | Formerly directed by the late prolific Roman actor Gigi Proietti, this theater replicates the London original inaugurated in 1576. Rome's homage to Shakespeare is built entirely of wood, and seats 1,250 with standing room for 420 groundlings (following Elizabethan custom). Performances run July–September and are usually works by Shakespeare translated into Italian. Set in the Villa Borghese park, it is roughly midway between the Bioparco and the Museo Carlo Bilotti. ■TIP➜ **Check the website for admission, as prices vary.** ✉ Largo Aqua Felix on Viale Pietro Canonica, Villa Borghese ☎ 3314619622 box office, 06/0608 tickets ⊕ www.globetheatreroma.com Ⓜ Flaminio.

Villa Medici

(The French Academy of Rome)

HISTORIC HOME | Purchased by Napoléon to create an academy where artists could study Italian art and put it toward the (French) national good, the villa originally belonged to Cardinal Ferdinando I de' Medici, who also laid out the immaculate Renaissance garden to set off his sculpture collection. In 1803, the building became the official host to the French Academy of Rome. Garden tours in English are offered, allowing you to walk in the footsteps of Subleyras, Fragonard, and Ingres, who all worked here. You can visit during special exhibitions or take a guided tour to see the gardens and the incredibly picturesque garden facade, which is studded with mannerist and rococo sculpted reliefs and overlooks a loggia with a beautiful fountain devoted to Mercury. There is also a pleasant cafeteria (daily 8 am–7 pm) at the loggia level, by the Galleria del Cardinale Ferdinando de' Medici. ✉ Viale Trinità dei Monti 1, Villa Borghese ☎ 06/6761200 ⊕ www.villamedici.it ⚲ €10, exhibits; €12, guided tour of the garden and villa; €14, includes garden tour and exhibit ⊗ Closed Tues. Ⓜ Spagna.

ⓧ Restaurants

One of Rome's two large parks borders the famed-but-faded Via Veneto, the former haunt of the Hollywood-on-the-Tiber scene. The upscale neighborhood is home to historic dining destinations as well as the caffè culture that formed the backdrop for those living *la dolce vita,* the sweet life.

Al Ceppo

$$$ | ITALIAN | The well heeled, the business-minded, and those of refined palates frequent this outpost of tranquility. The owners hail from Le Marche, the region northeast of Rome that encompasses inland mountains and the Adriatic coastline, and these ladies dote on their customers as you'd wish a sophisticated Italian mamma would. **Known for:** excellent wine list; authentic Le Marche cuisine; grilled meat and fish. $ *Average main: €30* ✉ *Via Panama 2, Villa Borghese* ☎ *06/8419696* ⊕ *www.ristorantealceppo. it* ◷ *Closed 3 wks in Aug.*

☕ Coffee and Quick Bites

Caffè delle Arti

$$$ | CAFÉ | Attached to the Galleria d'Arte Moderna, inside the Villa Borghese, this elegant caffè with a pretty terrace is a favorite all-day rendezvous both for Romans from nearby upscale Parioli and for visitors to the Villa Borghese park and museums. **Known for:** good coffee and desserts; excellent, if expensive, pastas; popular shaded terrace. $ *Average main: €32* ✉ *Galleria d'Arte Moderna, Via Gramsci 73, Villa Borghese* ☎ *06/32651236* ◷ *No dinner.*

🛏 Hotels

The area around the Villa Borghese gardens is a relaxing retreat from the hustle and bustle of the Eternal City. You won't get tired of waking up to views of the park.

Parco dei Principi Grand Hotel & Spa

$$$$ | HOTEL | The 1960s-era facade of this large, seven-story hotel designed by Gio Ponti contrasts with the turn-of-the-20th-century Italian court decor and the extensive botanical garden outside, resulting in a combination of traditional elegance and contemporary pleasure. **Pros:** quiet location on Villa Borghese; fitness room with wide variety of equipment; biosauna and sensory showers at spa. **Cons:** staff can be distant and unhelpful; a bit of a hike to caffè and restaurants; beyond the city center. $ *Rooms from: €360* ✉ *Via Gerolamo Frescobaldi 5, Villa Borghese* ☎ *06/854421* ⊕ *www.parcodeiprincipi. com* ⇥ *177 rooms* ⓧ *Free Breakfast.*

🎭 Performing Arts

FILM

Casa del Cinema

FILM | Casa del Cinema is Rome's hub for all things film, with multiple screening rooms, a resource center with DVD library, laptops for private viewings, plus a caffè and restaurant. Yearly programming includes new and retro films from its vast archives as well as many original-language films often showcased from several festivals, including Rome Film Fest. In summer, the cinema heads outdoors to show a wide array of movies. ✉ *Largo Marcello Mastroianni 1, Villa Borghese* ☎ *06/0608* ⊕ *www.casadelcinema.it.*

Cinema dei Piccoli
(*Mickey Mouse Cinema*)
FILM | FAMILY | This tiny quaint theater in the middle of the park has only 63 seats, and plays children's films during the day and adult new releases at night. Opened in 1934, many Romans still refer to it as "Casa di Topolino," thanks to the giant Mickey Mouse sign that appeared on the building until the 1970s. Warning to the very tall: leg room is minimal. ⊠ *Viale della Pineta 15, Villa Borghese* ☎ *06/8553485* ⊕ *www.cinemadeipiccoli.it.*

Piazza del Popolo

The formal garden terraces of the Pincio, on the southwestern side of Villa Borghese, give way to a stone staircase down to Piazza del Popolo, a mercifully traffic-free piazza that is one of Rome's best people-watching spots. Very round, very explicitly defined, and very picturesque, the Piazza del Popolo (the People's Square) is one of Rome's biggest. Papal architect Giuseppe Valadier laid out this square around 1820 with twin churches at one end and the Porta del Popolo, Rome's northern city gate, at the other. Part of an earlier urban plan, the three streets to the south radiate straight as spokes to other parts of the city, forming the famed *tridente* that gives this neighborhood its nickname. The center is marked with an obelisk taken from Egypt, one so old it makes the Pantheon look like the Sears Tower; it was carved for Ramses II in the 13th century BC. Today, the obelisk is guarded by four water-gushing lions and steps that mark the end of many a sunset *passeggiata* (stroll). The most fascinating pieces of art—including masterpieces by Raphael and Caravaggio—are hidden within the northeast corner's often-overlooked church of Santa Maria del Popolo, snuggled against the 400-year-old Porta del Popolo.

Sights

★ Piazza del Popolo

PLAZA/SQUARE | With its obelisk and twin churches, this immense square is a famed Rome landmark. It marks what was for centuries the northern entrance to the city, where all roads from the north converge and where visitors, many of them pilgrims, would get their first impression of the Eternal City. The desire to make this entrance to Rome something special had been a pet project of popes and their architects for more than three centuries. The piazza, crowded with fashionable carriages and carnival revelers in the past, is a pedestrian zone today. At election time, it's the scene of huge political rallies, and on New Year's Eve, Rome stages a mammoth alfresco party here. ⊠ *Piazza del Popolo* Ⓜ *Flaminio.*

Porta del Popolo (*City Gate*)

NOTABLE BUILDING | The medieval gate in the Aurelian walls was replaced by the current one between 1562 and 1565, by Nanni di Bacco Bigio. Bernini further embellished the inner facade in 1655 for the much-heralded arrival of Queen Christina of Sweden, who had abdicated her throne to become a Roman Catholic. ⊠ *Piazza del Popolo and Piazzale Flaminio, Piazza del Popolo* Ⓜ *Flaminio.*

Santa Maria dei Miracoli

CHURCH | A twin to Santa Maria in Montesanto, this church was built in the 1670s, started by Carlo Rainaldi and completed by Bernini and Carlo Fontana as an elegant frame for the entrance to Via del Corso from Piazza del Popolo. The church is dedicated to "Our Lady of the Miracles." Inside there is a gorgeous stucco, designed by Bernini pupil Antonio Raggi. ⊠ *Via del Corso 528, Piazza del Popolo* ☎ *06/3610250* Ⓜ *Flaminio.*

★ Santa Maria del Popolo

CHURCH | Standing inconspicuously in a corner of the vast Piazza del Popolo, this church often goes unnoticed, but the treasures inside make it a must for art lovers. Bramante enlarged the apse, which was rebuilt in the 15th century on the site of a much older place of worship. Inside, in the first chapel on the right, you'll see some frescoes by Pinturicchio from the mid-15th century; the adjacent Cybo Chapel is a 17th-century exercise in decorative marble. Raphael designed the famous Chigi Chapel, the second on the left, with vault mosaics—showing God the Father in Benediction—as well as statues of Jonah and Elijah. More than a century later, Bernini added the oval medallions on the tombs and the statues of Daniel and Habakkuk. Finally, the Cerasi Chapel, to the left of the high altar, holds two Caravaggios: *The Crucifixion of St. Peter* and *The Conversion of St. Paul.* Exuding drama and realism, both are key early baroque works that show how "modern" 17th-century art can appear. Compare their style with the much more restrained and classically "pure" *Assumption of the Virgin* by Annibale Carracci, which hangs over the altar of the chapel. ⊠ *Piazza del Popolo 12, near Porta del Popolo, Piazza del Popolo* ☎ *3923612243* ⊕ *www.smariadelpopolo. com/it* Ⓜ *Flaminio.*

Santa Maria in Montesanto

(*Church of the Artists*)

CHURCH | Located on the eastern side of the Piazza del Popolo, Santa Maria dei Miracoli's baroque "twin church" was built in the 1660s–70s. It was originally designed by Carlo Rainaldi and finished by Carlo Fontana who was supervised by his brilliant teacher, Bernini (whose other pupils are responsible for the saints topping the facade). On the last Sunday of the month from October to June, a Mass is held in tribute to artists, with live musical accompaniment, earning the church its nickname of the Church of the Artists. ⊠ *Piazza del Popolo 18, Piazza del Popolo* ☎ *06/3610594* ⊕ *www.chiesadegliartisti.it* Ⓜ *Flaminio.*

🍴 Restaurants

This high-traffic shopping and tourist zone has both casual pizzerie and upscale eateries, as well as classic caffè where you can have a restorative espresso and a light bite.

Acquolina

$$$$ | MODERN ITALIAN | This This Michelin-starred restaurant turns out delicious and high-quality seafood dishes that surprise and evoke a sensory experience. Tortelli are served with cheese, black pepper, eel, and onion, and all the dishes are artfully presented. **Known for:** sophisticated desserts; linguine with clams; elaborate tasting menus. ⑤ *Average main: €50* ⊠ *The First Roma Arte, Via del Vantaggio 14, Piazza del Popolo* ☎ *06/3201590* ⊕ *www. acquolinaristorante.it* ⊗ *Closed Sun. and Tues. No lunch* Ⓜ *Flaminio.*

Brillo Restaurant

$$ | WINE BAR | The location near Piazza del Popolo makes Brillo especially convenient for lunch or dinner after shopping in the Via del Corso area. The menu is more extensive than the typical wine bar, with cured meats, crostini, pastas, grilled meats, and pizzas. **Known for:** more than 400 types of wine; open late, ideal for an after-show meal; squash blossom pizza. ⑤ *Average main: €16* ⊠ *Via della Fontanella 12, Piazza del Popolo* ☎ *06/3243334* ⊕ *www.ilbrilloparlante.com* Ⓜ *Flaminio.*

Il Margutta

$$ | **VEGETARIAN** | Parallel to posh Via del Babuino, Via Margutta was once a street of artists' studios (including Fellini's), and this chic vegetarian restaurant, with changing displays of modern art, sits on the far end of the gallery-lined street. They turn out tasty meat-free versions of classic Mediterranean dishes, as well as more daring tofu concoctions. **Known for:** marinated ginger tofu; arty atmosphere; organic fruit and vegetable juices. ⑤ *Average main: €14* ✉ *Via Margutta 118, Piazza del Popolo* ☎ *06/32650577* ⊕ *www.ilmargutta.bio* ⊘ *Closed Mon.* Ⓜ *Flaminio.*

☕ Coffee and Quick Bites

Canova

$$ | **ITALIAN** | Esteemed director Federico Fellini, who lived around the corner on Via Margutta, used to come here all the time and even had an office in the back. His drawings and black-and-white stills from his films remain on display in the hallway that leads to the interior dining room, but the best place to sit for people-watching with a coffee, light lunch, or *aperitivo* (aperitif) is on the terrace out front. **Known for:** Fellini's old hangout; sandwiches and other light fare; great people-watching on Piazza del Popolo. ⑤ *Average main: €15* ✉ *Piazza del Popolo 16, Piazza del Popolo* ☎ *06/3612231* ⊕ *www.canovapiazzadelpopolo.it* Ⓜ *Flaminio.*

Hotels

While Piazza del Popolo is still quite close to the *centro* action, it's just removed enough to feel relaxing after a day of sightseeing. Here, amid high-end boutiques and galleries, you'll find several smart, stylish hotels.

The First Roma Arte

$$$$ | **HOTEL** | Set in a 19th-century neo-classical palace, this cozy boutique hotel was remodeled to feature high-tech, elegant guest rooms while keeping the core structure, including unique windows and tall ceilings, intact. **Pros:** fitness room with Technogym equipment; more than 200 works of art on display from Galleria Mucciaccia; incredible staff that is eager to please. **Cons:** not a lot of in-room storage for luggage; many rates don't include breakfast; some rooms can be a bit dark. ⑤ *Rooms from: €450* ✉ *Via del Vantaggio 14, Piazza del Popolo* ☎ *06/45617070* ⊕ *www.thefirsthotel.com/arte* ⇨ *29 rooms* ⧈ *No Meals* Ⓜ *Flaminio.*

★ Hotel de Russie

$$$$ | **HOTEL** | Occupying a 19th-century hotel that once hosted royalty, Picasso, and Cocteau, the Hotel de Russie is now the first choice in Rome for government bigwigs and Hollywood high rollers seeking ultimate luxury in a secluded retreat. **Pros:** big potential for celebrity sightings; excellent Stravinskij cocktail bar also has tables in the garden; well-equipped gym and world-class spa with hydropool Jacuzzi, steam room, and sauna. **Cons:** expensive; breakfast not included; faster Internet comes at a fee. ⑤ *Rooms from: €710* ✉ *Via del Babuino 9, Piazza del Popolo* ☎ *06/328881* ⊕ *www.roccofortehotels.com/hotels-and-resorts/hotel-de-russie* ⇨ *120 rooms* ⧈ *No Meals* Ⓜ *Flaminio.*

Hotel Locarno

$$$$ | **HOTEL** | This hotel, originally established in 1925, is known for its charm, intimate feel, and central location off Piazza del Popolo. **Pros:** spacious rooms; complimentary bicycles; free Wi-Fi. **Cons:** cleaning fee of €30 per night for pets; some rooms are a bit noisy; some rooms are dark. ⑤ *Rooms from: €350* ✉ *Via della Penna 22, Piazza del Popolo* ☎ *06/3610841* ⊕ *www.hotellocarno.com* ⇨ *49 rooms* ⧈ *Free Breakfast* Ⓜ *Flaminio.*

Hotel Valadier

$$ | **HOTEL** | Located just a quick walk from the Spanish Steps, this hotel has captured the hearts of elite travelers over the years. **Pros:** excellent American-style breakfast; spacious marble and travertine bathrooms; discount if booking directly through website. **Cons:** fitness room is quite small; rooms can be very dark; pillows are flat and outdated. ⑤ *Rooms from: €150* ⊠ *Via della Fontanella 15, Piazza del Popolo* ☎ *06/3611998* ⊕ *www. hotelvaladier.com* ⇗ *60 rooms* ⦿ *Free Breakfast* Ⓜ *Flaminio.*

ⓨ Nightlife

Like nearby Piazza di Spagna, Piazza del Popolo takes a turn for the quiet once the sun sets.

BARS

★ **Stravinskij Bar at the Hotel de Russie**

COCKTAIL LOUNGES | The Stravinskij Bar, in the Hotel de Russie's gorgeous garden, is the best place to catch a glimpse of la dolce vita. Celebrities, blue bloods, and VIPs hang out in the private courtyard garden where mixed drinks and cocktails are well above par. There are also healthy smoothies and bites if you need to refuel. ⊠ *Hotel de Russie, Via del Babuino 9, Piazza del Popolo* ☎ *06/328881* ⊕ *www. roccofortehotels.com* Ⓜ *Flaminio.*

🛍 Shopping

★ Il Marmoraro

ANTIQUES & COLLECTIBLES | This tiny shop is a holdout of Via Margutta's days as a street full of artists and artisans. Sandro Fiorentino's father opened the shop in 1969 (he carved plaques like the one that marks Federico Fellini's house up the street) and Sandro still engraves the marble by hand. The shop is packed full of plaques, many with clever phrases, which make a great souvenir. Sandro will also engrave a message of your choice upon request. ⊠ *Via Margutta 53B, Piazza del Popolo* ☎ *06/3207660* ⊗ *Closed Sun.* Ⓜ *Spagna.*

Flaminio

The Flaminio neighborhood, in northern Rome near the Tiber, was the focus of urban renewal plans for many years. Renzo Piano's Auditorium Parco della Musica put the area on the map, and the MAXXI museum solidified the area as a destination.

⊙ Sights

MAXXI—Museo Nazionale delle Arti del XXI Secolo

(*National Museum of 21st-Century Arts*) **ART MUSEUM** | Designed by the late Iraqi-British starchitect Zaha Hadid, this modern building plays with lots of natural light, curving and angular lines, and big open spaces, all meant to question the division between "within" and "without" (think glass ceilings and steel staircases that twist through the air). The MAXXI hosts temporary exhibitions of art, architecture, film, and more. The permanent collection, exhibited on a rotating basis, boasts more than 350 works from modern and contemporary artists, including Andy Warhol, Francesco Clemente, and Gerhard Richter. ⊠ *Via Guido Reni 4/A, Flaminio* ☎ *06/3201954* ⊕ *www.maxxi.art* 💶 *€12* ⊗ *Closed Mon.* Ⓜ *Flaminio, then Tram No. 2 to Apollodoro.*

🍴 Restaurants

Long a residential area, Flaminio is starting to come into its own, with new and interesting bars and restaurants opening.

★ Ristorante All'Oro

$$$$ | **MODERN ITALIAN** | At this sleek Michelin-starred restaurant inside the Hall Tailor Suite hotel, chef/owner Riccardo Di Giacinto and his wife Ramona make fine dining a fun and entertaining experience. Di Giacinto worked with Ferran Adrià in Spain and uses some of his techniques without veering too far into the territory of molecular gastronomy.

Known for: playful riffs on Roman dishes; sleek, modern design; top-notch service. ⑤ *Average main: €42* ✉ *Via Giuseppe Pisanelli 25, Flaminio* ☎ *06/97996907* ⊕ *www.ristoranteallloro.it* ⊘ *No lunch weekdays* Ⓜ *Flaminio.*

Tree Bar

$ | **CAFÉ** | Tree Bar is, as the name suggests, set amid lush greenery and decorated in wooden tree house style. Functioning as a bar, restaurant, and enoteca all at once, it's open for lunch and dinner as well as for apertivi and late-night drinks and brunch on weekends. **Known for:** pasta e ceci (pasta with chickpeas); aperitivo served with snacks; organic wines. ⑤ *Average main: €12* ✉ *Via Flaminia 226, Flaminio* ☎ *06/49773501* ⊕ *www.treebar.it* ⊘ *Closed 2 wks in Aug.*

 Hotels

Palazzo Dama Hotel

$$$$ | **HOTEL** | This former Roman villa was once home to the Malaspina family, who hosted high society gatherings throughout the 18th century. **Pros:** drinks and bites available all-day in garden or main hall; Acqua di Parma toiletries; swimming pool is open year-round. **Cons:** room service is slow and portions are tiny; rooms can be noisy; standard rooms are small with little storage space. ⑤ *Rooms from: €430* ✉ *Lungotevere Arnaldo da Brescia 2, Flaminio* ☎ *06/89565272* ⊕ *www. palazzodama.com* ⟿ *29 rooms* ⊙⧄ *Free Breakfast* Ⓜ *Flaminio.*

 Performing Arts

CLASSICAL MUSIC

Accademia Filarmonica Romana

(*Roman Philharmonic Academy*)
MUSIC | Nearly two centuries old, this is one of Rome's historic concert venues, founded in 1821, featuring both symphonic and chamber-music presentations. The garden hosts occasional outdoor performances. ✉ *Via Flaminia 118, Flaminio* ☎ *06/3201752* ⊕ *www. filarmonicaromana.org* Ⓜ *Flaminio.*

Accademia Nazionale di Santa Cecilia

(*National Academy of Santa Cecilia*)
CONCERTS | One of the oldest conservatories in the world (founded 1585), this venue has a program of performances ranging from classical to contemporary and a lineup of world-renowned artists. The Renzo Piano–designed Auditorium Parco della Musica hosts Santa Cecilia's shows in its three music concert halls. ✉ *Viale Pietro de Coubertin 30, Flaminio* ☎ *06/80242501* ⊕ *www.santacecilia.it* Ⓜ *Flaminio, then Tram No. 2 to Apollodoro.*

★ Auditorium Parco della Musica

CONCERTS | Architect Renzo Piano conceived and constructed the Auditorium Parco della Musica, a futuristic complex made up of three enormous, pod-shaped concert halls, which have hosted some of the world's greatest music acts. The Sala Santa Cecilia is a massive hall for grand orchestra and choral concerts; the Sala Sinopoli is more intimately scaled for smaller troupes; and the Sala Petrassi was designed for alternative events. All three are arrayed around the Cavea (amphitheater), a vast outdoor Greco-Roman-style theater. The Auditorium also hosts seasonal festivals, including the Rome Film Fest. ✉ *Viale Pietro de*

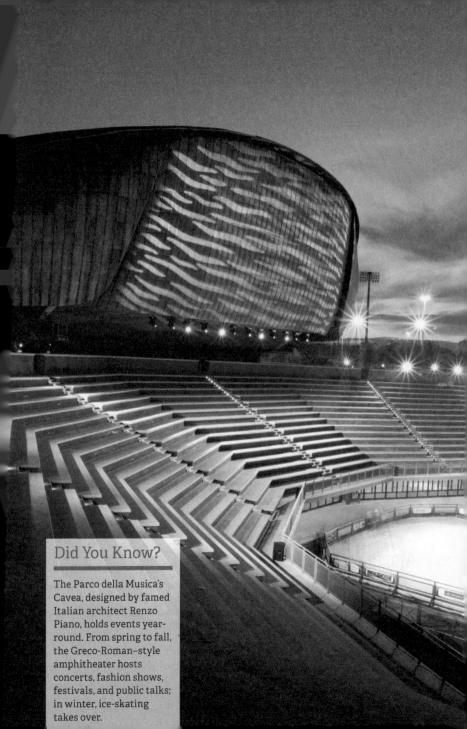

Did You Know?

The Parco della Musica's Cavea, designed by famed Italian architect Renzo Piano, holds events year-round. From spring to fall, the Greco-Roman–style amphitheater hosts concerts, fashion shows, festivals, and public talks; in winter, ice-skating takes over.

Coubertin 30, Flaminio ☎ *06/80241281* ⊕ *www.auditorium.com* Ⓜ *Flaminio, then Tram No. 2 to Apollodoro.*

DANCE
Teatro Olimpico
THEATER | Part of Rome's theater circuit, the 1930s-era Teatro Olimpico is one of the main venues for cabaret, contemporary dance companies, visiting international ballet companies, and touring Broadway shows. ✉ *Piazza Gentile da Fabriano 17, Flaminio* ☎ *06/32659916* ⊕ *www.teatroolimpico.it* Ⓜ *Flaminio, then Tram 2 to Mancini.*

Nightlife

Metropolita
COCKTAIL LOUNGES | Conveniently close to MAXXI and the Auditorium Parco della Musica, this hip lounge serves classic and creative cocktails as well as light bites in a two-story space with tables on the mezzanine, low sofas on the ground floor, and a disco ball above the bar. The tapas-style menu is international, with offerings like guacamole and hummus in addition to the popular *maritozzo salato*, a savory version of the Roman bun filled with tuna instead of cream, and a few heartier options, including a burger. Food is served until 1 am every night and brunch is available on weekends. ✉ *Piazza Gentile da Fabriano 2, Flaminio* ☎ *06/84381895* ⊕ *www.metropolita.it.*

Monte Mario

In the northwest part of Rome, perched on the city's highest hill, the neighborhood of Monte Mario has fabulous views. Although not the easiest to get to by public transportation, there are a few noteworthy hotels and restaurants here.

🍴 Restaurants

This neighborhood is home to some of Rome's fanciest restaurants.

★ La Pergola
$$$$ | MODERN ITALIAN | Dinner here is a truly memorable and romantic event, with incomparable views across the city matched by a stellar dining experience that includes top-notch service as well as sublimely inventive fare. The difficulty comes in choosing from among Michelin-starred chef Heinz Beck's *alta cucina* (high cuisine) specialties. **Known for:** weekend reservations that book up three months in advance; award-winning wine list; fagotelli La Pergola stuffed with pecorino, eggs, and cream with guanciale and zucchini. ⑤ *Average main: €69* ✉ *Rome Cavalieri, A Waldorf Astoria Resort, Via Alberto Cadlolo 101, Monte Mario* ☎ *06/35092152* ⊕ *www.romecavalieri.com/lapergola.php* ⊗ *Closed Sun. and Mon., 3 wks in Aug., and Jan. No lunch* 🔺 *Jacket for gentlemen.*

🛏 Hotels

Travelers looking for a relaxing getaway at a distance from the city center will appreciate staying in Monte Mario, but beware: public transportation is sparse in this area. It's a 20- to 30-minute drive to the centro storico—as much as an hour on public transport. Some hotels offer shuttles, but if you'd rather not have to rely on them or on taxi service, consider renting a car.

Rome Cavalieri, A Waldorf Astoria Hotel
$$$ | RESORT | A hilltop oasis in a quiet residential neighborhood a short ride from the centro storico, the Rome Cavalieri comes with magnificent views, three outdoor pools, one indoor pool, and a palatial spa perched atop the Monte

Mario amid 15 acres of lush Mediterranean parkland. **Pros:** famed art collection, including a Tiepolo triptych from 1725; impressive on-site restaurant; complimentary shuttle to city center. **Cons:** not all rooms have great views; outside the city center; you definitely pay for the luxury of staying here—everything is expensive. $ *Rooms from: €300* ✉ *Via Alberto Cadlolo 101, Monte Mario* ☎ *06/35091* ⊕ *www.romecavalieri.com* ↘ *370 rooms* ¶⊙¶ *No Meals.*

Parioli

The elegant residential neighborhood of Parioli, north of the Villa Borghese, is home to some of the city's poshest hotels and restaurants. However, it's not especially convenient if you're planning to do any sightseeing.

 Restaurants

Duke's Fine Casual Bar and Restaurant
$$$ | **AMERICAN** | It dubs itself an American West Coast–style restaurant, and the decor is very Malibu beach house, with a gorgeous patio out back. But the menu takes a few liberties: the California rolls contain tuna and carrot, and there are mint leaves in the Caesar salad. **Known for:** homemade bread and biscuits; Angus steak tartare; satisfying cravings for non-Italian food. $ *Average main: €26* ✉ *Viale Parioli 200, Parioli* ☎ *06/80662455* ⊕ *www.dukes.it* ⊘ *Closed Sun. and Mon.*

🛏 Hotels

Rome's poshest residential neighborhood attracts a well-heeled international crowd who are happy to be away from the centro storico hubbub. Luxurious lodgings and a great night's sleep might make you feel like you're in an elegant country home. Public transportation is limited in this area, but some hotels offer shuttles to major attractions.

Hotel Lord Byron
$$ | **HOTEL** | This art deco retreat has a jewelry-box charm and feels like a small country manor. **Pros:** luxury bathrobes and slippers; gorgeous bar; huge bathrooms, some with soaking tubs. **Cons:** not many caffè and shops in the area; cabs to the city center are expensive; too far to walk to sights. $ *Rooms from: €200* ✉ *Via Giuseppe de Notaris 5, Parioli* ☎ *06/3220404* ⊕ *www.lordbyronhotel.com* ↘ *30 rooms* ¶⊙¶ *Free Breakfast.*

The Hoxton, Rome
$$ | **HOTEL** | British brand The Hoxton's first foray into Italy is a design lover's dream filled with 1970s-inspired bespoke furniture, art tomes, and plants that transform the large lobby into intimate seating nooks perfect for socializing and co-working. **Pros:** stylish design; great food and drinks; friendly staff. **Cons:** no gym or spa; rooms have little storage space for clothes; location far from tourist sites, with no metro nearby. $ *Rooms from: €189* ✉ *Largo Benedetto Marcello 220, Parioli* ☎ *06/94502700* ⊕ *www.the-hoxton.com/rome* ↘ *192 rooms* ¶⊙¶ *No Meals.*

 Performing Arts

DANCE

Teatro Greco

MODERN DANCE | As part of Rome's rich and intense performance circuit, the Teatro Greco features international contemporary dance performances. Its own dance company, established in 1973, has performed all over the world. ✉ *Via Ruggero Leoncavallo 10, Parioli* ☎ *06/8607513* ⊕ *www.teatrogreco. weebly.com.*

Chapter 9

TRASTEVERE AND MONTEVERDE

Updated by
Natalie Kennedy

👁 Sights	🍴 Restaurants	🛏 Hotels	🛍 Shopping	🍸 Nightlife
★★★★★	★★★★☆	★★★☆☆	★★★☆☆	★★★★☆

NEIGHBORHOOD SNAPSHOT

MAKING THE MOST OF YOUR TIME

It's easy to get to Trastevere from Piazza Venezia: just take Tram No. 8 to the first stop on the other side of the river. You'll probably want to head right to the Piazza di Santa Maria in Trastevere, the heart of this lively area. Heading to the opposite side of Viale di Trastevere, though, is a treat many tourists miss. The cobblestone streets around Piazza in Piscinula and Via della Luce—locals peering down from balconies and the smell of fresh-baked bread floating from bakeries—are much more reminiscent of how Trastevere used to be than the touristic area to the north. Either way, remember that many of Trastevere's lovely small churches close, like others in Rome, in the afternoons. In the evenings, the neighborhood heats up with locals and students drinking, eating, and going for *passeggiate* (strolls)—a not-to-be-missed atmosphere, especially for those with energy to burn.

TOP REASONS TO GO

Santa Maria in Trastevere: Tear yourself away from the piazza scene outside to take in the gilded glory of one of the city's oldest and most beautiful churches, fabled for its medieval mosaics.

Isola Tiberina: Cross the river on the Ponte Fabricio—the city's oldest bridge—for a stroll on the paved shores of the adorable Isola Tiberina (and don't forget to detour for the lemon ices at La Grattachecca).

Nightlife: Trastevere has become one of Rome's hottest nighttime-scene arenas, with lively bars and people spilling into the streets at nearly every turn.

Get a feel for the Middle Ages: With cobblestone alleyways and medieval houses, the area around Trastevere's Piazza in Piscinula offers a magical dip into Rome's Middle Ages.

GETTING HERE

■ From the Vatican or Spanish Steps, expect a 30- to 40-minute walk to reach Trastevere. From Termini station, take Bus No. 40 Express or No. 64 to Largo di Torre Argentina, where you can switch to Tram No. 8 to get to Trastevere. If you don't feel like climbing the steep Gianicolo, take Bus No. 115 from Largo dei Fiorentini, then enjoy the walk down to the northern reaches of Trastevere or explore the leafy residential area of Monteverde Vecchio on the other side of the hill. Monteverde is a 10-minute tram ride from Trastevere.

VIEWFINDER

■ Trastevere is one of Rome's most enchanting neighborhoods, full of photo-worthy moments around nearly every corner. The start of Vicolo del Cedro, at the intersection of Via della Scala, is particularly perfect for a close-up. The small pedestrian street is bursting with blooming plants and a mishmash of ochre buildings, strung with colorful, freshly washed laundry languidly rippling in the Italian breeze.

Trastevere ("beyond the Tiber") can feel a world apart from the rest of Rome and despite galloping gentrification, the bohemian neighborhood remains about the most tightly knit community in the city.

Perfectly picturesque piazzas, tiny winding medieval alleyways, and time-burnished Romanesque houses all cast a frozen-in-time spell, while grand art awaits at Santa Maria in Trastevere, San Francesco a Ripa, and the Villa Farnesina. The neighborhood's greatest attraction, however, is simply its atmosphere—traditional shops set along crooked streets, peaceful during the day and alive with throngs of people at night. From here, a steep hike upstairs and along the road to the Gianicolo, Rome's second-highest hill, earns you a panoramic view of the city.

The inhabitants of Trastevere don't even call themselves Romans but Trasteverini, claiming that they, not the citizens east of the river, are the true remaining Romans. A visit here still feels a bit like entering a different time and place, as the district remains an enchanting mix of past and present.

Farther uphill along the 8 tram line, Monteverde is a quiet contrast to the bustle of trendy Trastevere. Between its sprawling parks and typical residential lanes, the neighborhood has become a destination for its growing culinary scene.

Trastevere

Sights

Gianicolo (*Janiculum Hill*)
VIEWPOINT | FAMILY | The Gianicolo is famous for its peaceful and pastel panoramic views of the city, a noontime cannon shot, the Fontana dell'Acqua Paola (affectionately termed "the big fountain" by Romans), and a monument dedicated to Giuseppe and Anita Garibaldi (the guiding spirit behind the unification of Italy in the 19th century, and his long-suffering wife). The view from the terrace, with the foothills of the Appennini in the background, is especially breathtaking at dusk. It's also a great view for dome-spotting, from the Pantheon to the myriad city churches. ⊠ *Via Servilia 43, Trastevere.*

Isola Tiberina (*Tiber Island*)
ISLAND | It's easy to overlook this tiny island in the Tiber, but you shouldn't. In terms of history and sheer loveliness, charming Isola Tiberina—shaped like a boat about to set sail—gets high marks. Cross onto the island via Ponte Fabricio, Rome's oldest remaining bridge, constructed in 62 BC; on the north side of the island crumbles the romantic ruin of the Ponte Rotto (Broken Bridge), which dates back to 179 BC. Descend the steps to the lovely river embankment to see a Roman relief of the intertwined-snakes symbol of Aesculapius, the great god of healing. In imperial times,

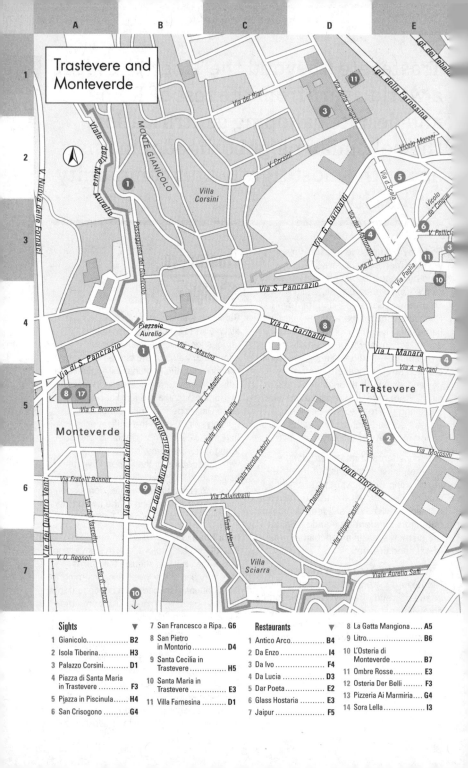

Trastevere and Monteverde

A B C D E

1

Via dei Riari

Via della Lungara

Lgt. della Farnesina

Lgt. del Tevere

11

3

2

MONTE GIANICOLO

Viale della Mura Aurelie

V. Nuova delle Fornaci

Villa Corsini

V. Corsini

Vicolo Moro

Via d. Scala

Via G. Garibaldi

Via dei Riari

Passeggiata del Gianicolo

Vicolo de' Cinque

5

Via dei Riari

4

Via d. Cedro

6 V. Petticia

11

3

Via Paglia

10

3 Via S. Pancrazio

4

Via di S. Pancrazio

Piazzale Aurelio

1

Via A. Masina

Via G. Garibaldi

8

Via L. Manara

Via A. Bertani

4

Trastevere

8 17

Via G. Bruzzesi

Via G. Medici

Monteverde

Viale Glorioso

Viale delle Mura Gianicolensi

Via Giacinto Carini

Viale Trente Aprile

Viale Nicola Fabrizi

Via Gaetano Sacchi

2

Via Morosini

5

Via dei Quattro Venti

Via del Vascello

Via Fratelli Bonnet

9

Via Calandrelli

Via Dandolo

Viale Wern

Via Fitipou Casini

6

V. O. Regnoli

Via G. Bezzi

10

Villa Sciarra

Viale Aurelio Saffi

7

Sights ▼

1	Gianicolo	B2
2	Isola Tiberina	H3
3	Palazzo Corsini	D1
4	Piazza di Santa Maria in Trastevere	F3
5	Piazza in Piscinula	H4
6	San Crisogono	G4
7	San Francesco a Ripa	G6
8	San Pietro in Montorio	D4
9	Santa Cecilia in Trastevere	H5
10	Santa Maria in Trastevere	E3
11	Villa Farnesina	D1

Restaurants ▼

1	Antico Arco	B4
2	Da Enzo	I4
3	Da Ivo	F4
4	Da Lucia	D3
5	Dar Poeta	E2
6	Glass Hostaria	E3
7	Jaipur	F5
8	La Gatta Mangiona	A5
9	Litro	B6
10	L'Osteria di Monteverde	B7
11	Ombre Rosse	E3
12	Osteria Der Belli	F3
13	Pizzeria Ai Marmiria	G4
14	Sora Lella	I3

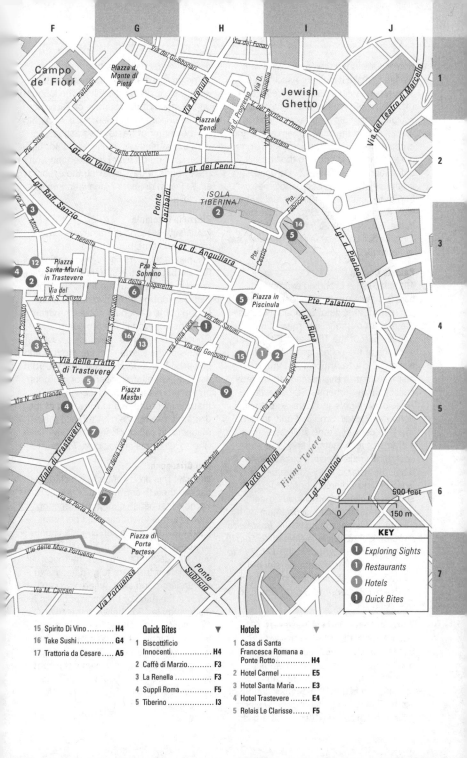

Romans sheathed the entire island with marble to make it look like Aesculapius's ship, replete with a towering obelisk as a mast. Amazingly, a fragment of the ancient sculpted ship's prow still exists. You can marvel at it on the downstream end of the embankment. Today, medicine still reigns here. The island is home to the hospital of Fatebenefratelli (literally, "Do good, brothers"). Nearby is San Bartolomeo, built at the end of the 10th century by the Holy Roman Emperor Otto III and restored in the 18th century. ⊠ *Trastevere* ✛ *Isola Tiberina can be accessed by Ponte Fabricio or Ponte Cestio.*

Palazzo Corsini

ART MUSEUM | A brooding example of baroque style, the palace (once home to Queen Christina of Sweden) is across the road from the Villa Farnesina and houses part of the 16th- and 17th-century sections of the collection of the Galleria Nazionale d'Arte Antica. Among the star paintings in this manageably sized collection are Rubens's *St. Sebastian Healed by Angels* and Caravaggio's *St. John the Baptist*. Stop in if only to climb the 17th-century stone staircase, itself a drama of architectural shadows and sculptural voids. Behind, but separate from, the palazzo is the University of Rome's Orto Botanico, home to 3,500 species of plants, with various greenhouses around a stairway/fountain with 11 jets. ⊠ *Via della Lungara 10, Trastevere* ☎ *06/68802323 Galleria Corsini, 06/32810 Galleria Corsini tickets, 06/49917107 Orto Botanico* ⊕ *www.barberinicorsini.org* ✉ *€12 Galleria Corsini, including entrance to Palazzo Barberini; €13 Orto Botanico* ⊗ *Closed Mon.*

Piazza di Santa Maria in Trastevere

PLAZA/SQUARE | **FAMILY** | At the very heart of the Trastevere *rione* (district) lies this beautiful piazza, with its elegant raised fountain and sidewalk caffè. The centerpiece is the 12th-century church of Santa Maria in Trastevere, first consecrated in the 4th century. Across countless generations, this piazza has seen the comings and goings of tourists and travelers, intellectuals and artists, who lounge on the steps of the fountain or eat lunch at an outdoor table at Sabatini's. At night, it's the center of Trastevere's action, with street festivals, musicians, and the occasional mime vying for attention from the throngs of people taking the evening air. ⊠ *Piazza di Santa Maria in Trastevere, Trastevere.*

Piazza in Piscinula

PLAZA/SQUARE | One of Trastevere's most historic and time-burnished squares, this piazza takes its name from ancient Roman baths on the site (*piscina* means "pool"). It's said that the tiny church of San Benedetto on the piazza was built on the home of Roman nobles in which St. Benedict lived in the 5th century. Opposite is the medieval Casa dei Mattei (House of the Mattei), where the rich and powerful Mattei family lived until the 16th century, when, after a series of murders on the premises, colorful legend has it that they were forced to move out of the district, crossing the river to build their magnificent palace close to the Jewish Ghetto. ⊠ *Piazza in Piscinula, Trastevere.*

San Crisogono

CHURCH | This pretty church, which dates back to the 4th or 5th century, might be Rome's first parish church. The soaring medieval bell tower can best be seen from the little piazza flanking the church or from the other side of Viale di Trastevere. Inside, ring the bell of the room to the left of the apse to gain access to the underground area, where you can explore the ruins of the ancient basilica, discovered in 1907 beneath the "new" 12th-century structure. The eerie space is astonishingly large and dotted with gems like 8th-century frescoes, ancient marble sarcophagi, and even a 6th-century marble altar. ⊠ *Piazza Sidney Sonnino 44, Trastevere* ☎ *06/5810076* ✉ *€3 for underground area.*

San Francesco a Ripa

CHURCH | In a quiet part of Trastevere, south of Viale di Trastevere, this church's dedication refers to the fact that St. Francis of Assisi stayed nearby during a visit to Rome. The medieval church was rebuilt in the 17th century and houses one of Bernini's last works, a statue of the *Blessed Ludovica Albertoni.* This is perhaps Bernini's most hallucinatory sculpture, a dramatically lighted figure ecstatic at the prospect of entering heaven as she expires on her deathbed. The cell in which Saint Francis is said to have stayed (Il Santuario di San Francesco) is often visitable. Fans of Giorgio de Chirico can ask to visit his tomb in a chapel that contains three paintings by the 20th-century metaphysical painter. ⊠ *Piazza di San Francesco d'Assisi 88, Trastevere* ☏ *06/5819020* ⊕ *www.san-francescoaripa.it.*

San Pietro in Montorio

CHURCH | Built by order of Ferdinand and Isabella of Spain in 1481 near the spot where medieval tradition believed St. Peter was crucified (the crucifixion site at the Vatican is much more probable), this church is a handsome and dignified edifice. It contains a number of well-known works, including, in the first chapel on the right, the *Flagellation* painted by the Venetian Sebastiano del Piombo from a design by Michelangelo, and *St. Francis in Ecstasy,* in the next-to-last chapel on the left, in which Bernini made one of his earliest experiments with concealed lighting effects. The most famous work here, though, is the circular Tempietto (Little Temple) in the monastery cloister next door. This small sober building (it holds only 10 people and is a church in its own right) marks the spot where Peter was thought to have been crucified. Designed by Bramante (the first architect of the "new" St. Peter's Basilica) in 1502, it represents one of the earliest and most successful attempts to create an entirely classical building. The Tempietto is reachable via the Royal Spanish Academy next door. ⊠ *Piazza di San Pietro in Montorio 2 (Via Garibaldi), Trastevere* ☏ *06/5813940 San Pietro in Montorio, 06/5812806 Tempietto (Accademia di Spagna)* ⊕ *www. sanpietroinmontorio.it* ⊗ *Tempietto closed Mon.*

★ Santa Cecilia in Trastevere

CHURCH | This basilica commemorates the aristocratic St. Cecilia, patron saint of musicians. One of ancient Rome's most celebrated Early Christian martyrs, she was most likely put to a supernaturally long death by the Emperor Diocletian just before the year AD 300. After an abortive attempt to suffocate her in the baths of her own house (a favorite means of quietly disposing of aristocrats in Roman days), she was brought before the executioner. But not even three blows of the executioner's sword could dispatch the young girl. She lingered for several days, converting others to the Christian cause, before finally dying. In 1595, her body was exhumed—it was said to look as fresh as if she still breathed—and the heart-wrenching sculpture by eyewitness Stefano Maderno that lies below the main altar was, the sculptor insisted, exactly how she looked. Time your visit in the morning to enter the cloistered convent to see what remains of Pietro Cavallini's *Last Judgment,* dating to 1293. It's the only major fresco in existence known to have been painted by Cavallini, a contemporary of Giotto. To visit the frescoes, ring the bell of the convent to the left of the church entrance between 10 am and 12 pm. ⊠ *Piazza di Santa Cecilia 22, Trastevere* ☏ *06/5899289* ⊕ *www.benedettinesantacecilia.it/ htm/Basilica.html* 🎟 *Frescoes €2.50, underground €2.50* ⊗ *Access to frescoes closed in the afternoon.*

★ Santa Maria in Trastevere

CHURCH | Originally built during the 4th century and rebuilt in the 12th century, this is one of Rome's oldest and grandest churches. It is also the earliest foundation of any Roman church to be dedicated to the Virgin Mary. With a nave framed by a processional of two rows of gigantic columns (22 in total) taken from the ancient Baths of Caracalla, and an apse studded with gilded mosaics, the interior conjures the splendor of ancient Rome better than any other in the city. Overhead is Domenichino's gilded ceiling (1617). The 18th-century portico draws attention to the facade's 800-year-old mosaics, which represent the parable of the Wise and Foolish Virgins. They enhance the whole piazza, especially at night, when the church front and bell tower are illuminated. The church's most important mosaics, Pietro Cavallini's six panels of the *Life of the Virgin,* cover the semicircular apse. Note the building labeled "Taberna Meritoria" just under the figure of the Virgin in the Nativity scene, with a stream of oil flowing from it; it recalls the legend that a fountain of oil appeared on this spot, prophesying the birth of Christ. Off the piazza's northern side is a street called Via delle Fonte dell'Olio in honor of this miracle. ⊠ *Piazza Santa Maria in Trastevere, Trastevere* ☎ *06/5814802* ⊕ *santamariaintrastevere. it.*

★ Villa Farnesina

CASTLE/PALACE | Money was no object to the extravagant Agostino Chigi, a banker from Siena who financed many papal projects. His munificence is evident in this elegant villa, built for him about 1511. He was especially proud of the decorative frescoes in the airy loggias, some painted by Raphael himself, notably a luminous *Triumph of Galatea.* Agostino entertained the popes and princes of 16th-century Rome, impressing his guests at riverside suppers by having his servants clear the table by casting the precious silver and gold dinnerware into the Tiber (indeed, nets were unfurled a foot or two beneath the water's surface to retrieve the valuable ware). In the magnificent Loggia of Psyche on the ground floor, Giulio Romano and others worked from Raphael's designs. Raphael's lovely *Galatea* is in the adjacent room. On the floor above you can see the trompe-l'oeil effects in the aptly named Hall of Perspectives by Peruzzi. Agostino Chigi's bedroom, next door, was frescoed by Il Sodoma with the *Wedding of Alexander and Roxanne,* which is considered to be the artist's best work. The palace also houses the Gabinetto Nazionale delle Stampe, a treasure trove of old prints and drawings. ⊠ *Via della Lungara 230, Trastevere* ☎ *06/68027268 info, 06/68027397 tour reservations* ⊕ *www. villafarnesina.it* ⊠ *€10* ⊗ *Closed Sun.*

🍴 Restaurants

Trastevere has always been known for its Left Bank bohemian appeal. A hip expat enclave with working-class Roman roots, the neighborhood is lined with an abundance of trattorias and wine bars. The Gianicolo area, at the top of the hill, is more subdued, with breathtaking views.

★ Antico Arco

$$$ | MODERN ITALIAN | Founded by three friends with a passion for wine and fine food, Antico Arco attracts foodies from Rome and beyond with its refined culinary inventiveness. The location on top of the Janiculum Hill makes for a charming setting, and inside, the dining rooms are plush, modern spaces, with whitewashed brick walls, dark floors, and black velvet chairs. **Known for:** private dining options for romantic meals; molten chocolate soufflé cake; changing seasonal menu. $ *Average main: €29* ⊠ *Piazzale Aurelio 7, Trastevere* ☎ *06/5815274* ⊕ *www.anticoarco.it* ⊗ *Closed Tues.*

★ Da Enzo

$$ | ROMAN | In the quieter part of Trastevere, the family-run Da Enzo is everything you would imagine a classic Roman trattoria to be. There are just a few tables, but diners from around the world line up to eat here—a testament to the quality of the food. **Known for:** small space with long waits; boisterous, authentic atmosphere; cacio e pepe (pasta with pecorino-cheese sauce and black pepper), carbonara, and other Roman classics. ⑤ *Average main: €14* ✉ *Via dei Vascellari 29, Trastevere* ☎ *06/5812260* ⊕ *www.daenzoal29.com* ⊙ *Closed Sun. and 2 wks in Aug.*

Da Ivo

$$ | PIZZA | This always crowded pizzeria opens early and closes late, and in between it's packed with locals, tourists, and sports fans who know they can watch the Roma soccer team play on big, flat-screen TVs. The selection of pizzas is large, with delicious mains available as well. **Known for:** sports-friendly atmosphere; long, leisurely meals; mixed-vegetables pizza. ⑤ *Average main: €16* ✉ *Via di San Francesco a Ripa 158, Trastevere* ☎ *06/5817082* ⊕ *www.ivoatrastevere.it* ⊙ *Closed Tues., and 2 wks in Jan.*

Da Lucia

$$ | ROMAN | There's no shortage of old-school trattorias in Trastevere, but Da Lucia has a strong following among them. Both locals and expats enjoy the brusque but "authentic" service and the hearty Roman fare; snag a table outside in warm weather for the true Roman experience of cobblestone-terrace dining. **Known for:** beef rolls (involtini); spaghetti cacio e pepe; bombolotti (a tubular pasta) all'amatriciana. ⑤ *Average main: €14* ✉ *Vicolo del Mattonato 2, Trastevere* ☎ *06/5803601* ⊙ *Closed Mon. and Aug.*

Dar Poeta

$ | PIZZA | Romans drive across town for great pizza from this neighborhood institution on a small street in Trastevere. They offer both thin-crust pizza and a thick-crust (*alta*) Neapolitan-style pizza with any of the given toppings. **Known for:** dessert calzone with Nutella and ricotta cheese; no reservations, so expect to wait in line; "superformaggio" (i.e., cheese lover's) pizza. ⑤ *Average main: €12* ✉ *Vicolo del Bologna 45, Trastevere* ☎ *06/5880516* ⊕ *www.darpoeta.com.*

★ Glass Hostaria

$$$$ | MODERN ITALIAN | After 14 years in Austin, Texas, chef Cristina Bowerman returned to Rome to reconnect with her Italian roots, and her cooking is as innovative as the building she works in and Glass has received numerous recognitions for its design as well as its expertly executed cuisine. The menu changes frequently, featuring dishes like a standout steak tartare and pork neck. **Known for:** plates inspired by Italy from north to south; more than 600 types of wine; vegetarian tasting menu. ⑤ *Average main: €35* ✉ *Vicolo del 'Cinque 58, Trastevere* ☎ *06/58335903* ⊕ *www.glasshostaria.it* ⊙ *Closed Mon., Tues., and 2 wks in July. No lunch Wed.–Fri.*

Jaipur

$$ | INDIAN | Named after the Pink City in India, this restaurant serves the highest-quality curries in a large space just off the main Viale di Trastevere. It's a festive and fun destination if you're craving something quite different from Italian food. **Known for:** tasting menus for two people; outside seating; 10 varieties of chicken curry. ⑤ *Average main: €16* ✉ *Via di San Francesco a Ripa 56, Trastevere* ☎ *06/5803992* ⊕ *www.ristorantejaipur.com* ⊙ *No lunch Mon.*

Ombre Rosse

$ | WINE BAR | Set on lovely Piazza Sant'Egidio in the heart of Trastevere, this open-day-and-night spot is a great place to pass the time. You can have a morning cappuccino and read one of their international newspapers; have a light lunch; enjoy an *aperitivo* (aperitif) and nibbles at an outdoor table; or finish off an evening with friends at the bar.

Known for: well-made cocktails; live-music nights; free Wi-Fi. $ *Average main: €12* ✉ *Piazza di Sant'Egidio 12–13, Trastevere* ☎ *06/5884155* ⊕ *www.ombrerossein-trastevere.it.*

Osteria der Belli

$$ | **SEAFOOD** | **FAMILY** | One might overlook Osteria der Belli because of its proximity to the central square of Trastevere, Piazza Santa Maria in Trastevere—and that would be a crying shame. Leo, the owner, is Sardinian and has been running this place daily for over 35 years; while Roman dishes are on the menu, it excels at seafood and Sardinian cuisine. **Known for:** ravioli or fettuccine alla sarda (in a creamy mushroom sauce); large outdoor patio; sea bass carpaccio. $ *Average main: €18* ✉ *Piazza di Sant'Apollonia 11, Trastevere* ☎ *06/5803782* ⊙ *Closed Mon. and 3 wks in Jan.*

Pizzeria Ai Marmiria

$ | **PIZZA** | **FAMILY** | This place is about as lively as it gets—it's packed pretty much every night with diners munching on crisp pizzas that come out of the wood-burning ovens at top speed. It's best not to go during peak dining hours, so go early or late if you don't want to wait. **Known for:** open until midnight for a late-night bite; fried starters such as supplì (breaded fried rice balls); excellent wood-oven pizzas. $ *Average main: €12* ✉ *Viale Trastevere 53, Trastevere* ☎ *06/5800919* ⊙ *Closed Wed. and 3 wks in Aug. No dinner Sun.*

Spirito Di Vino

$$ | **ITALIAN** | At this restaurant, diners get to enjoy an evening of historical interest alongside an excellent meal. The building was constructed on the site of an 11th-century synagogue, and the spot is rich with history—several ancient sculptures, now in the Vatican and Capitoline museums, were unearthed in the basement in the 19th century. **Known for:** mostly organic ingredients; cavernous wine cellar in historic location; ancient Roman recipe for braised pork shoulder

with apples and leeks. $ *Average main: €18* ✉ *Via dei Genovesi 31 a/b, Trastevere* ☎ *06/5896689* ⊕ *www.ristorantespirito-divino.com* ⊙ *Closed Sun., and Aug. No lunch.*

Take Sushi

$$ | **JAPANESE** | An increasingly familiar sight on the streets of Rome are all-you-can-eat Japanese restaurants, popular for their inexpensive prices—but Take Sushi couldn't be further from this concept. It's all about top-quality, authentic food here. **Known for:** tasty algae salad; imported Japanese beer and sake; uni nigiri (sea urchin roe). $ *Average main: €20* ✉ *Viale di Trastevere 4, Trastevere* ☎ *06/65810075* ⊕ *www.take-sushi.it* ⊙ *Closed Mon.*

Sora Lella

$$$ | **ROMAN** | The draw here—in addition to the wonderful food—is the fact that this is the only restaurant on Isola Tiberina, the wondrously picturesque island set in the middle of the Tiber River between the Jewish Ghetto and Trastevere, that's open year-round. As for the food, try the delicious prosciutto and mozzarella to start, and move on to classics like pasta all'amatriciana, meatballs in tomato sauce, or Roman baby lamb chops. **Known for:** elegant setting; unique location; stuffed calamari in white wine sauce. $ *Average main: €26* ✉ *Via di Ponte Quattro Capi 16, Jewish Ghetto* ☎ *06/6861601* ⊕ *www.trattoriasoralella.it/it* ⊙ *Closed Sun. and 1 wk in Aug. No lunch Sun. in July and Aug.*

☕ Coffee and Quick Bites

Biscottificio Innocenti

$ | **ITALIAN** | **FAMILY** | The scent of cookies wafts out into the street as you approach this family-run bakery, where a small team of bakers makes sweet treats the old-school way in an oven bought in the 1960s. There are dozens of varieties of baked goods, mostly sweet but some savory. **Known for:** brutti ma buoni ("ugly but good") cookies; dozens of varieties of baked goods; old-school family-run bakery. $ *Average main: €3* ⊠ *Via della Luce 21, Trastevere* ☎ *06/5803926* ⊙ *Closed 2 wks in Aug.*

Caffè di Marzio

$ | **CAFÉ** | Over a coffee or a cocktail, sit and gaze upon Santa Maria in Trastevere's glistening golden facade at Caffè di Marzio. The outdoor seating is lovely but the interior is warm and welcoming, too. **Known for:** prime piazza views; sunny outdoor seating; American-style breakfast. $ *Average main: €8* ⊠ *Piazza di Santa Maria in Trastevere 15, Trastevere* ☎ *06/5816095* ⊙ *3 wks in Jan.*

La Renella

$ | **PIZZA** | This no-frills pizzeria *al taglio* (by the slice) and bakery is hidden a few minutes away from Piazza Trilussa. As in many traditional bakeries, pizza is sold by weight, so get yours sliced to the size you want. **Known for:** no additives or animal fats; homemade breads and sweets; classic Roman pizza from a wood-fired oven. $ *Average main: €6* ⊠ *Via del Moro 15, Trastevere* ☎ *06/5817265* ▭ *No credit cards.*

Supplì Roma

$ | **ROMAN** | Trastevere's best supplì have been served at this hole-in-the-wall takeout spot since 1979. At lunchtime, the line spills out onto the street with locals who've come for the namesake treats, as well as fried *baccalà* (salt cod) fillets and stuffed zucchini flowers. **Known for:** classic fried risotto ball with ragu or cacio e pepe; gnocchi on Thursday (the traditional day for it in Rome); old-fashioned baked pizza with zucchini and stracciatella cheese. $ *Average main: €5* ⊠ *Via di San Francesco a Ripa 137, Trastevere* ☎ *06/5897110* ⊕ *www.suppliroma.it* ⊙ *Closed Sun. and 2 wks in Aug.*

Tiberino

$ | **ITALIAN** | **FAMILY** | Named for the island that it sits on in the middle of the Tiber River, Tiberino is a historic caffè that

has gotten a modern makeover. In the morning, stop in for a pastry topped with slivered almonds or a savory panino with mortadella and arugula. **Known for:** unique setting in the center of Rome's only island; freshly squeezed seasonal juice; shady outdoor seating. $ *Average main: €6* ⊠ *Via di Ponte Quattro Capi, 18, Trastevere* ☎ *06/6877662* ⊕ *www. tiberinoroma.it.*

 ## Hotels

This former working-class neighborhood, once the stomping ground of artists and artisans, is now home to many of Rome's expats and exchange students. Its villagelike charm makes it an appealing place to stay, and you'll find plenty of moderately priced accommodations here, including converted convents and small family-run hotels.

Casa di Santa Francesca Romana a Ponte Rotto

$ | **HOTEL** | In the heart of Trastevere but tucked away from the hustle and bustle of the medieval quarter, this cheap, clean, comfortable hotel in a former monastery is centered on a lovely green courtyard. **Pros:** rates can't be beat; away from rowdy tourist side of Trastevere; excellent restaurants nearby. **Cons:** spotty Wi-Fi; few amenities besides TV room and reading room; a bit far from Metro, but there are tram and bus stops nearby. $ *Rooms from: €98* ⊠ *Via dei Vascellari 61, Trastevere* ☎ *06/5812125* ⊕ *www.sfromana.it* ⊷ *37 rooms* ⦿❘ *Free Breakfast.*

Hotel Carmel

$ | **HOTEL** | In the heart of Trastevere and across the Tiber from the main synagogue is Rome's only kosher hotel, a friendly and budget-friendly place to stay. **Pros:** lovely dining terrace outside; kosher breakfast can be arranged for €5 extra per person per day; nice location. **Cons:** air-conditioning is noisy; some rooms share a bath; no frills. $ *Rooms from: €100* ⊠ *Via Goffredo Mameli 11,*

Trastevere ☎ *06/5809921* ⊕ *www. hotelcarmel.it* ⇨ *11 rooms* ⏐◎⏐ *Free Breakfast.*

Hotel Santa Maria

$ | **HOTEL** | A Trastevere treasure with a pedigree going back four centuries, this ivy-covered, mansard-roof, rosy-brick-red, erstwhile Renaissance-era convent—just steps away from the glorious Santa Maria in Trastevere church and a few blocks from the Tiber—has sweet and simple guest rooms: a mix of brick walls, "cotto" tile floors, oak furniture, and matching bedspreads and curtains. **Pros:** a quaint and pretty oasis in a central location; lovely rooftop terrace; free bicycles to use during your stay. **Cons:** some rooms can be noisy; not the best value for money; tricky to find. ⑤ *Rooms from: €120* ⊠ *Vicolo del Piede 2, Trastevere* ☎ *06/5894626* ⊕ *www.hotelsantamariatrastevere.it* ⇨ *20 rooms* ⏐◎⏐ *Free Breakfast.*

Hotel Trastevere

$$ | **HOTEL** | This hotel captures the villagelike charm of the Trastevere district and offers basic, clean, comfortable rooms. **Pros:** good rates for location; friendly staff; convenient to tram and bus. **Cons:** standard rooms are quite small; few amenities; rooms are a little worn on the edges. ⑤ *Rooms from: €130* ⊠ *Via Luciano Manara 24/a, Trastevere* ☎ *06/5814713* ⊕ *www.hoteltrastevere. net* ⇨ *14 rooms* ⏐◎⏐ *Free Breakfast.*

Relais Le Clarisse

$$ | **B&B/INN** | Set within the former cloister grounds of the Santa Chiara order, with beautiful gardens, Le Clarisse makes you feel like a personal guest at a friend's villa, thanks to the comfortable size of the guest rooms and personalized service. **Pros:** spacious rooms with comfy beds; complimentary high-speed Wi-Fi; high-tech showers/tubs with good water pressure. **Cons:** no restaurant or bar;

check when booking as you may be put in neighboring building; this part of Trastevere can be noisy at night. ⑤ *Rooms from: €140* ⊠ *Via Cardinale Merry del Val 20, Trastevere* ☎ *06/58334437* ⊕ *www. leclarissetrastevere.com* ⇨ *17 rooms* ⏐◎⏐ *Free Breakfast.*

Nightlife

Trastevere is no longer the rough-around-the-edges neighborhood where visitors used to come to get a glimpse of "real" Rome. Years of gentrification have made this medieval "country within a town" a mecca for tourists and for Americans studying abroad. Its nightlife is a fun mix of overflowing piazzas filled with creative buskers, busy pubs, and great hole-in-the-wall restaurants that are packed into the wee hours of the morning.

BARS

★ Freni e Frizioni

CAFÉS | This hipster hangout has a cute artist vibe, and is great for an afternoon coffee, tea, or aperitivo, or for late-night socializing. Though the vibe is laid-back, the bartenders take their cocktails seriously—and have the awards to prove it. In warmer weather, the crowd overflows into the large terrazzo overlooking the Tiber and the side streets of Trastevere. ⊠ *Via del Politeama 4, Trastevere* ☎ *06/45497499* ⊕ *www. freniefrizioni.com.*

Rivendita

WINE BARS | The full name is "Rivendita: Libri Teatro e Cioccolata" and that's exactly what you'll find in this charming hole-in-the-wall: books and chocolate. Open only in the evenings, the used bookstore-bar combo offers wine, sweet cocktails, or coffee served in cups of pure chocolate, as well as theater-related texts for as low as €3. ⊠ *Vicolo del Cinque 11/a, Trastevere* ☎ *06/58301868.*

PUBS

Ma Che Siete Venuti a Fa

PUBS | Affectionately shortened to "Makke" by Romans, this tiny pub can't contain the number of beer lovers who flock here at all hours to indulge in a craft pint, or three. Drinkers spill out onto the sidewalk behind Piazza Trilussa, sipping the carefully selected artisan brews that arrive from around the world. ⊠ *Via Benedetta, 25, Trastevere* ☎ *06/42918213* ⊕ *football-pub.com.*

 Performing Arts

FILM

L'isola del Cinema

FILM | Every summer from June until September, the gorgeous open-air Cinema d'Isola di Tiberina hosts its own film festival on Tiber Island. The 450-seat Arena Groupama unfolds its silver screen against the backdrop of the ancient Ponte Fabricio, while the 50-seat CineLab is set against Ponte Garibaldi facing Trastevere. There's a mix of international films in their original languages, documentaries, and new Italian films as well as talks with cinematic greats. Screenings usually start at 9:30 pm; admission is €6 for the Arena Groupama, €5 for CineLab. ⊠ *Isola Tiberina, Piazza San Bartolomeo all'Isola, Trastevere* ☎ *06/58333113* ⊕ *www.isoladelcinema.com.*

THEATER

Teatro India

THEATER | Teatro India occupies a former soap factory, showcasing the best in contemporary theater from local and visiting artists. Most shows are in Italian, but they have occasional English-language performances. ⊠ *Lungotevere Vittorio Gassman 1, Trastevere* ☎ *06/87752210* ⊕ *www.teatrodiroma.net* 🎫 *Tickets €20.*

🛍 Shopping

Trastevere is filled with funky boutiques and the biggest open-air flea market in Rome. The neighborhood attracts a lot of tourist traffic and an international college-student crowd thanks to the bustling nightlife, but it's also a local favorite for low-key shopping.

BOOKSTORES

Almost Corner Bookshop

BOOKS | Bursting at the seams with not an inch of space left on its shelves, this tiny little bookshop is a favorite meeting point for English speakers in Trastevere. Irish owner Dermot O'Connell goes out of his way to find what you're looking for, and if he doesn't have it in stock he'll make a special order for you. The shop carries everything from popular best sellers to translated Italian classics, as well as lots of good books about Rome. ⊠ *Via del Moro 45, Trastevere* ☎ *06/5836942.*

CERAMICS AND DECORATIVE ARTS

Polvere di Tempo

OTHER SPECIALTY STORE | Collectors with a passion for rare and decorative timepieces should consider taking a stroll over to Polvere di Tempo. The owner and craftsman, Adrian Rodriguez, has a deep adoration for decorative sundials, watches, and even hourglasses—all entirely made by hand. Stop in at his store, and he'll tell you a story about how monks used candles to tell time and other interesting anecdotes related to timepieces. ⊠ *Via del Moro 59, Trastevere* ☎ *06/5880704* ⊕ *www.polvereditempo.com* ☉ *Closed Sun.*

FOOD AND WINE

Antica Caciara Trasteverina

FOOD | All of Trastevere comes to this deli to get their hands on some of the freshest ricotta in town. Step inside and you'll encounter giant helpings of ham, salami, Sicilian anchovies, and burrata cheese from Puglia, as well as Parmigiano-Reggiano and local wines all served with polite joviality. The savory delights can all be vacuum-sealed in case you want to pack some Italian specialties in your suitcase, even though not all the products can be imported into the U.S. ✉ *Via San Francesco a Ripa 140 a/b, Trastevere* ☎ *06/5812815* ⊕ *www.anticacaciara.it* ⊗ *Closed Sun.*

MARKETS

Porta Portese

MARKET | One of the biggest flea markets in Italy, Porta Portese welcomes visitors in droves every Sunday from 7 am to 2 pm. Treasure seekers and bargain hunters love scrounging around tents for new and used clothing, antique furniture, used books, accessories, and other odds 'n' ends. Bring your haggling skills, and cash (preferably small bills—it'll work in your favor when driving a bargain); many stallholders don't accept credit cards, and the nearest ATM is a hike. ✉ *Via Portuense and adjacent streets between Porta Portese and Via Ettore Rolli, Trastevere.*

Monteverde

Southwest of Trastevere, adjacent to the expansive Villa Pamphili Park, Monteverde is a residential area that's been getting more and more foot traffic from travelers in recent years. It has some destination-worthy dining spots.

🍴 Restaurants

La Gatta Mangiona

$$ | PIZZA | FAMILY | The pizza at this neighborhood spot is Roman-style—with a thin crust, charred on the edges. All the standard toppings are available, from margherita to buffalo mozzarella and prosciutto, but try one of the newfangled combinations like ricotta and pancetta and edible wildflowers. **Known for:** pizza-and-wine pairings; great craft beer selection; Thai pizza with tomato sauce,

cheese, and spices. Ⓢ *Average main: €15* ✉ *Via Federico Ozanam 30–32, Rome* ☎ *06/65346702* ⊕ *www.lagattamangiona.com* ⊗ *No lunch.*

Litro

$$ | WINE BAR | The idea for Litro started with a commitment to natural and organic wines served by the liter. The restaurant is open late, so there is ample time to explore the vast menu that includes everything from tasty salads to focaccia sandwiches. **Known for:** excellent wine selection and cocktails; outside garden seating; incredible meat and cheese boards. Ⓢ *Average main: €15* ✉ *Via Fratelli Bonnet 5, Rome* ☎ *06/45447639* ⊗ *Closed Sun. and 2 wks in Aug.*

L'Osteria di Monteverde

$$ | MODERN ITALIAN | FAMILY | Romans are starting to recognize Monteverde as a foodie hub, and this trattoria is one of the neighborhood's outstanding spots. The food ranges from the classics to carefully thought-out modern dishes, but whatever you order, the quality of the produce shines. **Known for:** good selection of dessert wines; classic Roman tripe; tagliolino (ribbon pasta) stuffed with duck. Ⓢ *Average main: €18* ✉ *Via Pietro Cartoni 163, Monteverde* ☎ *06/53273887* ⊕ *www.losteriadimonteverde.it* ⊗ *Closed 3 wks in Aug. No lunch Mon. No dinner Sun.*

Trattoria da Cesare

$$ | ROMAN | FAMILY | This beloved neighborhood trattoria does many things well, from the fried starters to the pastas to the meaty *secondi* (second course), so it's no surprise that it's won the hearts—and stomachs—of Romans all over town. The wine list is extensive, but the friendly waitstaff are happy to offer advice. **Known for:** hearty gnocchi with sugo alla coda alla vaccinara (tomato and oxtail sauce); outdoor seating on a leafy patio; stewed meatballs. Ⓢ *Average main: €15* ✉ *Via del Casaletto 45, Rome* ☎ *06/536015* ⊕ *www.trattoriadacesare.it* ⊗ *Closed Wed.*

Chapter 10

AVENTINO AND TESTACCIO

Updated by
Natalie Kennedy

● Sights	⑪ Restaurants	🛏 Hotels	🛍 Shopping	🍸 Nightlife
★★☆☆☆	★★★☆☆	★★★☆☆	★☆☆☆☆	★★★☆☆

NEIGHBORHOOD SNAPSHOT

MAKING THE MOST OF YOUR TIME

Travelers with limited time often see just one sight here: the Bocca della Verità, or "Mouth of Truth." There are other gems, though, especially on a nice day. The Giardino degli Aranci (Garden of the Orange Trees) has spectacular views over Rome and the Tiber. Next to the *giardino* is Santa Sabina, one of Rome's finest ancient churches, and the Piazza dei Cavalieri di Malta, whose keyhole has a special surprise.

Visit Testaccio in the evening, when locals take their *passeggiata* (stroll) and restaurants fill with diners. Admire the Piramide di Caio Cestio and duck into the Cimitero Acattolico, or "Non-Catholic Cemetery," one of the most atmospheric spots in Rome.

In addition to the allure of its mix of ancient ruins and 19th-century architecture, Romans know that this is where to come for a good meal. The area is famed for its restaurants and has a unique culinary history that dates back to a time when the city's slaughterhouse sat at the edge of the neighborhood.

TOP REASONS TO GO

Santa Maria in Cosmedin: Test your truthfulness at the Bocca della Verità and swoon over St. Valentine's relics.

Cimitero Acattolico "Non-Catholic Cemetery": Full of flowering trees and friendly cats, this romantic graveyard even has an ancient Roman pyramid.

Piazza Cavalieri di Malta: Peek through the keyhole of the Priorato di Malta for a perfectly framed view of one of Rome's most famous landmarks.

Roseto Comunale: Overlooking the Circo Massimo, this seasonal rose garden offers a fitting and fragrant vestibule to Rome's most poetic hill.

Baths of Caracalla: South of the lovely Villa Celimontana Park are the imposing ruins of the Terme di Caracalla, once the second-largest bathing complex of the Roman world.

PAUSE HERE

■ The beating heart of Testaccio is its central square, Piazza Testaccio. Shaded by trees and ringed with benches, this is where locals of all ages meet in the afternoons and evenings to play ball, share a coffee, or swap stories. At the center of the square is the Fountain of the Anfore, designed by Pietro Lombardi in 1926 and restored and reinstated to its rightful spot after the historic daily market that was once held here moved to its new location in 2015.

GETTING HERE

■ It's a spectacular 20-minute walk through ancient ruins like the Circo Massimo to reach the Aventine Hill from either the Roman Forum or the Campidoglio. There's a Metro stop by the same name at the foot of Aventino, too. If you're coming from the Colosseum or Trastevere, take Tram No. 3; from the Spanish Steps, take Bus No. 160; from Termini, Bus No. 175. For Testaccio, use the Piramide (Ostiense) Metro stop.

While Romans consider these neighborhoods central, they are just far enough off the beaten path to be little-known to tourists—and to have retained their unique character, from the well-heeled, garden-filled residential quarter of Aventino to the traditional-yet-trendy riverside neighborhood of Testaccio. For travelers who have a little extra time (or who simply want to see a Rome beyond the Trevi Fountain and Spanish Steps), making a visit to these areas allows a glimpse of what the Eternal City really means to its residents.

Aventino

One of the seven hills on which the city was founded, the Aventine Hill enjoys a serenity hard to find elsewhere in Rome. Trills of birdsong win out over the din of traffic—appropriate, since the hill's name derives from the Latin *avis*, or bird. Indeed, legend says that the sighting of eagles was used by Romulus and Remus to determine the prime spot for the city's foundation. In the end, though, Romulus's site on the Palatine Hill won, and Remus's Aventino was abandoned. It would remain for centuries thereafter the hill of the plebs, who looked across the valley to the grandeur of Palatine Hill.

Things have long since changed, however, and today this is a rarefied district, in which some houses still have their own bell towers, and private gardens are called "parks" without exaggeration. Like the emperors of old on Palatino, the fortunate residents here look out over the Circus Maximus and the Tiber, winding its way far below. Today's travelers still enjoy great views, famously including that from the peculiar keyhole at the gates to the headquarters of the Cavalieri di Malta (Knights of Malta), which may be the most peered-through in the world.

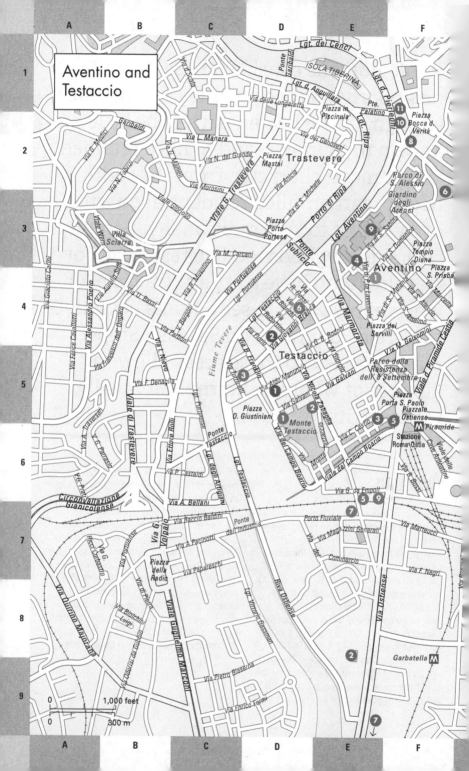

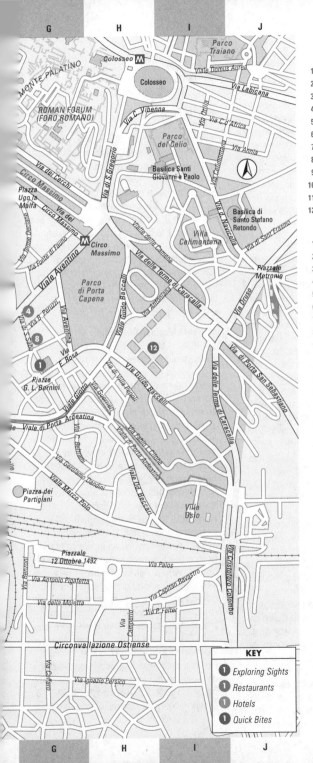

Sights ▼

1 Basilica di San Saba **G5**
2 Centrale Montemartini **E8**
3 Cimitero Acattolico **E5**
4 Piazza dei Cavalieri di Malta **E3**
5 Piramide di Caio Cestio **F5**
6 Roseto Comunale **F2**
7 San Paolo fuori le Mura............ **E9**
8 Santa Maria in Cosmedin.......... **F2**
9 Santa Sabina **E3**
10 Tempio di Ercole Vincitore......... **F2**
11 Tempio di Portuno **F1**
12 Terme di Caracalla................. **H4**

Restaurants ▼

1 Checchino dal 1887................ **D5**
2 Flavio al Velavevodetto **D5**
3 La Torricella **C5**
4 Marco Martini **G4**
5 Marigold **E6**
6 Pizzeria Remo **D4**
7 Porto Fluviale...................... **E7**
8 Queen Makeda Grand Pub **G4**
9 Trattoria Pennestri................. **E6**

Quick Bites ▼

1 Mordi e Vai **D5**
2 Trapizzino **D4**

Hotels ▼

1 Hotel San Anselmo **E4**

Sights

Basilica di San Saba

CHURCH | A former monastery, founded in the 7th century by monks fleeing Jerusalem following the Arab invasion, this is a major monument of Rome. The serene but rustic interior harbors 10th-century frescoes, a famed Cosmatesque mosaic floor, and a hodgepodge of ancient marble pieces. ⊠ *Piazza Gian Lorenzo Bernini 20, Aventino* ☏ *06/64580140* ⊕ *sansaba. gesuiti.it* Ⓜ *Circo Massimo.*

★ Piazza dei Cavalieri di Malta

GARDEN | Peek through the keyhole of the Priorato di Malta, the walled compound of the Knights of Malta, and you'll get a surprising eyeful: a picture-perfect view of the dome of St. Peter's Basilica, far across the city. The top of the church is flawlessly framed by trimmed hedges that lie beyond a nondescript, locked green door. The square and the priory within the walls are the work of Giovanni Battista Piranesi, an 18th-century engraver who is more famous for etching Roman views than for orchestrating them, but he fancied himself a bit of an architect and did not disappoint. As for the Order of the Knights of Malta, it is the world's oldest and most exclusive order of chivalry, founded in the Holy Land during the Crusades. Though nominally ministering to the sick in those early days—a role that has since become the order's raison d'être—the knights amassed huge tracts of land in the Middle East. From 1530 they were based on the Mediterranean island of Malta, but in 1798 Napoléon expelled them, and, in 1834, they established themselves in Rome. Tours with a private guide are usually available on Friday mornings if you would like to go inside; email for more information (tours must be prebooked by email). ⊠ *Via Santa Sabina and Via Porta Lavernale, Aventino* 🖼 *From €5 per person (min. of 10 people), plus the cost of the required guide, €80 in Italian, €100 in any other language). If a group has* already formed, then anyone may join for the regular entry fee 🖾 *Reservations required* Ⓜ *Circo Massimo; Tram No. 3.*

Roseto Comunale

GARDEN | As suggested by the paths shaped like a menorah, what is now the city's springtime rose garden was once a Jewish cemetery. The cemetery, save one tombstone, was moved and the space is now a municipal garden that is open during the brief weeks when the roses are in bloom. The garden is laid out to reflect the history of roses from antiquity to the present day and has sweeping views across the old chariot track of the Circus Maximus. ⊠ *Viale di Valle Murcia, Aventino* 🕑 *Closed July–late Apr.* Ⓜ *Circo Massimo. Bus Nos. 60, 81, 118, 160, 271, 628, and 715; Tram No. 3.*

★ Santa Maria in Cosmedin

CHURCH | FAMILY | Although this is one of Rome's oldest churches, with a haunting interior, it plays second fiddle to the renowned artifact installed out in the portico. The Bocca della Verità (Mouth of Truth) is in reality nothing more than an ancient drain cover, unearthed during the Middle Ages. Legend has it, however, that the teeth will clamp down on a liar's hand if they dare to tell a fib while holding their fingers up to the fearsome mouth. Hordes of tourists line up to take the test every day (kids especially get a kick out of it), but there is never a wait to enter the church itself, which was built in the 6th century. Head inside to stand before the flower-crowned skull of St. Valentine, who is celebrated every February 14th, but go ahead and pass on the trip down to the tiny, empty crypt. Heavily restored at the end of the 19th century, the church stands across from the Piazza della Bocca della Verità, originally the location of the Forum Boarium, ancient Rome's cattle market, and later the site of public executions. ⊠ *Piazza della Bocca della Verità 18, Aventino* ☏ *06/6787759* ⊕ *www.cosmedin.org* Ⓜ *Circo Massimo.*

Santa Sabina

CHURCH | This Early Christian basilica is stark and tranquil, showing off the lovely simplicity common to churches of its era. Although some of the side chapels were added in the 16th and 17th centuries, the essential form is as Rome's Christians knew it in the 5th century. Most striking are the 24 fluted Corinthian columns which line the classical interior. Once bright with mosaics, today the church has only one above the entrance door (its gold letters announce how the church was founded by Peter of Illyria, "rich for the poor," under Pope Celestine I). The beautifully carved, 5th-century cedar doors to the left of the outside entrance are the oldest of their kind in existence. ⊠ *Piazza Pietro d'Illiria 1, Aventino* ☎ *06/579401* Ⓜ *Circo Massimo; Bus Nos. 60, 75, 81, 118, 160, 175, and 715; Tram No. 3.*

Tempio di Ercole Vincitore

TEMPLE | The round layout of the Temple of Hercules Victor led it to be mistakenly identified for centuries as the Temple of Vesta, which has a similar shape but really sits in the Roman Forum. Now called by its correct name, it was built in the 2nd century BC around the same time as its neighbor, the Tempio di Portuno. The little park around the temples was once ancient Rome's cattle market, but now has benches to rest weary feet. ⊠ *Piazza Bocca della Verità, Aventino* Ⓜ *Circo Massimo; Bus Nos. 60, 75, 81, 118, 160, 175, and 271; Tram No. 3.*

Tempio di Portuno

TEMPLE | A picture-perfect, if doll-house-size, Roman temple, this rectangular edifice from the 2nd century BC is built in the Greek style. Positioned in a bend in the Tiber River and long known as the Temple of Fortuna Virilis ("Manly Fortune"), it was appropriately dedicated to Portunus, the protector of ports. It now sits on a slip of greenery between two well-trafficked roads and owes its fine state of preservation to the fact that it was consecrated as a church in the 9th century. ⊠ *Piazza Bocca della Verità, Aventino* Ⓜ *Circo Massimo; Bus Nos. 60, 75, 81, 118, 160, 175, and 271; Tram No. 3.*

Terme di Caracalla (Baths of Caracalla)

RUINS | FAMILY | The Terme di Caracalla are some of Rome's most massive—yet least visited—ruins. Begun in AD 206 by the emperor Septimius Severus and completed by his son, Caracalla, the 28-acre complex could accommodate 1,600 bathers at a time. Along with an Olympic-size swimming pool and baths, the complex also had two gyms, a library, and gardens. The impressive baths depended on slave labor, particularly the unseen stokers who toiled in subterranean rooms to keep the fires roaring in order to heat the water. Rather than a simple dip in a tub, Romans turned "bathing" into one of the most lavish leisure activities imaginable. A bath began in the sudatoria, a series of small rooms resembling saunas, which then led to the caldarium, a circular room that was humid rather than simply hot. Here a strigil, or scraper, was used to get the dirt off the skin. Next stop: the warm(-ish) tepidarium, which helped start the cool-down process. Finally, it ended with a splash around the frigidarium, a chilly swimming pool.

Today, the complex is a shell of its former self. Some black-and-white mosaic fragments remain, but most of the opulent mosaics, frescoes, and sculptures have found their way into Rome's museums. Nevertheless, the towering walls and sheer size of the ruins give one of the best glimpses into ancient Rome's ambitions. If you're here in summer, don't miss the chance to catch an open-air opera or ballet in the baths, put on by the Teatro dell'Opera di Roma. ⊠ *Viale delle Terme di Caracalla 52, Aventino* ☎ *06/39967702* ⊕ *www.coopculture. it* 🎟 *€8 (includes Villa dei Quintili and Tomba di Cecilia Metella)* 🕘 *Closed Mon.* Ⓜ *Circo Massimo.*

🍽 Restaurants

While there are no eateries to be found on the tree-lined streets of the Aventine Hill itself, you can take a short stroll down to Viale Aventino to find a range of restaurants and caffè that cater to the international staff at the nearby United Nations office. From French to Brazilian to Greek, the area has quick lunch stops and a few fine dining choices which tend to feel a world away from traditional Roman cooking.

Marco Martini

$$$$ | ITALIAN | With innovative Italian-inspired cuisine and one Michelin star, this intimate restaurant has a lovely terrace bar as well as a romantic plant-draped dining room. Twirl your fork into a bowl of spaghetti with a delightful oyster, sausage, and turnip-top sauce, or save room for the lamb with butter anchovies and pistachios. **Known for:** creative presentation; value-for-money tasting menu; whimsical garden setting. $ *Average main: €35* ⊠ *Viale Aventino 121, Aventino* ☎ *06/45597350* ⊕ *www. marcomartinichef.com* ⊗ *Closed Sun. No lunch Sat.* Ⓜ *Circo Massimo.*

Queen Makeda Grand Pub

$$$ | INTERNATIONAL | This gastropub has an international menu that ranges from Asian fusion appetizers to open-faced sandwiches on dark rye bread. With a rotating selection of 40 craft beers on tap, there is also a suggested drink pairing for every food item. **Known for:** craft beer menu; cool urban design; *yakitori* (Japanese-inspired grilled meat). $ *Average main: €25* ⊠ *Via di San Saba 11, Aventino* ☎ *06/5759608* ⊕ *www. queenmakeda.it* Ⓜ *Circo Massimo.*

🛏 Hotels

This affluent neighborhood full of trees, set on the Aventine Hill, attracts travelers looking for a green oasis removed from the *centro storico* (historic center). Hotels take advantage of the extra space, with gardens and courtyards where you can enjoy a little R&R alfresco, and where the only noise you'll hear in the morning is birdsong.

Hotel San Anselmo

$ | HOTEL | This refurbished 19th-century villa is a romantic retreat from the city, set in a *molto* charming garden atop the Aventine Hill. **Pros:** free Wi-Fi; garden where you can enjoy breakfast; historic building with artful interior. **Cons:** no full restaurant; limited public transportation; some rooms are quite small. $ *Rooms from: €80* ⊠ *Piazza San Anselmo 2, Aventino* ☎ *06/570057* ⊕ *www.aventinohotels.com* ⤳ *34 rooms* ⏀ *Free Breakfast* Ⓜ *Circo Massimo.*

🎭 Performing Arts

OPERA

Terme di Caracalla Ballet and Opera

OPERA | In the summer months, the 3rd-century-AD Baths of Caracalla are the spectacular backdrop for the Teatro dell'Opera's ballet and opera series. *Aida* is the most sought-after performance, thanks to its melodramatic flair and amazing props. The impressive productions keep the traditional sonatas and musical numbers untouched while incorporating contemporary elements into each show, including stage design that sometimes uses projections atop the ancient ruins. ⊠ *Viale delle Terme di Caracalla 52, Aventino* ☎ *06/481601* ⊕ *www.operaroma.it.*

Testaccio

Once considered to be on the periphery of the city, Testaccio is fast becoming a Roman destination in its own right. Testaccini locals claim that their neighborhood bleeds red and yellow, a reference to the colors of the A.S. Roma soccer team that has a passionate fan club located here. Formerly a bit tatty, Testaccio has undergone a trendy revival and is sometimes hailed as Rome's new "Left Bank" district. Most of the buildings date back to the late 19th-century, but nearly all were built on literal broken pots: the area takes its name from an eponymous hill made up of 53 million discarded ancient Roman amphorae that used to store oil, wine, and other goods loaded from the nearby Ripa, when Rome had a port and the Tiber was once a mighty river to an empire. Testaccio is a must for those seeking authentic and comparatively cheap Roman cuisine.

Sights

★ Centrale Montemartini

ART MUSEUM | A decommissioned power plant (Rome's first electricity plant) was reopened as a permanent exhibition space in 2005 and today houses the overflow of ancient art from the Musei Capitolini collection. After strolling Rome's medieval lanes, the Centrale Montemartini's early-20th-century style can feel positively modern. A 15-minute walk from the heart of Testaccio in one direction will lead you past walls covered in street art to the urban district of Ostiense. Head southwest and saunter under the train tracks to admire buildings bedecked with four-story-high murals until you reach the Centrale Montemartini. With Roman sculptures and mosaics set against industrial machinery and pipes, nowhere else in Rome is the contrast between old and new more apparent or enjoyable. A pleasure, too, is the fact that you're likely to be one of the few visitors here, making it the perfect stop for those feeling claustrophobic from Rome's crowds. Unusually, the collection is organized by the area in which the ancient pieces were found. Highlights include the former boiler room filled with ancient marble statues that once decorated Rome's private villas, such as the beautiful *Esquiline Venus*, as well as a large mosaic of a hunting scene. ⊠ *Via Ostiense 106, Testaccio* ☎ *06/0608* ⊕ *www.centralemontemartini. org* ✉ *€10* ⊗ *Closed Mon.* Ⓜ *Garbatella.*

★ Cimitero Acattolico

(*Non-Catholic or Protestant Cemetery*)
CEMETERY | Built up against the ancient Aurelian Walls, this famed cemetery was intended for the interment of non-Catholics. Poetic souls seek out the tomb of John Keats, who tragically died in Rome after succumbing to consumption at age 25 in 1821. The headstone is famously inscribed, "Here lies one whose name was writ in water" (the poet requested that no name or dates should appear). Nearby is the place where Shelley's heart was buried, as well as the tombs of Goethe's son, the founder of the Italian Communist Party and vehement anti-Fascist Antonio Gramsci, and America's famed beat poet Gregory Corso. What's more, the quiet paths of the cemetery are lined with fruit trees and prowled by shy cats from a nearby animal sanctuary. The tranquil spot is far from morbid and quite easy to find: simply catch the Metro Linea B from Termini station to the Piramide stop, which is just around the corner from the entrance to the cemetery. ⊠ *Via Caio Cestio 6, Testaccio* ☎ *06/5741900* ⊕ *www.cemeteryrome.it* ✉ *€3 suggested donation* ☞ *If door is closed, ring bell for cemetery custodian* Ⓜ *Piramide; Buses Nos. 23, 30, 60, 75, 118, and 715; Tram No. 3.*

Piramide di Caio Cestio

MONUMENT | **FAMILY** | Once a part of the Aurelian Walls and now a part of the Cimitero Acattolico, this monumental tomb was designed in 12 BC for the immensely wealthy praetor Gaius Cestius in the form of a 120-foot-tall pyramid. According to an inscription, it was completed in a little less than a year. Though little else is known about the Roman official, he clearly had a taste for grandeur and liked to show off his travels to far parts of the nascent empire. The pyramid was recently restored in a project funded by a €1 million donation from Japanese fashion tycoon Yuzo Yagi. At this writing, the interior was still closed due to COVID-19 precautions, but guided visits (when available on the second and fourth Saturday of each month) require a reservation. ⊠ *Piazzale Ostiense, Testaccio* ☎ *06/39967702* ⊕ *www.coopculture. it/it/poi/piramide-cestia* ⊗ *Closed Aug.* Ⓜ *Piramide; Bus Nos. 3, 30, 60, 75, 95, 118, 130, 175, and 719.*

San Paolo fuori le Mura (*St. Paul's Outside the Walls*)

CHURCH | A couple of Metro stops farther down Via Ostiense from Testaccio, in a rather dreary location near the river, St. Paul's is one of Rome's most historic and important churches. Its massive size, second only to St. Peter's Basilica, allows ample space for the 272 roundels depicting every pope from St. Peter to the current Pope Francis (found below the ceiling, with spaces left blank for pontiffs to come). Built in the 4th century AD by Constantine over the site where St. Paul had been buried, the church was later enlarged, but in 1823 a fire burned it almost to the ground. Although the outside lacks any real charm, the rebuilt St. Paul's has a sort of monumental grandeur that follows the plans of the earlier basilica. However, it's only in the cloisters (€4) that you get a real sense of the magnificence of the original building. In the middle of the nave is the famous baldacchino created by sculptor Arnolfo di Cambio. ⊠ *Piazzale San Paolo, Via Ostiense 190, Testaccio* ☎ *06/69880800* ⊕ *www.basilicasanpaolo.org* ⊠ *Cloister €4* Ⓜ *Basilica San Paolo.*

 Restaurants

This working-class neighborhood is where the old slaughterhouses once stood and where the butchers invented the (in)famous meat and offal dishes you can still find in authentic old-school restaurants. Relatively low rents have meant an influx of young people, which has made this one of the up-and-coming areas of the city.

Checchino dal 1887

$$ | **ROMAN** | Literally carved into the side of a hill made up of ancient shards of amphorae, Checchino is an example of a classic, upscale, family-run Roman establishment, with one of the best wine cellars in the region. One of the first restaurants to open near Testaccio's (now long closed) slaughterhouse, they still serve classic offal dishes (though the white-jacketed waiters can also suggest other options). **Known for:** *coda alla vaccinara* (Roman-style oxtail); old-school Roman waiters; old-school Roman cooking. Ⓢ *Average main: €23* ⊠ *Via di Monte Testaccio 30, Testaccio* ☎ *06/5743816* ⊕ *www.checchino-dal-1887.com* ⊗ *Closed Mon. and Tues., Aug., and 1 wk at Christmas* Ⓜ *Piramide.*

★ Flavio al Velavevodetto

$$ | **ROMAN** | It's everything you're looking for in a true Roman eating experience: authentic, in a historic setting, and filled with Italians eating good food at good prices. In this very *romani di Roma* (Rome of the Romans) neighborhood, surrounded by discos and bars sharing Monte Testaccio, you can enjoy a meal of classic local dishes, from vegetable antipasto to *cacio e pepe* (pasta with pecorino-cheese sauce and black pepper; said to be the best version in the city) and lamb chops. **Known for:** *polpette di* bollito (fried breaded meatballs); outdoor covered terrace in summer; authentic Roman atmosphere and food. $ *Average main: €16* ✉ *Via di Monte Testaccio 97, Testaccio* ☎ *06/5744194* ⊕ *www.ristorantevelavevodetto.it* Ⓜ *Piramide.*

La Torricella
$$ | SEAFOOD | FAMILY | This family-run institution has been serving seafood in the working-class Testaccio neighborhood for more than 40 years, and if you visit the local market early enough you may spot the owner on his daily rounds to select the freshest fish, which mainly arrives from Gaeta, south of Rome. The seafood menu changes every day, but look for house specialties like *paccheri* (a very large, tubular pasta) with *totani* (baby calamari), pasta with *telline* (small clams), and the wondrously simple spaghetti with lobster. **Known for:** relaxed but refined setting with outdoor seating; polpette di pesce al sugo (fish balls in tomato sauce); fresh, local seafood. $ *Average main: €18* ✉ *Via Evangelista Torricelli 2/12, Testaccio* ☎ *06/5746311* ⊕ *www.la-torricella.com* Ⓜ *Piramide.*

Marigold
$ | SCANDINAVIAN | Run by a husband-and-wife team (she's Danish, he's Italian), this hip restaurant blends the best of both their cultures with a Scandinavian-meets-Italian design and menù. It draws a young, international crowd who come for the sourdough, cinnamon buns, and veggie-forward dishes. **Known for:** minimalist design; weekend brunch; Danish breads and baked goods. $ *Average main: €13* ✉ *Via Giovanni da Empoli 37, Testaccio* ☎ *06/87725679* ⊕ *www.marigoldroma.com* ⊗ *Closed Mon., Tues., and 3 wks in Aug. No dinner* Ⓜ *Ostiense.*

Pizzeria Remo
$ | PIZZA | Arrive promptly at 7 pm or expect a line at this perennial-favorite pizzeria in Testaccio frequented by students and locals. There are no tablecloths or other nonessentials, just excellent classic Roman pizza and boisterous conversation. **Known for:** fried appetizers; perfectly charred pizza crusts; local crowds. $ *Average main: €10* ✉ *Piazza Santa Maria Liberatrice 44, Testaccio* ☎ *06/5746270* ▭ *No credit cards* ⊗ *Closed Sun. and 3 wks in Aug. No lunch* Ⓜ *Piramide.*

Porto Fluviale
$ | ITALIAN | This massive structure takes up the better part of a block on a street that's gone from gritty clubland to popular nightspot, thanks largely to Porto Fluviale. The place pulls double duty as a bar, caffè, pizzeria, lunch buffet, and lively evening restaurant. **Known for:** *cicheti* (Venetian-style tapas); pizza from wood-burning oven; good cocktails. $ *Average main: €13* ✉ *Via del Porto Fluviale 22, Testaccio* ☎ *06/5743199* ⊕ *www.portofluviale.com* Ⓜ *Piramide.*

Trattoria Pennestri
$$ | ROMAN | Sitting between Testaccio and Ostiense, Trattoria Pennestri manages to strike a careful balance between tradition and innovation. The thoughtful takes on Roman classics brighten up heavy dishes and add a more appetizing spin to some of the city's beloved entrails recipes. **Known for:** duck breast with peaches and wine; uncommon wines; modern Roman cooking. $ *Average main: €17* ✉ *Via Giovanni da Empoli 5, Testaccio* ☎ *06/5742418* ⊕ *www.trattoriapennestri.it* ⊗ *Closed Mon. No lunch Tues.–Thurs.* Ⓜ *Piramide.*

☕ Coffee and Quick Bites

★ Mordi e Vai
$ | ITALIAN | Sergio Esposito's stand at what will forever be called the "New" Testaccio Market (it moved in 2012) sells the best sandwiches in town. Meatballs, tongue, tripe, and other Roman classics are generously smothered on fresh bread, and there is always a vegetarian option, too. **Known for:** *alesso* (slow-cooked beef) sandwiches; breaded meatballs; long lines at lunch time.

$ *Average main: €5* ✉ *Testaccio Market Box 15, Via Beniamino Franklin, Testaccio* ☎ *339/1343344* ⊕ *www.mordievai.it* ⊘ *Closed Sun. No dinner.*

Trapizzino

$ | ROMAN | FAMILY | Stefano Callegari is one of Rome's most famous pizza makers, but at Trapizzino he's doing something a bit different. The name of the restaurant is derived from the Italian words for sandwich (*tramezzino*) and pizza, and the result is something like an upscale pizza pocket, stuffed on the spot with local specialties like chicken alla cacciatore, or *trippa* (tripe), or roast pumpkin, pecorino, and almonds. **Known for:** Italian craft beer; eggplant parmigiana and meatball sandwiches; casual setting, with seating available next door. $ *Average main: €4* ✉ *Via Giovanni Branca 88, Testaccio* ☎ *06/43419624* ⊕ *www.trapizzino.it* ⊘ *Closed 1 wk in Aug.* Ⓜ *Piramide.*

▼ Nightlife

Even if it is a bit outside the meandering medieval alleyways of the historic center, Testaccio is a hotbed for the Eternal City's nightlife scene. The rowdy clubs that dug into the side of Monte Testaccio have lost some of their appeal in recent years as the trendier dance clubs moved to old warehouses even farther out to the edge of Rome, but this has left space for new wine bars and hip street-food stops.

BARS

Ketumbar

CAFÉS | FAMILY | One of Rome's few "organic" happy hours, the price of a drink will buy you a spread of healthy and organic vegetarian appetizers. *Aperitivo* (happy hour) starts daily at 6:30 pm, but the modern minimalist restaurant also serves a great weekend brunch with a kids' area that includes a free babysitter. ✉ *Via Galvani 24, Testaccio* ☎ *06/57305338* ⊕ *www.ketumbar.it* ⊘ *Closed Mon.*

L'Oasi della Birra

PUBS | A long menu of imported brews make this a true beer oasis, although there are also good wines available by the bottle or the glass. Locals love the generous happy hour buffet that makes an appearance from about 6 pm to 8 pm every day, but come early to snag one of the outdoor picnic tables that overlook the piazza. Best known as a low-key drinking spot, the bar also doubles as a specialty food store that stocks Italian jams, chocolates, and pastas. ✉ *Piazza Testaccio 38/41, Testaccio* ☎ *06/5746122* Ⓜ *Piramide.*

Taverna Volpetti

WINE BARS | Most aperitivos tend to be more all-you-can-eat than refined pre-dinner stop, but that is not the case at Taverna Volpetti. The chic bistro-style wine bar and restaurant sources all its ingredients from the gourmet food store by the same name that sits just around the corner. The warm atmosphere, stellar wine list, and excellent cheese and salami make it the ideal place for a drink and a snack, or to stay put with a bottle and sip the night away. ✉ *Via Alessandro Volta 8, Testaccio* ☎ *06/5744306* ⊘ *Closed Mon.* Ⓜ *Piramide.*

★ Tram Depot

CAFÉS | A coffee stand by day and cocktail bar by night, this outdoor establishment began life as a city tram car back in 1903. Now the historic carriage has been converted to a kiosk permanently stationed on a park corner with retro tables and garden seating. A trendy crowd descends at sunset, and seats are at a premium until the wee hours of the morning. But since it is entirely outside, Tram Depot is only open in the warmer months of the year (April through November). ✉ *Via Marmorata 13, Testaccio* Ⓜ *Piramide.*

🛍 Shopping

Testaccio is Rome's original foodie neighborhood, with plenty of specialty food and wine shops, as well as an abundance of great Roman eateries. But look between the traditional working-class storefronts and you can also stumble upon trendy boutiques and artisan shops.

Assemblea

CRAFTS | This modest shop is brimming with fantastic small gifts ranging from ceramics to vintage fabrics remade into tote bags. Assemblea finds small artisans throughout the country and makes their quirky creations available in Rome, so every item featured is guaranteed to be made in Italy. ⊠ *Via Alessandro Volta 22, Testaccio* ☎ *06/5747696* ⊘ *Closed Sun.* Ⓜ *Piramide.*

Emporio delle Spezie

FOOD | Hardly larger than a walk-in closet, this tiny specialty shop is bursting with ingredients from every corner of the world. Specializing in high-quality spices, you can also find dried goods like legumes, nuts, and rice, along with ingredients to whip up almost any international cuisine. All are carefully scooped from the colorful glass jars that line the walls and measured out to your liking. ⊠ *Via Luca della Robbia 20, Testaccio* ☎ *327/8612655* ⊕ *www.emporiodellespezie.it* ⊘ *Closed Sun.* Ⓜ *Piramide.*

★ Volpetti

FOOD | A Roman institution for more than 40 years, Volpetti sells excellent cured meats and salami from its buzzing deli counter. The rich aromas and flavors are captivating from the moment you enter the store. The food selection also includes genuine buffalo-milk mozzarella, fresh pasta, Roman pecorino, olive oils, balsamic vinegars, and fresh bread. It's also a great place for assembling gift baskets, and they offer worldwide shipping. ⊠ *Via Marmorata 47, Testaccio* ☎ *06/5742352* ⊕ *www.volpetti.com* ⊘ *Closed Sun.* Ⓜ *Piramide.*

Chapter 11

ESQUILINO AND ENVIRONS

11

Updated by
Laura Itzkowitz

Sights ★★★★☆ Restaurants ★★★☆☆ Hotels ★★★★☆ Shopping ★★☆☆☆ Nightlife ★★☆☆☆

NEIGHBORHOOD SNAPSHOT

MAKING THE MOST OF YOUR TIME

Some of central Rome's least touristy and best-loved neighborhoods, these areas also have a great deal to explore. With its bustling food market and multicultural shops, Esquilino represents a more modern Rome. Its rich street life has attracted numerous artists, actors, and filmmakers who often gather at some of the popular caffè in the neighborhood. With Termini at its center, this is also your bus and Metro hub for reaching other parts of Rome or hopping on a train for a day trip out of the city. Nearby Pigneto with its hipster bars and galleries is also an example of the ever-evolving city.

San Giovanni is well worth the Metro trip to discover the Basilica of San Giovanni in Laterano, a cathedral that holds centuries of church history in its walls. This residential area also has great flea market shopping if you have the patience to browse. For a bustling night out, head to San Lorenzo, home to the Sapienza University of Rome and the crowds of young students that go with it. And no visit to Rome is complete without a tour of the catacombs on the Appian Way, one of the ancient republic's earliest and most strategically placed roads, built in 312–264 BC.

TOP REASONS TO GO

Arcibasilica di San Giovanni in Laterano: Before the Holy See made the Vatican its permanent home, leaders of the Catholic Church made the Lateran buildings their primary residence for nearly 1,000 years.

Catacomb country: Be careful exploring the underground graves of the earliest Christians—one wrong turn and it may be days before you surface.

Porta Maggiore: This white travertine "great gate" is an essential stop for understanding Rome's ancient aqueduct culture.

Teatro dell'Opera di Roma: If you've ever wanted to experience the Italian opera greats in their native land, from Verdi to Rossini to Puccini, this historic building with its charming rows of stacked theater boxes is the place to be.

VIEWFINDER

■ Fans of street art will find much to admire in San Lorenzo and Pigneto, with large-scale murals in both neighborhoods. There's a particularly impressive mural across from the new Soho House in San Lorenzo and several murals on and around Via Fanfulla da Lodi in Pigneto. To learn more about them and the neighborhoods they're in, you can take a Street Art tour with **Scooteroma** (⊕ *www. scooteroma.com*), which offers Vespa tours around Rome.

GETTING HERE

■ The Esquilino Hill can be reached via the Vittorio Emanuele subway station, one stop from Termini station. Pigneto is easily reached by the new Metro Line C.

Several neighborhoods come together here, just north of the Roman Forum and the Colosseum. They range from the bustling, multicultural Esquilino neighborhood to the hipster enclaves of Pigneto and San Giovanni. Most travelers will find themselves passing through at least part of the area, either when they come into the Termini train station or when they pay a visit to the Basilica of San Giovanni in Laterano, which offers everything from ancient monuments to baroque masterpieces. Head farther south for the evocative Via Appia Antica, dotted with ruins and ancient catacombs.

Esquilino

Rome's most sprawling hill—the Esquilino—lies at the very edge of most tourist maps. Even imperial Rome could not have matched this minicosmopolis for sheer internationalism. Right around Termini, sons of the soil—the so-called "romani romani"—mingle with Chinese, Sri Lankans, Sikhs, and a hundred nationalities in between. One highlight is the Nuovo Mercato Esquilino, a covered market hall where goods from the four corners of the Earth are bought and sold in a multitude of languages. This is also where you can find some of the city's largest variety of restaurants and cheapest bed-and-breakfasts—just not the cobblestone atmosphere that most think of when they think of Rome.

Sights

Porta Maggiore (*Great Gate*)
RUINS | The massive 1st-century-AD arch was built as part of the original Aqua Claudia and then incorporated into the walls hurriedly erected in the late 3rd century as Rome's fortunes began to decline; the great arch of the aqueduct subsequently became a *porta* (city gate). It gives an idea of the grand scale of ancient Roman public works. On the Piazzale Labicano side, to the east, is the curious Baker's Tomb, erected in the

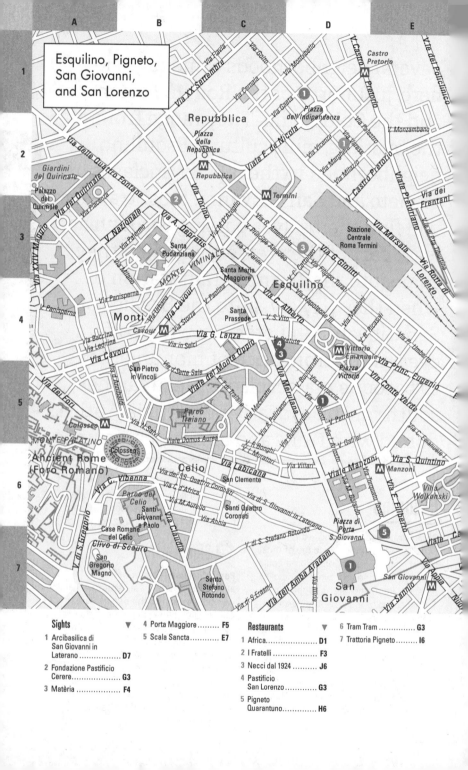

Esquilino, Pigneto, San Giovanni, and San Lorenzo

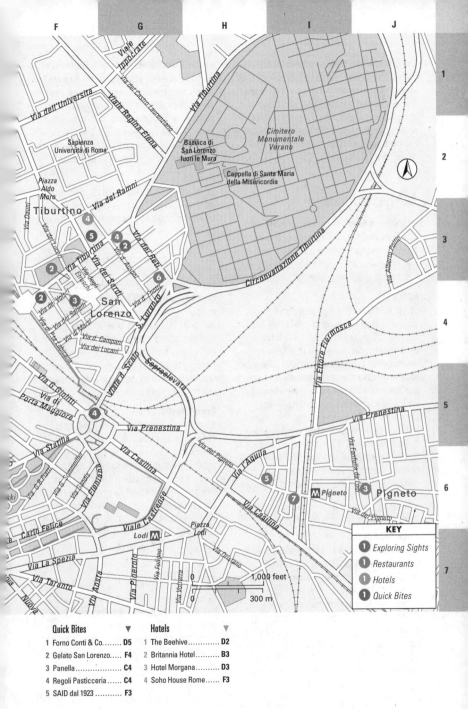

Quick Bites ▼

1 Forno Conti & Co........ **D5**
2 Gelato San Lorenzo..... **F4**
3 Panella.................... **C4**
4 Regoli Pasticceria **C4**
5 SAID dal 1923 .... **F3**

Hotels ▼

1 The Beehive.............. **D2**
2 Britannia Hotel........... **B3**
3 Hotel Morgana.......... **D3**
4 Soho House Rome...... **F3**

1st century BC by a prosperous baker (predating both the aqueduct and the city walls); it's shaped like an oven to signal the deceased's trade. The site is now in the middle of a public transport node, and is close to Rome's first tram depot (going back to 1889). ⊠ *Piazza di Porta Maggiore, Esquilino* Ⓜ *Tram No. 5, 14, or 19.*

🍴 Restaurants

Esquilino is Rome's main multicultural artery, with Mercato Esquilino, a great covered market for Italian, Asian, and African specialties. Tourist traps abound, but you can find some authentic Roman food.

Africa

$$ | ETHIOPIAN | For something very different from pizza and pasta, try this excellent Ethiopian restaurant where traditional food is served in a casual environment. Seating is at low tables, as is typical, and the spicy stews and salads are served with spongey *injera* bread, which is also used as a utensil—be prepared to eat with your hands. **Known for:** big portions; eclectic decor; vegetarian couscous. ⑤ *Average main: €20* ⊠ *Via Gaeta 26, Esquilino* ☎ *06/4941077* ⊕ *www.ristoranteafrica.com* ▤ *No credit cards* ⊘ *Closed Mon.* Ⓜ *Castro Pretorio.*

☕ Coffee and Quick Bites

Forno Conti & Co.

$ | BAKERY | At this new bakery on a quiet street near Piazza Vittorio, *Scandinavian-inspired* minimalist design is the backdrop for bread and pastries by fourth-generation baker Sergio Conti. You'll find staples like excellent croissants and pain au chocolat as well as special items like *maritozzi* (a typical Roman sweet consisting of a soft bun split in half and filled with whipped

cream), apple strudel, or brioche with salted caramel and peanuts. **Known for:** sleek minimalist design; sweet pastries and cakes; bread naturally leavened with sourdough starter. ⑤ *Average main: €3* ⊠ *Via Giusti 18, Esquilino* ☎ *339/2109591* ⊕ *www.fornoconti.co* ⊘ *Closed Sun.* Ⓜ *Vittorio Emanuele.*

Panella

$ | BAKERY | Opened in 1929, this nearly century-old spot is one of Rome's best bakeries and sells both sweet and savory baked goods, including over 70 types of bread. Line up for the pizza *al taglio* (by the slice) at lunchtime or sit down at one of the outdoor tables for a cappuccino and cornetto or an *aperitivo* (pre-meal drink) replete with mini sandwiches made on homemade buns. **Known for:** over 70 types of bread; crostata, tartlettes, and other sweet treats; one of Rome's best bakeries. ⑤ *Average main: €10* ⊠ *Via Merulana 54, Esquilino* ☎ *06/4872435* ⊕ *www.panellaroma.com* Ⓜ *Vittorio Emanuele.*

Regoli Pasticceria

$ | BAKERY | Established in 1916, this family-run pasticceria is famous for their maritozzi. If you want to try one, go in the morning—they often run out by lunchtime. **Known for:** cream-filled pastries like cream puffs and cannoli; maritozzi; wild strawberry tarts. ⑤ *Average main: €3* ⊠ *Via dello Statuto 60, Esquilino* ☎ *06/4872812* ⊕ *www.pasticceriaregoli. com* ⊘ *Closed Tues.* Ⓜ *Vittorio Emanuele.*

🛏 Hotels

Budget-conscious travelers who want to be near Rome's major transport hub, Termini station, often stay here. There are a number of cheap, clean, no-frills hotels and pensioni, as well as a few more-stylish options.

★ The Beehive

$ | HOTEL | This hostel run by an American couple is a welcoming, community-oriented place to stay near Termini Station offering some private rooms (some of those with shared bath) as well as regular hostel beds in dorms. **Pros:** owners make the best bagels in Rome; convenient to Termini station; very good prices (especially for beds in dorms) for variety of rooms, even in high season. **Cons:** standard rooms lack TV and air-conditioning; no 24-hour reception; some rooms do not have private baths. $ *Rooms from: €60* ✉ *Via Marghera 8, Esquilino* ☎ *06/44704553* ⊕ *www.the-beehive. com* ⌨ *8 rooms, 4 dormitories* �: *No Meals* ⌖ *Check-in hours are 9 am–9 pm* Ⓜ *Termini.*

Britannia Hotel

$$ | HOTEL | Situated in an elegant art nouveau palazzo dating back to 1876, this charming hotel feels like a luxurious private home. **Pros:** spacious, comfortable rooms; spacious marble bathrooms, many with Jacuzzi baths; great breakfast options. **Cons:** some furnishings are out of date; not very close to the city's main attractions; rooms can be noisy for light sleepers. $ *Rooms from: €194* ✉ *Via Napoli 64, Esquilino* ☎ *06/4883153* ⊕ *www.hotelbritanniaroma.com* ⌨ *34 rooms* �: *Free Breakfast* Ⓜ *Repubblica.*

Hotel Morgana

$ | HOTEL | A nice, cozy hotel just a stone's throw from Termini station sounds like some sort of a miracle, and yet the Morgana welcomes guests with elegant classically designed rooms and top amenities. **Pros:** practical base for public transportation; great breakfast; pet-friendly. **Cons:** removed from most sightseeing; some bathrooms are on the small side; run-down neighborhood. $ *Rooms from: €79* ✉ *Via Filippo Turati 33/37, Esquilino* ☎ *06/4467230* ⊕ *www. hotelmorgana.com* ⌨ *123 rooms* �: *Free Breakfast* Ⓜ *Termini.*

▼ Nightlife

The area around Termini can be a bit sketchy, especially at night, but there are a few pubs around Santa Maria Maggiore.

BARS
Fiddler's Elbow

PUBS | The oldest Irish pub in Rome, the proud Fiddler's Elbow is a rustic, traditional pub that probably hasn't changed since it first installed its wood panels in 1976. Expect raucous nights of beer and singing. ✉ *Via dell'Olmata 43, Esquilino* ☎ *06/4872110* ⊕ *www. thefiddlerselbow.com.*

▣ Shopping

Home to a variety of ethnic communities, the shops in Esquilino feel very authentic. The market here is a fabulous place to explore.

MALLS AND SHOPPING CENTERS
Roma Termini

DEPARTMENT STORE | Rome's handiest central shopping mall is this cluster of shops that stays open until 10 pm (even on Sunday), conveniently located directly inside Rome's biggest train station, Stazione Termini. In a city not exactly known for its convenient shopping hours, this "shop before you hop" hub is a good spot for last-minute goodies. Shops include ever-popular chains like Mango, Moleskine, and Sephora, and bookshops with a hearty selection of English-language best sellers, as well as a grocery store and well-stocked food court. ✉ *Piazza dei Cinquecento 1, Esquilino* ⊕ *www. romatermini.com* Ⓜ *Termini.*

MARKETS
Nuovo Mercato Esquilino

MARKET | This fabulous covered market is an excellent place to wander thanks to its sights and smells. There are plenty of Italian, Asian, and African specialties to be found, since the neighborhood is a cultural mix. Many of Rome's top restaurants get their main ingredients here. ⊠ *Via Filippo Turati 160, Esquilino* ⊙ *Closed Sun.* Ⓜ *Vittorio Emanuele.*

Pigneto

A hip neighborhood, famed for its street art and full of young people, Pigneto comes to life at night and is a good spot for cool restaurants and caffè. Connected to the rest of Rome by the new Metro Line C, the majority of bars and restaurants are clustered around the section of Via del Pigneto between Via l'Aquila and Circonvallazione Casilina, and around the junction of Via Braccio da Montone and Via Fanfulla da Lodi.

Restaurants

Pigneto is Rome's up-and-coming *zona*, or area: gritty caffè, artsy bars, and youth-driven, modern Italian restaurants are what you'll find.

★ Necci dal 1924

$$ | ITALIAN | Pigneto is full of hip restaurants and bars now, but Necci is the neighborhood's original hangout, the haunt of famed director Pier Paolo Pasolini, who grew up in Pigneto when it was still a rough-and-tumble working-class area. There's a full menu of pastas and other Italian fare, but it's also the kind of laid-back place where the servers won't bat an eyelash if you just want drinks or a small bite. **Known for:** laid-back hipster hangout; all-day dining and drinking; large patio with lots of outdoor seating. ⑤ *Average main: €16* ⊠ *Via Fanfulla da Lodi 68, Pigneto* ☎ *06/97601552* ⊕ *www. necci1924.com* Ⓜ *Pigneto.*

Pigneto Quarantuno

$$ | MODERN ITALIAN | Reservations are always a good idea at this popular spot for top-quality Roman food (especially if you'd like to sit outside). The constantly changing menu reflects seasonal produce; start off with one of their many foccacie, such as thyme, goat cheese, and grilled zucchini. **Known for:** homemade pasta; legendary meatballs; impressive local and Italian wine list. ⑤ *Average main: €15* ⊠ *Via del Pigneto 41, Pigneto* ☎ *06/70399483* ⊙ *No lunch weekdays* Ⓜ *Pigneto.*

Trattoria Pigneto

$$ | ROMAN | This casual home-style trattoria follows the style of a *fraschetta—a* type of countryside restaurant where the menu focuses on porchetta in a relaxed and casual atmosphere. Ordering the porchetta here is an obvious must—the waiter will serve it on butcher's paper according to how many people are in your party—but your meal needn't start, or end, there. **Known for:** old-school classics; rustic picnic table decor; affordable prices. ⑤ *Average main: €14* ⊠ *Via del Pigneto 68, Pigneto* ☎ *06/45650417* Ⓜ *Pigneto.*

Nightlife

Co.So. Cocktails & Social

COCKTAIL LOUNGES | This funky cocktail bar features street art–style murals and pendant lamps made from mixing glasses. The menu is inspired by Roman, Sicilian, and Japanese flavors, with a bento box *aperitivo* (aperitif) and a list of creative club sandwiches. Try something playful on the cocktail list like the Carbonara Sour, made with guanciale-infused vodka. ⊠ *Via Braccio da Montone 80, Pigneto* ☎ *06/45435428* ⊕ *cosoroma.business. site* Ⓜ *Pigneto.*

San Giovanni

The crown jewel of San Giovanni, just west of Celio, is the Basilica of San Giovanni in Laterano, Rome's cathedral. Today, it is a residential and commercial neighborhood with 19th- and 20th-century apartment buildings and modern shops. Reach San Giovanni by walking south along Via Merulana from the Colosseum.

Sights

★ **Arcibasilica di San Giovanni in Laterano** (*Basilica of St. John Lateran*)
CHURCH | The cathedral of Rome is San Giovanni in Laterano, not St. Peter's. The church was built here by Emperor Constantine 10 years before he built the church dedicated to Peter, making it the ecclesiastical seat of the Bishop of Rome (the pope). But thanks to vandals, earthquakes, and fires, today's building owes most of its form to 16th- and 17th-century restorations, including an interior designed by baroque genius Borromini. Colossal statues stand watch over the towering facade: the 12 apostles plus Christ, John the Baptist, and the Virgin Mary.

Some earlier fragments do remain: under the portico on the left stands an ancient statue of Constantine, while the central portal's ancient bronze doors were brought here from the Forum's Curia. The altar's rich Gothic tabernacle, holding what the faithful believe are the heads of Sts. Peter and Paul, dates to 1367. The last chapel on the left aisle houses the cloister, which is encrusted with 12th-century cosmatesque mosaics. Around the corner stands one of the oldest Christian structures in Rome: Emperor Constantine's octagonal baptistery. Despite several restorations, a 17th-century interior redecoration, and even a 1993 Mafia-related car bombing, the baptistery from AD 315 remains true to its ancient form. ⊠ *Piazza di San Giovanni in Laterano 4, San Giovanni* ☎ *06/69886433* ⊕ *www.vatican.va/various/basiliche/san_giovanni/index_it.htm* 🖾 *Basilica free; cloister €3* Ⓜ *San Giovanni.*

Scala Santa (*Holy Stairs*)
RELIGIOUS BUILDING | According to tradition, the Scala Santa was the staircase from Pilate's palace in Jerusalem—and, therefore, the one trod by Christ himself. St. Helena, Emperor Constantine's mother, brought the 28 marble steps to Rome in 326. As they have for centuries, pilgrims still come to climb the steps on their knees. At the top, they can get a glimpse of the Sancta Sanctorum (Holy of Holies), the richly decorated private papal chapel containing an image of Christ "not made by human hands." You can sneak a peek, too, by taking one of the (non-sanctified) staircases on either side. The splendid Sancta Sanctorum—the pope's private chapel long before the Sistine Chapel—is itself visitable, and well worth the price of admission. ⊠ *Piazza di San Giovanni in Laterano 14, San Giovanni* ☎ *06/7726641* ⊕ *www.scala-santa.com* 🖾 *Scala Santa free, Sancta Sanctorum €3.50* ☉ *Sancta Sanctorum closed Sun.* Ⓜ *San Giovanni.*

Shopping

San Giovanni has a wide selection of department stores and chains, as well as a great street market.

Marella
WOMEN'S CLOTHING | Part of the Max Mara group, Marella was born as a collection in 1976 and became its own brand in 1988. Sometimes described as Max Mara's little sister, the brand sells slightly more youthful and affordable clothes than the original. Expect elegant, high-quality coats and jackets, dresses, skirts, pants, and blouses in fun, colorful prints, and accessories including shoes, bags, scarves, and sunglasses. During semi-annual sales (in January and July), you can find especially good deals. There's also

a location near the Spanish Steps on Via Frattina. ✉ *Vià Appia Nuova 7, San Giovanni* ☎ *06/70491664* ⊕ *www.marella.com* 🕑 *Closed Sun.* Ⓜ *San Giovanni.*

Mercato di Via Sannio

MARKET | The *mercato* (market) on Via Sannio is a great place for flea-market junkies looking for something borrowed or something new. Rummage through piles of military surplus, leather jackets, cosmetics, and other bargains, and feel free to barter. You can find great deals on shoes, handbags, and accessories, although many booths have been overrun by hawkers selling new, cheaply made clothes. It's open Monday through Saturday 8 am–2 pm. ✉ *Via Sannio 65, near San Giovanni in Laterano, San Giovanni* 🕑 *Closed Sun.* Ⓜ *San Giovanni.*

Pifebo

SECOND-HAND | Vintage aficionados, university students, musicians, and the occasional costume designer looking for something a little offbeat all love browsing through the racks of the hip vintage clothing emporium Pifebo. The clothes fly off the racks quite quickly thanks to its eclectic selection of 1970s, '80s, and '90s apparel and shoes at hard-to-beat prices. The shop has another location on Via dei Serpenti in Monti. ✉ *Via dei Valeri 10, San Giovanni* ☎ *06/98185845* ⊕ *www.pifebo. com* 🕑 *Closed Sun.* Ⓜ *San Giovanni.*

San Lorenzo

This traditionally working-class neighborhood north of Termini station is close to the university. The area is inundated with students and faculty, which makes for quite a lively scene in the evening. It's also home to artist studios and galleries, which give the neighborhood a bohemian, creative flair.

◉ Sights

Fondazione Pastificio Cerere

ART GALLERY | This small nonprofit art foundation is housed inside the turn-of-the-century Cerere factory, which produced pasta until 1960 and embodies San Lorenzo's transition from industrial to artsy. The foundation was founded in 2004 to promote the work of young contemporary artists, but artists have been renting studio space in the factory since the 1970s. Check in advance to see if there's an exhibition on view, as they typically change every couple of months. Part of the exhibition space has remained raw, which makes for interesting site-specific installations. ✉ *Via degli Ausoni 7, San Lorenzo* ☎ *06/45422960* ⊕ *www.pastificiocerere.it* 🎟 *Free* 🕑 *Closed Sun. and Mon. Oct.–May; closed weekends Jun.–Aug.*

Matèria

ART GALLERY | If you're keen to delve deeper into Rome's contemporary art scene, this is a good place to go. This small, stark-white gallery represents local and international artists whose work gets shown at international art fairs and prestigious museums like MAXXI and MACRO. The gallery often works with the artists to present site-specific installations, with four exhibitions per year. ✉ *Via dei Latini 27, San Lorenzo* ⊕ *www.materiagallery. com* 🎟 *Free* 🕑 *Closed Sun. and Mon.*

🍴 Restaurants

San Lorenzo is a university quarter, where student budgets dictate low prices and good value. There are also a few hidden gems here.

I Fratelli

$$ | **SOUTHERN ITALIAN** | The four owners of this proudly Southern Italian pizzeria and restaurant come from the deep south (Sicily, Calabria, Campania, and Puglia), and the influence can clearly be seen in the menu, especially in the pizza, which is of the thicker Neapolitan variety. There are classic pizzas and interesting combinations like pear and Gorgonzola or Brie and speck. **Known for:** *cacio e pepe* (pasta with a pecorino-cheese sauce and black pepper) dressed up with black truffle; filetto di baccalà (fillet of salt cod) served with guanciale and honey; casual atmosphere popular with locals. Ⓢ *Average main: €15* ✉ *Via degli Umbri 14, San Lorenzo* ☎ *06/4469856* ⊕ *www. ristoranteifratelli.it* ⊘ *Closed 10 days in Aug. No lunch Sun.*

Pastificio San Lorenzo

$$ | **ITALIAN** | Not to be confused with the art foundation also located inside the former Cerere pasta factory, this industrial-chic restaurant wouldn't be out of place in New York or London. The menu balances traditional recipes with modern touches, like adding salted ricotta to the *fusilloni* pasta with smoked tomato sauce. **Known for:** house-made pastas; small and large portions of most non-pasta dishes; nicely priced wine list as well as cocktails. Ⓢ *Average main: €16* ✉ *Via Tiburtina 196, San Lorenzo* ⊕ *www. pastificiosanlorenzo.com.*

Tram Tram

$$ | **ROMAN** | The name refers to its proximity to the tram tracks, but could also describe the small, narrow interior of the restaurant, which is often packed with diners (in warmer weather there's a "side car" of tables along the sidewalk). Founded by Rosanna Di Vittorio and her two daughters, the restaurant adapts its cuisine from Rome with a slight Puglian influence, emphasizing meat and vegetables—pappardelle with a white ragù of lamb and artichokes, for example—as well as a variety of homemade pastas.

Known for: rigatoni *con pajata* (intestines of an unweaned calf); organic wine list; spaghetti with fresh anchovies. Ⓢ *Average main: €15* ✉ *Via dei Reti 46, San Lorenzo* ☎ *06/490416* ⊕ *www.tramtram. it* ⊘ *Closed Mon. No lunch Sun. in July and Aug.*

☕ Coffee and Quick Bites

Gelato San Lorenzo

$ | **ICE CREAM** | While San Lorenzo is filled with cheap fast food popular among students, this gelateria (open until 1 am) places quality above all else, and can easily rival some of Rome's most storied ice-cream shops. All flavors are properly labeled for special dietary restrictions. **Known for:** raspberry basil sorbetto; vegan and gluten-free options; local favorite spot. Ⓢ *Average main: €4* ✉ *Via Tiburtina 6, San Lorenzo* ☎ *06/4469440* ⊕ *www. gelatosanlorenzo.com.*

SAID dal 1923

$ | **DESSERTS** | Tucked away in a little alley, this historic chocolate shop and tearoom is heaven for chocolate lovers. Third-generation owner Fabrizio de Mauro carries on the tradition started by his grandfather, who lost his original factory during the bombings of WWII and started over in this location. **Known for:** thick hot chocolate with cinnamon or hot pepper; savory dishes made with chocolate; cozy atmosphere with industrial relics. Ⓢ *Average main: €12* ✉ *Via Tiburtina 135, San Lorenzo* ☎ *06/4469204* ⊕ *www.said.it* ⊘ *Closed Mon.*

Hotels

Soho House Rome

$$$ | **HOTEL** | The first international hotel brand to open in San Lorenzo, Soho House draws inspiration from the neighborhood's artsy ethos. **Pros:** sleek modern design with art from local galleries; cool events programming; rooftop pool and bar. **Cons:** only Soho House members can book; no-photo policy; far from the city's main sights, with no metro nearby. $ *Rooms from: €230* ✉ *Via Cesare de Lollis 12, San Lorenzo* ☎ *06/94808000* ⊕ *www.sohouse.com* ➩ *49 rooms* ⦿ *No Meals.*

Nightlife

Literally the other side of the tracks, just beyond Termini train station, San Lorenzo is a traditional university area with lots of inexpensive bars and restaurants, as well as art spaces. Evenings are always brimming with people and activity.

BARS

Black Market San Lorenzo

COCKTAIL LOUNGES | This bare-bones speakeasy-style bar offers top-notch cocktails expertly mixed with bitters or fruit, craft beer, organic wine, and a full spread of delicious appetizers. ✉ *Via dei Sardi 50A, San Lorenzo* ☎ *328/5629789.*

Shopping

This university district is a good place to hunt for unique boho-chic or secondhand clothing.

CLOTHING

L'Anatra all'Arancia

WOMEN'S CLOTHING | Colorful Chie Mihara shoes, chunky handbags, and funky dresses make L'Anatra all'Arancia one of the best local secrets of boho San Lorenzo. The shop showcases innovative clothes from local and international designers like Alice Marrone, Apuntob, and Rundholz. Leaning toward the alternative with an eclectic selection of handpicked Italian and French labels, Donatella also carries luxurious perfumes and boutique jewelry. ✉ *Via Tiburtina*

105, San Lorenzo ☎ 06/4456293 ⊕ www. lanatraallarancia.com ⊘ Closed Sun. Ⓜ Castro Pretorio.

BOOKS AND STATIONARY

Giufà Libreria Caffè

BOOKS | This funky little bookshop has a large selection of comics and graphic novels, the vast majority of which are in Italian. It also sells posters and prints by local artists, which can make a nice souvenir. The caffè inside serves coffee, cocktails, and light bites and has seating outside. ✉ *Via degli Aurunci 38, San Giovanni* ☎ *06/44361406* ⊕ *www. libreriagiufa.it.*

Via Appia Antica

Far south of Esquilino lies catacomb country—the haunts of the fabled underground graves of Rome's earliest Christians, arrayed to either side of the Queen of Roads, the Via Appia Antica (Appian Way). Strewn with classical ruins and dotted with grazing sheep, the road stirs images of chariots and legionnaires returning from imperial conquests. It was completed in 312 BC by Appius Claudius, who laid it out to connect Rome with settlements in the south, in the direction of Naples. Though time and vandals have taken their toll on the ancient relics along the road, the catacombs remain to cast their spirit-warm spell. Although Jews and pagans also used the catacombs, the Christians expanded the idea of underground burials to a massive scale. Persecution of Christians under pagan emperors made martyrs of many, whose bones, once interred underground, became objects of veneration. Today, the dark, gloomy catacombs contrast strongly with the Appia Antica's fresh

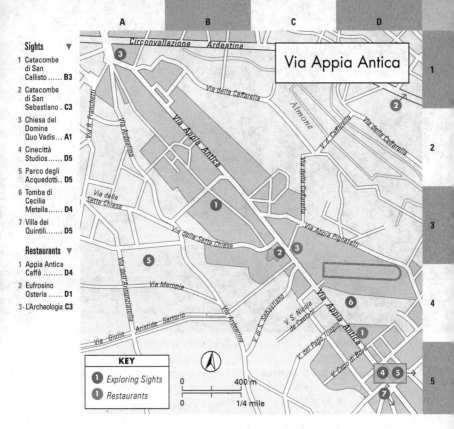

Sights

1 Catacombe di San Callisto **B3**

2 Catacombe di San Sebastiano . **C3**

3 Chiesa del Domine Quo Vadis... **A1**

4 Cinecittà Studios...... **D5**

5 Parco degli Acquedotti.. **D5**

6 Tomba di Cecilia Metella...... **D4**

7 Villa dei Quintili....... **D5**

Restaurants

1 Appia Antica Caffè **D4**

2 Eufrosino Osteria **D1**

3 · L'Archeologia **C3**

KEY

① Exploring Sights

① Restaurants

---

air, verdant meadows, and evocative classical ruins.

The initial stretch of the Via Appia Antica is not pedestrian-friendly—there is fast, heavy traffic and no sidewalk all the way from Porta San Sebastiano to the Catacombe di San Callisto. To reach the catacombs, take Bus No. 218 from San Giovanni in Laterano. Alternatively, take Metro Line A to Colli Albani and then Bus No. 660 to the Tomba di Cecilia Metella. Another attractive alternative is to rent a bike—for example, at the Appia Antica Caffè near the Cecilia Metella bus stop.

◉ Sights

Catacombe di San Callisto
(*Catacombs of St. Calixtus*)
CEMETERY | Burial place of several very early popes, this is Rome's oldest and best-preserved underground cemetery. One of the (English-speaking) friars who act as custodians of the catacomb will guide you through its crypts and galleries, some adorned with Early Christian frescoes. Watch out for wrong turns: this catacomb is five stories deep! ■ **TIP→ The large parking area means this is favored by large groups; it can get busy.** ✉ *Via Appia Antica 110, Via Appia Antica* ☎ *06/5130151* ⊕ *www.catacombe.roma.it* ⊠ *€8* ⊘ *Closed Wed. and mid-Jan.–Feb.*

Walk in the footsteps of St. Peter along the Via Appia Antica, stretches of which seem barely altered from the days of the Caesars.

★ Catacombe di San Sebastiano
(*Catacombs of St. Sebastian*)
CEMETERY | The 4th-century church was named after the saint who was buried in the catacomb, which burrows underground on four different levels. This was the only Early Christian cemetery to remain accessible during the Middle Ages, and it was from here that the term "catacomb" is derived—it's in a spot where the road dips into a hollow, known to the Romans as *catacumba* (Greek for "near the hollow"). ⊠ *Via Appia Antica 136, Via Appia Antica* ☎ *06/7850350* ⊕ *www.catacombe.org* 🎫 *€8* 🕐 *Closed Thurs. and Dec.*

Chiesa del Domine Quo Vadis
(*Church of Quo Vadis*)
CHURCH | This church was built on the spot where tradition says Christ appeared to St. Peter as the apostle was fleeing Rome and persuaded him to return and face martyrdom. A paving stone in the church bears an imprint said to have been made by the feet of Christ. ⊠ *Via Appia Antica 51, Via Appia Antica* ☎ *06/5120441* ⊕ *www.dominequovadis.com.*

Cinecittà Studios
FILM/TV STUDIO | **FAMILY** | Film buffs may want to make the trip out to Cinecittà Studios—stomping ground of Fellini, Audrey Hepburn, and Elizabeth Taylor and birthplace of such classics as *Roman Holiday, Cleopatra,* and *La Dolce Vita.* You can take a guided tour of the sets and see the exhibition *Cinecittà Shows Off,* with memorabilia like Elizabeth Taylor's *Cleopatra* gown and the dolphin-shaped statue that marked the chariot laps in *Ben-Hur.* Cinecittà is located about 25 minutes southeast of the city center on Metro Line A. Tours in English are available on weekends at 11:30. ⊠ *Via Tuscolana 1055, Via Appia Antica* ☎ *06/72293269* ⊕ *cinecitta.com* 🎫 *€15 exhibition and tour, €20 combined ticket with MIAC (Italian Museum of Moving Images)* 🕐 *Closed Tues.* Ⓜ *Cinecittà.*

Parco degli Acquedotti

CITY PARK | FAMILY | This massive park was named for the six remaining aqueducts that formed part of the famously elaborate system that carried water to ancient Rome. It's technically part of the Parco dell'Appia Antica and you can indeed walk on a piece of an ancient Roman road that once went all the way to Benevento, a city near Naples. The park has some serious film cred: it was featured in the opening scene of *La Dolce Vita* and in a rather memorable scene depicting some avant-garde performance art in *La Grande Bellezza*. On weekends, it's a popular place for locals to picnic, exercise, and bring their kids or dogs. ⊠ *Via Lemonia 221, Via Appia Antica* ⊕ *www.parcodegliacquedotti.it* Ⓜ *Giulio Agricola, Subaugusta.*

Tomba di Cecilia Metella

CEMETERY | For centuries, sightseers have flocked to this famous landmark, one of the most complete surviving tombs of ancient Rome. One of the many round mausoleums that once lined the Appian Way, this tomb is a smaller version of the Mausoleum of Augustus, but impressive nonetheless. It was the burial place of a Roman noblewoman: the wife of the son of Crassus, who was one of Julius Caesar's rivals and known as the richest man in the Roman Empire (infamously entering the English language as "crass"). The original decoration includes a frieze of bulls' skulls near the top. The travertine stone walls were made higher and the medieval-style crenellations were added when the tomb was transformed into a fortress by the Caetani family in the 14th century. An adjacent chamber houses a small museum of the area's geological phases. Entrance to this site also includes access to the splendid Villa dei Quintili, but you can get a super view without going in. ⊠ *Via Appia Antica 161, Via Appia Antica* ☎ *06/7886254* ⊕ *www.parcoarcheologicoappiaantica.it* 🎫 *€10, includes all the sites in the Parco dell'Appia Antica (Villa dei Quintili, Antiquarium di Lucrezia Romana, Complesso di Capo di Bove, Tombe della Via Latina, and the Villa dei Setti Bassi)* ⊗ *Closed Mon.*

Villa dei Quintili

RUINS | Even in ruins, this once splendid villa gives a real sense of ancient Rome's opulence, and the small on-site museum includes archaeological finds that add to the vision. Even today, two millennia later, it remains clear why Emperor Commodus—the villain in the 2000 film epic *Gladiator*—coveted this sumptuous property. To get the villa from its owners, the Quintili, he accused the family of plotting against him and had them executed, before moving in himself. He may have used the exedra for training for his fights with ostriches back in the Colosseum. Note that the villa is best included in a separate itinerary from the catacombs, being 5 km (3 miles) away. It is accessible from both the modern Appia Nuova and from the Appia Antica, the ancient road (by bicycle or on foot only). ⊠ *Via Appia Nuova 1092, Via Appia Antica* ☎ *06/7129121* ⊕ *www.parcoarcheologicoappiaantica.it* 🎫 *€10, includes all the sites in the Parco dell'Appia Antica (Villa dei Quintili, Antiquarium di Lucrezia Romana, Complesso di Capo di Bove, Tombe della Via Latina, and the Villa dei Setti Bassi)* ⊗ *Closed Mon.*

🍴 Restaurants

Appia Antica Caffè

$ | **ROMAN** | Strategically situated at the No. 660 bus stop on the corner of Via di Cecilia Metella, the Appia Antica Caffè, with its birdsong-filled atmosphere, is a rarity among Roman coffee bars. The food isn't particularly exciting (the usual array of sandwiches and pastries), but it's in a convenient location with lots of outside seating in the back. **Known for:** good people-watching; charming outdoor seating; classic Roman espresso. $ *Average main: €8* ✉ *Via Appia Antica 175, Via Appia Antica* ☎ *06/89879575* ⊕ *www.appiaanticacaffe.it* ⊗ *Closed Nov.–Mar.*

Eufrosino Osteria

$$ | **ITALIAN** | At this welcoming osteria run by three young owners, wood-paneled walls, terrazzo floors, and green pendant lamps evoke 1970s nostalgia. Romans come here to sample regional dishes from trattorias across Italy, like Tuscan fried chicken and Sicilian-style fusilli with broccoli, pine nuts, raisins, and anchovies. **Known for:** regional Italian dishes; nostalgic vibe; slow food principals. $ *Average main: €16* ✉ *Via di Tor Pignattara 188, Via Appia Antica* ☎ *348/5883932* ⊗ *Closed Tues.* Ⓜ *Malatesta, Porta Furba.*

L'Archeologia

$$ | **ITALIAN** | In this farmhouse just beyond the catacombs, founded around 1804, you can dine indoors beside the fireplace in cool weather or in the garden under age-old vines in summer. Specialties include spaghetti *aglio* (with garlic and olive oil), *olio e pepperoncini* (spaghetti with garlic, olive oil, and pepper) with raw shrimp, fillet of beef with onions, potatoes, and hazelnut sauce, and fresh seafood. **Known for:** romantic setting; hand-painted frescoes; ancient wine cellar La Cantina. $ *Average main: €24* ✉ *Via Appia Antica 139, Via Appia Antica* ☎ *06/7880494* ⊕ *www.larcheologia.it* ⊗ *Closed Tues. No lunch weekdays.*

Chapter 12

SIDE TRIPS FROM ROME

Updated by
Natalie Kennedy

⊙ Sights	🍴 Restaurants	🛏 Hotels	💼 Shopping	🍸 Nightlife
★★★★☆	★★☆☆☆	★☆☆☆☆	★☆☆☆☆	★★★☆☆

WELCOME TO SIDE TRIPS FROM ROME

TOP REASONS TO GO

★ **Ostia Antica:** This excavated port city of ancient Rome is brimming with ruins, mosaics, and structures, which convey a picture of everyday life in the empire.

★ **Tivoli's Villa d'Este:** Hundreds of fountains cascading and shooting skyward (one even plays music on organ pipes) will delight you at this spectacular garden.

★ **Castelli Romani:** Enjoy a raucous Roman lunch and an escape to the ancient hilltop wine towns on the city's doorstep.

★ **Viterbo:** This town may be modern, but it has a Gothic papal palace, a Romanesque cathedral, and the magical medieval quarter of San Pellegrino. It's also the gateway to the *terme* (hot springs) closest to Rome.

★ **Bizarre and beautiful gardens:** The 16th-century proto-Disneyland Parco dei Mostri (Monster Park) is famed for its fantastic sculptures; the stately Villa Lante, a few miles away, is a postcard-perfect Renaissance garden of swirling, manicured hedges.

1 Viterbo. The capital of Tuscia and a 13th-century time capsule with papal connections.

2 Bagnaia. The site of a 16th-century cardinal's summer home.

3 Caprarola. A quiet village that is also home to the huge Palazzo Farnese.

4 Bomarzo. The town with the eccentric Monster Park garden.

5 Ostia Antica. An ancient Roman port, now an archaeological site.

6 Tivoli. A fitting setting for the regal Villa Adriana and the unforgettable Villa d'Este, a park filled with gorgeous fountains.

7 Palestrina. Originally an ancient pagan sanctuary and home to the father of musical counterpoint.

8 Frascati. A historic getaway amid the Alban Hills and famed for its wine.

9 Castel Gandolfo. A lakeside town otherwise known as the pope's summer retreat.

10 Ariccia. Home to the grand Palazzo Chigi.

11 Nemi. A pretty hamlet, with an eagle's-nest perch above a volcanic lake.

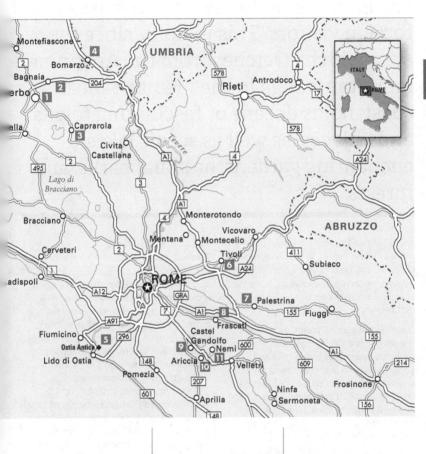

Less well known than neighboring Tuscany, Lazio, the region that encompasses Rome, is often bypassed by foreign visitors. This is a pity, since the area, which stretches from the Apennine mountain range to the Mediterranean coast, holds dozens of fascinating towns and villages, as well as scenic lakes, enchanting gardens, national parks, and forests.

A trip outside Rome introduces you to a more intimate aspect of Italy, where local customs and feast days are still enthusiastically observed and local gastronomic specialties take precedence on restaurant menus.

Despite these small towns' proximity to the capital and the increased commuter traffic congestion of today, they still each manage to preserve their individual character. Ostia Antica, ancient Rome's seaport, is one of the region's top attractions—it rivals Pompeii in the quality of its preservation, and it easily outshines the Roman Forum thanks to its beautiful setting and expansive, inspiring view on the past. Emperors, cardinals, and popes have long escaped to verdant retreats in nearby Tivoli, Viterbo, and the Alban Hills, and their amazing villas, palaces, and gardens add to nature's allure. So if the nonstop Vespa traffic and long lines at the Colosseum start to wear on you, do as the Romans do: get out of town. There's plenty to explore and experience.

MAJOR REGIONS

Tuscia. Tuscia (the modern name for the Etruscan domain of Etruria) is a region of dramatic beauty punctuated by deep, rocky gorges and thickly forested hills, with dappled light falling on wooded paths. This has been a preferred locale for the retreats of wealthy Romans for ages, a place where they could build grand villas and indulge their sometimes-eccentric gardening tastes.

The provincial capital, Viterbo, which overshadowed Rome as a center of papal power for a time during the Middle Ages, lies in the heart of Tuscia. The farmland east of Viterbo conceals small quarries of the dark, volcanic *peperino* stone, which shows up in the walls of many buildings here. Lake Bolsena lies in an extinct volcano, and the sulfur springs still bubbling up in the modern spas were once used by the ancient Romans. Bagnaia and Caprarola are home to palaces and gardens; the garden statuary at Bomarzo is in a league of its own—somewhere between the beautiful and the bizarre. The ideal way to explore this region is by car. From Rome you can reach Viterbo by train and then get to Bagnaia by local bus. If you're traveling by train or bus, check schedules carefully; you may have to allow for an overnight if you want to do a round of the region's sights.

Tivoli and Palestrina. Tivoli is a five-star draw, its main attractions being its two villas. There's an ancient one in which Hadrian reproduced the most beautiful monuments in the then-known world, and a Renaissance one, in which Cardinal Ippolito d'Este created a water-filled wonderland. Unfortunately, the Via Tiburtina from Rome to Tivoli passes through miles of industrial areas with chaotic traffic, so whether you are driving or taking the bus, take the A24 motorway to avoid it. Or take the train, which offers a slightly more scenic journey. Whichever way you decide to go, persevere and it'll be worth it for the small but charming city center, expansive park, and Tivoli's two gems that are rightly world famous. You'll know you're close to Tivoli when you see vast quarries of travertine marble and smell the sulfurous vapors of the little spa, Bagni di Tivoli. Both sites in Tivoli are outdoors and entail walking. With a car, you can continue your loop through the mountains east of Rome, taking in the ancient pagan sanctuary at Palestrina, spectacularly set on the slopes of Mt. Ginestro.

The Castelli Romani. These *castelli* aren't really castles, as their name would seem to imply. Rather, they're little towns that are scattered on the slopes of the Alban Hills just to the southeast of Rome. And the Alban Hills aren't really hills, but extinct volcanoes. There were castles here in the Middle Ages, however, when each of these towns, fiefs of rival Roman lords, had its own fortress to defend it. Some centuries later, the area was given over to villas and retreats, notably the pope's summer residence at Castel Gandolfo and the 17th- and 18th-century villas that transformed Frascati into the Beverly Hills of Rome. Arrayed around the rim of an extinct volcano that encloses two crater lakes, the string of picturesque towns of the Castelli Romani are surrounded by vineyards, olive groves, and chestnut woods—no wonder overheated Romans have always loved to escape here.

In addition to their lovely natural settings, the Castelli have also been renowned for their wine since the ancient Roman times. In the narrow, medieval alleyways of the oldest parts of the various villages, you can still find old-fashioned taverns where the locals sit on wooden benches, quaffing the golden nectar straight from the barrel. Traveling around the countryside, you can also pop into some of the local vineyards, where they will be happy to give you a tasting of their wines. Exclusive local gastronomic specialties include the bread of Genzano, baked in traditional wood-fired ovens, the *porchetta* (roast suckling pig) of Ariccia, and the *pupazza* biscuits of Frascati, shaped like women or mermaids with three or more breasts (an allusion to ancient fertility goddesses). Each town has its own feasts and saints' days, celebrated with costumed processions and colorful events. Some are quite spectacular, like the annual Marino Wine Festival in October, where the town's fountains flow with wine; or the Flower Festival of Genzano in June, when an entire street is carpeted with millions of flower petals, arranged in elaborate patterns.

Planning

Making the Most of Your Time

Ostia Antica is in many ways an ideal day trip from Rome: it's fascinating, it's not far from the city, it's reachable by public transit, and it takes about half a day to do. Villa d'Este and Villa Adriana in Tivoli also make for a manageable, though fuller, day trip. There's so much to see

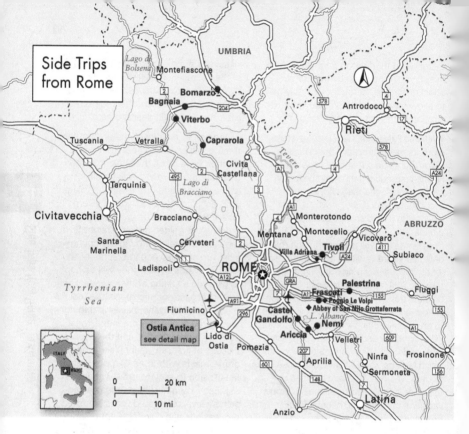

Side Trips from Rome

at these two sights alone, but also be sure to visit Tivoli's picturesque gorge, which is strikingly crowned by an ancient Roman temple to Vesta (which is now a part of the incomparable outdoor terrace at the famed Sibilla restaurant). Other destinations can be visited in a day, but you'll get more out of them if you stay the night.

One classic five-day itinerary that takes in the area's grand villas, ancient ruins, and pretty villages begins with Ostia Antica, the excavated port town of ancient Rome. You can then head north to explore Viterbo's medieval streets on Day 2. On Day 3, take in the hot springs or the gardens of Bomarzo, Bagnaia, and Caprarola. For Day 4, head to Tivoli's delights. Then on Day 5 take a relaxing trip to the Castelli Romani, where Frascati wine is produced. Admire the sparkling volcanic lakes, find a

spot at a family-style local restaurant, and explore the narrow streets of these small hill towns.

Getting Here and Around

There's reliable public transit from Rome to Ostia Antica, Frascati, Tivoli, and Viterbo. Castel Gandolfo is also reachable by train—so long as you don't mind a short uphill walk from the station. COTRAL is the regional bus company. For other destinations, having a car is a big advantage—going by bus or Trenitalia can add hours to your trip, and the routes and schedules are often puzzling.

CONTACTS COTRAL. ⊠ *Via Bernardino Alimena 105* ☎ *800/174471* ⊕ *www.cotral-spa.it.* **Trenitalia.** (*Italian National Railway System*) ☎ *199/892021, 06/68475475* ⊕ *www.trenitalia.com.*

Restaurants

You certainly won't go hungry when you're exploring the Roman countryside. Whether you choose a five-star establishment or a simple eatery, you can be sure of a fresh, clean tablecloth and friendly, attentive service. Odds are that the ingredients will come from down the road and the owner will be in the kitchen, personally preparing the time-honored dishes that have made Italian cuisine so famous.

Hotels

Former aristocratic villas with frescoed ceilings, *agriturismi* farmhouses, luxury spas, and cozy bed-and-breakfasts in the village center are just a few of the lodging options here. You won't find much in the way of big chain hotels, though.

WHAT IT COSTS in Euros

	$	$$	$$$	$$$$
RESTAURANTS				
	under €15	€15–€24	€25–€35	over €35
HOTELS				
	under €125	€125–€200	€201–€300	over €300

Visitor Information

Tourist information kiosks, which are scattered around Rome's main squares and tourist sights, can give you information about the Castelli Romani, Ostia Antica, and Tivoli. The Tuscia area is served by the central tourist office in Viterbo.

CONTACT Visit Lazio. ⊕ *www.visitlazio. com.*

Viterbo

104 km (64 miles) northwest of Rome.

Viterbo's moment of glory was in the 13th century, when it became the seat of the papal court. The medieval core of the city still sits within 12th-century walls. Its old buildings, with window boxes bright with geraniums, are made of dark peperino, the local stone that colors the medieval part of Viterbo a deep gray, contrasted here and there with the golden tufa rock of walls and towers. Peperino is also used in the characteristic and typically medieval exterior staircases that you see throughout the old town.

Viterbo has blossomed into a regional commercial center, and much of the modern city is loud and industrial. Nevertheless, in Viterbo's San Pellegrino district you'll get the feel of the Middle Ages—artisan shops and bottegas still operate in a setting that has remained practically unchanged over the centuries. The Papal Palace and the cathedral, which sit at the heart of the oldest part of the city, enhance the effect. The city has remained a renowned spa center for its natural hot springs just outside town, which have been frequented by popes and mere mortals alike since medieval times.

GETTING HERE AND AROUND

Viterbo is well-served by public transport from Rome. Direct train service from Stazione Trastevere takes 1 hour and 40 minutes, making frequent stops in the capital's more rural suburbs. Try to avoid peak hours, as many commuters live in towns along the line. By road, take either the old Roman consular road, the Via Cassia, which passes near Caprarola, or, if you are in a hurry, the A1 toll highway to the Orte exit and then the 204 highway, with a detour to Bomarzo. The trip can take a couple of hours or more, depending on traffic.

VISITOR INFORMATION

CONTACT Viterbo Tourism Office. ✉ *Piazza Martiri D'Ungheria,* ☎ *0761/226427* ⊕ *www.promotuscia.it.*

 Sights

Cattedrale di San Lorenzo

CHURCH | Viterbo's Romanesque cathedral was built over the ruins of the ancient Roman Temple of Hercules. During World War II, the roof and the vault of the central nave were destroyed, and you can still see the mark the shrapnel left on the columns closest to the pulpit. Subsequently, the church was rebuilt to its original medieval design, but it still has many original details, including a beautiful Cosmati floor that dates back to the 13th century. Three popes are buried here, including Pope Alexander IV (1254–61), whose body was hidden so well by the canons, out of fear that it would be desecrated, that it has never been found. The adjoining Museo del Colle del Duomo has a collection of 18th-century reliquaries, Etruscan sarcophagi, and a painting of the Crucifixion that has been attributed to Michelangelo. The ticket to the museum also grants you entrance to the Palazzo Papale, located on the same square. ✉ *Piazza San Lorenzo, Viterbo* ☎ *320/7911328* ⊕ *www.archeoares.it* 💶 *€9, includes tour of Cattedrale di San Lorenzo, Palazzo dei Papi, and Museo del Colle del Duomo.*

Palazzo dei Papi (*Papal Palace*)

CASTLE/PALACE | This Gothic palace was built in the 13th century as a residence for popes looking to get away from the city. At the time, Rome was notoriously ridden with malaria and the plague, not to mention rampaging factions of rival barons. In 1271 the palace was the scene of a novel type of rebellion. A conclave held that year to elect a new pope dragged on for months. The people of Viterbo were exasperated by the delay, especially as custom decreed that they had to provide for the cardinals' board and lodging for the duration of the conclave. To speed up the deliberations, the townspeople tore the roof off the great hall where the cardinals were meeting, and put them on bread and water. A new pope—Gregory X—was elected in short order. Today, you can visit the great hall, step out on the pretty loggia, and admire the original frescoes in the small adjoining room. ■TIP→ **An audio guided tour is free with the purchase of a ticket and lasts 45 minutes, starting from Museo del Colle del Duomo.** ✉ *Piazza San Lorenzo, Viterbo* ☎ *393/0916060* ⊕ *www.archeoares.it* 💶 *€9, includes tour of Cattedrale di San Lorenzo, Palazzo dei Papi, and Museo del Colle del Duomo.*

San Pellegrino

HISTORIC DISTRICT | One of the best-preserved medieval districts in Italy, San Pellegrino has charming vistas of arches, vaults, towers, exterior staircases, worn wooden doors on great iron hinges, and tiny hanging gardens. You pass many antiques shops and craft workshops, as well as numerous restaurants, as you explore the little squares and byways. The Fontana Grande in the piazza of the same name is the largest and most extravagant of Viterbo's Gothic fountains. ✉ *Via San Pellegrino, near Palazzo dei Papi and Cattedrale di San Lorenzo, Viterbo* ⊕ *www.promotuscia.it.*

★ Terme dei Papi

HOT SPRING | Viterbo has been a spa town for centuries, and this excellent spa not far removed continues the tradition, providing the usual health and beauty treatments with an Etruscan twist: try a facial with local volcanic mud, or a steam bath in an ancient cave, where scalding hot mineral water direct from the spring splashes down a waterfall to a pool beneath your feet. The Terme dei Papi's main draw, however, comes from the terme themselves: a 21,000-square-foot outdoor limestone pool, into the shallow end of which Viterbo's famous hot water pours at 59°C (138°F)—and gives a jolt with its sulfurous odor. Floats and deck chairs are for rent, but bring your own bathrobe and towel unless you're staying at the hotel. Tickets tend to sell out but can be booked online up to five days ahead of your visit. ■**TIP→ Shuttle buses operate between Rome's Piazza del Popolo and the Terme on weekends and holidays. Round-trip tickets cost €12; call or check website for travel times.** ⊠ *Strada Bagni 12, 5 km (3 miles) west of town center, Viterbo* ☎ *0761/3501* ⊕ *www.termedeipapi.it* 🛋 *Pool €18 weekdays, €25 weekends* ⊙ *Closed Tues.*

🍴 Restaurants

★ Osteria del Vecchio Orologio

$ | **ITALIAN** | Tucked away in a side street off the medieval Piazza delle Erbe, the Osteria del Vecchio Orologio offers top-quality Tuscia specialties in a warm and informal atmosphere. They're a member of the Slow Food movement, with a menu that changes according to the season. **Known for:** extensive wine list; local ingredients; cute, cupboard-lined walls. ⑤ *Average main: €14* ⊠ *Via Orologio Vecchio 25, Viterbo* ☎ *335/337754* ⊕ *www.alvecchioorologio. it* ⊙ *No lunch Mon. Closed Tues.*

Taverna Etrusca

$$ | **ITALIAN** | **FAMILY** | Located between the heart of San Pellegrino and Porta Romana, this friendly trattoria is known for its excellent home cooking and pizza. Be sure to admire the Etruscan-inspired decorations and check out the dessert— all the excellent gelato is made on-site. **Known for:** excellent gelato; *tagliolini* (ribbon pasta) with lemon; homemade pasta *alla viterbese* (spicy red sauce with fennel). ⑤ *Average main: €15* ⊠ *Via Annio 8, Viterbo* ☎ *0761/226694* ⊕ *www. tavernaetrusca.it* ⊙ *Closed Sun.*

Tre Re

$$ | **ITALIAN** | Viterbo's oldest restaurant— and one of the most ancient in Italy—has been operating in the *centro storico* (historic center) since 1622. The small, wood-paneled dining room, chummily packed with tables, was a favorite haunt of movie director Federico Fellini and, before that, of British and American soldiers during World War II. **Known for:** locals touch the Tre Re (Three Kings) sign outside for luck; roasted suckling pig; traditional local dishes. ⑤ *Average main: €15* ⊠ *Via Macel Gattesco 3, Viterbo* ☎ *0761/304619* ⊕ *www.ristorantetrere. com* ⊙ *Closed Thurs.*

Bagnaia

5 km (3 miles) east of Viterbo.

The quiet village of Bagnaia is the site of the 16th-century cardinal Alessandro Montalto's summer retreat, which is quite an extravaganza.

GETTING HERE AND AROUND

Local buses from Viterbo are one way to get here. By local train, it's 10 minutes beyond the Viterbo stop—few local trains actually do stop, though, so be sure to check beforehand. If you prefer to drive, take the A1 to the exit for Orte and follow signs for Bagnaia. There is free parking across the bridge from the main square.

👁 Sights

Villa Lante

CASTLE/PALACE | The main draw in this otherwise sweet but underwhelming village is the hillside garden and park that surround the two small, identical residences built by different owners in the 16th century, more than 30 years apart. The first belonged to Cardinal Gianfrancesco Gambara, but it was Cardinal Alessandro Montalto who built the second and soon commissioned the creation of a stunning garden filled with grottoes, fountains, and immaculately manicured hedges. The garden and the park were designed by the virtuoso architect Giacomo Barozzi (circa 1507–73), known as Vignola, who later worked with Michelangelo on St. Peter's. On the lowest terrace a delightful Italian garden has a centerpiece fountain fed by water channeled down the hillside. On another terrace, a stream of water runs through a groove carved in a long stone table where the cardinal entertained his friends alfresco, chilling wine in the running water. That's only one of the most evident of the whimsical water games that were devised for the cardinal. The symmetry of the formal gardens contrasts with the wild, untamed park adjacent to it, reflecting the paradoxes of nature and artifice that are the theme of this pleasure garden. ⊠ *Via Jacopo Barozzi 71, Bagnaia* ☎ *07/61288008* ⊕ *www.polomuseale-lazio.beniculturali.it/index.php?it/243/villa-lante* ⚲ *€5* ⊗ *Closed Mon.*

Caprarola

21 km (13 miles) southeast of Bagnaia, 19 km (12 miles) southeast of Viterbo.

The wealthy and powerful Farnese family took over this sleepy village in the 1500s and had the architect Vignola design a huge palace and gardens to rival the great residences of Rome. He also rearranged the little town of Caprarola to enhance the palazzo's setting.

GETTING HERE AND AROUND
Caprarola is served by COTRAL bus, leaving from Rome's Saxa Rubra station on the Roma Nord suburban railway line.

◉ Sights

★ Palazzo Farnese
CASTLE/PALACE | When Cardinal Alessandro Farnese, Pope Paul III's grandson, retired to Caprarola, he intended to build a residence that would reflect the family's grandeur. In 1559, he entrusted the task to the leading architect Giacomo Barozzi da Vignola, who came up with some innovative ideas. A magnificent

spiral staircase, lavishly decorated with allegorical figures, mythical landscapes, and grotesques by Antonio Tempesta, connected the main entrance with the cardinal's apartments on the main floor. The staircase was gently inclined, with very deep but low steps, so that the cardinal could ride his horse right up to his bedchamber. A tour of the five-sided palatial villa includes the Hall of Farnese Triumphs, the Hercules Room, and the Antechamber of the Council of Trent, all painted by the Zuccari brothers. Of special interest is the Hall of the Maps, with the ceiling depicting the zodiac and the walls frescoed with maps of the world as known to 16th-century cartographers. The palace is surrounded by a formal Renaissance garden. ⊠ *Piazza Farnese 1, Caprarola* ☎ *0761/646052* ⊕ *www.polomuseale lazio.beniculturali.it* ⚲ *€5, includes garden* ⊗ *Closed Mon.*

Restaurants

Antica Trattoria del Borgo
$$ | ROMAN | FAMILY | Visitors to Caprarola's landmark Palazzo Farnese often round out the experience with a hearty meal at this celebrated trattoria. There's a cozy, familial atmosphere inside, and when the weather permits, a pleasant seating area outside. **Known for:** homemade desserts; expansive wine cellar; local *salumi* (cured) and grilled meat. ⑤ *Average main: €20* ⊠ *Via Borgo Vecchio 107, Caprarola* ☎ *0761/645252* ⊕ *www.anticatrattoriadel-borgo.it* ⊗ *Closed Mon. No dinner Sun., Tues., or Wed.*

Bomarzo

15 km (9 miles) northeast of Viterbo.

Once a fief of the powerful Orsini family, Bomarzo is home to the Parco dei Mostri, the town's main attraction, which was created to amuse and astound the Orsinis' guests. The 16th-century Palazzo Orsini is now the seat of the town council.

Inside, there is a princely hall, frescoed by Pietro da Cortona, the famous Italian baroque fresco painter and architect.

GETTING HERE AND AROUND

Bomarzo is easily reached by car from the A1 autostrada. If you want to go there directly, carry on to the Attigliano exit. Parco dei Monstri is some 6 km (4 miles) from that point. Alternatively, come out at Orte and branch off at Casalone on the Viterbo road. A COTRAL bus also goes here, from Viterbo.

 Sights

Parco dei Mostri (*Monster Park*)

GARDEN | FAMILY | This eerie fantasy, originally known as the Village of Marvels, or the Sacred Wood, was created in 1552 by Prince Vicino Orsini, with the aid of the famous artist Pirro Ligorio. The surreal park is populated with weird and fantastic sculptures of mythical creatures intended to astonish illustrious guests. The sculptures, carved in outcroppings of mossy stone in shady groves and woodland, include giant tortoises and griffins and an ogre's head with an enormous gaping mouth and a table with chairs set inside. Children love it, and there are photo ops galore. The park has a self-service caffè (open Sunday only, in winter) and a gift shop. ⊠ *Localita Giardino, 1½ km (1 mile) west of Bomarzo, Bomarzo* ☎ *0761/924029* ⊕ *www.sacrobosco.it* ⊠ *€13.*

Ostia Antica

30 km (19 miles) southwest of Rome.

Founded around the 4th century BC, Ostia served as Rome's port city for several centuries until the Tiber changed course, leaving the town high and dry. What has been excavated here is a remarkably intact Roman town. To get the most out of a visit, fair weather and good walking shoes are essential. To avoid the worst extremes of hot days, be here when the gates open or go late in the afternoon. A visit to the excavations takes two to three hours, including 20 minutes for the museum. Inside the site, there's a snack bar and a bookshop, but the best idea is to plan to have lunch outside the archeological area, in the town's nearby medieval quarter.

GETTING HERE AND AROUND

The best way to get to Ostia Antica is by train. The Ostia Lido train leaves every 15 minutes from the Porta San Paolo station adjacent to Rome's Piramide Line B Metro station, stopping off at Ostia Antica en route; the trip takes 35 minutes. By car, take the Via del Mare that leads off from Rome's EUR district. Be prepared for heavy traffic, especially at peak hours, on weekends, and in summer.

 Sights

Castello di Giulio II

CASTLE/PALACE | The distinctive castle, easily spotted as you come off the footbridge from the train station and part of the medieval *borgo* (old town), was built in 1483 by the future Pope Julius II when he was the cardinal bishop of Ostia. The structure's triangular form is unusual for military architecture. The castle is typically open on the weekends, but it is best to check updated days and times for available visits are listed on the official website. Even if you can't get inside, its towers and walls add to the atmosphere of the charming old town. ⊠ *Piazza della Rocca 13, Ostia Antica* ⊕ *www.ostiaantica.beniculturali.it* ⊠ *Free* ⊙ *Closed weekdays.*

★ Scavi di Ostia Antica

(*Ostia Antica Excavations*)

RUINS | Today some of Rome's most impressive ruins, the ancient port town was covered by tidal mud and windblown sand and lay buried until the 19th century, when it was extensively excavated. The massive archaeological site can be

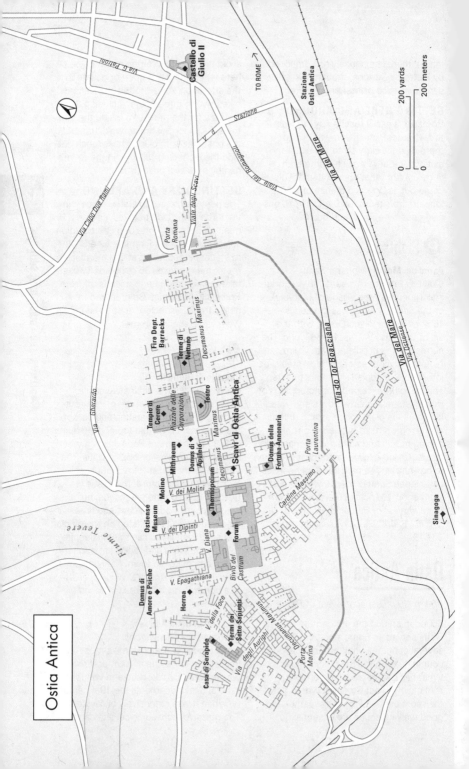

Ostia Antica

explored on foot and is brimming with curious corners, mosaic floors, fallen columns, and a huge Roman amphitheater. At its peak, it was home to a cosmopolitan population of rich businessmen, wily merchants, sailors, slaves, and their respective families. Great warehouses were built here in the 2nd century AD to handle goods that passed through the town, notably huge shipments of grain from Africa; the port did so much business that it necessitated the construction of *insulae* (apartment buildings) to provide housing for the city's growing population. The increasing importance of nearby Portus and the inexorable decline of the Roman Empire eventually led to the port's abandonment. Over the last two millennia the coastline has retreated, and a 16th-century flood diverted the course of the Tiber, so only a glimpse of the river (near the caffè) can be seen today. The on-site Museo Ostiense displays sculptures, mosaics, and objects of daily use found here. There's a cafeteria on-site.

■ **TIP** ➔ **The recently excavated ports of Tiberius and Claudius are nearby and also well worth visiting.** ⊠ *Viale dei Romagnoli 717, Ostia Antica* ☎ *06/56358099* ⊕ *www.ostiaantica.beniculturali.it* ⊠ *€12, includes Museo Ostiense (small increase if there is an exhibition); free 1st Sun. of month* ⊘ *Closed Mon.*

🍴 Restaurants

Arianna al Borghetto

$$ | **ROMAN** | **FAMILY** | This cozy trattoria is tucked away in the charming walled medieval borgo of Ostia Antica next to the Castello di Giulio II. A short walk from the excavations, it's an ideal spot to restore your energy with some seasonal dishes and Roman specialties. **Known for:** charming outdoor seating; homemade pastas; traditional Roman food. ⑤ *Average main: €15* ⊠ *Via del Forno 11, Ostia Antica* ☎ *06/56352956* ⊘ *Closed Mon. No dinner Sun.*

Tivoli

36 km (22 miles) northeast of Rome.

In ancient times, just about anybody who was anybody had a villa in Tivoli, including Crassus, Trajan, Hadrian, Horace, and Catullus. Tivoli fell into obscurity in the medieval era until the Renaissance, when popes and cardinals came back to the town and built villas showy enough to rival those of their extravagant predecessors.

Nowadays Tivoli is small but vibrant, with winding streets and views over the surrounding countryside. The deep Aniene River gorge runs through the center of town and comes replete with a romantically sited bridge, cascading waterfalls, and two jewels of ancient Roman architecture that crown its cliffs—the round Temple of Vesta (or the Sybil, the prophetess credited with predicting the birth of Christ) and the ruins of the rectangular temple of the hero-god Tibur, the mythical founder of the city. These can be viewed across the gorge from the Villa Gregoriana Park, named for Pope Gregory XVI, who saved Tivoli from chronic river damage by diverting the river through a tunnel, weakening its flow. An unexpected side effect was the creation of the Grande Cascata (Grand Cascade), a waterfall formed by the huge jet of water that shoots picturesquely into the valley below. You may also want to set your sights on the Antico Ristorante Sibilla, set up against the Temple of Vesta. From its dining terrace you can take in one of the most memorably romantic landscape views in Italy.

GETTING HERE AND AROUND

Unless you have nerves of steel, it's best to skip the drive to Tivoli. Hundreds of businesses line the Via Tiburtina from Rome and bottleneck traffic is nearly constant. You can avoid some, but not all, of the congestion by taking the Roma–L'Aquila toll road. Luckily, there's abundant public transport (although leaving your own car behind does make it slightly more inconvenient to visit Hadrian's Villa). Buses leave every 15 minutes from the Ponte Mammolo stop on Metro Line B; the ride takes an hour. Regional Trenitalia trains connect from both Termini and Tiburtina stations and will have you in Tivoli in about an hour, or 30 minutes if you plan to take one of the few express trains each day. Villa d'Este is in the.town center, and there is a bus service from Tivoli's main square to Hadrian's Villa.

VISITOR INFORMATION

CONTACT PIT (Punto Informativo Turistico). (*Tivoli Tourist Office*) ⊠ *Piazzale Nazioni Unite,* ☎ *0774/313536* ⊕ *www.visittivoli. eu.*

Sights

★ **Villa Adriana** (*Hadrian's Villa*)
RUINS | An emperor's theme park, this astonishingly grand 2nd-century villa was an exclusive retreat below the ancient settlement of Tibur, where the marvels of the classical world were reproduced for a ruler's pleasure. Hadrian, who succeeded Trajan as emperor in AD 117, was a man of genius and intellectual curiosity, fascinated by the accomplishments of the Hellenistic world. From AD 125 to 134, architects, laborers, and artists worked on his dreamy villa, re-creating some of the monuments and sights that the emperor had seen on his travels in Egypt, Asia Minor, and Greece. During the Middle Ages, the site was sacked by barbarians and Romans alike, and many of the statues and architectural features ended up in the Vatican Museums. Nonetheless, the colossal remains are impressive: the ruins rise in a garden setting of green lawns framed with oleanders, pines, and cypresses. Not surprisingly, Villa Adriana is a UNESCO World Heritage site, and it's one that has not yielded up all its secrets. Archaeologists recently discovered the site of the Temple of

Isis, complete with several sculptures, including one of the falcon-headed god Horus. ■**TIP→ A visit to the villa, which sits outside town, takes at least two hours (carry water on hot days); maps dispensed at the ticket office will help you get your bearings.** ⊠ *Largo Margherite Yourcenar 1, 6 km (4 miles) southwest of Tivoli, Tivoli* ☎ *0774/382733* ⊕ *www.levillae. com/en* ⊡ *€10; free 1st Sun. of month Oct.–Mar.*

★ **Villa d'Este**
GARDEN | One of Italy's UNESCO World Heritage sites, Villa d'Este was created by Cardinal Ippolito d'Este in the 16th century. This villa in the center of Tivoli was the most amazing pleasure garden of its day, and it still stuns modern visitors with its beauty. Cardinal d'Este (1509–72), a devotee of the Renaissance celebration of human ingenuity over nature, was inspired by the excavation of nearby Villa Adriana. He paid architect Pirro Ligorrio an astronomical sum to create an extraordinary garden filled with nymphs and grottoes. But water is the true artistic centerpiece here, and the Aniene River had to be diverted to water the garden and feed the several hundred fountains that cascade, shoot skyward, imitate birdsong, and simulate rain. The musical Fontana dell'Organo has been restored to working order: the water dances to an organ tune every two hours starting at 10:30 am. Romantics will love the night tour of the gardens and floodlit fountains that takes place on Friday and Saturday in summer. ■**TIP→ Allow at least an hour for a visit, which involves steep inclines and many stairs. There are vending machines for refreshments by the bookshop.** ⊠ *Piazza Trento 5, Tivoli* ☎ *0774/332920* ⊕ *www.levillae.com/en* ⊡ *€10; free 1st Sun. of month Oct.–Mar.*

Restaurants

★ Antico Ristorante Sibilla

$$ | ITALIAN | Founded as a hotel and restaurant in 1720 beside the striking Roman Temple of Vesta and the Sanctuary of the Sybil, the idyllic wisteria-draped terrace has a spectacular view over the deep gorge of the Aniene River, with the thundering waters of the waterfall in the background. Standards are high, and the trip to Tivoli is worth it even if you do nothing more than order a lunch of upscale versions of local dishes in this unforgettable setting. **Known for:** homemade pasta with seasonal ingredients; special take on fried zucchini blossoms; beautiful terrace with a super view. ⑤ *Average main: €20* ⊠ *Via della Sibilla 50, Tivoli* ☎ *0774/335281* ⊕ *www.ristoran-tesibilla.com* ⊗ *Closed Mon.*

🛏 Hotels

Torre Sant'Antonio

$ | B&B/INN | Set inside a tower that dates back to the 1300s, this small but cozy hotel offers two private rooms on the edge of the historic center. **Pros:** historic setting; easy walk to most major sites; modern interior design. **Cons:** no 24-hour front desk; old windowpanes let in some street noise; limited parking nearby. ⑤ *Rooms from: €80* ⊠ *Vicolo Sant'Antonio 35, Tivoli* ☎ *347/8037983* ⊕ *www.torresantantoniotivoli.it* ⇵ *2 rooms* ⑩ *No Meals.*

Palestrina

27 km (17 miles) southeast of Tivoli, 37 km (23 miles) east of Rome.

Except to students of ancient history and music lovers, Palestrina is little known outside Italy. Set on a steep hillside, Romans flock to the small town of sherbet-colored houses in summer, when its country breezes offer a refreshing break from the hot city. In addition to the relatively cooler weather, the town is best known for its most famous native son, Giovanni Pierluigi da Palestrina, born here in 1525, and considered the master of counterpoint and polyphony. He composed 105 Masses, as well as madrigals, Magnificats, and motets. There is a small museum dedicated to his life and work in the town center.

Ancient Praeneste (modern Palestrina) flourished much earlier than Rome. It was the site of the Temple of Fortuna Primigenia, which dates from the 2nd century BC. This was one of the largest, richest, most frequented temple complexes in all antiquity—people came from far and wide to consult its famous oracle. In modern times no one had any idea of the extent of the complex until World War II bombings exposed ancient foundations occupying huge artificial terraces, which stretch from the upper part of the town as far downhill as its central duomo.

GETTING HERE AND AROUND

COTRAL buses leave from the Anagnina terminal on Rome's Metro Line A and from the Tiburtina railway station. Alternatively, you can take a train to Zagarolo, where a COTRAL bus takes you on to Palestrina. The total trip takes 40 minutes. By car, take the A1 (Autostrada del Sole) to the San Cesareo exit and follow the signs to Palestrina. The drive takes about an hour.

Sights

Palazzo Barberini

RUINS | A bomb blast during World War II exposed the remains of the immense Temple of Fortune that covered the entire hillside under the present town. Large arches and terraces are now visible and you can walk or take a local bus up to the imposing Palazzo Barberini, which crowns the highest point. The palace was built in the 17th century along the semicircular lines of the original Roman temple. It now contains the Museo

Nazionale Archeologico di Palestrina, with material found on the site that dates from throughout the classical period. There is a well-labeled collection of Etruscan bronzes, pottery, and terra-cotta statuary as well as Roman artifacts, but all of these take a distant second place to the main event, a massive 1st-century BC mosaic depicting a buzzing scene on the Nile River, complete with ancient Egyptian boats, waving palm trees, and intricately crafted African animals. This highly colorful and detailed work is worth the trip to Palestrina by itself. But there's more: a model of the temple as it was in ancient times helps you appreciate the immensity of the original construction. ⊠ *Piazza della Cortina 1, Palestrina* ☎ *06/9538100* ⊕ *www.polomusealelazio. beniculturali.it* 🎫 *€5.*

Restaurants

Il Piscarello

$$ | ITALIAN | FAMILY | Tucked away at the bottom of a steep side road, this elegant dining room immersed in a garden comes as a bit of a surprise. Specialties of the house include meat carpaccio and fish, seafood, and meat dishes with white and black truffles, and the pasta can even be made gluten-free if you call at least one day ahead of time. **Known for:** outdoor seating in summer; fresh seafood; truffle-topped dishes. $ *Average main: €20* ⊠ *Via delle Pratarine 2, Palestrina* ☎ *06/9574326* ⊕ *www.ristoranteilpiscarello.it* ⊗ *Closed Mon. No lunch Tues.–Thurs. No dinner Sun.*

Frascati

20 km (12 miles) south of Rome.

Frascati is one of the easiest villages of the Castelli Romani to get to from Rome, as well as one of the most enjoyable to navigate. After climbing the stairs from the train station or driving uphill to the entrance of the town, it's worth taking a

stroll through Frascati's lively old center. Via Battisti, leading away from the looming presence of Villa Aldobrandini, takes you into Piazza San Pietro with its imposing gray-and-white cathedral. Inside is the cenotaph of Prince Charles Edward, last of the Scottish Stuart dynasty, who tried unsuccessfully to regain the British Crown and died an exile in Rome in 1788. A little arcade beside the monumental fountain at the back of the piazza leads into Market Square, where the smell of fresh baking will entice you into the Purificato family bakery to see the traditional honey-flavored *pupazza* biscuits, modeled on old pagan fertility symbols.

Take your pick from the caffè and trattorias fronting the central Piazzale Marconi, or do as the locals do: buy fruit from the market gallery at Piazza del Mercato, then get a huge slice of porchetta from one of the stalls, a hunk of *casareccio* bread, and a few *ciambelline frascatane* (ring-shaped cookies made with wine), and take your picnic to any one of the nearby *cantine* (homey wine bars) to settle in for some sips of tasty, inexpensive vino. Or continue on to nearby Grottaferrata to take in its one-of-a-kind abbey.

GETTING HERE AND AROUND

An hourly train service along a single-track line through vineyards and olive groves takes you to Frascati from Stazione Termini. The trip takes 45 minutes. By car, take the Via Tuscolano, which branches off the Appia Nuova road just after St. John Lateran in Rome, and drive straight up.

VISITOR INFORMATION

CONTACT Frascati Point (Tourism Office). ⊠ *Piazza G. Marconi 5,* ☎ *06/94184406* ⊕ *www.comune.frascati.rm.it.*

Sights

Abbey of San Nilo Grottaferrata

CHURCH | In Grottaferrata, a busy village a couple of miles from Frascati, the main attraction is a walled citadel founded by St. Nilo, who brought his group of

Basilian monks here in 1004, when he was 90. The order is unique in that it's Roman Catholic but observes Greek Orthodox rites. It is the last surviving Byzantine-Greek monastery in Italy, and has a distinctive blend of art and architecture. The fortified abbey with its soaring bell tower, considered a masterpiece of martial architecture, was restructured in the 15th century by Antonio da Sangallo for the future Pope Julius II. The abbey church, inside the second courtyard, is a jewel of Oriental opulence, with glittering Byzantine mosaics and a revered icon of Mary with child set into a marble tabernacle designed by Bernini. The Farnese chapel, leading from the right nave, contains a series of frescoes by Domenichino. If you make arrangements in advance you can visit the library, which is one of the oldest in Italy. The abbey also has a famous laboratory for the restoration of antique books and manuscripts, where Leonardo's *Codex Atlanticus* was restored in 1962 and more than a thousand precious volumes were saved after the disastrous Florence flood in 1966. ⊠ *Corso del Popolo 128, Grottaferrata* ☎ *06/9459309* 💲 *Free.*

★ Poggio Le Volpi

WINERY | Lazio's wines may not be as famous as those of Tuscany or Piedmont, but this award-winning family-run winery is leading the way for the region. The family's wine-making roots stretch back to 1920, but it was third-generation winemaker Felice Mergè who turned the winery into a destination with two restaurants: the casual Epos bistro and the fine-dining Barrique, where a tasting menu is served in the barrel aging room. Tours of the winery are available by appointment only, but the best way to experience this place is to book a table at one of the restaurants and request a tour. ⊠ *Via Fontana Candida 3/C, Monte Porzio Catone* ☎ *06/9426980* ⊕ *www.poggiolevolpi.com* 💲 *Tours available by appointment* 🕐 *Closed Mon.*

🍴 Restaurants

Antica Fontana

$$ | ROMAN | Across the road from the Abbey of San Nilo, this is one of Grottaferrata's most esteemed restaurants, and it tends to be slightly higher priced than other nearby eateries. Run by the Consoli family since 1989, the decor is rustic but stylish, with plants hanging from the ceiling and rows of polished antique copper pans and molds decorating the walls. **Known for:** pleasant outdoor terrace; fettuccine with porcini; homemade pizza with excellent dough. 💲 *Average main: €22* ⊠ *Via Domenichino 24, Grottaferrata* ☎ *347/4044492* 🕐 *Closed Mon.*

★ Cacciani

$$ | ITALIAN | The Cacciani family has been running this stylish restaurant in the heart of Frascati old town since 1922, when it was a popular hangout for the likes of Clark Gable and Gina Lollobrigida. Perched high on a rise overlooking the town and the Roman plain, there are spectacular views from the Cacciani terrace, but you can also keep an eye on the gorgeous food being prepared in the open kitchen. **Known for:** welcoming, family-run vibe; great views; tonnarelli *cacio e pepe* (prepared with a pecorino-cheese sauce and black pepper) prepared at the table. 💲 *Average main: €18* ⊠ *Via Armando Diaz 13, Frascati* ☎ *06/9420378* ⊕ *www.cacciani.it* 🕐 *Closed Mon. No dinner Sun.*

Il Grottino Frascati

$$ | ITALIAN | This former wine cellar just beyond Frascati's market square is now an old-fashioned and cheerful trattoria serving traditional Roman dishes and pizza. In summer you can sit under an awning outside and enjoy the sweeping view over the plain toward Rome. **Known for:** extensive wine list; casual atmosphere; pasta alla gricia (with pecorino cheese, black pepper, and guanciale). 💲 *Average main: €15* ⊠ *Viale Regina Margherita 41–43, Frascati* ☎ *06/94289772.*

★ Osteria del Fico Vecchio

$$ | ITALIAN | Only a couple of miles outside Frascati, this 16th-century coaching inn has a tastefully renovated dining room and an old fig tree (its namesake) that shades the restaurant's charming garden filled with outdoor tables. Long known for its excellent cooking, the classic restaurant still prepares typical Roman dishes, among them *pollo al diavolo* (spicy braised chicken) and *abbacchio allo scottadito* (sizzling grilled lamb). **Known for:** typical Roman dishes; classic cacio e pepe; pretty garden for outdoor dining. ⑤ *Average main: €20* ✉ *Via Anagnina 257, Grottaferrata* ☎ *06/9459261* ⊕ *www.alfico.it* ⊘ *No lunch Thurs.*

 Hotels

★ Park Hotel Villa Grazioli

$ | HOTEL | One of the region's most famous residences, this patrician villa halfway between Frascati and Grottaferrata is now a first-class hotel, though the standard-issue guest rooms are a bit of a letdown amid the impressive frescoed salons of the main building. **Pros:** incredible frescoes in the main building; wonderful views of the countryside; elegant atmosphere. **Cons:** Wi-Fi connection can be poor; not all rooms are in the main building; situated at the end of a long, narrow lane. ⑤ *Rooms from: €120* ✉ *Via Umberto Pavoni 19, Grottaferrata* ⊹ *Narrow turnoff from the SP216 road going from Grottaferrata roundabout to Frascati* ☎ *06/945400* ⊕ *www.villa-grazioli.it* ⇥ *62 rooms* ⦿ *Free Breakfast.*

Castel Gandolfo

8 km (5 miles) southwest of Frascati, 25 km (15 miles) south of Rome.

This scenic little town has been the preferred summer retreat of popes for centuries. It was the Barberini Pope Urban VIII who first headed here, eager to escape the malarial miasmas that afflicted summertime Rome; before long, the city's princely families also set up country estates around here.

The 17th-century Villa Pontificia has a superb position overlooking Lake Albano and is set in one of the most gorgeous gardens in Italy. Fortunately, these treasures are now open to the public as papal audiences are no longer held at Castel Gandolfo. There's a fountain on the little square in front of the palace by Bernini, who also designed the nearby Church of San Tommaso da Villanova, which has works by Pietro da Cortona.

The village has a number of interesting craft workshops and food purveyors, in addition to the souvenir shops on the square. On the horizon, the silver astronomical dome belonging to the Specola Vaticana observatory—one of the first in Europe—where the scientific Pope Gregory XIII indulged his interest in stargazing, is visible for miles around.

GETTING HERE AND AROUND

There's an hourly train service for Castel Gandolfo from Termini station (Rome–Albano line). Otherwise, buses leave frequently from the Anagnina terminal of Metro Line A. The trip takes about 40 minutes, and the village is reachable by a 10-minute uphill walk from the station. By car, take the Appian Way from San Giovanni in Rome and follow it straight to Albano, where you branch off for Castel Gandolfo (about an hour, depending on traffic).

VISITOR INFORMATION

CONTACT PIT Tourist Office Castel Gandolfo. ✉ *Via Massimo D'Azeglio,* ⊹ *A green kiosk on your right as you walk up the road, just outside the town walls* ⊕ *www. comune.castelgandolfo.rm.it.*

👁 Sights

Lakeside Lido
BEACH | FAMILY | This waterside promenade below the pretty town is lined with restaurants, ice cream parlors, and caffè and is a favorite spot for Roman families to relax on summer days. No motorized craft are allowed on the lake, but you can rent paddleboats and kayaks. In summer, you can also take a short guided boat trip to learn about the geology and history of the lake, which lies at the bottom of an extinct volcanic crater. The deep sapphire waters are full of swans, herons, and other birds, and there is a nature trail along the wooded end of the shore for those who want to get away from the crowds. Deck chairs are available for rent; you might also want to stop for a plate of freshly prepared pasta or a gigantic Roman sandwich at one of the little snack bars under the oak and alder trees. There's also a small permanent fairground for children, and local vendors often set up temporary shops selling crafts, toys, and snacks on the warmer weekends. ✉ *Lake Albano, Castel Gandolfo* 🔁 *Free.*

Palazzo Apostolico di Castel Gandolfo
CASTLE/PALACE | For centuries the Apostolic Palace of Castel Gandolfo was the summer retreat of popes, who kept the papal villa and extensive grounds completely private. Luckily for tourists, Pope Francis decided that he was too busy to use it and had it opened to the public. Inside you can view the Gallery of Pontifical Portraits, ceremonial garments, and the imposing papal throne in the Sala degli Svizzeri. The private area of the palace with the pope's bedchamber, his library, study, and offices are also open to visitors. ✉ *Piazza della Libertà, Castel Gandolfo* ☎ *06/69863111* ⊕ *www.musei-vaticani.va* 🔁 *€11* ⊙ *Closed Sun. and on Catholic holidays.*

⭐ Pontifical Gardens Villa Barberini
GARDEN | In 2016 Pope Francis opened the 136-acre pontifical estate and its glorious gardens to the public. Once rarely accessible, the pontifical gardens of Villa Barberini can now be visited in a 60-minute tour by an eco-friendly electric vehicle. The tour takes in the landscaped gardens as well as the archaeological remains of the palace of the Roman Emperor Domitian (dating back to the 1st century AD) and the home farm, which supplies the Vatican with fresh dairy products and eggs. Multilingual audio guides are included in the price. ✉ *Via Massimo D'Azeglio (entrance gate), Castel Gandolfo* ⊕ *www.museivaticani.va* 🔁 *€20 Villa Barberini gardens with minibus tour; €12 gardens only; €19 gardens and Apostolic Palace* ⊙ *Closed Sun.* ⚠ *Reservations required.*

🍴 Restaurants

Antico Ristorante Pagnanelli
$$$ | ITALIAN | One of the most refined restaurants in the Castelli Romani has been in the same family since 1882. Its dining-room windows open onto a breathtaking view across Lake Albano to the conical peak of Monte Cavo. **Known for:** famous wine cellar and wine museum in basement; elegant and cozy interior with an open fire in winter; homemade gnocchetti with clams and black truffles. $ *Average main: €30* ✉ *Via Gramsci 4, Castel Gandolfo* ☎ *06/9360004* ⊕ *www.pagnanelli.it.*

Hotels

Hotel Castelgandolfo
$ | HOTEL | Overlooking the volcanic crater of Lake Albano and a minute's walk from the Apostolic Palace, this intimate hotel in the heart of Castel Gandolfo makes an ideal retreat for romantics. **Pros:** convenient location; ideal for romantics; intimate. **Cons:** stunning terrace sometimes closed for private events; balconies

The Monumental Bridge connects Ariccia to Albano and offers beautiful views of Palazzo Chigi and Santa Maria Assunta.

are small and narrow; some rooms have street views. $ *Rooms from: €120* ✉ *Via De' Zecchini 27, Castel Gandolfo* ☎ *06/9360521* ⊕ *www.hotelcastelgandolfo.com* 🍽 *18 rooms* 🍴 *Free Breakfast.*

Ariccia

8 km (5 miles) southwest of Castel Gandolfo, 26 km (17 miles) south of Rome.

Ariccia is a gem of baroque town planning. When Fabio Chigi, scion of the superwealthy banking family, became Pope Alexander VII, he commissioned Gian Lorenzo Bernini to redesign his country estate to make it worthy of his new station. Bernini restructured not only the existing 16th-century palace, but also the town gates, the main square, with its graceful loggias and twin fountains, and the round church of Santa Maria dell'Assunzione (the dome is said to be modeled on the Pantheon). The rest of the village was coiled around the apse of the church down into the valley below.

Ariccia's splendid heritage was largely forgotten in the 20th century, and yet it was once one of the highlights of every artist's and writer's Grand Tour. Corot, Ibsen, Turner, Longfellow, and Hans Christian Andersen all came to stay here.

GETTING HERE AND AROUND
For Ariccia, take the COTRAL bus from the Anagnina terminal of Metro Line A. Buses on the Albano–Genzano–Velletri line stop under the monumental bridge that spans the Ariccia Valley, where an elevator whisks you up to the main town square. If you take a train to Albano Laziale, you can proceed by bus to Ariccia or go on foot through the first town and over the bridge (it's just under 1½ km [1 mile]). If you're driving, follow the Via Appia Nuova to Albano and carry on to Ariccia.

◉ Sights

★ Palazzo Chigi

CASTLE/PALACE | This is a true rarity: a baroque residence whose original furniture, paintings, drapes, and decorations are largely intact. The Italian film director Luchino Visconti used the villa, which sits just at the end of Ariccia's famous bridge, for most of the interior scenes in his 1963 film *The Leopard.* The rooms of the *piano nobile* (main floor)—which, unlike Rome's Palazzo Chigi, does open to the public, but only on guided tours—contain intricately carved pieces of 17th-century furniture, as well as textiles and costumes from the 16th to the 20th century. The Room of Beauties is lined with paintings of the loveliest ladies of the day, and the Nuns' Room showcases portraits of 10 Chigi sisters, all of whom took the veil. You can get a close look at Le Stanze del Cardinale (Cardinal's Rooms), the suites occupied by the pleasure-loving Cardinal Flavio Chigi, with a guide on most days. The upper floors contain the Museo del Barocco (Baroque Museum), with an important collection of 17th-century paintings with largely religious themes. The expansive park stretching behind the palace is the last remnant of the ancient Latium forest, where herds of deer still graze under the trees. Be sure to check the website for the hours when various rooms are open to the public, and plan to book ahead to secure a tour in English. ⊠ *Piazza di Corte 14, Ariccia* ☎ *06/9330053* 🖅 *€19 full villa tour (when possible), €8 piano nobile, €6 Cardinal's Rooms, €6 Baroque Museum, €6 park* ⊘ *Palazzo closed Mon. Park closed Oct.–Mar.*

Santa Maria Assunta in Cielo (Church of the Assumption)

CHURCH | Directly across from Palazzo Chigi is the Church of the Assumption, with its distinctive blue dome and round shape designed by none other than Gian Lorenzo Bernini. The artistic architect had his best students execute most of the work of building and decorating the Pantheon-inspired church, creating porticoes outside and an intricately plastered cupola inside, which steals the show in the otherwise simple interior. ⊠ *Piazza di Corte, Ariccia* ⊕ *www.chiesediariccia.it.*

◉ Restaurants

A visit to Ariccia isn't complete without tasting the local gastronomic specialty: porchetta, a delicious roast whole pig stuffed with herbs, that is best with a side of local Romanella wine. The shops on the Piazza di Corte will make up a sandwich for you, or you can do what the Romans do: head for one of the *fraschetta* (a casual, boisterous countryside restaurant) wine cellars, which also serve cheese, cold cuts, pickled vegetables, olives, and sometimes a plate of pasta. Pass Palazzo Chigi and turn left under the arch to find several in a long row on the other side of the street. Take your pick and ask for a seat on a wooden bench at a trestle table covered with simple white paper; be ready to make friends and maybe join in a sing-along.

L'Aricciarola

$ | ITALIAN | FAMILY | This fraschetta around the corner from Palazzo Chigi is great for people-watching, which you can do while enjoying a platter of cold cuts and mixed cheeses, washed down with a carafe of local Castelli wine. Order your own appetizers and slices of porchetta at the counter near the door, snag a table on the patio, flag down a waiter if you want to order pasta, and then settle into the rustic setting surrounded by Roman families who've come to enjoy the local food. **Known for:** very casual and friendly atmosphere; local cold cuts; classic porchetta. ⑤ *Average main: €12* ⊠ *Via Borgo S. Rocco 9, Ariccia* ☎ *06/9334103* ⊕ *osterialaricciarola.it* ⊘ *Closed Mon. and 2 wks in Jan.*

Nemi

8 km (5 miles) east of Ariccia, 34 km (21 miles) south of Rome.

A bronze statue of Diana the Huntress greets you at the entrance to Nemi, the smallest and prettiest village of the Castelli Romani. It's perched on a spur of rock 600 feet above the little oval-shaped lake of the same name, which is formed from a volcanic crater. Nemi has an eagle's-nest view over the rolling Roman countryside as far as the coast, some 18 km (11 miles) away. The one main street, Corso Vittorio Emanuele, takes you to the baronial Castello Ruspoli (not open to the public), where there's an 11th-century watchtower, and the quaint Piazza Umberto I, lined with outdoor cafés serving desserts made with the town's famous tiny wild strawberries which are harvested from the woodlands that line the crater bowl.

GETTING HERE AND AROUND

Nemi is difficult to get to unless you come by car. COTRAL buses from the Anagnina station on Metro Line A go to the town of Genzano, where a local bus travels to Nemi every two hours. If the times aren't convenient, you can take a taxi or walk the 5 km (3 miles) around Lake Nemi. By car, take the panoramic route known as the Via dei Laghi (Road of the Lakes). Follow the Appia Nuova from St. John Lateran and branch off on the well-signposted route after Ciampino airport. Follow the Via dei Laghi toward Velletri until you see signs for Nemi.

◉ Sights

Museo delle Navi Romane

(*Roman Ship Museum*)

HISTORY MUSEUM | In the 1930s, the Italian government drained Nemi's lake to recover two magnificent ceremonial ships, loaded with sculptures, bronzes, and art treasures, that were submerged for 2,000 years. The Museo delle Navi Romane, on the lakeshore, was built to house the ships, but they were burned during World War II. Inside are scale models and finds from the Bronze Age Diana sanctuary and the area nearby. There's also a colossal statue of the infamous and extravagant Roman emperor Caligula, who had the massive barges built on the pretty lake. Italian police once snatched the marble sculpture back from tomb robbers just as they were about to smuggle it out of the country. ✉ *Via del Tempio di Diana 13, Nemi* ☎ *06/9398040* ⊕ *www.beniculturali.it* 🎟 *€4* ⊘ *Closed Mon.*

🍴 Restaurants

★ La Fiocina

$$ | ITALIAN | With its privileged position on the tranquil shores of Lake Nemi next to the Roman Ship Museum, La Fiocina has been serving local specialties, including lake fish and homemade gnocchi with wild boar sauce, for more than 50 years. The dining room is elegant and welcoming, and there's a terrace on which you can dine alfresco, overlooking the small lakeside garden. **Known for:** tiny wild Nemi strawberries; garden terrace with lake views; coregone lake fish. ⑤ *Average main: €15* ✉ *Via delle Navi di Tiberio 9, Nemi* ☎ *06/9391120* ⊘ *Closed Mon. and Tues.*

Locanda Specchio di Diana

$ | ITALIAN | Halfway down the main street on the left is the town's most historic inn, where Byron stayed when visiting the area. Today it's a wine bar and caffè on street level, and a full restaurant on the second floor with marvelous views over the lake. ■ TIP→ **It also has several small apartments and rooms available to rent by the night in the village center.** **Known for:** local Nemi strawberries when in season; spectacular lake views; fettucine *al sugo di lepre* (hare sauce). ⑤ *Average main: €14* ✉ *Corso Vittorio Emanuele 13, Nemi* ☎ *06/9368714* ⊕ *www.albergodiffusonemi.it.*

Index

316

Photo Credits

Notes

Fodor's ROME 2023

Publisher: Stephen Horowitz, *General Manager*

Editorial: Douglas Stallings, *Editorial Director;* Jill Fergus, Amanda Sadlowski, *Senior Editors;* Kayla Becker, Brian Eschrich, Alexis Kelly, *Editors;* Angelique Kennedy-Chavannes, *Assistant Editor*

Design: Tina Malaney, *Director of Design and Production;* Jessica Gonzalez, *Graphic Designer;* Erin Caceres, *Graphic Design Associate*

Production: Jennifer DePrima, *Editorial Production Manager;* Elyse Rozelle, *Senior Production Editor;* Monica White, *Production Editor*

Maps: Rebecca Baer, *Senior Map Editor;* David Lindroth, Mark Stroud (Moon Street Cartography), *Cartographers*

Photography: Viviane Teles, *Senior Photo Editor;* Namrata Aggarwal, Neha Gupta, Payal Gupta, Ashok Kumar, *Photo Editors;* Eddie Aldrete, *Photo Production Intern;* Kadeem McPherson, *Photo Production Associate Intern*

Business and Operations: Chuck Hoover, *Chief Marketing Officer;* Robert Ames, *Group General Manager;* Devin Duckworth, *Director of Print Publishing*

Public Relations and Marketing: Joe Ewaskiw, *Senior Director of Communications and Public Relations*

Fodors.com: Jeremy Tarr, *Editorial Director;* Rachael Levitt, *Managing Editor*

Technology: Jon Atkinson, *Director of Technology;* Rudresh Teotia, *Lead Developer*

Writers: Laura Itzkowitz, Natalie Kennedy

Editor: Douglas Stallings

Production Editor: Monica White

13th Edition

ISBN 978-1-64097-531-6

ISSN 0276-2560

All details in this book are based on information supplied to us at press time. Always confirm information when it matters, especially if you're making a detour to visit a specific place. Fodor's expressly disclaims any liability, loss, or risk, personal or otherwise, that is incurred as a consequence of the use of any of the contents of this book.

SPECIAL SALES
This book is available at special discounts for bulk purchases for sales promotions or premiums. For more information, e-mail SpecialMarkets@fodors.com.

PRINTED IN CANADA

10 9 8 7 6 5 4 3 2 1